LINA AND SERGE

BOOKS BY SIMON MORRISON

*Russian Opera and
the Symbolist Movement*

*The People's Artist:
Prokofiev's Soviet Years*

Lina and Serge

Lina *and* Serge

The Love and Wars of Lina Prokofiev

Simon Morrison

HOUGHTON MIFFLIN HARCOURT
BOSTON   NEW YORK
2013

For information about permission to reproduce selections from this book,
write to Permissions, Houghton Mifflin Harcourt Publishing Company,
215 Park Avenue South, New York, New York 10003.

www.hmhbooks.com

Library of Congress Cataloging-in-Publication Data
Morrison, Simon Alexander, date.
Lina and Serge : the love and wars of Lina Prokofiev / Simon Morrison.
pages cm
ISBN 978-0-547-39131-1
1. Prokofiev, Lina, 1897–1989. 2. Sopranos (Singers)—Biography.
3. Composers' spouses—Biography. 4. Prokofiev, Sergey, 1891–1953. I. Title.
ML420.P9753M67 2013
780'.922—dc23
[B]   2012042185

Printed in the United States of America
DOC 10 9 8 7 6 5 4 3 2 1

For Serge Prokofiev Jr.

LINA AND SERGE

Introduction

AMONG THE FEW possessions to survive from Lina Prokofiev's eight years in the Soviet gulag is a battered burlap sack. The makeshift purse is just large enough to hold the scores of the French, Italian, and Russian arias that the once-aspiring operatic soprano sang in prison and taught to other women in the barracks.

Among the pieces of remembered music was a song by Chopin called "The Wish." It tells the tale of a woman so devoted to her beloved that if she were the sun, she would shine only for him, and if she were a bird, would sing for him alone. For Lina the song offered an escape into the memories of an earlier time; she had learned it long before. And in the extreme north of the Soviet Union where she was imprisoned, it spoke to the power of imagination in a place of mind-numbing barrenness.

The sack's twine handles wrap around two small wooden plates, one twice the size of the other, with the smaller set into a dented metal frame. Each plate bears her name—LINA PROKOFIEV—the letters etched into the wood and underscored in pencil. Since Lina did not have a conventional Russian patronymic—a middle name derived from the father's first name—her captors assigned her one, also adding a feminine ending to her surname. She became known as Lina Ivanovna Prokofieva, her former self lost with her freedom but safe there in the sack.

Her initials, L. P., are stitched into the middle of each side, surrounded by crosshatches in red, yellow, orange, and gray. Having learned needlecraft in the camps, she labored hard over the embellishments that personalized her belongings. Save for a small dark stain at the bottom, the sack remains in excellent condition. Decades later, it ended up in the care of her older son, Svyatoslav.

Lina was born in Madrid, spent her youth in Brooklyn, studied singing in Paris, and sought to make a name for herself in Milan. She spoke the languages of all of these places as well as Russian, her mother's tongue. She married Serge Prokofiev, one of the great musical geniuses of his time, when she became pregnant by him in 1923, and together they traveled back to Stalin's Soviet Union for the first time in 1927, as much anxious as excited. Serge had originally left Russia in 1918, before Stalin's ascent to power, and Lina had not been within its borders since childhood. Soviet cultural officials sought to reclaim Serge for the socialist experiment, to lure the modernist phenomenon back to his modernizing homeland. The potential benefits of the trip were immense. Serge had been promised prestigious commissions, performances of works that had languished in the West, enthusiastic receptions, even a professorship with the Moscow Conservatoire. He pledged—haughtily, condescendingly—to change the course of Soviet music.

The former Russian capital of St. Petersburg, called Leningrad at the time of the Prokofievs' return, retained its palaces and estates, pastel façades, and frozen canals; it had not changed since Serge's youth, and seeing it again, he was overcome. In contrast, the new capital of Moscow was undergoing shocking change. The skyline had been cleared of onion domes to make way for imposing utopian monuments to Soviet power; their foundations were still being poured. The city had its seductions but also a palpable darkness the Prokofievs chose mostly to ignore. Lina paid no attention to the telltale buzz on the phone in the Metropole Hotel, which signaled that the line was bugged, and banished thoughts of who might be listening on the other side of the thin door connecting their room to another. Told there might be microphones, Serge made a joke of cupping his hands and whispering into her ear in bed at night.

But success fostered self-delusion as Serge received repeated standing ovations and spectacular reviews as a pianist in Soviet concert halls. He unleashed an inferno at the keyboard, playing his Third Piano Concerto with a conductorless ensemble in Moscow—his forearms strong enough to crack apart the soundboard, his immense hands generating vast sonorities at earsplitting dynamics. Lina basked in the attention lavished on the elegant couple at banquets given in their honor. Stalinist cultural officials could not countenance Serge's music yet recognized its power, its potential as a weapon of propaganda. Lina was complimented on her singing—calculated praise, of course, but appreciated nonetheless—and told that if the couple returned to Moscow, as the Soviet government hoped they would, she could have the career that had eluded her in the West.

Serge's subsequent trips to the Soviet Union were not as triumphant yet less obviously scripted, a better indication of what Soviet life might really be like for him, should he choose to stay. He turned crimson and bristled, in his three-piece tailored suit and multicolored leather shoes, when drab proletarian musicians attacked him for mocking Soviet economic progress in one of his ballets, *Le pas d'acier* (*The Steel Step*). Lina did not need to be present at the debate to know how her husband reacted to his critics—by reminding them, in staccato outbursts, of their trifling politics and his greater artistic concerns.

In Paris, where the couple then lived, Lina received invitations to soirees at the newly opened Soviet embassy, the first in the world. The Soviet ambassador to France took the lead in convincing her to relocate, while continuing his promises to Serge about "the privileges awaiting him in the Soviet Union."

It was easier to believe the promises than doubt them, and in 1936 they moved to Moscow. Lina, tired of merely being the great artist's wife, deluded herself into thinking that her life would suddenly be more fulfilling than it had been in Paris. The City of Lights had not been particularly glamorous for her, and she had grown tired of the endless talk of the economic crisis and the threat posed to Europe by Hitler.

But the lie was soon exposed. Lina and Serge's neighbors turned paranoid and tight-lipped. The disappearances that soon became obvious to the newcomers were caricatured in *Pravda* as a campaign to liquidate industrial saboteurs and anti-Communist "enemies of the people." Those whose psyches had been stained by imperialist dogma needed to be reeducated (Serge's imprisoned cousin, Shurik, apparently among them). The suicide rate exploded; children orphaned themselves, denouncing their parents in the service of the greater family called the Communist Party.

Lina played the role of Soviet loyalist as long as she could, but aimlessness and listlessness took hold. Serge lived in denial much longer. Tensions between them increased, and the problems in their marriage could no longer be masked by travel and child rearing. During the summer of 1938, while staying in a resort for the Soviet elite in Kislovodsk, Serge became attracted to a woman twenty-four years his junior, Mira Mendelson.

Lina and Serge's marriage unraveled as, almost daily, they heard about people disappearing without explanation from apartments, factories, and institutes. The English-language school that their sons attended abruptly closed down. The parents of some of the students were repressed; likewise the teachers. The din of construction outside their apartment in Moscow became louder as a quiet desolation took over the household.

Serge left Lina for Mira just three months before the start of the Soviet phase of the Second World War. Lina locked herself in the apartment and refused to socialize. Even in her grief, she remained proud and pulled together, dreading the thought of sympathetic looks. She would not admit to her devastation. Aided by her faith and the sheer force of her mercurial personality, she persevered.

Once she had absorbed the blow, she emerged and mobilized her foreign contacts to try to do what Serge himself could not: she would get out. The French, British, and American embassies had long been her connection to the outside world, her refuge from Stalin's madness. Betrayed by her husband, needing to support her children, she tried to obtain a foreign passport, an exit permit, this stamp, that stamp. But nothing could be done — and her actions raised suspicions.

At first, it was easy for her to shake off the pursuers sent to shadow her: step onto a tramcar, wait for the doors to start closing, then bolt at the last second, leaving the agent trapped inside until the next stop. Later she had to adopt more elaborate ruses, such as entering the tunnel that linked the Metro lines, which had dimmer lighting than the cathedral-like platforms, and changing her clothes there. One day, while purchasing a ticket, she glimpsed her shadow. Upon entering the tunnel and rounding a corner, she removed one summer print dress, revealing another worn beneath it. Lina refused to acknowledge the likelihood of her arrest.

The night before the horror began, Anna Holdcroft, an employee with the press office of the British embassy, stopped by Mrs. Prokofiev's apartment to see how she was managing on her own. They had first met in 1945 at a cocktail party arranged by the British at the Hotel Metropole in Moscow, where Anna was staying. Lina was a pleasure to talk with—learned, desirous of attention, and vivacious. She was sharp-tongued without being mean-spirited, except when referring to people who she believed had wronged her. At a time when foreigners lived and worked under surveillance, and when Russians with any foreign contacts were automatically accused of sedition, her interactions with foreign workers and visitors to the Soviet Union who might help her get to France did her no good. Anna's visit to Lina's apartment on February 19, 1948, was rare and perilous.

On the way, Anna was spotted by someone she had seen before —a low-level agent, as she tersely informed Lina upon arriving. They agreed that Anna would telephone if she thought she was being watched or followed after leaving the apartment. Before saying goodbye, Lina asked if they could meet again the next day at a neutral location, far from her eavesdropping neighbors. On the morning of the twentieth, however, Holdcroft herself received a call warning her not to go to the meeting place. She anticipated the worst and did not leave her hotel.

Alone at home that evening, Lina received an unexpected telephone call. Could she collect a parcel outside? She hesitated, feeling tired and unwell, but the unknown caller insisted. After dressing hurriedly, she neatened her chestnut hair and swiped on some lipstick. Gathering her coat and keys, she took the elevator to the first floor, exited, and walked through the empty inner courtyard to the front of the building, where she expected to find a uniformed courier. Instead she started a twenty-year prison sentence for treason.

Lina did not recognize the man who strode up that night to meet her, without a package. He was not one of the people who had sidled up to her on the buses or trains and stalked her through the underpasses of the massive roadways of the city, including her own — Chkalov Street. As the estranged wife of an eminent musician, wartime government employee, and European transplant to Moscow connected to foreign diplomats and officials, Lina was a person of interest being tracked by semiliterate agents of the OGPU, NKVD, MGB, and MVD. The acronyms of the agencies changed, but the work remained the same: fulfilling arrest quotas by targeting people whose names appeared on their lists and dragging them from their apartments, as the neighbors cowered behind closed doors.

The man who met Lina in the courtyard that night was not in uniform, nor was he alone. His accomplices had not been standing around in the slush, she noticed; their black boots remained clean. Had Lina thought to demand his pink identification card, as was the right of Soviet citizens facing interrogation, her caller would have produced it. Not that it mattered. What happened was not to be forestalled.

Lina was thrust into a car and driven from her building along the broad, deserted avenue toward the old center of Moscow. She did not return to the four-room apartment where she had lived, with and without her husband, for twelve years.

As the car slinked through the sullen city streets, she realized that the worst had come to pass. Her name had appeared on a detention list and her arrest ordered. Fear stopped her from screaming, but she gained enough bearing to challenge her abductors. "What's happened? Why am I in this car? Why have you taken my purse away, with my keys?" she demanded. "Let me go, let me tell my children. I can't just go with you like this."

They drove past the Kursk train station, onto Pokrovka Street, and into the center of Moscow and Lubyanka Square, the heart of the Soviet police state. The most ornate building in the ever-expanding complex was a mud-brown edifice with a columned façade, once the home of an insurance firm and now headquarters of the MGB, the Ministry of State Security (Ministerstvo gosudarstvennoy bezopasnosti). Along with the MVD, or Ministry of Internal Affairs (Ministerstvo vnutrennikh del), the MGB was tasked with administering the vast labor-camp system in Siberia. On the same square, just across from a department store called Children's World (Detskiy mir), stood a dull-yellow neoclassical fortress, the Lubyanka prison. Its gates opened to allow the car past the guard station, then closed.

Neighbors who witnessed Lina's arrest would later recount the details to Svyatoslav, then twenty-three years old, and her younger son, Oleg, nineteen, who had returned home to watch helplessly as the family apartment was plundered. A photograph survives of the entranceway after the search: papers litter the floor; Oleg sits on a kitchen footstool, staring blankly at the list of items removed. Police seized paintings, jewelry, and photographs, along with other mementos and treasured possessions, including Serge's coveted Förster grand piano. Lina's gold and emerald ring would also go missing, along with a prized floral painting by Natalia Goncharova, an artist affiliated with the Ballets Russes. A recording of *La bohème* was smashed while being hauled down the stairs. The Duke Ellington records were tagged for later collection. Interior doors were sealed, shrinking the apartment to half its original size.

Svyatoslav and Oleg turned in vain to family friends for help. They then trudged through the snow to Prokofiev's dacha outside of Moscow with the grim news. They had not seen their father for months. He listened in silence before stammering, enigmatically, "What have I done?" That evening, he and Mira searched his belongings to purge anything potentially incriminating from his cosmopolitan past. He burned foreign-language magazines, books, and letters at the kitchen stove. Lina would later assume that he too had been imprisoned.

First at Lubyanka, then at Lefortovo prison, Lina suffered nine months of sustained interrogation. Investigators spat on her, kicked her, and threatened her children. Needles were stuck into her arms and legs. For the first three months, she was deprived of sleep, pushing her to the brink of madness. Two of every five days she spent crouched in a cell for hours on end until her legs shook and buckled from the pain. In the deep winter cold, she was made to walk outside without a coat to face another round of questioning, as the screams of other inmates echoed in the central square. Hers would be louder, one of her torturers growled into her ear.

Information about Lina's arrest, trial, and imprisonment in the gulag comes from personal letters and other unpublished documents currently in the possession of her grandson Serge Prokofiev Jr., a resident of Paris. These materials, including papers from Soviet police files and the embroidered sack that held her music, provide those details of Lina's life that she kept secret from interviewers, kept secret even from herself. Other materials used in this book come from the Russian State Archive of Literature and Art (RGALI) and the Serge Prokofiev Archive at Goldsmiths, University of London — the latter housing scattered interview transcripts (here fact-checked and filled in) and "closed" letters from the 1930s. Most of the archival sources consulted in the first half of this book are from RGALI collection 1929, section 4, which to this day remains "categorically forbidden" (*kategoricheskoye zapryoshcheniye*) to researchers. Exclusive permission to access all of these materials was granted by the Serge Prokofiev Estate.

This book chronicles a totalitarian nightmare but begins with a young woman's dreams. The pledges that the Soviet Union made to Lina — of material comfort and social status, of a cosmopolitan life secured by the socialist state, of individual freedom and special privilege — mirror those it made to itself, its citizens, and its sympathizers. But the regime was nothing if not a tangled network of criminals, and its business was not the business of the people but the machinations of immoral leaders who secured power through coercion and violence. Lina never came to terms with the tragedy of her life, nor did the country that was its stage for many years.

Chapter 1

LINA RARELY SPOKE about her arrest and eight years in prison. Silence was a condition of her release, but she would have chosen it anyway. American journalists were the most tactless, and British journalists the most persistent, in the pursuit of details about that time, but no one learned much, though she sat for interviews. Lina had perfected the art of evasion and used her skills against those with the hubris to write about things that they did not understand. She would, she decided, revise her life on her own in an autobiography, but she never wrote more than scattered notes and an outline.

The list of forbidden subjects grew as she aged. The events after her arrest were suppressed, then too her experiences with her children during the Second World War. Soon the silence spread across the entire period between 1936, when she moved to Moscow, and 1974—the year of her de facto defection to the West. She papered over the period with élan, making it seem as if she had never even lived in the Soviet Union, that she had not been forsaken by her husband. She slipped, however, in an interview for the *New York Times* by mentioning "eight years in prison and in the north" even while insisting that her life had not been "a tragic one." Still, the trauma could not be suppressed. Jumbled memories haunted her nights and fueled the paranoia of her days.

The past for Lina included Paris in the 1920s and 1930s, and her upbringing in New York, where she learned about world politics from

Russian émigrés. More often she transported herself to the distant past, harking back to her relatives in nineteenth-century France, Poland, Russia, and Spain. But these people and places were so long lost that she could no longer remember who was who, when was when, or where was where. Her memories, or memories of memories, came out confused and fragmented. There was the engineer uncle who laid underwater cables until he contracted malaria in a swamp, and the doting Polish Lithuanian grandfather who became a high-ranking councilor in the Russian government (Poland being part of the Russian empire at the time). Grandpa Vladislav, her mother's father, favored Lina, taking her to fancy restaurants where the waiters glided like ghosts over the floor; he presented her with bouquets of flowers and watched her dance when she was four years old. The erudite, spiritual Grandma Caroline, Lina's namesake, helped the little girl overcome her fear of the dark. "Can't we turn on the light because I'm afraid?" Lina pleaded during a thunderstorm. "But you know everything in this room," her grandmother cooed. "Nothing has changed. And the quietness . . . Listen to the quietness in the dark, and the thunderstorm, it's wonderful."

Lina reveled in these flickering memories, recalling image after image of her mother's family, despite her interviewers' lack of interest. She described scarily mystical childhood summers in the Caucasus, the southernmost part of Russia, where fragile wooden houses huddled on mountain plateaus from which torrents of water cascaded. Her aunt Alexandra lived there with her Welsh husband, who might have been the cable layer. The place was wild, and the howls of the jackals and the savage barking of the wolfhounds that guarded the houses made Lina cower at night. Later, when she heard this same barking in the barracks, she escaped into thoughts of her girlhood, willing herself to remain unafraid of the dark.

Of all the places she had visited or lived in, Russia remained a dominant and powerful attraction. It stood out in her recollections of her childhood, even though the time she spent there was trivial compared to her years in Spain, Switzerland, Cuba, and the United States. She remembered her peripatetic upbringing as an adventure.

· · ·

Born on October 21, 1897, on Calle de Bárbara de Braganza in Madrid, Lina inherited her chestnut hair and dark, heavy-lidded eyes from her father, but otherwise she was very much her mother's daughter: courageous, impetuous, and relentless once committed to something—though that something was often hard to find. Her father, Juan Codina, who began his musical career singing at the Catedral Basílica de Barcelona, became a professional tenor and amateur composer of songs with a Catalan flavor. He took lessons with Cándido Candi, a prominent composer, organist, and arranger of folksongs. From Barcelona Juan went to Madrid, where he studied at the Royal Conservatoire. His voice dropped from countertenor to tenor range during this period but retained its delicate thinness. Later in the United States he taught American students to sing solfège, the do-re-mi system of musical syllables.

In Madrid, Juan met and fell for Olga Nemïsskaya, a fair-haired, gray-eyed soprano from Odessa, Ukraine. She had trained in St. Petersburg, Russia, before traveling to Italy and on to Spain for lessons with the eminent tenor Giorgio Ronconi, who was then in his seventies but still accepting students. Juan and Olga married in 1895 or 1896, despite protests from her parents about his being Catholic and from his about her Calvinist Protestant origins. Juan had six brothers who made their living on the sea, plus a sister, Isabella, a late addition to the Codina family much beloved by her parents. But Olga never got to know them, having been coarsely branded an *herética*, and Juan never spoke of his family, save for the occasional suggestion that his mother had studied Asian languages and some of his brothers ended up in South America. His financial prospects as a musician worried Olga's father, who grumbled that she would have done better to marry a caretaker. In truth, Juan was something of a dabbler, a jack-of-all-trades but master of none, too much the artist to succeed in business. And as an artist, he suffered terrible stage fright.

As a very young girl, Lina traveled with her parents to Russia. This was long before the radical upheaval known as the Russian Revolution, before even the First World War and the rise of the communist movement. The basement execution of the Russian tsar Nicholas II, his wife, and their five children still lay a decade in the future.

· · ·

Perhaps in the Russian capital of St. Petersburg, perhaps in Moscow or somewhere else, Juan sang a few recitals under the Russian equivalent of his name, Ivan. Olga did not perform with him, even though her talent rivaled—or even exceeded—his. In the early 1890s, she carved out a niche for herself in the regional theaters of Italy. A notice from 1894 places her in the role of the coquettish peasant girl Micaela in *Carmen*, staged at the Teatro Sociale in the northern Italian town of Montagnana. Engagements with opera troupes in Moscow and Milan would follow. She sang under the stage name Neradoff, which, as her teacher advised her, was much easier to spell and pronounce than Nemïsskaya.

While her parents were busy performing, Lina was left in the care of her maternal grandparents in the Caucasus. Her bond with them intensified during successive visits, and there she formed some of her strongest childhood memories. There was a beekeeper who, warning Lina of the dangers of the creatures in his care, placed a mask over her face before she approached the hives. She retrieved eggs from her grandfather's henhouse, and with a shovel chased geese around the yard, imitating their hissing and honking. At some point around 1906 she was in Moscow at a fashionable department store, where her parents or grandparents presented her with a pleated coat and velvet beret imported from Paris. She kept one of the leaf-embossed buttons long after outgrowing the coat.

Lina was there when her grandmother died. Her parents had made the fortnight trek from Switzerland in hopes of seeing her one last time. At the wooden house, her grandfather took eight-year-old Lina by the hand and guided the girl to her grandmother's bedside. She watched as he bent to caress the weathered face. He then asked Lina to do the same, explaining that Grandma Caroline was about to leave. "Kiss her on the forehead, or on the cheek," he said, guiding her. Lina complied but wondered aloud, "But she's so cold. Why doesn't she get well?" "Well, she's going away, to another world."

This was the beloved grandmother who had taught Lina not to fear the night and who had also introduced her to ancient fables as told by Jean de La Fontaine. Reciting them in the original French, she encouraged Lina to learn their elegant phrasing by heart—which she did, though much later in life. Her grandmother was also an accomplished scholar of French literature and an author: she read Lina the stories she herself had written. Most of them dwelled on religious conflicts that were difficult for a six- or seven-year-old to understand. One of the grimmer tales concerned the St. Bartholomew's Day massacre and seemed to refer, perhaps by allegorical extension, to the persecution of Caroline's Huguenot relatives. In gratitude to her grandmother, Lina recalled as an adult the moral of the La Fontaine tale about a butterfly that leaves its hiding place, only to be torn apart by children. "To live happily one must live hidden," she offered as a clue to understanding her experiences in the Soviet Union.

Lina's life became sadder when her grandfather, whose beard she would remember twirling in her fingers, decided that he could not continue on his own. His metabolism was weakened by various nagging ailments; he contracted pneumonia and made it worse by throwing open the windows of his house and breathing in the frost. He died in November 1907. Juan and Olga never returned to Russia after his death.

Home for Lina was now Switzerland, in the quaint Grand-Saconnex suburb of Geneva. She recalled a park and a lake, with skaters in the winter, a pair of bakeries, one much more elaborate than the other, and outdoor parties arranged by the local mayor. Neighbors alternately called her La Petite Espagnole or La Petite Russe, unable to decide from which corner of Europe the exotic child with the long dark braids had emerged. She attended kindergarten in the village, frowning at its strictness and struggling with French grammar. This setback, which her mother helped her to overcome, belied what would prove to be a phenomenal talent for languages. During her early years, Lina would hear and absorb five: Russian from her mother and maternal grandfather, English from the nannies, French from her maternal grandmother, and Spanish and Catalan from her father. German came in dribs and drabs. This exposure was the greatest blessing of her cosmopolitan background, fitting her for a likely career as an interpreter. Near the end of her life, she went back to see the kindergarten schoolhouse again, only to find that it had been razed, along with the entire village, to build the Geneva international airport.

Juan and Olga pursued their musical careers, performing in and around Switzerland. There survive short reviews of recitals at the Conservatoire de Musique de Genève, where Juan performed Italian arias on a mixed program in January 1904. According to a paragraph in *Le Journal de Genève*, he capably interpreted songs by Paolo Tosti, an Italian English composer still active at the time and very much in demand in drawing rooms and salons. Olga also performed, and attracted her admirers. One of them made a profound impression on Lina and, thanks to his connections, became a crucial contact for her, years later. This was Serge M. Persky, a prominent Russian-to-French translator who worked for a dozen years as secretary to the prime minister of France, Georges Clemenceau. His admiration for Olga and her mother, Caroline (Lina's grandmother), was longstanding. Having arranged several concerts for Olga in Europe, he expressed frustration that she had not achieved the fame that, in his estimation, she deserved. Nor could he quite understand her decision to curtail her musical activities in order to raise her daughter.

Lina benefited from his chivalrous largesse and looked forward to his visits and the beautiful tins of chocolate-covered biscuits he presented to her in an effort to sweeten his relationship with Olga. When, in 1920, Persky learned that Lina was living in France, he sought her out, lavishing chocolate truffles on her as if she still had ribbons in her hair and asking, "Avez-vous une aussi belle voix que votre mère?" (Do you have as beautiful a voice as your mother?) Deaf to Lina's protests, he imagined marrying her off to one of his millionaire friends.

Juan and Olga were not poor, but their finances were precarious and they found themselves having to draw on Olga's family money. When discussing this and other sensitive matters in Lina's presence, they would write notes to each other in languages she had not yet learned to read. During one of these exchanges they decided to accept an offer of help from Olga's Swiss uncle to sail to New York City, where it was hoped they could further their careers. This was naive, since Juan at forty was past his prime as a singer and Olga, thirty-five, had let her skills slide. They promised each other and their daughter that the move would not be permanent.

On December 21, 1907, the family sailed from Boulogne-sur-Mer on the ocean liner *Statendam*, listing Juan's brother Paul as their nearest living relative in Spain and an unnamed hotel as their destination in New York. They disembarked at Ellis Island on New Year's Day,

1908, becoming part of a vast wave of immigration that would, by 1910, bring the population of the five boroughs of New York to some five million people. Nearly two million residents were foreign born, including the thin-lipped, top-hatted mayor, George B. McClellan Jr., a native of Dresden. McClellan earned as much fame for the architectural wonders he muscled into being between 1904 and 1909 as he did for his puritanical campaign against the rising fad known as the moving picture. The same man who oversaw the building of Grand Central Station and the Chelsea Piers revoked the licenses of the hundreds of nickelodeons that operated at the time in concert halls, restaurants, and bars. Other forms of entertainment, for both the masses and the elite, remained safe: Lina and her parents arrived in New York during the opening run of George Cohan's vaudeville entertainment *The Talk of the Town* at the Knickerbocker Theatre, and just ten days before the Viennese composer Gustav Mahler conducted the Metropolitan Opera. (Mahler would soon be replaced at the Met by Arturo Toscanini and pivot to the New York Philharmonic and Carnegie Hall.)

For assistance, the Codinas at first relied on Olga's uncle, who had sailed on the *Statendam* with them. Frederic Charles Verlé had long since emigrated from Europe with his wife, Mary; she had died on Christmas Day, 1898, at the age of fifty-four. The widower, whose surname was Americanized to Wherley, rented an apartment on Division Avenue in Brooklyn for a while, later relocating to the Williamsburg area. He taught German in the evenings at Public School No. 19. And in an effort to supplement his income, he took out postage-stamp-sized ads in the *Brooklyn Daily Eagle* under the name Professor Frederick C. (or F. C.) Wherley. These offered lessons in French, German, and Spanish at moderate rates.

Lina and her parents squeezed into his lodgings at 206 Rodney Street. Wherley was an insistent and petulant man whose only real passion, according to Lina, was the "made-up language" of Esperanto, which he foisted on the unconverted with revivalist zeal. For his efforts, he would be elected vice president of the Brooklyn Esperanto Society, which he helped to found. Living with him was unpleasant, and his repeated efforts to indoctrinate Lina in Esperanto precipitated an argument with her mother that almost landed the immigrant family on the street. Olga complained that her daughter had more than enough languages to contend with, and besides, Esperanto sounded terrible.

The conflicts motivated the family to travel to Havana, Cuba, where Juan had friends. That was the last time Lina remembered seeing her irascible uncle, but in fact she lived with him again when she returned from Cuba. She would also lodge with him in her early teens while her parents traveled abroad to perform. The separations were painful, hence forgotten. Since his cherished Esperanto was banned by Olga, Wherley resolved to force some of his second-favorite language—German—onto his niece. The experiment proved successful, though Lina continued to begrudge his presence in her life. She would not see the last of him until she was in her midteens. Wherley mysteriously disappeared from his apartment; unable to find any trace of him through mutual friends, Lina's mother concluded that he had committed suicide.

The family ventured to Havana by steamship, a cheaper option than the rail-and-ferry service through Key West, Florida. They found temporary lodging on Tulipán Street, in a market-filled neighborhood of transients not far from the port and near the soon-to-be-demolished Tulipán train station. Cuba, which was under American naval occupation, remained a magnet for Spanish immigrants, who operated their own banks, social services, and daily newspaper—the conservative *Diario de la Marina*. Havana catered to a chimerical assortment of conventioneers, servicemen, sugar barons, and entertainers. Juan planned to improvise a living as a Catalan folk musician or an opera singer with the National Theater.

Soon, however, Lina and her mother quit Havana, steaming back to New York without Juan on May 27, 1908. Meanwhile he made contact with Adolfo Bracale, impresario of the National Theater, a connection that would later lead to performances throughout Latin America and South America. When Juan returned to New York, the family rented their first apartment: a five-room flat in a walkup at 404 Gold Street in Brooklyn, a block over from the major thoroughfare of Flatbush Avenue Extension and still reasonably close to Wherley's apartment. Lodgings in the narrow red-fronted building ranged from eighteen to twenty-five dollars per month; the janitor who lived in the basement handled all inquiries and complaints. The place had little going for it besides quick access to the Brooklyn Bridge and trams into Manhattan.

Among their neighbors were a few other Russian immigrants, but most were locals—Brooklyn had a higher percentage of native-born residents than did Manhattan. Two boarders lodged with the Codina family at least briefly: a middle-aged dockhand and his daughter, another Lina; the girls were the same age, as were a couple of boys in the building. The children could walk five minutes east to Fort Greene Park, a hilly expanse of thirty acres with impressive views of the Navy Yard and Manhattan. A few minutes more to the west lay Borough Hall and the busy shopping district of Fulton and Court Streets.

Construction of the new Fourth Avenue subway, running across the Manhattan Bridge south along the avenue, meant that Lina had to make her way everywhere with care. Trenches ran a hundred feet wide and thirty feet deep. Workmen were almost entombed on Gold Street when the embankment gave way near Myrtle Avenue, smothering them in sand and gravel; they escaped with minor injuries. The same noise, smell, and danger—from the same source, subway construction—would confront her and her own children some three decades later outside their new apartment in Moscow.

Lina entered grade school in Brooklyn at Public School No. 5, on the corner of Tillery and Bridge Streets, just two blocks from home. At fourteen years of age, she was in sixth grade. The years of traveling had slowed her education in the basics, and English was not her strongest language. But she studied hard and, thanks to her mother's prodding, earned good marks. On Memorial Day, 1911—two months after the worst industrial tragedy in New York's history, the Triangle Shirtwaist Factory fire—Lina took part in a patriotic school pageant on the subject of the American Civil War. Her role was to recite by heart the anonymous nineteenth-century tale "Foes United in Death," in which tragically wounded soldiers, a Northerner and a Southerner, resolve to forgive each other in their final moments. "The Southerner tried to speak, but the sound died away in a murmur from his white lips; but he took the hand of his fallen foe, and his stiffening fingers closed over it, and his last look was a smile of forgiveness and peace."

Meanwhile Juan maintained a catch-as-catch-can career, performing throughout New York. The city remained, to his modest benefit, musically conservative, importing modernism rather than generating it. The dominant forms of mass entertainment were vaudeville and syncopated dance orchestras. The jazz age had yet to begin. From the newspapers that catered to immigrants, Juan would have learned about the opening of the Winter Garden Theater, the Folies-Bergère, and the banishment of the tango from the ballrooms, but these events, like the high-society-driven intrigues at the opera and the philharmonic, were of little relevance to him as he struggled to make ends meet.

Some of the venues where he performed offered programming that tended toward the diverse and eclectic. On January 21, 1909, Juan sang popular arias by Leoncavallo (from *Pagliacci*) and Mascagni (from *Cavalleria rusticana*) as well as Luigi Venzano's irresistible "Valse brillante" as part of a program arranged by the Chiropean Women's Club. Formed in 1896, the club brought together accomplished women in the eastern district of Brooklyn for meetings on the first and third Thursday of each month, from October to May. Its odd name stemmed from the Greek words for hand (*chiros*) and song (*peon*). But it was also an elaborate acronym standing for Christianity, Heaven, Independence, Industry, Republic, and a handful of other slogans, coyly kept secret. Its organizers encouraged intellectual and professional opportunities for women, so that they would be recognized as not merely equal but indeed superior to men. Olga was involved with the club and doubtless helped arrange for her semi-employed husband to sing at the January 21 meeting. The headline speaker that afternoon was Madame Marie Cross Newhaus, a fine arts patron and a prominent advocate for justice for women. She gave a talk titled "Italy, or Some Italians," on the subject of Italian American culture—hence the Italian composers on Juan's program—and also rallied support for the victims of the devastating Italian earthquake and tsunami of the preceding year.

Olga sought bookings of her own in New York. In 1908 she signed with Carlo E. Carlton and his Metropolitan Musical Association, a talent agency in midtown Manhattan. The firm was in financial trouble and would collapse in the early spring of 1909, but Carlton worked hard for Olga. He touted her as a renowned talent in an advertisement in the *New York Clipper* and arranged some singing for her; he even presented her with the chance to appear on screen. Lina remembered her mother being hired as an actress for a silent film about a green but gifted immigrant singer. Olga was to play a despoiled and dishonored version of herself for distribution to the nickelodeons, and according to Lina's exceedingly partial recollection, Olga was to have lip-synced a brilliant aria from *La traviata* as part of the role. But as soon as the contract had been signed and the announcement prepared, Olga took sick and pulled out, infuriating everyone involved. Her agent suspected that the illness was feigned and moved her name from the top to the bottom of his talent roster. Lina believed that her mother had succumbed to pride, deciding that acting the part of a naif just off the boat was beneath her — an insult to her sophisticated upbringing.

Thereafter Olga's musical activities in the United States were limited to teaching. She would not return to the stage there nor fulfill the promise that she demonstrated in Europe. Friends of the family, including her devoted benefactor Serge Persky, were saddened and surprised to learn of this withdrawal. After 1912 she and Juan earned the bulk of their income as voice teachers. To generate business, they advertised in the *Brooklyn Daily Eagle* and the *New York Evening Telegram*, marketing themselves as experienced international professionals.

The couple taught for about a dollar an hour at 88 Herkimer Street, their second Brooklyn apartment, which Lina called home until graduation. The four-story brick building, adjacent to the exotically ornate Ancient Arabic Order of the Mystic Shrine (the Shriners, an American branch of the Freemasons), was advertised as having "the cheapest high-class apartments in the vicinity" and boasted hot water as well as steam heat. It was one room bigger than the family's previous rental on Gold Street, and the extra room became the teaching studio. Lina, hiding under the piano on the floor, sometimes listened to the lessons, pretending that her parents could not see her. She absorbed some of the Italian opera repertoire from Olga and basic music theory from Juan, and she began to study voice with them herself.

In 1913 Lina completed her elementary education at Public School No. 3. She was in eighth grade and would soon turn sixteen, the age that marked the end of compulsory education for girls in New York; henceforth she continued her schooling at night. Her graduation, held at the nearby Commercial High School on the warm, clear evening of June 24, 1913, coincided with the school's 250th anniversary. (It remains the oldest continually operating public school in New York City.) To honor the occasion, the commencement exercises featured historical reenactments, processionals, choral singing, and ballroom dancing. Bearing the title "The Call of the Centuries," the pageant was reported in lavish detail in the *Brooklyn Daily Eagle*.

Thanks to her strong voice, Lina was chosen to participate in the third scene, which re-created an eighteenth-century colonial singing school. The fourth scene — the actual graduation — featured synchronized marching and the announcement, from a member of the local school board, that Misses Gladys Cook and Carolina Codina had won the prizes for German, each receiving a silver medal from the German-American National Alliance. Wherley's lessons had paid off.

Lina herself remembered the event in patchwork detail. She hoarded chiffon for an elaborate hand-sewn graduation gown. Her mother refused to risk her elegant hands with needle and thread, so Lina had to fashion the dress by herself from a simple pattern. There was a formal dance for the class (102 strong, almost equally divided between boys and girls), during which the ill-tuned school orchestra performed a Mozart minuet.

Much of the rest of Lina's education was vocational, and it took her out of Brooklyn into Manhattan and, she sometimes claimed, the suburbs of northern New Jersey. By 1916, she had relocated with her parents to Manhattan: first to Morningside Heights, where the family took an apartment at 161 Manhattan Avenue, near Central Park at 107th Street, and then farther north to 145th Street in Washington Heights. Most of their neighbors were native-born Americans of modest professions, including salesmen and clerks, teachers, and a handful of actors and actresses of limited success. Juan and Olga continued to travel, leaving their daughter in the care of kindhearted friends of greater means.

In 1912, before Lina's eighth-grade graduation, her parents sailed to Bermuda, performing on one of the three ocean liners that, during Lent, conveyed the well-heeled of New York to the island retreat. That winter turned severe, and the demand for reservations on the boats and in Bermuda's hotels exceeded capacity, meaning that Juan and Olga had large audiences. In 1916 both Lina and her mother were left behind when Juan went on tour to Guatemala City with an opera troupe. Lina knew little of his activities on this junket or any of his subsequent travels to Latin and South America. The details of his 1920 trip to Lima and Panama with the Bracale Opera Company were long forgotten, if she ever even knew of them.

A calm, kind person, Juan was much less involved in his daughter's upbringing than was his wife. He presided contentedly over an apartment full of music and musician friends, but remained a distant figure in Lina's life. Olga, in contrast, hovered over the girl, pressing a glass of milk into her hand each time she moved to leave the apartment and constantly overfeeding her, fearing that she might become anemic. Since Olga considered the subways and elevated trains to be incubators of infection, Lina was discouraged from using them. But her lips never turned blue, the dreaded sign of iron depletion, and she escaped the massive flu epidemic of 1918 without a sniffle. Olga even at one point suggested that her daughter preserve her figure by forswearing exercise. "People," Lina recalled, "had strange ideas then."

The most that Lina learned about her father's career was the undated recording he made for Columbia Records, accompanying himself on the guitar. She kept it her entire life, along with a beautiful sepia photograph of him sprawled in a palm tree in Cuba, nattily attired in a three-piece suit and Havana straw hat. The 78 had two very old songs on it, part of the wistfully sensuous folk and flamenco repertoire that Juan took to Havana. He liked to sing one of them, "Para jardines Granada," to Olga, perhaps reminding her of his triumphant courtship. "For gardens, Granada; for women, Madrid; but for love—your eyes, when they look at me." Lina jotted down these lines in a notebook and learned the song herself.

Among the people who cared for her while her parents were away was Vera Danchakoff, a remarkable woman scientist lauded at the time for her study of tumors and more recently noted for her pioneering work on stem cells. Lina remembered her as a researcher for the Eli Lilly pharmaceutical company, but she was much more. Danchakoff had studied medicine in her native Petrograd (St. Petersburg) before immigrating to the United States in 1915—a year after Russia's ruinous entry into World War I. She worked first at the Rockefeller Institute in New York City and later the College of Physicians and Surgeons of Columbia University. She was also a journalist and politically active humanitarian, serving as the New York correspondent for the Moscow paper *Utro Rossii* (Russian Morning) and assisting the American Relief Administration in the early 1920s to publicize the plight of Soviet scientists in Russia during and after World War I. Her energetic example—she was written up in the feminist *Who's Who* of the day—might have helped inspire Lina's own ambitions.

Yet the connection was more cultural than professional. A devoted amateur pianist, Danchakoff participated in the musical soirees that Juan and Olga hosted in their apartment. She in turn invited the family to her summer rental in Woods Hole, Massachusetts. Danchakoff and her husband presided over lavish dinners with successive generations of relatives and friends carefully arranged around the table. The patriarchal vignette remained in Lina's mind, testament to the important social connections that her parents had forged in Russian émigré circles in New York. When Lina was nine, the Russian émigré population stood at 500,000; by the time she was twenty-one, the number of political, economic, and cultural refugees had increased to 750,000. They brought with them descriptions of the chaos that followed the Revolution: the abdication of the Russian tsar in February 1917 and the Bolshevik (Communist) takeover in November of that same year. Her parents hoped that she would become part of the vast network, and in this they would not be disappointed.

Lina would, for example, twice encounter the Russian composer Serge Rachmaninoff, a tall, lean figure, suave with the ladies but otherwise sullen. For the sake of ticket sales in America, he did not mind having his music described as melancholic and sentimental, as though burdened with the woes of his homeland. He dispelled these mawkish clichés as soon as he placed his preternaturally large hands on the keyboard, however. Rachmaninoff overpowered his audiences as a performer, even dominated the orchestras that played his piano concertos with him.

The first time Lina met him was in 1909, during Rachmaninoff's first visit to the United States. It was a successful trip, yet nonetheless made him miserable. (He declined successive offers to tour until after the Russian Revolution.) Through mutual friends, Lina and her mother received an invitation to meet him backstage at the Academy of Music on East Fourteenth Street, the grande dame of the Gilded Age concert scene and the nineteenth-century home of the Metropolitan Opera. Olga made sure that her eleven-year-old daughter looked her prettiest for the occasion, dressing her in a sailor suit and plaiting her long hair down the back. Rachmaninoff professed an intense dislike for American children but took to Lina straightaway, stroking her head and murmuring nostalgically, "You're such a polite little Russian girl."

Coming into her own as a young woman, Lina found a ready home in Russian émigré circles, trading on her mother's connections while forging her own. As soon as she finished grade school, Lina was instructed to find a profession, a métier, rather than relying on marriage and motherhood. As Juan and Olga themselves had learned, life was unstable and anything could happen; Lina needed to be able to support herself, perhaps in the employ of a professional lady or teaching French. Income was less important than establishing independence, Olga claimed. She had a feminist streak, fueled by the activities of her own mother and involvement in organizations like the Chiropean Women's Club. So Lina trekked to business school to learn basic secretarial skills while also continuing with the singing lessons she had started with her mother.

Thanks to Olga, Lina could read and write Russian as well as speak it, and these skills offered her entry into the world of well-connected émigrés, many of them impressive women—including three Veras. Besides Vera Danchakoff, there was Vera Johnston, an affluent socialite involved in Russian relief efforts during World War I; she took singing lessons with Lina's parents and shared news of Russia with Olga. Johnston had impressive pro-immigrant political connections with the Democratic political machine known as Tammany Hall, but what most fascinated Lina was the unusual, even bizarre, mix of nationalities and persuasions among Johnston's relatives. Her mother had been a pioneering science fiction writer, famous in Russia for her stories about children with occult powers. The fascination with the supernatural, which peaked in Russia in the eerie twilight of the tsarist era, extended to her aunt, Helena Blavatsky, a clairvoyant and spiritualist who established the Theosophical Movement. She was rumored to perform amazing psychic feats and attracted a passionate following in the United States. Though Lina was not drawn into Theosophy, she would later become a passionate devotee of another spiritual woman, Mary Baker Eddy, and the faith she founded, Christian Science.

Vera was married to Charles Johnston, whom Lina also found fascinating. He was a leading expert in Sanskrit, and his translations of Hindu scripture, including the Bhagavad Gita, became standard reading for converts to Theosophy. Before meeting Vera in England (at the London home of her Aunt Helena) and relocating to the United States, he had briefly worked in India for the Bengal Civil Service in 1888. There he contracted "jungle fever" and received a medical discharge, returning to Europe to become a scholar and writer.

In the United States, he held various temporary appointments: as a faculty member at the University of Wisconsin in 1908, an instructor at the Russian Seminary in New York, and even a captain in the Military Intelligence Division from 1918 to 1919. Charles claimed the eminent poet W. B. Yeats as a longtime personal friend; they had gone to school together in Ireland and had similar religious outlooks. In 1914, through Charles, Lina herself met Yeats, who was in New York on a lecture tour. She described him as "ruddy faced" and a true "cock of the walk."

Charles adored Lina, alternately nicknaming her "Buttons" and "Baalaa," the latter a Sanskrit word meaning "little girl." His wife, whom Lina remembered as an old-fashioned Russian matron, discouraged his fawning and let on that she had grown tired of her husband, as he had of her. They distracted themselves with the theater and shared their tickets to operettas by Gilbert and Sullivan and a play by W. B. Yeats with Lina and her parents. Lina enjoyed *The Mikado* and *Pirates of Penzance* but could not grasp the arcane Celtic drama. Though Charles sought to explain it to her, her sole grade-school impression was of helmeted swashbuckling.

In February 1915, Lina was, through the Johnstons, among the cosmopolitan company at a reception and banquet aboard the Russian

American ocean liner *Kursk*, docked at the Bush Terminal port in Brooklyn. It was the launch of a fundraising campaign, organized by the recently formed Russian War Relief Society and sponsored by the wife of the Russian ambassador, Madame Bakhmeteff. Vera Johnston was a member of the executive committee, and Lina her special guest. On an unseasonably warm winter evening, women boarded the ship dressed in fur-trimmed coats and full-length velvet gowns in deep jewel tones, many cut in the stylish mode of the "moyen âge." Along with the dancing after dinner, a troupe of Domba players in Bozar costumes presented a program of Eastern folk music. That they hailed from India rather than Russia suggests that Vera had enlisted her husband's help in arranging the musical entertainment.

The third Vera who shepherded Lina into the workplace was Vera Janacopoulos, a Brazilian singer of Dutch and Greek descent. She was romantically involved with a Russian many years older than her, named Aleksey Stahl, a lawyer who arrived in the United States in 1918 from Russia, where he had served as a magistrate. Lina described him as a former mayor of Moscow, but he was, in fact, a member of the short-lived provisional government that succeeded the abdication of the Russian tsar in 1917. He had to flee when the Bolsheviks came to power nine months later; otherwise he would have been hunted down and shot. What was considered the real revolution was led by Vladimir Lenin, not the bourgeois holdovers who had formed the provisional government. To its members, and to Tsar Nicholas II and his family, no mercy was shown. Stahl was accordingly full of inflated stories about his survival, which he shared with friends and acquaintances over too many glasses of vodka at his house on Staten Island.

Lina admired him from a distance, recognizing danger in his charms and mischief in his twinkling eyes. His ginger beard enhanced the impression of foxlike cunning. Stahl's paramour, Vera — he called her "Diva" — was utterly different: enchanting, kindhearted, fluent in French. For Lina, she was the ideal role model.

Through such contacts, Lina landed her first job at the age of twenty-one. Much of the position was clerical, but it provided a unique education in international politics. In 1919 she was hired for a month as an assistant to Yekaterina (Catherine) Breshko-Breshkovskaya, nicknamed the "Grandmother of the Revolution." Twice imprisoned in Siberia for her involvement in militant anarchist and socialist organizations in Russia, she had agitated for the overthrow of Tsar Nicholas II and served in the provisional government that succeeded his abdication. Reportedly executed in Russia in 1918, Breshkovskaya had obviously escaped. She was seventy-five when she came to the United States, with some three decades of militant political activism behind her and fifteen years still ahead. Breshkovskaya made her way across the Pacific to the United States in January 1919, arriving in Seattle to begin a coast-to-coast tour of sorts to report on the famine, plunder, and violence in her homeland. She was a guest at Hull House in Chicago, a settlement dedicated to the welfare of new immigrants and to the cause of cosmopolitan pluralism. Speaking to a massive gathering of supporters at Union Station, she described the suffering of the Russian people in anguished and frightening detail and urged Americans to redouble their efforts on behalf of her Orphans Fund Council. Her supporters, including progressive women activists such as Lillian Wald, Jane Addams, and Alice Stone Blackwell, lionized Breshkovskaya for her selfless fundraising.

Ten days later, she arrived at Grand Central Terminal in New York, where she was greeted by cheering admirers bearing flowers. She was then whisked to the Henry Street Settlement, a sister institution of Hull House serving the immigrant community of New York's Lower East Side. Breshkovskaya made it her local headquarters.

Her story was the same as that of Lina's Staten Island host, Aleksey Stahl; both fled Russia to save their lives. Unlike Stahl, however, Breshkovskaya never lost her activist streak. Even in exile, she continued to campaign for change in Russia. While the beloved babushka lobbied for American humanitarian aid, she also spoke out forcefully against the danger of Bolshevism and in support of the League of Nations. She denounced the Bolsheviks and their leader, Lenin, as reckless fanatics under the control of German agents. The Russian Revolution was actually a coup d'état, she argued, that had subverted the cause of socialism.

The twenty-one-year-old Lina Codina worked as her typist and occasional interpreter, regarding her employer with bemusement. Breshkovskaya assumed an innocent, modest manner despite her astonishing range of experiences. She made a paradoxical impression on Lina: the "very old lady" pretended to be apolitical, "certainly not

Bolshevik," and "far from totalitarian." But as Breshkovskaya labored to explain to her American handlers, there was a difference between socialists and Bolsheviks; to her, the latter were just another brand of dictators, worse than the tsars. "It is difficult to speak of Russia unless you understand Russia," she concluded.

Lina was also struck by her feminism, though she would not have characterized it as such. Breshkovskaya believed that women, especially staunch American women, represented the best hope for humankind. She lauded the struggle for women's suffrage and stressed the importance of education in the pursuit of a just, goodhearted life. As she put it to Lillian Wald, education prevented people from being "enticed, tempted, and mislaid." Lina, still rather naive herself, recalled a much vaguer stress on "fundamental good foundations" and "humanitarian principles."

The job was temporary and intermittent, since Lina was just one of Breshkovskaya's assistants tending to her overfull calendar. At the invitation of the Executive Committee of the Friends of Russian Freedom, the Grandmother spoke on February 10 at Carnegie Hall —raising almost $11,000. She explained to the audience that what Russia needed most was a constitutional, representative government. After that she journeyed to Washington to appear before a congressional subcommittee on Bolshevism, testifying until exhausted and advised by her physicians to rest.

Some of her audiences on the left were skeptical and, to her amazement, she found herself caricatured as a lackey of capitalism. In Boston, her foes shouted impertinent questions in Russian from the balconies. A near riot erupted in Providence, with radicals in the rafters singing a revolutionary march while supporters on the floor countered with "The Star-Spangled Banner." Sensing that she had perhaps outworn her welcome, Breshkovskaya left the United States for France on June 28—but not before warning that there were some three million Bolshevik sympathizers in the United States who needed to be monitored.

Again tapping into the Russian network that was now as much hers as her mother's, Lina parlayed the experience with Breshkovskaya into another position, this one more regular and routine, in New York's financial district. Every morning she paid five cents to ride the IRT

West Side subway, newly extended to Lower Manhattan, from Washington Heights down to 136 Liberty Street. She earned from sixteen to twenty dollars a week—the typical salary for a young woman stenographer or office assistant—at the American Committee of the Russian Cooperative Unions.

The American Committee was part of the All-Russian Central Union of Consumer Societies, a trade organization known to the Russian community by its opaque acronym Tsentrosoyuz. It published a monthly English-language magazine called *Russian Cooperative News*, which reported on the activities and aspirations of the organization in fuzzy detail. The first issue explained the economic and diplomatic purpose of the American Committee: "The Cooperatives will endeavor to make America's share in the commerce and the industry of Russia as important and significant as the international trade position of the United States demands at the present time." But of course the real interests served were Russian. Consider that the declaration of the end of the First World War was greeted with anything but euphoria. Russia remained war-torn, so there was nothing to celebrate. "The peace treaty has been signed by Germany and the blockade of that country has been lifted. A strong and powerful rival has appeared in the world market and has to be reckoned with. Other nations are now shaping their economic policies on a footing totally different from that in vogue during the war 'that was.'" The economic reforms that the Bolsheviks had introduced in an effort to rescue the Russian economy from chaos were now under threat from, of all things, peace.

The American Tsentrosoyuz (there was of course one in Moscow, located in a building designed by Le Corbusier) housed a telegraph office along with a branch of the Moskovskiy narodnïy bank (Moscow People's Bank). Lina worked on the fourth floor under the supervision of Eugene Somoff, a friend of a friend who was also the personal assistant of the composer Serge Rachmaninoff. He was a little sweet on Lina and liked to tease her from his desk on the other side of a glass partition. Sometimes he picked up the telephone receiver to eavesdrop on her personal calls.

One of the clients at the bank was a blue-eyed, blond-haired composer and pianist visiting New York from Russia. He was well on his way to controversial fame in Europe and the United States, and he made no secret of his disdain for the pompous music of the Romantic composers whom New York audiences still held dear. The American media dwelled on his ferocious, mechanistic technique at the piano and the cacophonies of works like his Second Piano Concerto and *Scythian Suite*. In person he was much less bizarre and eccentric than the musician who loped across the stage to wreak havoc on Steinways. He was beleaguered by a touring schedule that taxed his strength, leaving him frail, even gaunt, but his icy intellect allowed him to remain focused on his purpose—the musical conquest of the New World. Rachmaninoff stood in the way in this city, but he was a generation older, a generation less modern.

Now and again the newcomer came to the bank to wire funds to his mother, who was trapped in Russia during the Revolution. As far as he knew she had traveled southward with her nephew's family. The journey was treacherous, since the nephew was a member of the retreating White Army and thus on the losing side of the civil war that had followed the Bolshevik eradication of the provisional government. The hope was that they would both be evacuated by boat on the Black Sea. The composer, who had very little money, was trying desperately to reach her. He had sent letters to all of the Russian consulates, enclosing small amounts of cash with a plea for information and instructions as to how his mother might contact him.

Lina thought him vaingloriously rude at first, but then became smitten. He gradually became curious about her. By the summer of 1919, they had been out a few times to concerts and dinners. Stahl was a mutual friend and, seeming to encourage the match, extended invitations to gatherings on Staten Island. Lina's mother voiced concern about the nascent relationship and advised her daughter against getting involved with a musician, as she herself had once been warned by her father. But Olga admitted that the lad was charming, and she enjoyed his talk of Russia, past and present.

His name was Serge Prokofiev. Lina first saw him on December 10, 1918, at a performance at Carnegie Hall that featured his First Piano Concerto. Vera Danchakoff had telephoned her mother with the news that an iconoclastic composer just arrived from Russia would be giving an orchestral concert. Neither she nor Olga liked new music, but they thought it might be interesting to hear a "Bolshevik" musician rumored to be a mad genius. Having overheard the conversation, Lina exclaimed, "Oh, I'd like to go too!" So she went to the raucously received concert, and another one after that, where she met the composer backstage. Thus began the next phase of her life, which proved to be even more of an adventure than her childhood.

Chapter 2

NEW YORK AUDIENCES had long been entertained by touring musicians, but Serge Prokofiev was a special draw in 1918—a modernist virtuoso who performed his own startlingly innovative music.

A child prodigy comparable to Mozart, he had studied at the St. Petersburg Conservatoire, whose first famous graduate was Tchaikovsky. Much younger and certainly more arrogant than his classmates, Serge taunted them by counting up their mistakes in harmony and counterpoint, while also telling anyone within earshot that he considered his classes boring to the point of bewilderment. His teachers groused, sighed, and tut-tutted in exasperation at the wrong notes in his scores and his strange orchestrations. He was too beholden to the noise-making, degenerate expressionists, futurists, and primitivists, he was told; he had no respect for tradition. Most of the time he brushed off the criticism, taking it as a point of pride that his grades were lower than those of his dutiful peers. Still, the scolding he regularly received from Nikolay Rimsky-Korsakov, Anatoliy Lyadov, and Alexander Tcherepnin could be tough, even mean-spirited, and he felt it.

His doting mother, Mariya Prokofieva, gave him tremendous confidence, however, and promised him a trip to Paris for graduation. Serge finished his exams in composition in 1909, and those in piano in 1914, winning first prize in a duel with four other pianists with a performance of his own First Piano Concerto—a tension-filled, percussive work that shattered the nerves of the Conservatoire's stout, red-faced director, Alexander Glazunov. He continued his studies to avoid conscription into the Imperial Army, producing his Second Piano Concerto as well as a cluster of shorter piano works with disarming titles: "Diabolic Suggestion," "Sarcasms," "Fugitive Visions." To "tease the geese," as he put it, referring to the fuddy-duddies of the Conservatoire, he also composed the old-fashioned *Classical Symphony* (Symphony no. 1). To his surprise, it would become one of his most famous works.

Prokofiev found Paris "astonishingly beautiful, alive, gay and seductive," as much for the iconoclastic artists it attracted as for its sights: the Eiffel Tower, from which he sent postcards to jealous friends back home; the silk top hats worn to the performances of the ballets *Petrushka, Daphnis et Chloé*, and *Scheherazade*; the Académie des Beaux-Arts; the boulevard cafes where he developed a taste for whiskey and soda. As soon as Serge Diaghilev, the impeccably tailored impresario of the Ballets Russes, granted him an audience, Prokofiev knew that his future lay in the West.

But by the time his plans to leave Russia had solidified, the route to Paris and its chic arts scene was cut off. Russia was in turmoil. The horrific events of February 1917 — the shootings on the streets of Petrograd, as St. Petersburg had been renamed; the flow of mutinous imperial soldiers into the center; the snipers on the roofs; the political leaflets blowing down the street; the acts of vandalism and the bonfires — unfolded in Serge's capacious imagination as if they were merely moves on a political chessboard. Though he saw these things himself, he did not feel them. Self-obsessed, and blessed with phenomenal powers of concentration, Serge shut out the chaos, closed off the world, and focused on his music.

In the spring of 1918, having left his mother behind in the Caucasus, he began a long journey east, first to Japan and then to America. He taught himself English en route (it lagged far behind his knowledge of French) and began work on his second opera, *Love for Three Oranges*, commissioned by the Chicago Lyric Opera.

Serge pursued his career in the West with the permission of Russia's Bolshevik (Communist) government. The head of cultural affairs under Vladimir Lenin, Anatoliy Lunacharsky, sanctioned his journey abroad with the understanding that Serge would serve as a kind of cultural diplomat. The Bolsheviks were destroyers, Lunacharsky admitted, whereas Serge was a creator. The regime needed him. He honored the agreement, keeping his assessment of post-revolutionary Russia positive in conversation with American reporters, never risking his good relationship with the Bolshevik regime and its foreign agents.

His trip to the United States was sponsored by the industrialist Cyrus McCormick, whom Serge met in June 1917, when McCormick visited Russia as a member of an American diplomatic delegation. It was a fraught sojourn, beginning with an unpleasant customs interview at Angel Island, California, on August 24, 1918, and ending on April 27, 1920, with the composer in the midst of a quarrel with the Chicago Opera. In between, he traveled America as a concert pianist, performing his own scores more than the shopworn favorites of the Romantic era beloved by his audiences.

Serge was homesick for Russia even as he privately reacted with disgust to reports of the Bolshevik execution of the tsar and the confiscation of private property by the Communists. He fretted that he had forsaken his country at a crucial—if brutal—period of transition and feared that he would be punished for seeking success abroad. The fate of his mother, who had nurtured his talent and overseen his education, was a pressing concern, as were his own prospects for returning. Yet there was no time for reflection, since he was living on borrowed money and had to hustle to secure commissions, performances, and publications in America. McCormick's money was running out, and Serge found himself in hock to various Russian contacts.

He suffered a myriad of stress- and fatigue-induced ailments throughout 1918 and 1919: nagging colds, migraine headaches, toothaches, scarlet fever, rheumatism, and a "plague of abscesses," one of which lodged in his throat. Although he was not yet out of his twenties, his hair thinned, his heart weakened, and he lost weight. Despite these hardships and the haggling with his tightfisted manager, M. D. Adams, over contracts and receipts, he remained certain of himself and of his genius. As confirmation, he obsessively added up the number of curtain calls he received after his recitals—ten or twelve (he couldn't remember exactly) in Chicago on December 8, 1918—and calculated the relationship between the loudness of the applause he received, the time of day of the performance, and whether the ladies in the audience were wearing gloves and thus unable to produce the volume he thought they should.

There was much more to his pursuit of fame than egotism. From his readings in philosophy—Serge steeped himself in Kant, Hegel, and Schopenhauer during his teens—he had come to the conclusion that his music existed outside time and space, that his talent was truly God-given. How else could he explain that melodies, harmonies, indeed entire forms just came to him, appearing in his mind, demanding to be written down? He had no choice but to devote his whole being to his music, no interruptions allowed.

His single-mindedness took different forms, including arrogant outbursts and occasional bouts of melancholia. If rejected or otherwise disappointed by the ladies he squired around—Lina included—his jaw would tighten and his face would redden as he accused them of being banal, superficial. His lack of basic human feeling could be shocking, as was the strange comfort he found in transferring matters of the heart to the mind. Of his father's death in 1910, Prokofiev reflected, chillingly: "Did I love him? I do not know . . . He served me, his only son, unstintingly, and it was thanks to his tireless work that I was provided for so long with all my material necessities." Sentiment, in his relationships as in his music, was anathema.

The composer maintained a daily diary of his travels in the United States, and he recalled the sights and sounds of his initial months in New York during the late summer of 1918 in coarsely colorful detail, from the "gloomy-looking Negro" who lived a floor below him in his shared rental on 109th Street to the "beautiful, flat-chested, and unresponsive" young woman whose professional services he enlisted. He soon relocated from uptown Manhattan to the more central, if still sketchy, Wellington Hotel on Seventh Avenue and Fifty-fifth Street, where he occupied two furnished rooms, with a piano. He joked in his diary that the walk-in closets provided sufficient space to conceal "other people's wives if furious husbands forced their way in through the door," but confessed that his love life was "limping badly." Circumstances improved once he entered the New York social scene and began to frequent the mansions of his sponsors. Besides various coquettes, he flirted with Harriet Lanier, founder and president of the Society of Friends of Music, at one of the teas she and her husband, a broker, held at their Beaux Arts–style mansion at 123 East Thirty-fifth Street. Lanier dedicated her life to the society—even after heart disease confined her to her bedroom at the Savoy Plaza Hotel, she continued to plan concerts—and so she promised, after Serge had "conquered" her with his playing, to sponsor his debut. But Lanier was put off by the outrageous fee he demanded, and changed her mind.

On the evening of October 19, 1918, Serge walked one block from the Wellington to Carnegie Hall to participate in a Russian Liberty Loan Committee concert. A fundraising event was not the debut he had imagined for himself in New York, and he worried about blemishing his reputation before it was even established. He was spared, however, by the organizers, who placed him at the end of the program. When the concert ran overtime, his appearance was scrapped. And so his actual debut came ten days later, on October 29, at the Brooklyn Museum. Members were invited to preview an exhibition of paintings and theater designs by Boris Anisfeld. (Anisfeld was a former Ballets Russes artist who later supplied the designs for the Chicago and New York premieres of *Love for Three Oranges*.) Preceding the reception was a concert of Russian piano and vocal music, but the two hundred guests in attendance did not even know that anyone worth noticing was at the piano. He was just the entertainment. After surveying the dowagers in the room and deciding that barbarism would neither be to their taste nor open their pocketbooks, he held back, playing to match his appearance: well-dressed, with carefully trimmed hair and polished nails. His aggressive Toccata sounded reticent, and he skipped notes to deaden its impact. "Prokofiev may well be the lion of the musical revolutionists," complained a disappointed reviewer in the *Brooklyn Daily Eagle*, "but yesterday that lion roared as gently as the gentlest dove." The "musical extremes"—avalanches of chromaticism on the black keys and oases of calm on the white—that had been promised in advance were nowhere to be heard. Perhaps, the reviewer sighed, Prokofiev "had been warned to treat the afternoon audience in his kindliest manner. For the music of the future we must perforce wait until other and more auspicious times."

That occasion arrived on November 20. Thanks to a loan of $450 from a Russian émigré benefactor, Serge managed at the last minute to arrange a recital in Aeolian Hall, located across from Bryant Park and the New York Public Library on the third floor of a seventeen-story skyscraper. He anticipated a small crowd of envious local pianists, but to his amazement, his manager delivered. Serge was greeted by an almost full house (the Aeolian seated thirteen hundred) of enthusiastic listeners. As the performance unfolded, the crowd pressed closer and closer to the stage to hear Serge's scintillating rendition of the scherzo and finale of his Second Piano Sonata. The stiff action of the piano flustered him; his hands took a wrong turn at one point and landed in the key of C major—not where he should have been. He recovered by rewriting a transition in his head and pounded on the Steinway until it produced the fortissimo he needed. He shredded his fingers, losing feeling in them halfway through, but he triumphed.

The program included works by Scriabin and Rachmaninoff, the latter intended to lure Rachmaninoff himself to the concert. He had just arrived in New York, and Serge sought the attention of his elder compatriot, a fellow pianist and composer who had achieved the kind of success Serge still longed for. Respect too would have been nice, but Rachmaninoff did not show it and failed to appear, leaving Serge to conclude that he simply had no interest in "the thoughts of the young." Apparently, he had "sold his soul to the devil for American dollars," Serge sniffed, by turning what should have been serious recitals into pops concerts.

Nonetheless, Serge achieved the intended impression—ultramodernist, cerebral, intolerant of tradition. During the three breaks in the concert, Serge bowed ten times, and the next day tallied eleven reviews. He had braced himself for withering critiques—the twentieth-century logic of his works confused nineteenth-century ears—and reasoned that, in the grand scheme, his career could survive a subpar appearance before a conservative crowd. Besides, he was better able to judge the success of his performance than was the press. The reviews were unflattering, as he had predicted, with the *New York Times* declaring him a "psychologist of the uglier emotions. Hatred, contempt, rage—above all, rage—disgust, despair, mockery and defiance legitimately serve as models for mood." The critic for the *Tribune* had the gall to describe his music as a "hell-broth" mixed in a "witches' caldron," only to retract the comment the next day. Apparently he had another ultra-modernist in mind.

Missing from the audience that evening was Serge's new friend and mentor Aleksey Stahl, who was sick in bed. (Lina also knew Stahl, through his girlfriend Vera Janacopoulos, a dramatic soprano.) They saw each other several times a week, but Serge was forced to stay away when Stahl came down with the Spanish flu, "coughing like a lunatic" as his fever shot up to 104 degrees. The composer was sure that he too would contract the potentially fatal disease, as had thousands of other New Yorkers in the fall of 1918. A mild head cold sent him into a panic, and so he refused to visit until he received written assurance that Stahl's home had been decontaminated.

The two had met by chance in the summer of 1918 in Yokohama, Japan, while both were en route to the United States—albeit for entirely different reasons.

Stahl had witnessed and, in a sense, become a victim of the political turmoil in Russia between 1905 and 1917. Having served in the provisional government that followed the abdication of the Russian tsar, he found himself marooned in Japan after the Bolshevik coup. The former Moscow and St. Petersburg magistrate nonetheless managed to maintain his political connections in Russia. In New York, Stahl nurtured good relations with the Russian consul—a potential employer for him and, for Serge, a possible financial lifeline. Serge sated his desire for news of Russia by visiting Stahl at his various Upper West Side apartments (he bounced from West 133rd to West 86th to West 112th Street before renting a grand house with Vera on Staten Island). Their evenings together were spent debating the Bolshevik takeover of the Kremlin and the brutal ongoing conflict between the Reds and the Whites, which had placed Serge's mother in danger. Stahl also regaled Serge with stories about his colorful career before the Revolution. He had lobbied for the release of political prisoners and participated in militant socialist organizations such as the Liberation Union and Peasant Movement, leading to his arrest in 1905 as an agitator. Exiled to France in 1906, he was granted a pardon and so returned to Russia in 1913. All the while Stahl was an active member of French and American Masonic lodges and involved in the establishment of the Russian Red Cross. In 1917 he went to Japan on business as a member of the Far East Committee of the provisional government, but after the coup kept heading east around the globe to the United States, where he met up again with Serge. He never returned to Russia.

Nor, for all his international connections, did he ever find a footing in the United States, except as a member of the Grand Masonic Lodge of New York. Instead he concentrated his energies on promoting Janacopoulos's singing career, twice accompanying her to Rio de Janeiro before they relocated to Paris in 1921. Once there, his fortunes took a strange turn. Stahl founded Les Craquantes (Golden Girls), a french-fry factory in the northeastern suburbs. The proceeds from this culinary enterprise helped bankroll Janacopoulos's career, as did his legal work, which he resumed full-time in the early 1930s.

For Serge, as for Lina, Stahl was a stimulating presence with tremendous stamina. His counsel on a broad range of personal and professional issues proved invaluable, and their friendship had more than its fair share of odd adventures. Serge recalled once going out with Stahl in Paris to "a sort of nightclub where they sing a requiem mass over you, put you in a coffin and then, by means of mirrors, spots start appearing all over your body which then turns into a skeleton." Yet a dispute between Serge and Janacopoulos over a recital of his music precipitated a falling-out in 1924. Vera backed out of performing his desired program—an injury to his pride he could not forgive, coming at a time when he was already disappointed with Paris and second-guessing his career. The City of Lights was not, he decided, what it had been before he had left Russia.

Serge admired Stahl's cunning, but he could not imagine how he had managed to seduce Janacopoulos, who had just turned twenty-five when she arrived in New York in 1918. Stahl was not only twenty-one years older, but also married to another woman at the time. He divorced her to be with Vera. Born in Brazil, Janacopoulos grew up and received her musical training in Paris, first as a violist, then as a singer. Her French was so much superior to her Portuguese that Serge assumed she was a French national when they first met. And in 1919, he enlisted her and Stahl to jointly translate the libretto of *Love for Three Oranges* from the original Russian into French. Stahl took on the task because he had time on his hands and needed the income, Janacopoulos because she owed Serge a rather large favor. For her New York debut on December 14, 1918, she performed three songs by him. And at a subsequent performance at Aeolian Hall just after Christmas, on December 29, she sang the vocal part of Serge's orchestral arrangement of a beloved Rimsky-Korsakov romance. He admired her exuberance on stage, even if, as critics never tired of noting, it merely masked the problems in her technique.

Janacopoulos performed the Rimsky-Korsakov romance ("The Rose and the Nightingale") under the baton of Modest Altschuler, who conducted a motley orchestra of out-of-work Russian musicians. That, at least, was Lina's description of the group, having heard them play at another concert on December 10 at Carnegie Hall—Serge's first New York appearance with an orchestra, which included an "Etude in Rhythms," his First Piano Concerto.

The twenty-one-year-old Lina, who sat beside her mother and Vera Danchakoff, was thrilled by the concerto and awed by Serge's rhythmic control at the keyboard. Nothing else on the program impressed her—not Serge's Humoresque Scherzo, a crowd-pleaser for a quartet of bassoons, nor Rachmaninoff's Second Symphony. She was mesmerized by Serge's phlegmatic demeanor and blistering technique at the keyboard as well as his odd manner of accepting applause. He popped straight up from the piano and so abruptly folded in half, like a jackknife, that she thought he might split in two. Danchakoff and her mother were much less enamored of the spectacle; over polite clapping they joked that Lina seemed more attracted to the man than his music—not that he had the looks to inspire love at first sight, especially from the back rows. Lina was indignant, defending her musical, rather than romantic, interest. "Don't you understand? This is wonderful . . . the rhythm, the beauty of the theme." The teasing continued at home, leading to an argument with her mother.

Serge, for his part, relaxed with a small group of friends after the performance, drinking beer and eating cheese at a local restaurant.

Serge and Lina first met some two months later, on February 17, 1919, following a solo recital at Aeolian Hall before a less stunned and more appreciative audience. Lina's invitation came from Stahl, and she accepted it without telling her mother, which avoided further teasing but violated a household rule: her parents were always to know her whereabouts. Because Lina had gushed to Stahl about Serge's music, he promised to introduce them—a simple enough matter, since he and Janacopoulos were busy translating his opera libretto at the time. After the performance, the couple beckoned her to the green room to meet the composer. Lina pretended to decline but then followed them, her bashfulness a feint. When she peered into the room to find her friends in conversation with Serge, he looked up to meet her gaze and smiled, taking note of her appealing face and generous smile. Stahl introduced the two with a graceful flourish, but Lina found herself tongue-tied, a condition she could not attribute to her subpar Russian. The tall, thin composer was surrounded by attractive ladies that evening, including one who hung possessively on his arm. Once the crowd thinned, Serge bid his farewells and joined a friend, Boris Samoylenko, for tea at Sherry's, a landmark restaurant favored by the New York social elite just a few blocks south of the hall. Afterward, he played bridge. There was no mention of Lina in his diary entry that evening.

She went unnoticed among the women at Serge's beck and call. Some were wise enough to hold themselves in check, but all were capable, as older ladies warned him, of ruining his life, should he be seduced. Lina's ambition in this regard was checked by her mother's strict rules of conduct, which for the moment she respected. Serge toyed with the rather proper Gertrude Liebman until she declared her love for him with characteristic American straightforwardness. Alarmed, he backed away, though he continued to see her when he visited her parents, who were prominent supporters of the arts in New York.

The audacious twenty-one-year-old who had clung to his arm after the February 17 recital was more formidable. This was Dagmar Godowsky, the dark-haired, sloe-eyed daughter of the Polish pianist and composer Leopold Godowsky. Dagmar acquired her social skills from her father, a maniacal host who plied a constant stream of guests with food and drink at his Riverside Drive apartment.

Dagmar was just starting her career as a silent film actress. A femme fatale both on screen and off, she would later be romantically linked to Rudolph Valentino, Charlie Chaplin, and Igor Stravinsky, among others. Like the other celebrities in her life, Serge succumbed to her sexual advances, declaring her a "hell of a girl" in a late-night diary entry and expressing mirthful sympathy for her distracted father, who had no chance of keeping her under control. The affair ended as soon as it began, however, leaving him unaware of her mercurial temperament and self-destructive potential. "I lived only for my pleasure," Dagmar later wrote in her autobiography, lamenting the dreadfulness into which her obvious former glamour had morphed, "and spoiled my own fun."

Gertrude rescued Serge from the unabashed Dagmar (and the gossip pages) by introducing him to yet another admirer, the eighteen-year-old Stella Adler. Assured that she was ravishing, Serge allowed Gertrude to summon Stella into his apartment from the street. He was instantly smitten. She too was an actress, of the stage more than the screen, and her career was slower to flourish than Dagmar's. But it took her further and had more significance, both in the United States and in Europe. The daughter of two stars of the Yiddish theater, Stella appeared on stage at only four years of age, often at the Grand Theater on the Lower East Side, attending public school whenever her work schedule allowed. Years later, in the mid-1920s, she studied the theories of Konstantin Stanislavsky of the Moscow Art Theater, first in New York City and then in Paris with Stanislavsky himself. From him, she developed what would be dubbed Method acting. After building a reputation on stage and screen as a member of the left-wing Group Theater and gaining some experience as an acting teacher at the New School for Social Research in New York City, she opened the Stella Adler Theatre Studio in 1949. Among her students were Marlon Brando and Robert De Niro, who learned from her to project the emotional core of a script. "Your talent is in your imagination," she insisted. "The rest is lice."

From the start, Serge found her enchanting, describing her in terms evocative of an impressionist canvas. She fell hard for him too, but their personalities clashed and circumstances pulled them apart. By the fall of 1919, they were no longer a couple, the relationship no sooner begun than ended. Leaving Serge depressed and distraught, Stella boarded a steamer with her parents for a run of performances in London. Even Serge's work suffered a slowdown. He sought traces of her by spending time with mutual friends and lamented the breakup for several years—even while courting Lina on the rebound. Nothing dimmed the memories of Stella, even as the chances of reconnecting faded. By 1921, their contact had been reduced to sardonic notes from ships that were quite literally passing in the night. "Lately I have thoughts about you a little," Stella wrote to him, awkwardly (she too had finished school at age sixteen). "You inquired after me. So now you take the consequences — this silly note." Serge's hurried response: "I arrived to New York one week ago and was very unhappy to find your note instead of yourself. That is just like you: when I am in New York, you are hurrying to London; when I am going to Europe, you return to New York; when I am in California, you are here; when I come back, you are on your way to San Francisco; when I adore you, you are as nonchalant as a devil." "Anyway," he confessed, "I am missing you very much."

Though it went unstated, each had moved on to other relationships in other places, with Lina increasingly at the center of Serge's personal life, if not his career. For him the divide between those two realms — the intimate and the professional — would never be reconciled.

Lina and Serge were brought together by Stahl, who invited Lina to Staten Island on successive weekends in the fall of 1919. The pretext for his matchmaking was that Serge had few friends his own age. Music would bring them together; Lina was progressing with her singing lessons, and Stahl imagined taunting her into performing an aria or two — though doubtless the superior Janacopoulos (not to mention Serge) would show her up. Lina's mother was against her making the trek, suspecting that Serge's intentions were not wholesome. But the composer behaved himself at a gathering on October 18. Stahl lived with Janacopoulos in the Prince's Bay neighborhood on the south shore of the Island, close to the Great Kills Masonic Lodge. At the time, the south shore featured pristine beaches, upscale amusements, and, as the original Dutch word for the area (kille) denotes, freshwater streams.

Serge, Lina, and some of the other guests took to the water on that first afternoon, on flatboats in Wolfes Pond Park, a picnic area located just inland from the shore. He thumped his vessel into hers, threatening her with an unexpected swim as she lurched to and fro, almost capsizing. He used a similar juvenile attention-getting tactic alongside the commuter railroad, pushing her into sight of an oncoming locomotive before pulling her back and boasting, "Look, I saved your life!"

His "new admirer," as he self-assuredly described her, seemed too demure for his liking, but Stahl promised him that Lina was not—rushing to prove the point by inviting her to sing one of the arias that she was learning with her mother. She performed the brooding, beckoning "Night" by Anton Rubinstein. Yet no sooner had she completed the opening stanza, well before she could impress the crowd with her command of the climactic high C, than Serge interrupted her, complaining that she had botched the lyrics. He offered his own version with his reed-thin voice, plinking out the accompaniment on the piano, but failed to convince Lina that he was correct. Since neither of them knew or would admit that different versions of the aria existed, the moment was spoiled. Lina found Serge rude and said so to his face. He agreed, asserting that insolence was his preferred mode.

Stahl invited them to his house again, but Lina declined. She had admired Serge from afar but did not like what she saw up close. Eventually she changed her mind, and he improved his manners. On their subsequent excursions to Prince's Bay he was well behaved, chatting in Russian (though hers remained less than perfect) as they rambled through the woods together. She listened to him describe his education in St. Petersburg and the long and hazardous trip he took east through Japan and Hawaii to California. He also spoke with desperation about his mother and the chances of securing her passage either from Russia or at least beyond the zone of conflict between the Reds and the Whites. (Lina would not learn the hair-raising details of Mariya Prokofieva's ordeal until much later.)

A November afternoon ended with the two piling up leaves and dried corn stalks in the garden behind Stahl's large house and lighting a bonfire. Someone had a camera. One of the photographs shows the dark-suited composer towering over the smoking lawn, with his left hand on Lina's covered head in imitation of a scene from Wagner's *Die Walküre*. The rake in his right hand substituted for a spear, the grinning Lina for a rescued warrior maiden. Even without the photograph, Lina remembered the episode in detail, screening the day's events in her mind's eye when she was apart from him, dreamily asking Serge by letter, *"Vidish'-li ti inogda etot cinema?"* (Do you ever see the same film?)

Returning to Manhattan, she provided the details to her mother. Olga, ever distrustful of Lina's gentleman callers, decided that she had no choice but to assess Serge in person by inviting him to dinner. At the Codinas' apartment uptown, he turned on the charm, flattering Olga and indulging her anecdotes about Russia while contributing his own. She could not help but like him, especially when he voiced concern about his mother. Additional dinner invitations followed, which Lina badgered him into accepting to keep up appearances. Her father did not register an opinion on the match until much later, after he had heard Serge's music. "My child," Juan told her toward the end of his life, "you don't know it but you have married a genius." Before the wedding, however, he exhorted her to remind her suitor that she had been "brought up as a young girl should be brought up."

Olga sanctioned the relationship, but not before warning her daughter about being seen with Serge in public and suggesting that they meet under her supervision at home. Lina defied her, accepting Serge's infrequent invitations to afternoon strolls, dinner, and the theater. If he wanted to unwind when she could not, he played bridge or indulged his greater recreational passion—chess—at the Manhattan Chess Club at Broadway and Seventy-first Street. Both of them also liked to frequent New York's cinema palaces. Romantic features rife with class-based conflict—*His Official Fiancée, Her Kingdom of Dreams, Almost a Husband,* and *The Temperamental Wife*—became favorites. Admission also included one or two shorts, a comedy sketch, and an in-house orchestral performance of a shopworn classic such as *The Hungarian Fantasy* or *The William Tell Overture.* Being out in public with Serge did not concern Lina; she was much more apprehensive about going to his apartment. He lived in the Hotel Calumet at 340 West Fifty-seventh Street between Eighth and Ninth Avenues —not the nicest neighborhood at the time. Despite, or perhaps because of, the courtesans residing in the area, it was popular among artists. The apartment was shabbily furnished, as Lina enjoyed teasing him, but the price—fifteen dollars a week, including hotel-like service—could not be beat. The rooms received enough sunlight, and he could afford to rent an upright piano and practice cacophonously.

Lina feared being spotted entering and was apprehensive about what might happen inside. Serge was not, after all, someone with much interest in formal dating; he lacked patience for such courtesies. At first, she came by only when he had other guests. When he finally harried her into visiting by herself, she purchased a veil to hide her face. The ruse did little except amuse the store salesclerk. Once the door had closed and they were alone, Lina became anxious, repelling his advances and halfheartedly protesting the insult to her honor. "Just what do you think you're doing?" "Everyone does it . . . well, most everyone." "But for young girls it's not allowed." "They just say it isn't." Negotiations broke down when Lina found herself willingly pinned to a table.

Possessing a strong sense of decorum, thanks of course to her mother, Lina was not afraid to assert herself. After one chaste evening at the movies, Serge left Lina at the entrance to the Times Square subway station before returning to the Hotel Calumet to do some work. Instead of boarding a train, Lina pulled herself back up the subway stairs and lit into him for treating her like a tramp. "Do you know what time it is? My mother would have a stroke if she knew! I can't image what kind of women you've been going out with!" He apologized, shamefaced, and accompanied her home by taxi.

These initial weeks of courtship were full of ambivalence. Lina was torn about being alone with Serge but found herself at his place ever more frequently (and making excuses to her mother) while he checked his baser instincts with romantic effusions. He recorded the first time they stole a kiss (November 2) and the few hours he contrived to be alone with her at Stahl's (November 9). Serge nurtured the thought that she was the perfect partner for him, the woman he had long been seeking. When coarser instincts prevailed, however, he treated her like just another conquest, tracking his progress in breaking down her resistance.

And he continued to taunt her. When Lina refused an invitation one evening, he quipped that he would easily find someone else to accompany him. The next day, she phoned to ask what he had done the night before; Serge refused to tell her anything. To appease him, she offered to visit that afternoon, later called and canceled, then phoned again to apologize. By December 9 he knew she adored him, writing in his diary that "it is a long time since anyone loved me as this dear girl seems to do." Lina, full of earnest affection, endured the mild mockery, indulged his moods, and offered herself as a source of support. She wanted to be more than a fetching accoutrement, a charming chatterbox, but she had yet to imagine what sort of role she might have in his future. And she wanted such a role, acutely, for she was now in love, both with the artist and his art — their conviction, purpose, and disdain for the ennui that, she could now see, had been her parents' curse. Lina did not want to live an apathetic life.

Serge was too self-involved to consider Lina's needs but thought she was beautiful and collapsed into her laughter. Perhaps, she thought, she could be the one person to break through his cerebral exterior and enchant him. Or perhaps, given that all of his love went into his art, he would make her his muse.

The relationship solidified as he pushed through the orchestration of *Love for Three Oranges*. They spent Christmas together, taking in the view of the New York skyline from the frigid summit of the Woolworth Building. She sported a new, fetching gray coat, a present from her parents; he was underdressed in a town suit. It does not seem that they gave gifts to each other. The next day Serge boarded a train to Chicago to attend to affairs there. Lina skipped work to have lunch with him at the Pennsylvania Hotel beforehand, offering her boss, Mr. Somoff, a feeble excuse for her absence at Tsentrosoyuz. Serge departed on the Broadway Limited, convinced of her loveliness and her commitment to him, but preoccupied with what he knew would be distressing negotiations with Chicago Opera executives. These would not be concluded until the spring of 1921, and *Love for Three Oranges* reached the Chicago stage only at the end of that year, for just two performances.

Serge shared his irritation about the ordeal with Lina and played through his music at the piano. He explained that the opera was a send-up of opera itself, treating satirically the conventions of the genre and the behavior of its audiences. The plot concerns a hypochondriac prince who takes ill after overindulging in Jean Racine's tragic verse. Laughter is the cure, but it comes at the expense of an accident-prone sorceress, Fata Morgana, who curses the convalescent prince with the need to find and consume three fantastically oversized oranges. These conceal beautiful princesses, one destined to become the prince's bride, though not without additional shenanigans from Fata and a sidesplitting encounter with a giant cook in drag.

Lina did not offer an opinion about the raucous, march-driven score in her reminiscences, except to note that Serge renamed one of the characters after her. The Princess Nicoletta became Linette. Lina found the gesture chivalrous, but her mother was suspicious. "Oh, he did that for effect," Olga complained. "Wait until it's published and then you'll see if he meant it."

He did, but his intentions remained uncertain. By mid-February he and Lina had made tentative plans to spend the summer together in Paris, he fulfilling a commission with the Ballets Russes, she perhaps taking voice lessons. But Stella Adler's return to New York from London clouded his thinking and stirred his latent passion. Stella stoked it by convincing Serge to give her piano lessons, a development that irritated Lina beyond measure. Dagmar Godowsky had also re-emerged, this time on the screen in *The Peddler of Lies*, which depicted an ingénue much like Dagmar herself.

Serge took in the film on February 27, just after a performance of Liszt's Piano Concerto by the New York Philharmonic, with Rachmaninoff as soloist. Lina joined him at the concert, sharing a private box that had been offered to him by Gertrude's parents, the arts patrons Henry and Zelda Liebman. Once again, Lina's mother expressed pointed disapproval, and once again, Lina rebuffed her, accepting the invitation and then joining Serge in the green room to congratulate Rachmaninoff. His wife and daughters helped revive the pianist, who despite playing immaculately—even Serge admitted as much—seemed fed up. As soon as they were introduced, Rachmaninoff assured Lina that he remembered their first meeting so many years ago. He nodded his approval to Serge, something that he had seldom done when it came to his music. Then, prodded by his inquisitive younger daughter, Rachmaninoff asked Lina the question that her mother had long feared: "So, are you getting married?" Lina blushed; Serge said nothing.

Professional pursuits always trumped personal exploits, and perhaps to escape his competing affections for Stella and Lina, Serge immersed himself in work, drinking cups of hot chocolate and fighting through tension headaches as he outlined the musical structures that he had dreamed or imagined, using melodies jotted down in sketch-books and allowing his intuition to guide him through the harmonies. The notes spilled onto the page from the piano, on which, as his neighbors protested, he made a hellish racket. Sometimes, he realized, the music came out too fast, especially that of *Love for Three Oranges*, which he had conceived in such fantastic detail that he himself could not make sense of the torrents of sounds. The music had a life of its own.

He maintained a punishing schedule in the spring of 1920, beginning another opera, *The Fiery Angel*, before the ink was dry on *Love for Three Oranges*. He also accepted several concert engagements and fulfilled his contract with the Aeolian Company by recording piano rolls of his shorter pieces. He saw Lina less frequently and continued his pointless dalliance with Stella; the conflict between the two women sapped his patience more than it burdened his conscience. "I revolve between Stella and Linette as the earth spins between the moon and the sun," he wearily confessed to his diary on March 13.

In April he embarrassed himself by sending roses to both women, which the courier mislabeled, so that Lina received Stella's, and vice versa. He did little to settle the matter but placed his trust in circumstance, perhaps simply hoping one or the other would give up on him. Neither did, and ultimately he resolved to control himself in Stella's presence. Having weighed the odds of forging a relationship with the actress, he decided that their chances for success were about as slim as the possibility that the hero of his new opera, an obtuse knight, would find happiness with the heroine, a maiden apparently possessed by the devil.

And so an invitation to dinner at the Bohemian Club on April 3 went to Lina. Typically the club hosted stag parties, but on this august occasion—in honor of the pianist Harold Bauer—its members were permitted to invite women. Lina thought it prudent for Serge to first approach her mother, but he mishandled the overture by explaining that the event at the Biltmore Hotel was intended for the fiancées, wives, and sisters of members. Olga, whose ears pricked up at the word *fiancée*, prohibited her daughter from attending on the grounds that she did not have a proper gown to wear.

Serge pleaded his case—asking, "Olga Vladislavovna, don't you trust me?"—and vowed to have Lina back home by half past eleven. As soon as he left the apartment, however, Olga changed her mind. "You don't really think you're going to that dinner, do you?" she scolded her daughter. "Oh, Mama," Lina protested, "I need an evening dress and I won't, after all, be alone with him all evening. A lot of musicians are attending." "Yes, but people will assume that you're his lady friend."

Lina pressed the subject of the dress, reasoning (without saying as much to her mother) that even improper girls needed to look good on occasion. She and Olga agreed on a pink-and-silver lamé gown with tulle. At the dinner, Lina felt predictably self-conscious, since she and Serge were seated at the front table, near the guest of honor and the club president, Franz Kneisel. The discussion ranged from Serge's music to the other celebrities honored by the Bohemians: Mahler, Toscanini, Ferruccio Busoni, Pablo Casals. The Polish-born pianist Arthur Rubinstein, then on tour in the United States, leaned over to Serge to whisper, "Where did you hook such a beauty?" Lina blushed, her mother's imprecation ringing in her ears.

Sixty years later, Rubinstein would remind Lina of the embarrassment and her reaction to it. "I'm probably one of the only people alive who knew you before you were married."

Marriage, at this juncture, was unthinkable. First the couple needed to see about spending the summer together in Europe. Serge left New York for Paris on April 27, 1920, after having enjoyed a final tryst with Lina in the city of Orange, New Jersey, and its three townships (a fitting location, given the title of his opera). He left her with $150 and a dozen roses, describing the funds, not altogether in jest, as down payment for her translation of the libretto of *Love for Three Oranges* into English. He had in mind not the production in Chicago but a hypothetical one at Covent Garden in London.

Throughout May, Lina wrote effusive letters to him, but she did not indicate whether or not she was coming to France. She seemed to want to but complained of difficulties in obtaining a ticket. Serge interpreted this as hesitation or, worse, cold feet, even though she made it clear that she hoped the relationship would not wither. Where there's a will, there's a way, he admonished Lina, and suddenly a ticket was obtained for a June 10 departure aboard the *Touraine*, arriving at Le Havre ten days later.

Things worked out only because Olga, whose eyes welled up with tears at the mere thought of saying goodbye to her daughter, received word that Lina would be met in Paris by trusted family friends. Zelda and Henry Liebman were in Europe for an extended summer holiday, dividing their time between Florence and Paris. They agreed to meet Lina dockside upon arrival. Then in the early fall, Carita Spencer and Gussie Hillyer Garvin would be in Europe to keep an eye on her. The thirty-eight-year-old Spencer was a colleague of Charles Johnston, the doting theater lover, Sanskrit expert, and friend of W. B. Yeats. During World War I, she became involved in relief efforts, and Lina somehow got it into her head that she had been a pilot, one of the first women to fly a plane. Spencer's actual career was less spectacular but not without excitement. As the national chairwoman of the Surgical Dressings Committee of the National Civic Federation, she traveled throughout Europe, eventually narrating her experiences in a self-published memoir, *War Scenes I Shall Never Forget*. Later she served as chairwoman of the Food for France Fund, with the extremely wealthy, forty-three-year-old Gussie Garvin as secretary. Lina admired Miss Spencer and Mrs. Garvin to the extent that her mother became rather jealous of them. They were good and kind, the perfect minders for Lina in Europe.

Even so, in the first week of June when the matter seemed to be settled, Olga exercised her talent for emotional blackmail, becoming ill with a mysterious ailment just as Lina was about to purchase the ticket. An x-ray was taken, but surgery ruled out. Serge saw the ploy for what it was. It convinced him more than ever of the need for Lina to get away from her overbearing mother, if only for a few months.

Finally Lina sailed to France alone, though she met plenty of people aboard and the captain invited her to dine with him. When she arrived, she was whisked away by the Liebmans for some sightseeing and then some pampering at their residence in Paris, a Haussmann townhouse on rue du Bassano, while Serge waited anxiously for word from her. Lina was free—she no longer had to report her whereabouts to her mother or listen to her warnings about falling, unmarried, into the clutches of a musician with a wandering eye. Little did she know, however, that escaping her own mother would result in her looking after someone else's — Serge's. And unlike Olga, who was sick only with worry, Mariya Prokofieva was truly in need of medical care.

Emaciated, sallow-skinned, and almost blind from cataracts, Mariya had managed to escape southern Russia, her worldly belongings reduced to two suitcases and a satchel containing refugee identity papers and some of her son's manuscripts. From Novorossiysk, the main port on the Black Sea, she had traveled with defeated White Army soldiers to Constantinople. There she stayed in a refugee camp on the Princes' Islands, off the coast of Constantinople, eating watery soups brought in pails for large groups of people and, she claimed, enduring harassment from ruffian children who had nothing better to do than torment a fearful old woman.

Meanwhile, Serge navigated the Belgian and then French bureaucracies in an effort to secure travel papers for her. Stahl and his other contacts in Paris, including Igor Stravinsky, offered crucial advice. Once she had obtained her visa and a ticket, Mariya endured eighteen days in the hold of an overcrowded steamer as it dragged itself from Constantinople to Marseille. She arrived, as her son had hoped, on the *Sourieh* on June 20. Serge found his mother cramped, helpless, in steerage, awaiting the medical check that would allow her to disembark. Her back was turned to him and she was wearing sunglasses, which made it hard for him to recognize her. Reunited after two years apart, they spent the day in Marseille, swapping tales of Russia and America. The next day they returned to Paris, where, to Serge's relief, he was handed a telegram with news that Lina was also in the city.

He first introduced her to his mother at the three-story summer house he rented in Mantes-sur-Seine, papering over the details of their relationship. Lina was one of his American friends, he hedged, who just happened to be in Paris taking voice lessons and, for a modest fee, was translating the text of his opera for the English conductor Albert Coates. Mariya, certainly no fool, chose not to fret the details of the relationship, since she found Lina pleasant and much more attentive to her needs than her distracted son was. Lina felt sorry for her. Mariya's looks were gone, and she seemed, because of all she had recently endured, much older than her sixty-five years. (She always gave her age as forty-five.) Also, Lina saw in Serge's mother the key to his heart. In the weeks and months ahead, throughout the summer in Mantes and the fall in Paris, Lina showed her devotion to him by running errands for her, teaching her English, and applying compresses to her eyes following the cataract operations in October that were intended to delay the inevitable onset of blindness.

Back in Paris, Serge arranged for the three of them to live at the Hôtel du Quai Voltaire, surprising himself by successfully negotiating a favorable rate. He could no longer conceal the nature of his relationship with Lina from his mother, and she could no longer pretend to be ignorant of its inappropriateness—even if Lina insisted on staying on a separate floor.

But Serge soon escaped the awkwardness, departing, with a kiss for each of them, for the United States on October 16. He had arranged a series of concerts in Chicago and was intent on seeing *Love for Three Oranges* brought to the stage. (He would not succeed for another year.) Lina, while continuing to tend to Mariya, took lessons with Félia Litvinne, a famous dramatic soprano originally from St. Petersburg. She had found her teacher thanks to Serge, who extracted a pledge from Litvinne to make "un petit bijou" (a little gem) out of Lina's voice, though Litvinne had her doubts and quickly lost interest. Meanwhile those three accomplished ladies—Mrs. Liebman, Miss Spencer, and Mrs. Garvin—kept close watch.

Lina's only contact with Serge came through letters, hers much longer and more frequent than his. These trailed each other in the post by up to two weeks, narrating his journey from New York to Chicago to the West Coast, and hers from Paris to Milan. She nicknamed him "Bus'ka" (Russian, of sorts, for "Kissy Face") in energetic dispatches that brought together English, French, and Russian in arcane combinations. He kept his responses short and to the point, often ignoring her questions and making her feel as if she was just one on a long list of pesterers to whom he owed a tired, generic reply. But she persisted, and the "many miles of briny deep" that separated them inspired her to indulge his inattention. The occasional bickering was quickly forgotten, replaced in her letters with loving scolds about his periods of silence.

There was, however, a bigger chasm, one that both of them should have recognized as fraught with personal and professional danger. Lina had turned out like her parents—exotic, impulsive, scattered—

while Serge was focused and obsessive in his creative pursuits. Lina believed she could bridge the divide between their temperaments by becoming someone special, by making a name for herself. But her initial inclination, encouraged by Serge, to pursue music was deeply fraught. No matter what she achieved as a singer, nothing could compare to Serge's gifts as composer and pianist. Even if things did not work out for her, Lina reasoned, sharing the highs of his career would more than allow her to absorb the lows of her own. She would seek to play roles on the stage and in his life. The first of these was that of the long-suffering lady in waiting.

Chapter 3

WHILE LINA APPLIED herself to her singing lessons, Prokofiev crossed the Atlantic, his thoughts flitting from the delayed opera premiere to the recitals he would be presenting up and down the coast of California in the winter of 1920–1921. As the only superstar composer touring the state, he had audiences to himself. Rachmaninoff had visited California in 1919 (he posed for a photo in front of a redwood tree) but by now had returned to his home in New York; Stravinsky, Prokofiev's main competition in Paris, would eventually settle in Los Angeles, but not until World War II.

Serge was also anticipating the arrival in New York of the Ukrainian soprano Nina Koshetz, a close friend whose impassioned singing (especially in her rich, warm lower range) made him melt. They had met in St. Petersburg, and though Serge was initially indifferent, eventually he looked past her dramatic persona and persistent flirtations to see that she was a serious artist destined, if she handled herself correctly, for international renown. Her constant fawning seemed harmless enough, at least until revelations surfaced of her affair with Serge's rival Rachmaninoff. Koshetz was single and carefree; Rachmaninoff had a wife and family. Even after she married the visual artist Alexander von Schubert, she never missed the chance to remind Serge that she remained devoted to him. Nor was she dissuaded upon hearing (false) rumors from Lina's erstwhile employer Somoff that Serge and Lina had been secretly married. Reports of his romance with the young singer in Paris merely buttressed Koshetz's ardent belief that her love for Serge would last "to the grave!!!!!!!" But he doubled over in laughter when she announced, with characteristic extravagance, that her psychic had predicted their romance.

Serge dedicated an early cycle of songs to Koshetz and completed another, at her eager request, while giving his concerts in California. This was the group known as *Five Songs Without Words*, which Koshetz impatiently awaited "like a lover for a rendezvous." It was a minor opus, but the composer hoped that it would appeal to American audiences by showing them, through Koshetz's voice, the limpid, lyrical side of his musical persona. He was eager to demonstrate that he was not the Bolshevik barbarian the critics had imagined him to be.

Serge also pressed for Koshetz to be given a starring role in *Love for Three Oranges* when it finally premiered at the end of 1921. He convinced Mary Garden, the profligate director of the Chicago Opera, that Koshetz possessed the dramatic control required for the part of the klutzy yet menacing Fata Morgana. She did not disappoint in the role, though she made a nuisance of herself by pestering Serge to track down special shades of makeup for her while he was in Paris — along with, of course, her favorite perfume (La Rose Jacqueminot) and complexion powder (Rachel Clair). Much later, she would also sing the part of the fortuneteller in a concert of excerpts from Prokofiev's opera *The Fiery Angel*. Her talent exceeded Vera Janacopoulos's, and altogether eclipsed Lina's. Although Lina harbored hopes of a legitimate singing career, one that at least equaled her mother's success, she banished the thought that she could somehow compete with Koshetz — at least on stage. Her voice simply did not have the power or depth.

Instead Lina's battle with Koshetz would be for Serge's attention, a frustrating contest, given not only his wandering eye but also his self-obsession. She had succumbed to his magnetism and had the wiles to maintain his affection, so she braved the broad range of other women in his life without protest. His indifference to her needs was, and would always be, the greater affront to her pride.

On October 26, 1920, just before the start of the California tour, Serge enjoyed the sight of Koshetz descending from the deck of the ocean liner *Pannonia* when it docked in New York Harbor. She flowed down the gangplank among a tattered gaggle of Greek, Italian, and Spanish passengers—1,135 in all—unmistakable in her garish jewels and furs, framed by two beaming, smitten members of the crew. Her ostentatious arrival disguised the fact that she had traveled second class. On the dock Koshetz wrapped herself around Serge, enveloping him in her fragrance, and boisterously thanked him for freeing her and her family from the ravages of Russia (in truth, he had merely advised her on the best route to America). They took a taxi to the fashionable French-styled Brevoort Hotel in Greenwich Village, where he had booked a suite for her, her eight-year-old daughter, Marina, and her out-of-sight, out-of-mind husband. Serge had himself arrived from Europe only the day before, after perspiring through a week of near-seasickness and anxieties over a lost suitcase. He too was staying at the Brevoort, though in a more modest room. In his diary he recalled that he had once had an assignation with Stella Adler there.

He was in New York for only a few days before heading to Chicago and farther on to Oakland, where he performed, with minimal practice, the first of his California concerts. The cavernous halls were less than full, but audiences hailed him and the run was extended. Koshetz remained behind, resentful, in the care of Serge's agent, Fitzhugh Haensel, who failed to lavish enough attention on her. Temper tantrums aside, her American career took off in 1921. She sang twice in Cleveland, once in Detroit, and seven times in New York—her Town Hall appearance with the Schola Cantorum on March 27 garnered significant press coverage. Bookings included private soirees at the residences of New York's most prominent families, the Astors and Vanderbilts.

Three time zones away, Serge put Koshetz out of his mind as best as he could. He received regular letters from her, chaotically handwritten over several days across dozens of pages, furnishing the details of her conflicts with Haensel, her rebuffs from Rachmaninoff, her practice regime, and her new American friends. She complained of impoverishment even as she settled into a furnished apartment at 610 Riverside Drive (at 138th Street) for some $200 a month, leaving Serge to wonder just where the truth lay. But the chronicles of her New York adventures were irresistible in their outrageousness. So too were her predictions for the future, aided, as always, by soothsayers. "The spirits told me that I'll be singing at the Metropolitan Opera in two months," she gushed in a letter that December. "There'll be a concert in Carnegie, I'll be in contact with Rachmaninoff in two weeks and he'll even be accompanying me this season, in two years I'll go to Paris, and a year after that to Moscow, where it'll be wonderful." Additional predictions concerned diplomatic relations among England, Russia, and India.

Serge read with bemusement up to the part where Koshetz announced that she had received *Five Songs Without Words.* Apparently they were not quite what she had expected. "One of them (the longest) has an appealing, remarkable melody, but, frankly, the harmonies frighten me," she confessed. "Three others are enchanting but . . . better for St. Petersburg. I think I can only sing two of them in my recital, the one in A minor and the one in 12/8. I'm afraid that the song in A major is beyond me technically. I still haven't managed to sing it with full voice." She suspected that the composer would be irked by her response and hastened to add, "For goodness sake don't bite off my head but the song in A major is frightful in places." Serge's respect for Koshetz immediately declined. He had written the songs with her eloquence (and its appeal to his critics) in mind, only to have them capriciously rejected. In the end, she would perform just one of the five at Town Hall on March 27, 1921, sticking instead to simpler pieces by Musorgsky and Rimsky-Korsakov, along with a rarity by Scriabin. Lina heard nothing of this incident until much later, though she would benefit from it as a singer when Serge began to write for her voice instead.

Lina knew that Koshetz was in New York and in touch with Serge. Wary of the relationship, she made sure to express her reservations — often through secondhand reports. "It's strange," she disingenuously wrote from Paris, "but lately I've heard a lot about Koshetz." She mentioned a friend of her mother, who had studied at the Moscow Conservatoire with the singer, and an acquaintance of her own in Paris, who declared Koshetz a "scoundrel" and an "unbelievable show-off."

The slander came from the young soprano and actress Elaine Amazar (she used the stage name Elvira), who had also trained in Moscow and was in Paris performing in a cabaret while also looking for work in film (she had appeared in two movies in the United States in 1919, playing the role of a seductive foreigner). Amazar was not in any position to criticize someone for showing off. Besides acting and singing, she earned a living as a model, posing for pinups. She was certainly entertaining, but not to be trusted.

When Lina found out from Amazar that Koshetz was Jewish, she couldn't help but add her own slur. She crudely joked to Serge, in a mixture of Russian and English, "Bus'ka, I must warn you that I don't have a single drop of Jewish blood in me. This is evidently a big minus but that's the way it is—you must take me as I am—without the genial blood!" Lina's lifelong anti-Semitism came from her father, and she would, in Serge's presence, struggle to suppress it.

While Koshetz enjoyed her success in New York and Serge his in California, Lina began to make her way in Paris, taking advantage of the strong dollar and weak franc to rent a room near the Paris Opera at 3, rue des Italiens. Like other expats, she also visited the newly opened jazz clubs. Lina was garrulous, if sometimes temperamental, and quickly found company.

Much of her neighborhood, the ninth arrondissement, has vanished; the sights and sounds that greeted her did not survive beyond the 1920s. Missing are the arcades that housed Café Certa and Du Petit Grillon, the hangouts of the founders of the Dadaist movement; gone too is the restaurant, in the eighth arrondissement, that became Le Boeuf sur le Toit (The Ox on the Roof), the gathering place for the most avant-garde of the avant-gardists. Lina's neighborhood housed many transients and was populated with bars and *maisons de tolérance*. It certainly did not have the bohemian feel of Montmartre and Montparnasse, the artist enclaves where several of her contacts lived. In her first letters from Paris to Serge, Lina mentions fraternizing with the nineteen-year-old demimondaine Alice Prin, nicknamed "Kiki de Montparnasse." Kiki came from a broken home. Her mother, who did not raise her, encouraged her to apprentice as a chef or baker; instead, she became an iconic figure in the nightclubs and a much-sought-after fashion and portrait model. (Kiki's performances, in matchstick-blackened eyebrows, garters, and stockings, and her titillating repertoire, soon attracted the attention of the Dadaist Man Ray, whom she took as a lover.) Neither she nor, for that matter, Elaine Amazar were the kind of company Lina's mother would have wanted her to keep, which was just the point.

Late nights in the cafes ended once Lina threw herself into her singing lessons with Félia Litvinne. She found them stressful and suffered insomnia and, when she did close her eyes, nightmares of stage fright. To overcome them, Lina sought some real performing experience. She turned to her friends for advice and in November 1920 joined the same cabaret that employed Amazar. It was a start-up enterprise called La Chauve-Souris (The Bat), headed by the Russian showman Nikita Balieff. He had come to Paris all the way from Moscow and offered an esoteric alternative to the cancans, feathers, and nearly naked women of the Montmartre music halls. Lina felt from the start that she had compromised herself by signing with Chauve-Souris, but his cabaret, which had previously operated out of a basement in Moscow, was not like the Folies-Bergère. Kiki would descend into the lower depths of Parisian society, the substratum of drugs and pimps; the chaperoned, well-mannered Lina would not.

Her new employer, Balieff, was little known in Paris at this time; the beautiful neo-nationalist sets and costumes, integrated song-and-dance routines, and souvenir programs that would make Chauve-Souris famous were still to come. He arrived in Paris in 1919 (the Bolsheviks imprisoned him for five days before his escape from Russia), thereafter reopening his cabaret in December 1920 at the Théâtre Femina, with actors from the former Russian imperial theaters. Located on the Champs Élysées, the Femina had served as a gathering spot for American servicemen during the armistice. It was a little rough around the edges but suited Balieff's needs.

Finances initially forced him to depend on word of mouth to attract the fickle Parisian public to his shows. The performances in which Lina appeared began at 8:45 P.M., an unusual hour but not unsuitable to Parisian theatergoers. In Moscow, Balieff had scheduled his shows for the post-theater crowd — meaning performers themselves — to unwind after hours. Lina was part of a bill that would have featured, according to the bulletins that appeared in French newspapers in 1921, a dozen or so skits, some as short as three minutes; Russian songs and choruses; a ballerina imitating a wind-up doll; and various popular dances (nothing risqué). The sets were modest — a table and chairs, a picture frame that doubled as a window, a black curtain, and lighting. The skits ranged from the grotesque to the sentimental; for example, one ruminated on the power of gypsy song to defrost a soldier's heart. Between numbers, the avuncular, round-faced Balieff would do standup comedy.

Lina rehearsed twice a day in the chorus, appearing incognito in a red wig under the stage name Verlé. Amazar assumed one of the main roles (despite being shockingly unmusical, according to Lina) and so needed an understudy. When Balieff prompted Lina to learn the part, Litvinne helped her prepare, but felt that Lina should conserve her easily taxed voice until her technique improved. Lina also learned Jacques Offenbach's showcase aria "Chanson de Fortunio" under her teacher's guidance. She sang the number—her star turn—two or three times before Balieff changed the show's repertoire, sending her back to the chorus.

Balieff moved his performers around like this all the time—there were no headliners in his company—but Lina was wounded by the change and decided that Balieff was an ignoramus when it came to music. And she resented hearing that she had more talent as a mime artist than a singer. Wary of Serge's response and fearing his disapproval, she repeatedly told him that she had joined Chauve-Souris solely for the experience and the income, which was modest but better than the pittance she would have earned as an office worker or sales clerk in Paris. He agreed that the solo singing was good training, but the time spent in the chorus futile. If nothing else, Lina had proved to herself that she could appear on stage and "contrôler le trac" (keep her composure). But she ended up feeling debased. The "Midnight Frolics," the name she used to ridicule Balieff's enterprise (the title of a Ziegfeld Follies show running in New York City at the time), seemed beneath her. After just a month she returned her wig and resigned, informing Serge in a letter of January 5, 1921, that she couldn't forgive herself for getting mixed up with Balieff, who openly disdained singers. "'Takaya gadost'—such vileness—on the whole," she concluded, "and nothing to show for it besides exhaustion."

By quitting the show, however, she had unknowingly forfeited the chance to be part of an international phenomenon. After a slow start, Les Spectacles de la Chauve-Souris became such a sensation that rival theatrical groups fretted they had fallen behind in the march of chic. Once Balieff gained traction in France, he and his artists toured Spain, England, and the United States. Reviewers were hyperbolic in their praise.

Lina returned to her lessons and took comfort in her teacher's satisfaction with her progress; thankfully, her time with Balieff had inflicted no lasting damage on her voice. But the sixty-year-old Litvinne seemed increasingly distracted and detached, owing, Lina rationalized, to an overload of students. She could not fail to notice that the "old dear" contradicted herself and assigned her one aria after another without allowing her to properly learn any of them. When she signaled to Lina that her voice might not be suited for opera, certainly not coloratura roles, and that the best she might hope for were low- or medium-range character parts, Lina questioned her judgment.

She filled her letters to Serge with news of her career (such as it was), generally upbeat reports on the health of his mother following her eye operations, the latest Parisian social gossip, and expressions of how much she missed him.

The extant letters do not provide the details of her ski trip to Switzerland, but a quirky series of photographs does; the gentlemen in her entourage apparently braved the slopes in suits and ties. Now and again Lina saw her designated chaperone, Zelda Liebman, who rather hypocritically advised her to be more idealistic and less materialistic (this as she packed up a colossal assortment of toiletries for a vacation on the French Riviera). Lina envied the material success, grumbling, "How lucky some people are! Why?" She also saw her other minders, Miss Spencer and Mrs. Garvin, but felt constrained in their presence, unable to open up about her long-distance relationship with Serge. Yet she could hardly share her feelings with him, or expect any reassurance. "You never make any reference to whatever I write you," she scribbled in good-humored but palpable frustration. "Ponyal— do you get it— Seryozhka! You naughty boy!" For Christmas she sent him a new pair of gloves, size 8¼.

Serge kept most of his letters businesslike, excluding the more colorful details of his time in California in favor of drier matters like the teaching offer he received from the San Diego Conservatoire. He glossed over his fraternizing in Los Angeles with a young émigré actress whom he nicknamed "Frou-Frou" and his encounters with Dagmar Godowsky, also a recent arrival out west. On January 12, 1921, he and Frou-Frou (whose real name was Mariya Baranovskaya) showed up late for a screening of the John Ford western *Hitchin' Posts*, starring Dagmar in the role of the wild-eyed, uncontrollable Octoroon. Her lover is the southern riverboat gambler Jefferson Todd, played, true to life, by the very manly Frank Mayo. Dagmar and her leading man were engaged in a heated affair at the time, and though she claimed to be trying to extricate herself, the two married in Tijuana later that year. Serge enjoyed her stories and became increasingly convinced that her life was merely a simulacrum of the plots of the silent films she was making. She even spoke in melodramatic phrases resembling inset titles.

Serge's letters did go into detail about his New Year's revelries, and here he had no choice but to entertain Lina with tales of Dagmar, since he had spent most of the evening at a costume party she hosted. In her response, Lina parried, "I understand that your successes have aroused Dagmar anew, but since she is a first-class vamp and very attractive it's not worth describing your dates with her!" The pangs of jealousy subsided when she read that Serge longed to see her. From Los Angeles he would head back to New York and then to London, where he insisted that Lina meet him. She declined the invitation at first, claiming that she had no friends in London and fearing that Serge would abandon her while attending to his affairs — as he had in the past. Moreover, while he could change cities as easily as "posting a letter," she would need to obtain an entry and exit visa for England (difficult because she did not yet have a French *carte d'identité*), rearrange her music lessons, and explain to her friends why she suddenly needed to travel abroad. There was also the question of accommodations.

In the end Lina braved the bureaucracy and reunited with Serge at Victoria Station in London on February 10. They booked separate quarters at the nearby National Hotel, with Serge doing his part to make the relationship look proper by mussing the bed sheets in his smaller room each morning. He attended to his business and, as Lina predicted, excluded her from his meetings. The slight continued in Paris, where Serge had to supervise the upcoming staging of his ballet *The Buffoon*, the first of what would be three exceptionally hard-to-secure productions with Diaghilev and the illustrious Ballets Russes. The complete title of the absurdist, fairy-tale-inspired ballet gives a fair sense of the plot: *Skazka pro shuta, semerikh shutov pereshutivshago*

(*The Tale of the Buffoon Who Outwits Seven Other Buffoons*). It was almost as important to Serge as his absurdist, fairy-tale opera *Love for
Three Oranges,* and he heeded every request from Diaghilev for revisions—to the extent that he would still be orchestrating the final two
scenes and an entr'acte in the spring. The premiere would take place
on May 17, 1921, with Serge conducting, at Le Théâtre de la Gaîté
Lyrique in Paris.

Lina certainly understood that Serge needed to discuss the production with the choreographer and set designer, but she resented
being ignored at dinner parties and left out of his evenings of bridge
and chess. Why the awkwardness about their relationship—or what
she more heatedly called their "stupid situation"? What was his reluc-
tance, his ambivalence? If he was so embarrassed of her and cared so
little for her company, then why had he arranged for them to spend
the summer together with his mother? Lina longed to be as important to Serge as his Russian friends, with whom he seemed to prefer to
spend his time. She was neither "a freak nor an idiot," she sadly protested, which was exactly how he made her feel. Plus she was not well,
not at all.

At the end of February, in the middle of discussions about the
ballet, Lina was diagnosed with appendicitis. She had developed a
cough and a low-grade fever, found it difficult to swallow, and in general felt run-down despite gamely maintaining her social calendar,
which meant spending a cold late winter afternoon with Mrs. Garvin
at Marie Antoinette's chateau at Versailles. Her physician conducted
an exam and, discovering an inflammation in her abdomen, recommended either an operation or a twelve-month course of treatment
that required a radical change in diet and restricted activities.

Lina turned to Serge for advice; the crisis at once drew them closer
and interrupted the difficult discussions they had started on the subject of marriage. He arranged for her to see a top-tier American-born
surgeon (Charles Winchester du Bouchet), who confirmed that she
was suffering from appendicitis. Noting the potential for rupture, he
recommended immediate extraction. Serge booked Lina a second-
floor room in a small, quiet clinic at a convent and saw her through
the March 17 procedure. She stayed calm until she was placed on a
stretcher and rolled into the hall toward the operating room, at which

point she began to shriek in terror. Serge heard about this incident from Lina's lady friends, who had gathered to offer moral support. Fortunately the anesthesia took immediate effect.

As soon as Lina was on the mend and convinced that she would quickly be up and about, Serge left Paris for Nantes and then Saint-Brevin-les-Pins, installing his mother in a large stone house that he had rented for the summer on the Bay of Biscay. Lina would join them as soon as Bouchet cleared her to sit on a train (the trip to the coast took half a day). Having to explain to her surgeon that she no longer had a home in Paris—she had surrendered her short-term rental—only added to her list of indignities. She would have to stay in a hotel or with acquaintances until she was well enough to travel. Despite Bouchet's assurances, her convalescence took much longer than either of them anticipated, and she remained in the hospital. Each of the ten days she was in the clinic she wrote to Serge with updates, jocularly signing one of the letters "Lina (not Nina)." He wrote her a letter just once and sent one- or two-line telegrams the rest of the time.

Acute nausea kept her up the first night after her operation. Though it dissipated after forty-eight hours, sleep continued to elude her. Her hands trembled, and she had to pause while writing her letters to recover from bouts of dizziness. Lina's social life remained essentially unaffected by her condition, however. One could even say it improved. The gentle nurses allowed visitors from late morning to early evening, and among the callers were Miss Spencer (as Lina always called her) and her new husband, Warren Fisher Daniell, along with Lina's teacher, Litvinne, who presented her with a bouquet of forget-me-nots.

Later, Mrs. Garvin visited, followed by Janacopoulos and Stahl, whose merciless teasing caused Lina to laugh and then cry out in pain as she hurled a pillow at him to make him stop. The painter and Ballets Russes costume designer Natalia Goncharova stopped by, as did Somoff's ex-wife Mariya Argunova, whom Lina had not seen for two years and who she had assumed was living in Russia. Goncharova, true to form, assembled a bouquet that harmonized with the colors of Lina's eyes and lips. Her room became filled with roses, lilacs, violets, and (from Serge) additional forget-me-nots, together with perfume, chocolate, fruit, and kefir—the latter a special request smuggled in by Miss Spencer, who lavished the most attention on her. Lina smiled for photographs on March 23 and 27. Several of them, including a drowsily winsome portrait amid the flowers, survive. Mr. Daniell, in a buttoned-up suit, is shown at her bedside, as is one of the nurses.

In the absence of real news or changes in her routine (she had yet to brave the move from bed to chaise longue, never mind the corridor outside), Lina provided intricate descriptions of the hospital menu and the much-delayed reappearance of her appetite: "In the morning I drank coffee, for lunch soup, mashed potatoes and a very small piece of ham and cooked cherries." She mocked her trashy reading habits, blaming Miss Spencer for getting her addicted to the detective stories that she had been reading aloud to Lina during her visits. "I finished reading by myself a detective tale called 'The Double Traitor.' Imagine how exciting."

The bandage itched day and night, and Lina scratched it in her sleep, making her stomach and side look like the barracks of "an entire battalion of fleas." Once it was removed, she would report that the scar was "2½ inches long, pleasantly pain-free but unpleasant to look at." Though Serge was not at her bedside, she insisted that he at least pretend as much by writing a letter to her mother in New York, informing her of the unqualified success of the operation. Her mother's name, she sternly reminded him, lest he had forgotten, was Olga Vladislavovna, and he needed to refer to her in the letter as "Linette" rather than "Ptashka"—his latest nickname for her, meaning "little bird." Serge did as he was told, sending the letter on March 29.

After a week, Lina began to hobble around her room and, with Miss Spencer's help, stand at the balconied window and venture into the garden outside. On March 28, the day after her second post-op photo shoot, Bouchet released her from his care, confirming that she would be able to swim in the summer. She stayed for two days with Janacopoulos and Stahl in Paris while waiting for Serge to arrive and accompany her to Saint-Brevin-les-Pins. He appeared on March 30, full of news about his still-unfinished ballet and the forthcoming performance of his hyper-dissonant *Scythian Suite* of 1915, an orchestral score on a mythological subject. Success with Diaghilev, the arbiter of artistic chic, seemed to be at hand. From Paris they traveled to Les Rochelets, the name of the beach on which the summer rental was located. Lina remained in considerable discomfort, but she managed to resume her singing. When she arrived at the house, a cypress-framed villa, she insisted that Serge tell the housekeeper and the neighbors that the two of them were married.

Soon he had to head back to Paris and then on to Monte Carlo to attend to *The Buffoon*. Lina wrote to him on April 23, his thirtieth birthday, sending him tender hugs and kisses and wishing him, in English, "to acquire all the sense that you may lack!" He pledged during his absence not only to see the ballet to the stage (no easy task, given the colossal mess the copyist had made of the orchestral parts) but also to try to finish his opera *The Fiery Angel* and a new group of songs. These settings of verses by the symbolist poet Konstantin Balmont would serve Lina's—rather than Nina's—voice. Koshetz, Lina gladly noted, had declined in Serge's opinion for several reasons, not least of all her reconciliation with Rachmaninoff back in New York.

Serge resisted the seductions of Paris, both in choice of neighborhood (he preferred the area around Les Invalides in the seventh arrondissement over Montmartre and Montparnasse) and entertainment (bridge and chess rather than vaudeville and girlie shows). He reserved his licentiousness for his music, and despite his endless travels, stuck to his routines. Paris was a place of work, not pleasure, and he generally did not respect what French musicians produced. He insisted on escaping Paris for his summer rental, where Lina, who loved the city, tended to his mother on his behalf.

Lina briefly slipped away from this chore and escaped Saint-Brevin-les-Pins on April 29, traveling to Paris to hear the performance of *Scythian Suite* the next day. She left Mariya Prokofieva to her needlework in the company of the part-time housekeeper. Judging from the ovation, the performance was a success, though Lina sensed condescension in the compliments Serge received from Stravinsky, who was to him in Paris what Rachmaninoff had been in New York —the competition.

On May 1, the couple returned to Saint-Brevin-les-Pins, where they stayed for only a week, until Serge was summoned back to Paris, this time for *The Buffoon*. It was a crucial moment in his career, the chance to create the kind of raucous theatrical sensation that had eluded him but defined the Ballets Russes, and he wanted Lina and his mother to be with him. The weather had improved and the temperature in the house with it, so leaving was sadder than the three of them thought it would be. In Paris, Mariya returned to the clinic where her eye operations had taken place, while Serge and Lina checked into separate rooms at a faded hotel located just across the street from the faded theater—the Gaîté Lyrique—where the ballet would premiere. (Diaghilev had not been able to book a more prestigious hall, a sign that his influence over the Parisian arts scene had begun to wane.) Serge needed to practice his conducting and relearn the complicated score, so the decision to sleep apart from Lina was, on this occasion, legitimate.

Extra last-minute rehearsals ensured that *The Buffoon* went off without any major complications. Although the dazzling, violent score did not approach the *succès de scandale* of Stravinsky's ballet *Le sacre du printemps* (*The Rite of Spring*) in 1913, it generated enough heckling from the well-heeled but conservative audience to confirm Prokofiev anew as a bona fide modernist. Diaghilev was satisfied; his investment in Prokofiev had not gone to waste.

The composer basked in the limited applause (he had arrived late on stage for his awkward bow) and allowed himself to drink during the post-curtain celebration in Montmartre, a crescendo of Russian-style toasts and counter-toasts amid platters of food, Japanese paper animal balloons, and "alarmingly *décolletées* cocottes." Lina proudly joined him; his mother did not. Though Serge found it hard in general to relax, it was a night to savor. He did so until Lina overindulged and needed, for the sake of her dignity, to be escorted back to their hotel.

The next day it was back to work, with Serge's mild hangover exacerbated by the wrong notes that crept into the score during the second performance of *The Buffoon*. After two more performances in Paris, the ballet moved on to London with a different conductor. Drained by the Paris performances, Serge decided against crossing the English Channel with Diaghilev's dancers and musicians for the rehearsals. Instead he collected his mother and took the train back to Saint-Brevin-les-Pins, intent on full-time composing and looking forward to the tranquil setting.

That was on May 26. The next day, Lina joined them at the house. She had remained behind in Paris to attend to a major change in her career—a new teacher, the eminent French soprano Emma Calvé. Best known for her devastating interpretation of the title role in

Georges Bizet's *Carmen*, Calvé was nearing the end of her glorious career, having performed for the last time at the Paris Opera in 1919. Leisurely farewell tours of the British Isles and the United States were still to come. She could be ill-tempered, but she had a soft spot for young singers and took them under her wing during the off-season.

At Calvé's invitation, Lina arranged to spend the middle of the summer taking private lessons at the chateau the singer owned in southern France. Miss Spencer and Mrs. Garvin, delighted at Lina's new chance for success, promised to drive down to see her. For Lina, the opportunity meant additional travel and another separation from Serge, which he pretended to complain about but actually encouraged; he stressed in his diary, if not to Lina herself, his desire that she forge an independent career. Her own ambition had ebbed, given the fiasco with Chauve-Souris and the fierceness of the competition. Lina sobbed as she packed to leave, and his mother pouted, but he assured both that the time apart would whisk by. Lina had planned to be in the south for three weeks, though she remained for six.

Lina traveled with Calvé, her accompanist, and another student to the medieval town of Millau in the Midi-Pyrénées. The trip was meant to last sixteen hours, but the train ahead of theirs derailed, so it ended up taking two days. Calvé's residence, which she had purchased at the height of her fame in 1894, was perched on a mountain plateau twelve kilometers from the town and two thousand feet above sea level. It bore all of the features of a rehabilitated medieval castle: panoramic views, ramparts dating back to 1050, gardens, sheep, and cold drafts that Calvé, unlike her students, never seemed to mind. She loved the place to the extent that she called the three mountains that surrounded it after the operas that had brought her the most fame and that had funded its purchase: Carmen, Cavalleria, and Navarraise.

Had Lina visited Millau in later years, she would have been able to stay in a charming full-service boutique hotel named after her teacher, a local hero. Instead, she felt like a damsel in distress, stuck on an inaccessible pile of rock among the eagles, hoping Calvé's chevalier would appear with letters in his satchel. She slept the first night in an eerie room where Henry IV had once lodged; in the morning she relocated to a brighter space with a cabinet de toilette located in a round tower with a balcony. The winds moaned, and water rushed somewhere below.

Lina was well cared for, but her teacher's strict meal, exercise, and sleep regimen (up at 8 A.M. and in bed by 10 P.M.) left her feeling all the more isolated. The accompanist, a meek French girl, proved dull-witted and thus not much of a conversationalist, and Lina despised the other student at the chateau, subjecting her to a withering critique that brought out Lina's least attractive traits. Her name was Frida Manasevich, but to Lina she was nothing more than a "conniving little Yid, so affected." She carped to Serge about "the way she hovers around Mme Calvé, it's completely nauseating," and Frida spitefully reported that she "acts like a total idiot in order to please her, and she's unfortunately also a coloratura." Calvé tempered Lina's irrational ire by assuring her that, in her opinion, she was "plus avancée" (more advanced) than Frida.

Lessons tended to be just fifteen minutes long, once or twice a day, and were often conducted jointly with Frida in an elegant music room with excellent acoustics. Calvé had stuffed it with mementos and souvenirs and couldn't resist sharing with Lina anecdotes about her encounters with kings and queens. Some of the lessons were tiring without being productive, others productive without being tiring, and still others both, depending on the extent to which Calvé was in the mood to teach. Lina's one faux pas came at the start, when she had to admit that she had been working with another teacher. Calvé and Litvinne had performed together, Lina quickly learned, and had suffered a disastrous falling-out. Thus it was no surprise that Calvé found all sorts of things wrong with Lina's technique, starting with the fact that she forced air through her vocal cords rather than breathing naturally. And, contrary to Litvinne's assessment, she was not a dramatic soprano but a "pure coloratura."

Lina took the news in stride and even felt vindicated—her displeasure with Litvinne seemed justified. Soon, however, she became equally disenchanted with Calvé. Her lessons were unfocused, her taste in music old-fashioned, and, like all celebrities, she was vainglorious, devoted to herself. Her anecdotes about her stunning rise to fame and the dashing men in her life, including her Italian baritone husband, grew tiresome. The accompanist advised Lina not to expect very much from Calvé, explaining in strictest confidence that "she's a marvelous person but you're wasting your time with her."

"How encouraging," Lina responded, suddenly feeling as if she'd been duped. The rest of her time in the chateau would find her mood fluctuating wildly between pessimism and optimism. Other singers appeared, including an Australian-born, English-trained mezzo-soprano who was soon to have her debut at the Monte Carlo Opera. "I owe it all to Mme Calvé," the new arrival, Marguerite Gard, enthused, reflecting on her successful performances in London and Paris, where she had assumed the surname Vécla, an anagram of Calvé. "I assure you that if you stay with her she will make something of you and get you engagements because she knows so many people."

That boosted Lina's spirits, as did the compliment she received from Calvé after a performance in the town of Rodez, some four hours from Millau. The concert had been organized by local dignitaries as part of a banquet in Calvé's honor, and Lina sang in a large choral piece. She was one of 150 performers, but her solo was a highlight.

Lina's mood crashed, however, when she thought about her predicament with Serge, who was still shuttling back and forth between Les Rochelets and Paris. The relationship was her greatest concern; at times, she knew, she was just playing the part of an aspiring soprano. Serge was obviously unwilling to make a commitment to her and was satisfied with just half of a relationship—the physical half. His composing always took priority, with everything (and everyone) else falling far behind. At the moment, he was completely absorbed in work at different stages on the ballet, the opera *The Fiery Angel*, the Balmont songs, and the Third Piano Concerto. He seemed content with the company of the amateur poet and philosopher Boris Bashkirov, a childhood friend who had only just left Russia. Serge invited him to spend the summer at Les Rochelets, where Bashkirov whiled away the days swimming, playing chess, and keeping Serge's mother entertained.

Serge recounted his activities throughout June to Lina, and while she was consoled he wrote at all, his one-page letters provoked anxieties. Apparently he was doing just fine without her. "Your letter from the 17th is perhaps the nicest one that you've yet written to me," Lina replied on the twenty-first. "You describe your life so well and it's so clear that everything is going so smoothly for you that I'm afraid that I'd bring disorder into it and that, besides you being dissatisfied I'd be dissatisfied being ignored, etc."

But she talked herself out of the malaise. "If only you knew how wonderful it is here. When I sit in the evening on the terrace contemplating the beautiful view, how I wish you were here beside me, how much more beautiful it would be. How you would like it here! If only we could have such a castle to ourselves, you and I!" Then back to worrying in a bilingual appendix: "Hélas, no tebe bïlo bï skuchno" (Alas, but you'd find it boring).

Lina tried to concentrate on her studies, but only because the dominant figures in her life—first her distant, despondent mother and then Serge—had imposed on her their own need for her to have a career. Plus she had her pride, and so she implored Serge not to relay her difficulties to Janacopoulos or Stahl. She was struggling to find her own future and a greater purpose, but resigned herself to doing it alone, because the meaning that she might otherwise find in marriage was not in the offing. "It seems to be the only thing for me to do, as you don't consider me worthy to do it for me," she lamented to Serge. Not worthy of marrying, she meant. "Oh, you have no idea what I suffer morally when I think things over!"

Serge was unmoved by the effusions, at least that summer, and chose to attribute Lina's discontent to capriciousness. Perhaps her next letter would find her in better spirits. Perhaps she should visit. Or perhaps the problem would somehow resolve itself, despite her threats about ending the relationship. Lina considered returning to her mother in New York, but she did not have the means to do so. Calvé and the other singers who turned up at the chateau in June and July tried to convince her to continue with her lessons, even if she couldn't actually afford to pay for them. The cost of her room and board—twelve francs per day—was to be settled in the fall. Lina's unhappiness was plain, however, and her teacher sensed flagging commitment. So too did Marguerite, the mezzo-soprano from Australia, whom Lina had befriended.

After much agonizing about how Serge and her friends would react, Lina decided to leave the chateau. The lessons would resume at the end of October in Paris, but by then Calvé had lost interest in her. She would say as much to Lina's mother in New York at the end of the year, between performances at the Metropolitan Opera and Carnegie Hall. Lina had a beautiful voice that suited opera, Calvé vaguely reassured Olga, but "j'ai peur qu'elle n'a pas assez de patience et de vouloir

d'arriver" (I fear she lacks the patience and the will). Lina did not record her mother's reaction, but it could not have been good, even if it
gave Olga hope that Lina would soon return home.

The rest of the year was miserable. Following a few days of vacation in Fontainebleau at Marguerite's suggestion, Lina returned to
Paris and took an inexpensive one-room flat at 119, bis rue Notre
Dame des Champs, in the sixth arrondissement. The fireplace was
difficult to light and produced very little heat; the drafts and damp
only worsened the colds and sore throats that plagued her throughout the fall. Serge's mother, now also living in Paris, tallied up Lina's
trips to the doctor for treatment: twenty-five. For lack of better options, she continued her lessons with Calvé despite the "confounded
colds," as she called them, breaking down in tears of frustration both
with her health and her teacher. Get-well wishes came in the form
of postcards and letters from warmer places. Then, on December 5,
when Calvé left for New York and another appearance in her signature role of *Carmen*, the relationship was terminated. She left Lina
with a signed photograph that complimented her enchanting singing
but disenchanting attitude. "The old witch," Lina grumbled.

Marguerite and other experienced singers, meanwhile, had planted
the idea in her head to enroll in a formal program of studies at the
Milan Conservatoire. The curriculum was conservative but well-re-
spected, offering students private lessons, master classes, and exposure to the practicalities of operatic staging. Lina mulled it over for
three months before deciding to give it a try—she had no better options. If nothing else, studies in Milan would please her parents, reminding them of their own time there, and would likely lead to some
professional experience, which (Chauve-Souris aside) she had yet to
achieve.

It meant another move, farther away from Serge, and living on a
tight budget, though she had become used to that. For much of the
year, including her time with Calvé at the chateau, she had depended
on money from Serge. It arrived at the Guarantee Trust bank, often
along with funds for his mother. Lina did not ask for the help—her
circle included doting benefactors like the Liebmans—and she always had the option to decline it. But it was something, even if the
real support she craved from him was not financial, but emotional.

Not that she was abandoned in Europe. Besides Marguerite, she socialized with Serge Persky, the former assistant to Prime Minister Georges Clemenceau, and with Janacopoulos, Stahl, and the well-heeled ladies and gentlemen who attended afternoon teas at the American embassy. In November, she attended two of these events, battling bronchitis at the second but making a positive impression. The hostess held her back to tell her that the men had paid her "nice" compliments, one of them even ruffling decorum by deeming her "dangerously attractive." She returned in December, this time with an accompanist, and sang a selection of arias by Debussy, Rimsky-Korsakov, Delibes, and Gounod.

Appealing to the Americans in the crowd, she encored with the ever-popular "Drink to Me Only with Thine Eyes," a staple of the American recital circuit. Lina acknowledged to Serge that she did not feel prepared to sing his songs in public, even though the most recent set had been dedicated to her. His music was difficult; it required much more preparation than "Drink to Me," and the texts of the songs had yet to be translated from Russian into French. The problem of finding a competent translator was compounded by the nature of the texts — Balmont's recherché symbolist poetry. The teas were the sole pleasure of the final weeks of 1921.

Throughout the fall and winter, Lina paid social calls to Janacopoulos and Stahl, but they pressed her into the service of Janacopoulos's career. The two of them cared only for themselves, Lina decided, after weeks of silence. Finally in November, she received an invitation to their gracious apartment for breakfast, and Stahl turned on the charm, chatting amiably and sharing anecdotes about his business dealings. The next time she saw him, however, he put her to work addressing a stack of envelopes with the names of everyone she knew in New York — some fifty people in all, her parents included. Stahl then stuffed the envelopes with Janacopoulos's latest recital programs and put them in the mail. That the people in Lina's address book learned all about Janacopoulos's musical triumphs in Paris from her husband and business manager seemed only to draw attention to the paltriness of her own achievements.

She felt cheated. No one offered her support — she had only herself, and even she neglected her own needs. Instead she served Serge's career, acting as his part-time assistant, collecting reviews and articles about him in the French press, and summarizing them in her letters to him. These included reviews—some positive, some negative—of additional performances of *Scythian Suite* under the baton of Serge Koussevitzky, a Russian émigré who landed first in Paris before becoming, in 1924, the conductor of the Boston Symphony Orchestra.

Lina was not against helping Serge in this way, but her role in his life seemed limited to what she could do to benefit his life and work, whether providing companionship when he was lonely, caring for his mother, or clipping press notices. The relationship remained precarious even in the eyes of his mother, with whom she often went to concerts. Lina felt alone, both mentally and physically; the famous figures in Serge's world were generally not part of hers, leaving her to fantasize in absentia about the cafes, nightclubs, and salons to which they retired, the scent of cigarettes and perfume, the canvases on the walls. The parade of musical greats with whom Serge competed and (occasionally) fraternized were, for Lina, observable only from a distance. The dainty composer Maurice Ravel sat across from her at one of the Koussevitzky performances but instantly vanished from the theater after his one piece on the program (*La valse, un poème chorégraphique*) had been heard. Lina also encountered Diaghilev, stouter and grayer (the hair color was obvious) than Serge had described him, as well as the artists of the Ballets Russes—an impoverished but fashion-conscious clique much enamored with the breaking of taboos.

Though she grew increasingly resentful of the time and energy—emotional and otherwise—that she poured into the relationship with Serge, she hid her true feelings until she made up her mind about Milan. When she had, she informed him that she was putting her affairs in order, was leaving Paris, and could not continue to trawl the newspapers and magazines looking for his name. She would leave the reviews and articles that she had already gathered in the care of his mother.

Of course this news was sent by letter, as Serge was far away again. He had steamed on the *Aquitania* to the United States for the rehearsals and premiere of *Love for Three Oranges* in Chicago, which felt as if it had been in the works for decades, rather than just two years. Serge was also booked to perform his Third Piano Concerto—a masterpiece destined for a permanent place in the repertoire. In New York he looked up his old flame Stella Adler, but he avoided Nina Koshetz, knowing that he would soon see her in Chicago. She had a lead role in his opera. The last thing he needed was to be drawn into one of her personal dramas, even as he admitted to himself that he enjoyed attending her séances and communing with the table-tapping spirits that served as her muses. Lina, unaware of his continued interest in Adler, was relieved to hear about his undercover existence and jokingly suggested he enlist a friend in Chicago as a "bodyguard" to protect himself from Koshetz's advances. Throughout his American tour, she continued to write to Serge, to banter with him, and express her concern for his well-being. Lina had not actually ended the relationship, as she pretended she wanted to do.

Serge arrived in Chicago on October 29 to conduct rehearsals. He also appeared with orchestras in the Midwest as piano soloist, a "string of $1,000 dates," his agent boasted, that made him less churlish and more confident with reporters. The composer granted long interviews on subjects ranging from his love of flirting to the terror he felt at having to give a lecture on his music in English and the futuristic opera that he might one day write about the game of chess. (He had won a chess tournament en route to America.) The upcoming premiere of *Love for Three Oranges* absorbed his thoughts, and he threw his head from side to side in nervous excitement as he described the apoplectic music and disorienting decor. More time had been devoted to the staging of his opera, he cued the *Chicago Evening Post*, than "anything else the company has ever given." Hearing the news of his adventures at the podium, Lina teased that the tennis he had played during the summer had gotten his conducting arm into shape. She worried about his back, though, and asked after the health of his teeth.

The dreaded reunion with Koshetz was benign, though the two of them quickly resumed the impassioned disputes that defined their relationship. He delivered the perfumes and powders that she had insisted he bring from Paris, swapped stories with her, and then got back to work—as did she. The premiere of the opera on Friday, December 30, was a success, better than he and the creative team expected. Hoots and hollers greeted his arrival at the podium for the last act. Serge basked in the afterglow of a performance three years in the making. Even though the ending was a mess and the chorus lacked coordination, there was uproarious laughter throughout— all in all an auspicious way to close out 1921. *Love for Three Oranges* earned a second performance in Chicago on January 5, with the composer sitting in the audience rather than leading the orchestra. The rough spots remained, but it also came off well.

The reviews, however, were derisive; the critics refused to embrace the public's fascination with the "prophet of the music of the future" and his "Russian jazz with Bolshevik trimmings." Noting the huge amount expended on the opera in gangland Chicago, the reporter for the *Chicago Daily Tribune* identified just "two tunes" in the score, one a "very good march." But "for the rest of it, Mr. Prokofieff might well have loaded up a shotgun with several thousand notes of varying lengths and discharged them against the side of a blank wall."

Excluding some imaginative descriptions of the "hurdy-gurdy rhythms" and "fantastic lollipops" of the opera, the best thing Serge read appeared a month before the premiere and complimented his fashion sense rather than his music. Enamored of his well-pressed three-piece suits, a journalist for the *Daily News* dubbed him the "best-dressed man in Chicago."

Serge responded with snobbish indifference to the criticism, attributing it to Midwestern parochialism, but it definitely stung. He counted on a stronger positive reception elsewhere—something comparable to his all-conquering recitals. The opera would be performed in New York on February 14 (postponed from February 6, owing to illnesses in the cast), but there too the reviewers gleefully pounced on him. Additional performances in the United States and Europe were discussed. There was no thought of Russia.

During rehearsals in Chicago, Serge sometimes pondered what it would be like to have Lina perform the part of her namesake in *Love for Three Oranges;* back in Paris, Lina indulged the same fantasy—despite not actually knowing the music. Her namesake was the beautiful, seductive Princess Linette, who materializes in the penultimate act. She and two other fair maidens are being held prisoner in the castle of the old witch Creonta. The Prince and the court jester Truffaldino manage to free her, but she dies of thirst in the blazing desert when the bumbling rescuers fail to heed her pleas for water. Her ethereal arioso lines expire with her. The Prince knew this might happen, since the same thirst had felled another Princess who had also sprung from an orange. Slowly learning his lesson, the Prince manages to save a third Princess, Ninetta, by absurdly drenching her in water. The two of them fall in love and find happiness—though not before some additional mischief-making by Fata Morgana. Princess Linette hangs limp over the side of the giant fruit from which she sprang. The role suited Lina's range, and she might have been able to do something with the part. But Serge concluded that he did not have sufficient knowledge of her voice to know if she could handle it, and that even if she could, he would never have enough clout to cast her on his own.

While Serge relished his popular success in Chicago and New York, Lina spent the holidays alone in Paris. Even Marguerite had forsaken her to spend Christmas and New Year's in London with her parents. By letter on December 8, Lina again stressed to Serge that she could no longer tolerate living under false pretenses, without personal or professional support. She was tired of his ambivalence. For his part, Serge was increasingly aware that their long-distance relationship —long-distance even when they were together, it seemed—was at a crossroads. Either she would have to accept a less prominent role in his life, or he would have to make additional room for her.

In the past she could count on her mother, but Olga could not be reached. "It's impossible," Lina complained, "to struggle alone." But that is just what she continued to do. Surrendering the future of the relationship to Fata Morgana, Lina packed her suitcase and moved to Milan.

Chapter 4

B Y 1922, THE CIVIL WAR between pro- and anti-Bolshevik forces had come to an end in Russia and the lands it controlled, but sporadic fighting continued. Some nine million people had died since the Revolution, most from famine and disease. The peasant revolts in Ukraine were suppressed with mass executions; the Red Army gained control of Siberia and the south. Far Eastern Russia, the lawless terrain Serge passed through en route to Japan and the United States in 1918, was treacherous territory. The Cheka, the "Emergency Commission" tasked by Vladimir Lenin with liquidating counterrevolutionaries, oversaw a growing network of labor camps. In May 1922, Lenin suffered a crippling stroke. His life was near its end.

These events went vaguely reported in their time, and Serge followed the news from home as best he could. But the situation in Russia (especially outside Petrograd and Moscow) remained unclear to him. He assumed the worst as he achieved greatness in the West. Although *Love for Three Oranges* was not the success Serge had hoped it would be, he had been admitted into the inner circle of Diaghilev's Ballets Russes and finally triumphed over Rachmaninoff with his Third Piano Concerto.

Lina moved from Paris to Milan in February 1922, the deterioration of her relationship with Serge a pressing concern for both of them. The negotiations ahead, in letter and in person, would mix his ego and renown with her desire to be more than average, if only through the bond with him. It was the central problem of their relationship, and it interfered with their otherwise passionate attraction.

In the week preceding Lent, Milan hosts the world's longest Carnival—longest because the city follows the calendar of the Ambrosian rite, rather than the more familiar Roman. Whereas parades, parties, feasts, and street fairs in other cities cease on Ash Wednesday, after the excess of Mardi Gras (Fat Tuesday), the Milanese keep going until the first Sunday in Lent. Citizens gorge themselves on local pastries, including *tortelli di Milano* (fried sweet dough dusted with powdered sugar and cinnamon) and chocolate-covered *chiacchiere*, while dressed in masks and historical costumes. On Saturday, the carnival festivities culminate in a procession to the Duomo, which begins in the afternoon and ends with a raucous street party on the piazza lasting well into the night. The streets are crammed with people reveling in a blizzard of confetti and streamers.

This was one of the first events that Lina experienced in the city after she arrived. With her ambition renewed, she came to Milan to work on her vocal technique, expand her repertoire, and audition for the opera. In her lessons, she worked from a collection of twenty-four vocalises composed by the renowned nineteenth-century tenor Marco Bordogni. A stamp on the cover of her score indicates that she acquired the treasured collection in Paris. She held on to it throughout her life, even during her years in the Stalinist variant of Lenin's labor camps. Other music to have survived the experience includes piano-vocal editions of Verdi's *Rigoletto* and Gounod's *Roméo et Juliette*, with Russian translations of the texts. These were published in Moscow and came to Lina either from her mother or Serge. Besides Chopin's "The Wish," she also maintained a sentimental attachment to Charles Wakefield Cadman's "At Dawning (I Love You)," an American parlor song composed in 1906.

Although Lina anticipated an anonymous, friendless existence in Milan, her boarding house, populated by aspiring tenors and sopranos, provided endless distraction. She took a room in a pension for musicians at Piazza del Duomo 8, in the boisterous heart of the city just a block from the massive Gothic cathedral, and for a few weeks relished the theatrical atmosphere. Excitement faded into weariness during Carnival, however, though Lina could not help but be impressed by the final procession. The alfresco masquerade, she recounted to Serge with wonderment, mirrored the grand balls held in the theaters, which she could not afford to attend.

In the spring, her room became warmer and noisier, and when all of her neighbors were practicing at the same time with the windows open, the residence felt like a musical madhouse. The chatter improved her Italian to the point that she could attend local plays and understand everything, but Lina grew tired of the constant gossip and intrigue in the building. Following a four-day trip to see Miss Spencer in Florence at the very end of May, she relocated with a New York girlfriend, Consuelo Eastwick, to Via Stella 38A, in a much quieter area just west of the inner ring of Milan. (The street was renamed after the unionist Filippo Corridoni in November 1922, right after Benito Mussolini, the head of the Italian Socialist Party and future fascist dictator, seized control of the government.)

A few stark, bleached-out photographs survive from this period, some taken that fall in Milan, others in the summer in the park in the town of Monza and on Lake Como. Lina poses between her unnamed teachers, arm in arm with them, or idles with a book on a park bench, or cuddles a puppy named Porríto; the stately Consuelo appears stern-faced.

The rent was cheaper on Via Stella than at the boarding house, which was good since Lina's funds were dwindling. The apartment boasted comfortable furniture and a sitting area generous enough for the two girls to have guests over for tea on Saturdays, host bridge games during the week, and even throw the occasional party. Among their guests were musicians at the Conservatoire and local artistic celebrities, including Filippo Marinetti, the founder of the Italian futurist movement.

Seeking to build a network of potential supporters, Lina sought out critics, conductors, the director of the Ricordi music publishing house, and the chief stage designer of La Scala, Giovanni Grandi, whose Russian wife was (as chance would have it) acquainted with Somoff. Somehow her former New York employer never seemed to leave her life. Nor did Dagmar Godowsky, whose close friend Eva Didur lived adjacent to Lina at the boarding house. She was a true diva, the daughter of the great Polish basso Adamo Didur. Her debut in New York had, according to the reviewers, won over the crowd, despite

Eva being as "temperamental as her Bernhardt hair." In Milan, she successfully sang the lead role of Mimi in Puccini's *La bohème* at the Teatro Dal Verme, no doubt provoking Lina's jealousy.

Lina's studies were calibrated for auditions with professional opera companies. She enjoyed her teachers much more than the canonic Italian operas they assigned her. For the first two months, her repertoire included Gilda from *Rigoletto* and the title role of Catalani's *La Wally*. The parts were challenging, but she found the operas stale and tired compared to the music she had studied in France under Litvinne and Calvé—including, of course, Serge's own Balmont songs.

La Wally came in for her harshest critique, despite it being a favorite of the principal conductor of La Scala at the time, Arturo Toscanini. It was rubbish, she declared—a rash judgment that presumably excluded its most famous aria, the celestial "Ebben? Ne andrò lontana" of the first act, wherein the heroine expresses her intention to leave her mother's happy home, perhaps never to return. Lina learned the part under the direction of a conductor and rehearsal coach. Both earned her praise, as did the émigré Russian director Victor Andoga (his real surname was Zhurov), with whom she had been acquainted in Paris and who became intimately involved with her roommate Consuelo. Andoga had just staged Musorgsky's opera *Boris Godunov* at the newly reopened La Scala, with Toscanini conducting, and Lina was overwhelmed at having the chance to receive instruction in mise en scène from him. Her progress was such that she hoped to have her professional debut in the early fall, maybe September or October.

Meanwhile, Serge returned to Europe, arriving in Boulogne from New York on February 25, thereafter traveling by train for a hectic series of engagements in Paris and Berlin. He had steamed across the Atlantic on the *Noordam* with his dissolute poet and philosopher friend Boris Bashkirov, and the two of them decided, in Lina's absence, to hunt for a summer rental in the Bavarian Alps. His own finances being tight, Serge ruled out renting in southern France as he had the summer before. (The economic crisis in Germany meant living there cost a fraction of what it would in France.) Bashkirov promised to find a proper rental for them in Bavaria, but in the end, Serge had to lead the search. His mother would of course join them once they settled. Bashkirov, who besides eating and sleeping aspired to finish a collection of poems, even pledged to read Nietzsche to her in the evenings. The hope was that Lina would come as well. Anxieties about losing touch with her had penetrated Serge's distracted mind, but her desire to get married clashed with his fears of being pinned down, confined. And he had long convinced himself that marriage would not bring him contentment. His mother's experience made him wary of making such a commitment. After getting married and settling in Sontsovka, Ukraine, the village of Serge's birth, she had struggled to maintain the trappings of her previous cosmopolitan existence.

Serge and Bashkirov found a large house in the village of Ettal, some ninety-five kilometers south of Munich, high in the Bavarian Alps. Villa Christophorous, as the house was dubbed, was delightful —so much so that Serge decided to stay through 1923. It featured a first-floor library with books in three languages, couches, and rich-hued carpets; balconied bedrooms on the second story; electric lighting, a cold-water bath, futurist paintings on the walls, and a marvelous view onto the Ettal Kloster and the surrounding meadows. There was no piano at first, so Serge had to practice on an instrument owned by a local shopkeeper for his upcoming performances, in London and Paris, of the Third Piano Concerto.

Convincing Lina to visit the idyllic retreat proved a challenge. Neglected for months and jaded by the five-to-one ratio in their correspondence, she had fallen nearly silent, sending but a few curt updates on her studies. Serge tried to soothe her by complimenting her "very chic" promotional photograph, but the tactic backfired when he added Bashkirov's lustful assessment of her neckline. Lina repeatedly resisted visiting, claiming that she was too absorbed in her improvised Milan Conservatoire curriculum and that she had changed her outlook on life. Philosophy had come to her aid, reinforcing her increasing conviction that, as she haughtily explained to him, "for me it is the spiritual union that counts most—the primitive plays a lesser part, and if the first does not exist, what is the second worth?"

Plus, she quipped, it would be a shame to disturb the peace in Villa Christophorous, since Serge, Bashkirov, and his mother seemed perfectly content. "So if I do decide to take a vacation," she wrote, "it will be a short one and not for more than a couple of weeks . . . so that's how matters stand!" She even took a jab at Serge's general interest in mysticism and the occult-based opera he was struggling to complete, *The Fiery Angel.* Trying to best him, she reported that "I'm reading *Le Grand Secret*," Maurice Maeterlinck's meditation on mystic doctrine that invoked, to the extent that words allowed it to be invoked, a separate plane of being. "It's very profound. Have you read it?" He had not, though he had seen some reviews.

The businesslike tone of Lina's letter made an impression, as did her subsequent declaration that, despite "elements of growth" in their relationship, she needed to free herself of him. Her mother, she told him, could not understand why he had not proposed to her and why she still had to conceal their relationship. Though poor health prevented Olga from writing more than once a month, she grieved for her daughter. And Miss Spencer, along with some of Lina's other friends, considered Serge a cad. These reports of course served as stand-ins for her own frustrations and desires. She wanted to get married. Serge answered, as he had in the past, by reminding Lina that he was above all committed to his music — not to any person — and that he was not prepared to consent to marriage if it was not inscribed in his heart. This in a letter dated July 9, 1922. He offered other excuses. Scriabin and Wagner had not been legally married but respected their partners, he noted, while Stravinsky, who was much more his musical (if not personal) role model, had betrayed his wife by entering into a dalliance with Coco Chanel and an affair with Vera Sudeykina. Going on the offense, he also wondered if Lina herself might not succumb to temptation in the opera world.

He neither promised to propose nor gave her a date for a declaration of his intentions. "Such is possible only for a person who has built his life around the family hearth," he wrote, "but it is too foreign for a person living in the abstract world of sounds (and isn't this the reason you love me?)." And if she truly loved him, even if only so she could "pose before the world," a desire for status that he had inferred from her letter, then she had to think matters through before making a decision to leave him. Serge acknowledged that he had used her by having her tend to his affairs and look after his mother, but he believed that Lina had taken advantage of him too. For all of her unhappiness with the status quo, she continued to cling to the relationship because her desire for public recognition eclipsed her resentment at being subservient.

Her actual words to him were more nuanced than his tough-minded assessment of them. "I must feel that you accept me before the world as the woman of your choice," she wrote—hardly the preening sentiment he parroted back to her. Whereas he presumed she wanted to posture on his arm, Lina longed for him to openly acknowledge their relationship, to invite her to stand beside him rather than leave her to walk ten paces behind. She needed him to validate her. The romantic chess match between them had lasted two years. She could triumph by ending the relationship, he allowed, but the satisfaction would last no longer than the time it would take to pick up the pieces. And then she would spend the summer alone in the "frying pan" of Milan, while, he admitted, "I'd be sad in Ettal"—a modest display of discontentment on his part.

Lina fought back hard, dissecting his argument point by point. "I sincerely love and value your music," she wrote in slightly rusty Russian before switching to slightly rusty English. "But I love S. P. man and not S. P. composer—if I loved you only for your music I would not want you, but would attend your concerts—buy your works and have someone play them for me—that is quite feasible, you know." She rejected his metaphor of a chess match, since chess pieces are not flesh and blood but wood, made to move around the board without feeling. She also dismissed his other metaphor, comparing the relationship to unripe fruit, "green" or "sour apples," and defended herself against his insult to her character. "If I were the vain and empty creature you have involuntarily accused me of being, by calling my love for you 'a desire to pose before the world,' I am afraid my desire would have been crushed long ago by the last 2–3 years' circumstances. I haven't any desire to give you up, but if it must be it certainly won't be as you say 'like extracting an infected tooth.'" She then softened her tone. "Mal'chik moy—my boy—such a comparison is not fair."

Serge recognized the unfairness without apologizing for it and pleaded with Lina to spend "ein paar Wochen" in Ettal. But he only made matters worse by telling her that he hoped that she would return to being the "kind and gentle ptashka" with whom he had become smitten in New York, rather than a "bat grabbing at his hair" —as if any expression of her own feelings made her a nuisance. Unless she could be sweetly accommodating, he obliquely warned her, she would be swatted away. Despite this additional insult, she agreed to see him, at first thinking that she would present an ultimatum but then, in the days before her departure, deciding against it. The trip was delayed for a week by visa problems, which would recur on the way back. Lina needed to obtain both a transit and a visitor permit for her Spanish passport, a complicated procedure, given the fact that she was residing in Italy at the time. Having at last managed to secure the proper papers, she arrived in Munich through Switzerland on the morning of August 7. Serge met her at the station, finding her more attractive than ever, and was delighted—indeed relieved—to see her.

They took the two-hour train ride that afternoon to Oberammergau, an ornate if frayed Bavarian town that prided itself on its traditional crafts boutiques, stuffed with pottery and wood carvings, and, adorning the chalets, the frescoes showing scenes from the Bible or regional folklore. Oberammergau was renowned for its once-a-decade Passion play, which began in 1634 to celebrate the fact that the town had been spared the horrors of the bubonic plague. The villagers had prayed for salvation and apparently received it, so they expressed their gratitude in a reenactment of the sufferings of Christ. Once presented by and for peasants, the event now attracted international attention and thousands of spectators; the wooden benches on the theater grounds seated two thousand people, an audience about the same size as the population of Oberammergau. The prior performance had occurred in 1910, and a new production was set for May through September 1922—two years later than anticipated, owing to the German economic and political crisis. Since 1900, the famous local actor and craftsman Anton Lang had performed the role of Jesus, riding across the newly rebuilt stage on the donkey that grazed behind his studio. He was now forty-seven, much too old for the part, according to the biblical story and the opinion of some local officials. Still, he was able to bring the required pathos to the role, though he grumbled about the strain of hanging on the cross. (His fame was such that he would appear on the cover of *Time* magazine on December 17, 1923.)

The vast supporting cast included residents of the town who had lived there for two decades or more, long-haired youths, one or two babies, and a huddle of semi-domesticated animals. Some participants made their own peasant garb, brightening the local color of the event.

In anticipation of massive crowds of visitors arriving from abroad, the town had turned itself into a prototypical tourist attraction, putting up signs in English and German and opening a brand-new hotel and several bank outlets. Whittled icons were sold near the performance grounds. There was sufficient interest in the event for a Hollywood studio to offer to film a performance, but the town said no, fearing the production would lose its integrity. Later there would be talk of tours.

Serge and Lina attended the play that summer. For her, the eight-hour, afternoon-to-evening affair seemed less spiritual than theatrical, though, as they both remembered, the spirit world did exert its presence toward the end of the performance — in the form of a massive thunderstorm. The couple ended up befriending the actor who played Pontius Pilate, a local doctor. Later he would provide care to Serge's mother.

Ettal was four kilometers to the southeast of Oberammergau, an easy walk in pleasant weather but much more difficult, as Lina would learn at Christmastime, in the high-altitude snow. It was defined by its oldest building — the Kloster, dating from the fourteenth century. The abbey had once housed both men and women, and for a time had even been home to an assembly of Teutonic Knights. In 1744, it was converted into a boarding school, where the composer Richard Strauss installed his son Franz during the First World War. Serge and Bashkirov visited the abbey brewery, purported to produce the best beer in the region. They also took advantage of the hospitality of the monks by borrowing their driver for excursions into the mountains.

Lina spent August and September in Ettal, and Serge took pains to make her feel at home, decorating the window of her room with forget-me-nots forming the letter *L*. He taught her to play chess, accompanied her at the piano (having finally secured one for the house) while she sang his *Balmont Romances* as well as songs by Debussy and Poulenc, and shared news of his progress on *The Fiery Angel*. She restored relations with Serge's mother, whose health remained fragile, and learned to tolerate Bashkirov, who took to her appearance more than to her character. Recreation included bridge, chess, gardening, and tennis on the courts of the abbey. Serge and Bashkirov also engaged each other in a poetry translation contest.

While Serge was at work proofreading the piano-vocal score of

Love for Three Oranges and the arrangement of an orchestral suite from *The Buffoon*, Lina occupied herself by socializing with two of the Kloster monks. The younger of them was Father Joseph, who unpiously flirted with her when he stopped by to give Lina some goat's milk. He then confessed the matter to Serge: "Once when I was at your house, your wife saw me to the door and as I said goodbye I kissed her hand." Serge forgave him, barely able to keep from laughing. The older monk was Father Isadore, who behaved himself, limiting their conversations to liturgical matters.

Toward the end of her life, Lina would recount another event in Ettal, though it occurred the following summer. This was the purchase of an electric chick-brooder from an advertisement in a Munich newspaper. Their housekeeper advised them of a shortage of eggs in the area and encouraged them to make the acquisition, which sat on the balcony at Villa Christophorous, where they usually hung their clothes to dry. They stocked it with eggs from an Ettal farm. In the evenings, Serge presided over the incubator like a proud father-to-be, watching for motion within the shells. Twenty-one eggs hatched, the chicks looking feeble, unconvinced by the heat lamp. Most of them died, Lina recalled, blaming Serge for not tending to them properly. Serge gave the others to the neighbors. The last egg did not hatch for a few more days. A duckling emerged.

Rested, and temporarily rid of the stomach ailments that she had long been battling, Lina left Ettal for Milan on the morning of October 7. The extended trip back offered an unwelcome lesson in economics (the disastrous devaluation of the German mark versus the Austrian crown), the kindness of strangers (the divorced man who got her through customs in Innsbruck without a visa and found her a room there in the middle of the night), and the vexing Italian rail system. She arrived in Milan at three in the afternoon the next day, the heavens opening up as her train pulled in.

At Via Stella 38A, Lina found ten letters and nine postcards waiting for her — along with a different roommate. Consuelo, newly pregnant by and wed to Andoga, had suddenly moved to Paris. She was replaced by the Russian Tanya Kalashnikova. An aspiring pianist, Tanya did not impress Lina as a musician — her sight-reading needed considerable improvement — but she could claim insider knowledge of events in Russia, from the anarchic violence of the Revolution to Lenin's frantic consolidation of power during the civil war. It turned out that Tanya had a brother who lived in Tbilisi, Georgia, and her first cousin, Mikhaíl Karpovich, worked at the Russian embassy in New York. Karpovich had been a member of the provisional government in Russia (as had Stahl) before its collapse forced him to relocate to Washington and then New York, where he worked as a midlevel diplomat at the embassy. The Bolsheviks deprived him of his post in the summer of 1922. He could not return to Russia for fear of arrest and so became a freelance translator and lecturer. Karpovich was destined for a distinguished career in the history department at Harvard University.

Tanya discussed with Lina the stunning news of the creation of the Soviet Union at the end of 1922, following the merger of the RSFSR (Russian Soviet Federative Socialist Republic) with the Ukrainian, Belorussian, and Transcaucasian states. Lina, in turn, shared what she heard from Tanya with Serge, including her brother's prediction that within five years the Russian ruble would be gold-backed and the economy would stabilize. Serge, in response, described the letters he had started to receive from officials in the Soviet government, including a note of congratulations on the premiere of *Love for Three Oranges*. He also offered Tanya some tips on performing his music; she was playing the march from that same opera—and not badly, in Lina's opinion.

Soon Lina and Tanya were joined by Marguerite Gard, the Australian mezzo-soprano with whom Lina had lived at Emma Calvé's chateau. She had come to Milan to take lessons with Giannina Russ, and her presence in the apartment enhanced the convivial atmosphere. In December, however, the three roommates learned that they would have to move, since the owner of the apartment wanted it for herself. Lina and Marguerite decided to take rooms in a pension at Via Fratelli Bronzetti 27, a half-hour walk to the east of the previous address, while Tanya left for Rome to see her sister.

The sole attributes of the new residence were its cleanliness and the amenities of the avenue. Marguerite did not stay long, having decided it would be more exciting and less expensive to live in the center of town. Lina declined to join her (she had not forgotten her experience during Carnival), and found herself bored and alone, save for

the occasional outing with Marguerite to La Scala. The neighbors—
young lovers on one side, and a sixteen-year-old pianist who played
wrong notes from eight in the morning to eleven at night on the other
—stole her sleep, so she needed to change rooms. Outside it drizzled,
blackening the streets of the disenchanting city, along with Lina's
mood. She complained of nerves, fevers, and worse. "Do you know
I am becoming a bit worried—quite worried," she wrote in English
to Serge in a letter otherwise composed in Russian. Lina had taken
to the habit of highlighting personal matters in English and professional ones in Russian or French. Later, she would reverse the pattern. She never explained what was wrong, but an appointment with
an unnamed specialist about the unnamed condition apparently set
her mind at rest.

Separated from Serge again, Lina began to doubt anew his commitment to her. The obvious question—how much he cared about
her well-being—raised others. She asked him to reveal his thoughts
about the relationship, honestly and frankly; he only reiterated his
ambivalence about the institution of marriage. Of course he loved
her, yet he could not, would not, propose to her. The comment preceded several lines about the hazards that marriage posed to positive relationships. What, Serge asked Lina, could be more mundane,
more prosaic, than the words "my wife" and "my husband"? Either
he did not realize or did not care that those were the very words she
longed to hear.

Lina was confused and directionless, unsure of her personal
or professional future. She declined Serge's invitation to visit Ettal over Christmas because she and Marguerite had made plans to
travel to Berlin on the invitation of the eminent Wagnerian soprano
Lilli Lehmann, author of a classic book on singing methods called
Meine Gesangskunst (published in English as *How to Sing*). But then
Lina learned she might be scheduled to perform in Verona, which
ruled out traveling anywhere except to the rehearsal studio. To make
matters worse, as she despaired about her relationship with Serge,
Consuelo and Andoga returned to Milan for a few days, trumpeting
their romantic bliss. Then Marguerite revealed her romance with the
La Scala designer Giovanni Grandi, who was newly estranged from
his wife. They would soon marry, and she assumed his surname for
the stage. At opera houses in England, the Netherlands, Hungary,

Italy, and Egypt, Marguerite Gard performed as Mme Margherita Grandi before cheering audiences.

Lina would never have Marguerite's career, and in that glum December of 1922, she confronted her admittedly ambivalent desire for the stage, and the prospect of satisfying it, which seemed dubious. The prospective Verona performance fell through, since the opera in which she was supposed to sing had been replaced by another. She considered returning to Paris, then thought about New York. But she paused at the travel office, resisting rashness. Her aggrieved pride advised her against retracing the train route to Ettal and Serge but, in the end, that is what she did. An unadventurous decision, prompted by stubbornness. Lina arrived at Villa Christophorous on Christmas Eve. Her gifts included a picture of Mussolini for Serge's mother.

Serge had not been expecting her, since the telegram confirming her travel plans did not arrive until after she did, but the reunion was a relief to both of them, and it cast a glow over the start of 1923. After the brief holiday together, they saw each other again in Milan that February, staying at the Como Hotel near the train station rather than at her pension. Three days there were followed by two more in Genoa. Serge was en route to Spain, but Lina could not accompany him, as she had fleetingly fantasized doing, even though he would be appearing in her birthplace or, as both of them liked to put it in their letters, her "hometown" of Barcelona. During the brief visit in Italy, their relationship strengthened, the disagreements concerning a permanent commitment eclipsed by the pleasure of the moment. When Serge left for his international engagements, Lina returned to her pension and endeavored to secure her still elusive debut.

She was motivated as much by Serge as by the gossip that each of them received in the mail and through mutual friends. Everyone was full of news. Serge's actress friend Mariya Baranovskaya, otherwise known as Frou-Frou, had married a classmate of his at the St. Petersburg Conservatoire, the pianist Alexander Borovsky. Stahl and Janacopoulos had visited Ettal and toured the surroundings in high style. The Somoffs, Lina learned through her mother, relocated to Riverside Drive in Manhattan and purchased an automobile. Then something serious from Miss Spencer: a letter voicing profound concern for Lina's well-being and suggesting she return to New York. Lina's mother was in ill health. Olga appeared "very well poised in mind, but none too strong in body," Miss Spencer reported, to Lina's extreme distress. "She longs for you as you can little realize, but she dare not go to Europe. To say that we are all worried about her is to put it mildly, Linette dear. Of course, I am deeply conscious of your own aims and ideals. But, dear little girl, you have fallen on a difficult road in a difficult time."

The "difficult time" was not a reference to Lina's personal life, but to political circumstances in Europe. The year 1923 witnessed the consolidation of Soviet power in Russia and surrounding territories, hyperinflation in central Europe, the rise of Mussolini, and the birth of the Fascist movement in Italy. Lina followed these events with a sort of girlish curiosity and relished being in the center of the storm. She saw Mussolini once, in the company of King Victor Emmanuel III, who had asked him to assume control of the Italian government in an effort to prevent further social unrest after the Italian General Strike of 1920 and thwart a potential Communist takeover. Lina remembered going into the center of Milan at 8:30 A.M. one April morning to witness a parade. "Il Re—the King—came with his entire retinue in parade uniform, even more splendid than last year. I had a good view of the King and Mussolini, who sat beside him in the carriage. The city was decked out . . . everyone lost their head in the patriotic fervor."

And whatever the difficulties around her, things actually seemed to be looking up—at least in terms of her singing career. In mid-February 1923, Lina received a contract for three performances as Gilda in *Rigoletto*, meaning that her unhappy tussle with the role in her lessons had paid off. The contract mentioned additional bookings for other operas, but these would not come through, since her repertoire did not match that of the theater, the Carcano. Founded in 1803 on the grounds of a forsaken monastery, it claimed an impressive number of premieres and at times rivaled La Scala as the crown jewel of the Milan opera scene, though its luster faded after 1900. Lina was hired as the understudy and alternate for Gilda, meaning she did not actively participate in orchestral rehearsals, but the young maestro worked with her at the piano so she could learn his tempos.

The contract pleased her less than it should have, since she was battling a cold at the time and feeling extremely lethargic. On certain days she was unable even to get out of bed, succumbing to self-pity, if not depression. "There are times when I hate all mankind," she moped, "and like to be alone but on the whole I believe I was not made to be alone."

Tanya came around to collect her letters and tried to engage her in conversation, but Lina grimly joked that her voice had dropped into the range of a basso profundo on account of her congestion. The foul weather further vexed her that February, as did the tumult of Carnival. When she managed to venture out of the apartment, Lina found the streets unbearable. She reacted angrily when the crowd threw confetti in her face, flailed in frustration when she was caught in a serpent banner, and even declined an invitation to attend one of the balls. She had had enough of Milan.

The thought of finally reaching the stage provoked anxiety as much as excitement. Lina was told she had until March 7 or so to prepare for her debut. But after the secretary at the Teatro Carcano confirmed that she would first appear on March 10, the date was pushed back to March 15. Her stage name, Lina Llubera, appeared on the large street signs advertising the opera season, prompting fear in her heart. Noting the announcement, the director at the Ricordi music publishing house summoned her to his office with an offer to help her secure additional auditions by providing a personal letter of recommendation. Lina found him a little bit too attentive, however, and concluded that his intentions might not be pure.

Suddenly on March 5 she was summoned to the Carcano with news that the principal singer, Marina Campanari, had fallen ill. Lina would take the stage on March 6. Already nervous, she was distressed to learn that there would be no time to rehearse with the orchestra before the performance. The best the theater could do was schedule a run-through with the conductor at the piano. Moreover, she needed to be fitted for her costume and wig, so she would not have the chance to rest up. The very next evening she found herself on stage, and only then did she realize how risky it all was.

She got off to a bad start. In act one, scene two, during her first duet with the seasoned baritone Arturo Romboli, she lost her place. The duet finds Rigoletto, played by Romboli, joyfully reuniting with Gilda, whom he has been concealing from the philandering Duke of Mantua. Lina fell behind in the music, and the conductor did not hold the orchestra back to allow her to catch up; it took her until the middle of the number to regain her bearings. The fault, she felt, resided with the baritone, who almost deafened her by shouting in her ear. Her complaint about Romboli may have been justified. In a review of the March 3 premiere in Milan's major newspaper, *Corriere della Sera*, Romboli was tagged for his "tendency towards excess, overstretching the tempos to better flaunt his voice, which does him harm insofar as it makes his inconsistencies more manifest."

Lina's error nonetheless demoralized her and made her feel like a disgraced impostor. Once she managed to recover, her subsequent duet with the duke (during his semi-successful attempt to seduce Gilda) went well enough. But nerves had dried her throat to the point that she could sing with only a third of her usual force during the showcase aria, "Caro nome" ("Dearest Name"), about the first flush of love. She finally found her voice toward its end.

In the interval between the first and second acts, she hurriedly changed costumes while downing two cups of coffee in an effort to lubricate her vocal cords. Her throat remained dry throughout the performance, but her entrances improved. By the famous quartet of the third act, which features Gilda and Rigoletto outside a tavern, with the duke and the contralto Maddalena inside, her singing was almost error-free—she missed "just one note," she claimed—and was able to enhance her acting. The rest of the act leading up to her tragic death came off fine. (Here Rigoletto believes that the assassin enlisted to kill the duke has succeeded in his task, but when he opens the sack presumed to contain the duke's corpse, he discovers his daughter instead—a horrific event ascribed to a curse.) At the end Lina almost collapsed in exhaustion, and she had no recollection of the respectable applause or curtain calls. Just one rehearsal with the orchestra would have enabled her to perform the part without incident, she rued.

The conductor, Giovanni Patti, complimented her singing but advised her to make better eye contact with him next time. Other members of the cast, including the baritone, congratulated Lina, praising her acting skills in particular. A few friends whisked her away to celebrate at Savini, a restaurant near the theater with a view of the Duomo. There she swallowed a glass of beer and some cold pullet—an odd mix for a celebratory meal. There were no reviews of her impromptu performance, since the critics had focused their attention on the premiere featuring Campanari, now bedridden with the flu. (Campanari was praised in the *Corriere della Sera* for her "gracious," "precise," and "tasteful" singing.) Plus a magnificent new production of *Boris Godunov* was running at La Scala; the staging of *Rigoletto* at the Carcano, with its modest sets and costumes, could hardly compete. All in all, the experience proved a real education, and despite the botched first act, Lina felt that she had it in her to make a name for herself.

The theater scheduled her next performances for the thirteenth and fifteenth. The first of these was canceled when it appeared that the other soprano had recovered, then reinstated when she suffered a relapse. Though the juggling of the dates upset Lina, she performed extremely well, singing the first-act duet with assurance. An acquaintance confirmed that the difference between her first and second outings was black and white, and Lina received a couple of mentions in the press. The theater assigned her the rest of the run, and on the fifteenth, she performed without bad nerves, hearing cheers in the middle of "Caro nome." The doting baritone Romboli, who twice did her stage makeup for her, asked her to travel with him to Perugia for a paid performance, and the conductor hinted at an event in Genoa. The plans, Lina realized, were tentative at best and would not pan out. The Teatro Carcano concluded its season with other operas, and the tour went unrealized.

Yet for the moment, Lina's career in Milan seemed on the rise. On March 17 she posed for one of the best photographers in town, who snapped a dozen shots of her in costume. Later in the month, she returned for another photo session, since only half of the original images were usable, and the photos ended up being exhibited in Torino that May. Her role in *Rigoletto* concluded with a performance on March 21, which went well, she felt, though nerves once again bedeviled her in the first act. "Under the circumstances," Lina reported to Serge in English at the end of the month, "I didn't do so badly all in all. I hope to do much better some day and earn a real triumph." She sought to resume lessons with her teacher in Milan and expand her repertoire, which remained pitiably small.

Serge did not witness her modest success, which left Tanya with the task of describing it to him (she heard Lina three times and would be seeing Serge at one of his Belgian or French tour stops). He blamed his absence on his own schedule of performances, Lina on the challenge of arranging "stupid visas . . . the hell with them."

The visa problem plagued them once more in April, when Lina convinced Serge to perform a joint recital with her in Milan. She had resumed her lessons in hopes of auditioning again for the opera, but had no immediate prospects. For the recital, she found a backer in the editor, writer, and director Enzo Ferrieri, whom she regarded as so set in his ways that she all but dragged him by the coattails to Palazzo Chigi in Rome to apply for a visa for Serge. Besides the visa, they argued over the date of the concert, the program, and whether or not there should be an intermission. Lina mocked Ferrieri as just another "helpless Italian businessman," without appreciating his prominence in the press. "Oh, queste donne sono terribili" (Oh, women are so terrible), Ferrieri wailed in response, tugging at his hair.

He recommended his own salon, Il Convegno (The Meeting Place), as the venue for the concert. It was located close to La Scala on Via Borgospesso (which is now a stretch of designer boutiques). After attending a concert in the space given by the harpsichordist Wanda Landowska, Lina fretted over the difficult acoustics. Il Convegno was better suited to the debates and lectures it usually hosted.

Planning the program proved a challenge, owing to Ferrieri's last-minute insistence that it be expanded to include works by Musorgsky and Borodin. Though Serge had final say over the content of the program, Ferrieri and Lina tentatively agreed on a ninety-minute recital featuring Serge's *Balmont Romances*, with Lina singing the French translation of the poems; the Second Piano Sonata; selections from *Love for Three Oranges*; the Toccata for piano; and one of the *Visions fugitives*. Ferrieri suggested April 27 as the ideal date: La Scala would be closed that evening, and more reviewers would thus be able to attend. It would be Lina's first performance with Serge as her accompanist, but hardly the last.

Lina hoped that Serge would arrive a few days before the performance and linger after, allowing them to escape the din and the polluted air of central Milan to relax in the quieter suburbs. Beforehand, he could save money by staying at her residence; her piano was in good condition and her new neighbors quiet. His next engagement was to follow in Paris, and Lina suggested that he go there directly from Milan without returning to Ettal. He should bring a tuxedo, she wrote, but not his mother. "She needn't be jealous because I won't go to Paris with you, but for your sake you ought to choose the easiest way. I am sure that one of her reasons for going is to get a new hat and several other little things. I can get everything for her here and bring it with me [to Ettal]." To firm up the plot to have Serge all to herself, Lina sent a note to Mariya Prokofieva, asking for her hat size.

Ferrieri did not come through with the visa, which meant going through a Russian contact in Rome and postponing the recital until the beginning of May. But as of May 1, the visa had still not been issued. Nor did it come through in the first and second weeks of the month, despite a promise received secondhand from one of Mussolini's secretaries that it had in fact been sent. Ferrieri joked that "evidently your Prokofiev is a dangerous person." Lina then realized, though it should have been obvious, that the Italian government had all but suspended the issuing of visas to Russians, to prevent "Communist infiltration." Her contacts at La Scala rescued her, enacting a bureaucratic deus ex machina that allowed Ferrieri to schedule the appearance of the couple—"Sergio Prokofieff" being the obvious main draw, "signora Llubera" the appendage—at 9 P.M. on May 18, the tenth and final concert of the season at Il Convegno, and a date that, miraculously, fit Serge's schedule (one hundred lira would vanish from the agreed-upon fee, however). He arrived with the precious visa from Paris, where he had performed a concert with Balmont.

To his delight and Lina's relief, the recital was a success. Serge informed Stahl that he "had little hope of Verdi's descendants having a taste for my music. However it didn't matter as they liked us and the reviews are proof of this." Clippings of those reviews eventually reached Stahl and his wife, the "diva" Janacopoulos, whom Lina was glad to show up for once. Stahl noted, while nearly keeling over in jealousy, that the Milan programs featured Lina singing the premiere of Serge's *Five Poems for Voice and Piano*.

By the end of May, Lina was exhausted—for reasons that she had yet to divine but would prove decisive. Serge too was unwell, suffering chest discomfort that his doctor attributed to an overstrained heart. The villa in Ettal beckoned. There he fell into recuperative silence, causing Stahl to send a mildly concerned letter in July: "Could it be you have nothing to report to your adopted parents? . . . Have the

Bavarian mountains and Bavarian beer had the effect of committing you to quiet idleness?" Eventually Serge's heart ceased its pirouettes, calmed by afternoons amid the dandelions in the garden and what he called the "dulcet rhythm of the life of vegetables."

Bashkirov remained in Ettal, but his friendship with Serge had suffered, owing in part to the poet's unwillingness to contribute to the household. Yet he represented a connection to Russia—a Russia that no longer existed, but that Serge pined for nonetheless. This longing explains his immersion in the literature of the Russian "mystic" symbolists, who exerted their greatest influence on Russian culture in the twilight of the tsarist era, before the Bolshevik takeover. Serge had made the acquaintance of two prominent symbolist poets: Konstantin Balmont, who immigrated to France in 1920 and who provided the texts for Serge's *Five Poems for Voice and Piano*; and Andrey Belïy, who came to Germany in 1921, spending two years there before returning to Russia. (The homecoming turned nightmarish when he was denounced in print by Leon Trotsky.) Serge met Belïy several times in Berlin in the first half of 1922, with the composer making sure to express his admiration for the poem "First Encounter," which Lina also came to appreciate. On hearing of their meetings, Lina asked Serge repeatedly for his impressions of the writer, and whether or not the poet had visited Ettal, as he promised Serge he would. It seems he did not.

The connection to Belïy reached beyond the personal into "the abstract world of sounds" and influenced Serge's five-act opera *The Fiery Angel*, which he was struggling to complete in Ettal. It was based on a novel of the same name that featured a thinly disguised Belïy as one of the characters. Serge had been introduced to the novel in New York and found it a compelling, if problematic, subject for an opera. The thought became a creative obsession, one that had the composer seeking out as much information as possible about the sources of the novel, its setting, and its mystical message. He chose to live in Bavaria in part because it came close to the setting of the novel: Renaissance Cologne at the time of the Spanish Inquisition. The mountains of Bavaria, the Passion play of Oberammergau, and the Cathedral of Our Lady of Ettal—all were potent, if geographically distant, sources of inspiration. So too were Lina's descriptions of Milan's raucous carnivals.

The novel was written by Valeriy Bryusov, and it parodied a bizarre real-life love triangle involving Belïy, the rather unproductive poet Nina Petrovskaya, and the erudite, prolific Bryusov. The affair played out between 1904 and 1913 (before and after the writing of the novel) in the claustrophobic ranks of the "mystic" symbolists, who were notorious for their decadent self-indulgences. Immersion in the occult, substance abuse, and games of pretend were integral to their daily lives, the result being a rather explosive exchange between life and art. Suicides were common among the crowd. Serge knew little of these activities. He was of a later modernist generation, more rationalist than decadent in outlook. But his operatic treatment of Bryusov's novel represented a sincere attempt to manufacture a supernatural atmosphere through densely chromatic melodic and harmonic writing. It is one of the most dissonant operas ever composed—dissonance being a cipher in the score for forces beyond human comprehension—and it stood little chance of being produced. Yet he persisted with it, since at its heart lay the effort to overcome constraints of time and place.

In the novel, Bryusov wove a plot of real-or-imagined demonic possession around three characters. He cast himself as the kindhearted but hapless knight Ruprecht, who falls in love with the maiden Renata, the fictional stand-in for Nina Petrovskaya. She is obsessed with a beautiful flaming angel named Madiel, who is the fictional stand-in for Belïy. It all ends badly, with Renata locking herself up in a convent in hopes of exorcising her visions, only to be sentenced to death by the Inquisition. Ruprecht arrives in time to rescue her but she chooses execution. Renata becomes a tragic victim of an ideal—of immaterial, preternatural love. Something of this ending would replay itself in real life in 1928, to both Lina and Serge's amazement.

In Ettal, Serge discussed the opera at length with Lina. He played Renata's music for her at the piano, and she sang some of it back to him. The exchange compelled Serge to extract a vocal suite from the opera. True to "mystic" symbolist form, the couple engaged in roleplaying games, strolling through Ettal and its surroundings while acting out scenes from the score. Doubtless they continued their own personal discussions about spiritual and physical love, this time with the opera as focal point. It was a romantic period in their lives—perhaps the most romantic period, which allowed Lina to forget, for at least a moment, the ordeals of the past three years in Paris and Milan. In May, the physical side of their relationship triumphed over the spiritual. Lina learned that she was pregnant. Midway through her term, on October 8, 1923, she and Serge were married.

The vows were exchanged at the Ettal Rathaus in the presence of the *Bürgermeister*, the mayor. Bashkirov and Serge's mother were witnesses, along with two of Serge's benefactors from Munich, Colonel Evald and his companion. It was an innocuous event, except for one detail: Lina and Serge were both foreigners. The colonel helped them navigate the paperwork and get permission for the wedding. But the fact of their foreignness proved fateful. Many years later in Moscow, their marriage would be declared null and void on the flimsiest of pretexts — that it had not been registered at a Soviet consulate. The decision was incomprehensible, and not in some mystical sense.

Chapter 5

A FTER A TRANQUIL prenatal confinement, spent in a private house for paying guests in Sèvres, Lina gave birth to a son—Svyatoslav. Prokofiev picked the name, though it was not his first choice. He preferred Askold, after the ruler of pre-Christian Kiev, but suspected that a child with that name would be refused a baptism. So the new parents settled on Svyatoslav, a blend of the Russian words for "holy" and "glory."

Lina had managed the last trimester of her pregnancy on her own. Serge continued to tour—to Geneva, London, and Paris—with the edge-of-the-seat excitement of his Third Piano Concerto revealing more about his drive and temperament than his occasional imitations, in smaller works, of Dada- and jazz-inspired French composers like Francis Poulenc. In his 1924 circus ballet *Trapeze*, Prokofiev's harmonies became less piquant, and blues lines supplanted spinning ostinato patterns. *The Fiery Angel* maintained its macabre designs, and the flames of Revolution continued to burn in his Second Symphony, completed in 1925, a huge flop with the Parisian public. But Serge also embraced French decorum and restraint, producing a limpid sound that he dubbed "New Simplicity." He began to think of himself as doing "what Mozart did after Bach": reducing counterpoint from numerous simultaneously unfolding lines to just two or three, limiting the number of nonharmonic pitches, stressing a "simpler melodic element." Dissonance for its own sake was no longer in fashion. Despite his references to European masters, however, on the road Prokofiev continued to be touted as a distinctly Russian virtuoso, and he continued to describe himself as a product of the Russian soil—at least before the Bolsheviks had plowed through it. It was a confusing time in his career.

The expense and logistical headaches of touring irritated him no less than the border guards who harassed him about visas and *cartes d'identité*. Serge seriously began to resent the lack of attention paid to his larger, theatrical scores: there was little interest in Europe in his beloved operas, and *The Buffoon* was a short-lived wonder. Although he remained boyishly energetic, he began to think about reducing the amount of travel, both to concentrate on composition and to give greater support to Lina. The crisis in their relationship, the brinksmanship of July 1922, was long past; his affection for her had increased through the first months of their marriage and her pregnancy.

Mariya Prokofieva remained in Bavaria because her frail heart prevented her from traveling to France, where her son hoped to find a nursing home for her. She was living with Bashkirov in a modest rental in Oberammergau (the villa in Ettal having been sold by its owner in 1923). Serge arrived there in February 1924, the same month Lina was due; he found his mother in a dreadful state, unable at times to speak or lift her head from the pillow and slipping in and out of consciousness. Her caregivers suspected that she had just a few days left to live, and he worried that her condition would prevent him from being with Lina in Paris for the birth. Lina reassured him over and over again that she was in good care and that he needed to be with his mother.

On the advice of Lina's obstetrician, Serge arranged for her to enter the French hospital before she was due, in the last week of February or first week of March. Lina had hoped to deliver in the American hospital, but the cost of a semi-private room there ruled it out; besides, she could not prove U.S. citizenship. Instead her obstetrician, the eminent specialist Gabriel Bouffe de Saint-Blaise, admitted her to the Hôpital Saint-Antoine.

Mariya rallied, allowing Serge to return to Paris, where Lina's own mother was expected any day, having dispatched a three-word telegram: "sail about 20." Olga arrived, disoriented and distressed, ahead of schedule, on February 24. Her first words to her new son-in-law predictably concerned her daughter's well-being. Lina had endured a difficult pregnancy. Yet she and her husband managed to so-cialize at table d'hôte dinners and even danced together one evening at a reception, the waistline on her dress concealing her condition. Although there had been signs of premature labor, she made it to full term. Two days before the birth, Stahl dragged Serge to a Montmar-tre cabaret to toast the baby's health with cheap champagne.

Svyatoslav was born at 8:45 A.M. on February 27, 1924. Neither Lina's husband nor her mother witnessed his birth, having been barred from the ward by the nurses in the final hours. (In his di-ary, Serge recalled playing cards with Lina between contractions.) He took Olga for a stroll outside in an effort to calm her nerves. Follow-ing the delivery, the attending physician congratulated him, handed him a surgical gown, and escorted him to Lina's room. She was ex-tremely sweaty, semiconscious, and "stomach-less," he recalled in his diary before launching into a description of the mechanics of breast-feeding. Lina's longtime benefactor Gussie Garvin sent gifts of two thousand and then three thousand francs toward the costs of experi-enced nannies, recognizing that Serge would insist on arranging full-time care for Svyatoslav in the summer to prevent the disruption of his work. She also offered to become the baby's legal guardian in the event of misfortune.

Once Lina and the baby were discharged, the new family abruptly relocated to an apartment at 5, rue Charles Dickens, near the Seine and a green space (the Gardens of the Trocadero). Serge found it through a Russian broker, who extorted eight hundred francs to set-tle the three-month lease. He had little choice but to sign, since it was clear that he could not remain in the apartment he and Lina had been sharing in central Paris with his actress friend Frou-Frou (Mariya Baranovskaya) and her husband, Alexander Borovsky. Their new place was adequately furnished and came with a view of the wa-ter, but the walls were paper-thin and the racket from the piano-playing "hoyden" downstairs compelled Serge to stomp on the floor in mock applause. The tasteless lumbering on the keyboard pre-vented him from sleeping even more often than Svyatoslav's night-time howling. He consoled himself with the knowledge that he did not have a pressing composition deadline for a couple of months. To help him sleep and keep him out of the cinematographs and cham-pagne bars that he continued to frequent with Stahl, Lina asked her mother to find him some earplugs. Olga was desperately needed in the household, but she was extremely sensitive about imposing. Lina likened her to a mimosa, a plant whose leaves closed when touched or exposed to heat.

A broken elevator in the building prevented Lina from leaving the apartment for a month because she could not manage the stairs post-partum. When it was finally repaired, she celebrated by reviving herself as a wife and woman, besides a mother. The first thing she did was go to a hair salon for a voguish cut that parted on the side, letting her dark hair fall in waves to her collar. She reentered the Parisian music scene in April, attending with her husband a gathering of composers at the home of the founder of *La Revue Musicale*. Post-concert receptions and evenings at Right Bank restaurants such as the oyster bar Prunier followed, with Lina entrusting Svyatoslav to the care of her mother. Serge took pride in his wife's superior social graces, fashion sense (wearing the black evening dresses, cloche hats, and Chanel faux pearls introduced in 1924 in *Vogue*), and her lighthearted cosmopolitanism. She admired Paris's top models, who posed in dramatic silhouette, and she worked to restore her slim-hipped, full-busted figure so that no one could tell she had ever been pregnant.

The bliss faded as Prokofiev increased the pace of his work. His greatest musical concern that spring was the preparation of his Second Piano Concerto for its Paris premiere under the baton of the Russian émigré Serge Koussevitzky, who had used his personal wealth (his second wife was heiress to a tea fortune) to bankroll his conducting activities in Europe. Koussevitzky's debut in Berlin in 1908 was self-financed, as were his publishing house, Édition Russe de Musique, and the Concerts Koussevitzky in Paris. Prokofiev learned the hard way that "couscous" (as he called him) was not a great conductor, but he nonetheless benefited significantly from him, both in Paris and in Boston, where Koussevitzky took charge of the symphony in the fall of 1924.

The manuscript of the concerto had been left in Russia before Serge's departure for the United States in 1918, but it disappeared in his vandalized former apartment; he had to reconstruct the piece based on the surviving piano reduction. He made a point of practicing the loudest passages when his downstairs neighbor was home, though the din had its greatest impact on Lina's overwhelmed mother, hastening her return to the United States on May 24, 1924, after she had provided countless hours of free child care. She would return in the fall of 1925, and Lina's father, Juan, would follow in the spring of 1926.

Looking ahead to the summer, Serge rented a villa in St. Gilles-Croix-de-Vie, not far from the Côte de Lumière resort where he and Lina had stayed in 1921. His mother advised Lina to leave Svyatoslav in the care of others, but the thought of being separated from her infant son for months at a time left Lina in tears. Instead they chose to hire a live-in nanny with the money from Mrs. Garvin. After interviewing a parade of Scandinavians from a local au pair agency, they settled on a deferential, clear-skinned Norwegian, Miss Mack, who stayed with the family through the summer. Serge's mother arrived with Bashkirov in Paris to journey with her family to St. Gilles. Fears about seeing her in a frightful condition disappeared when she stepped off the train. She was able to walk with his assistance, all were relieved to see, and demanded to see the grandson whom she would have left behind.

On June 23, the five of them departed for an unseasonably cold summer in the oceanfront town of St. Gilles, leaving Bashkirov behind in Paris to advance the art of idleness in what Ernest Hemingway called "the principal cafés." These were inexpensive magnets for penniless writers, but Bashkirov still turned to Serge for financial assistance. Lina could never understand her husband's attachment to the poet, though Serge's bond with Russia—which, emotionally and psychologically, he could not sever—had something to do with it. He mentioned missing his childhood friends and kept in contact with them. He also found the French arts scene paradoxically impoverished compared to what he remembered in St. Petersburg. Serge had no interest in the bohemian intellectual set or the extravagant parties that, until 1923, Cole and Linda Porter had hosted within the platinum-colored walls of their apartment on rue Monsieur. The Ballets Russes remained cutting-edge, losing little sheen despite competition from Chauve-Souris and the upstart Ballets Suédois, but Serge could not countenance the lustful lesbianism of Poulenc's ballet *Les biches* (otherwise known as *The House Party*) as staged by Diaghilev. Neither *la vie sans frontières* nor its choreographic satire interested him.

Like Stahl, Bashkirov reminded Serge of the horrible news from Russia; the poet did not feel the same pull home, despite frequenting the leftist establishments that Serge shunned, including Café de la Rotonde, home away from home for Marxist revolutionaries and local attraction for idle bohemians. Lina had no point of reference for her husband's longing beyond his sardonic, ill-tempered assessments of his Parisian competition and occasional declarations of weariness with life on the road. His longing was existential—for a guild of like-minded composers, a support network, the inspiration that direct access to Russia culture, of the distant and recent past, had given him. It increased during the long walks he took each day along the *quais*, past the booksellers and the fishermen, jotting down the melodies that entered his head in his pocketbook and mulling over abstract spiritual matters. He thought about the present, about his inability to escape the shadow of Stravinsky. The future too pressed in on him.

In October, Bashkirov helped the Prokofievs find a large winter house to rent in Bellevue, fifteen minutes southwest of Paris. Then he faded from their lives, having taken, it seemed, to gambling. Later he worked as a chauffeur and became involved with Russian fascists.

Serge described the Bellevue residence as having a "wondrous garden, with a lot of flowers nowhere to be found in St. Gilles. The house made quite a peculiar impression. Several rooms were of good size, others small, the staircases cramped, steps everywhere, and a multitude of rooms in an incredible arrangement. This is owing to the fact that the house is made up of three houses that had gradually become attached." The medieval-looking garden included urns and sarcophaguses, each of which, according to the owner, could fetch the value of the entire house. A photograph taken outside survives: Lina stands behind a wicker chair, clothed in a loose white skirt and blouse, round-faced and half grinning—perhaps less thrilled with life in the suburbs than her husband was. Serge, hair thinned, stands smiling on the other side, also dressed in white. He and Lina had just returned from playing tennis. His mother fills the chair, wearing a thick black dress, shawl, and scarf. She holds Svyatoslav, just eight or nine months old, in her large, splayed hands, looking away from the camera. This is the last known image of Mariya, who suffered a fatal heart attack on December 13. As in the case of his son's birth, Serge noted the event in his diary with clinical precision: "At 12:15 in the morning Mama died in my arms." He made no entries for the rest of the year. The blank pages spoke of grief. For several months, he hid his feelings — and even the fact of his mother's death — from those who asked after her.

He found solace in the faith he had discovered the summer before — Christian Science. Lina adopted the religion before her husband did, by way of elderly English acquaintances in Sèvres: a Mr. Price, a Mr. and Mrs. Wade, and several unnamed messieurs and mesdames. She began practicing in full faith after Svyatoslav's birth, having dropped a lot of weight and suffered a bout of postpartum depression. The Christian Science practitioner Caroline Getty, a congenial Boston native, took Lina into her care in June 1924, training her in positive thinking and prescribing meditation techniques that would, she repeatedly promised, allow her to deflect attention away from the mortal body toward the immortal mind and its connection to the divine. By rethinking her experience with childhood as a reflection of "God's motherhood," her sickness would be negated. "Turn thought away from the body," Caroline wrote to her in late July. "The body cannot feel, doesn't know anything. You need not think of it — it cannot think of you." The aphorisms were accompanied by references to scripture and suggestions for further reading in a textbook she provided to her clients.

Getty worked in central Paris at the Christian Science Committee on Publications but kept a home in Sèvres, where she had reportedly cured Mr. Price of a heart condition — or at least Mr. Price claimed as much, though his dotage prevented him from recalling the details. Getty introduced Lina to other practitioners as well as to the local Christian Science congregation, the Deuxième Église du Christ, Scientiste, at 58, boulevard Flandrin in Paris. Later, the practitioner Eve Crain entered Lina's life, as did Lawrence Creath Ammons, who would become a decisive influence.

Serge had long resisted religion, owing to its inherent illogic, but thanks to Lina had now discovered something apparently based on reason. Christian Science offered the appealing image of a clockwork universe. He also met with the practitioners and exceeded Lina's zeal when it came to attempts at self-healing. He complained to Getty of unprovoked sharp pains in his limbs, head, and chest. The neuralgia, he calculated, had been bothering him three times a month for a decade, and he feared for the health of his heart. Getty promised him a cure. She pressed a copy of the foundational text of Christian Science, Mary Baker Eddy's *Science and Health with Key to the Scriptures*, into his hands, directing him to several key passages and asking him to summarize them for her.

Serge left her office hopeful, offering her thirty francs for the session instead of her usual fee of twenty. Counseled by Getty throughout the summer and into the fall, he achieved partial success in relieving his chronic headaches. Sickness was but an illusion stemming from a lack of harmony with the divine, Christian Science taught him. Meditation did not eliminate the pain but certainly reduced it, and he was also able to occasionally battle back colds. His efforts to improve his vision failed, however, and the Science did not allow him to get by without glasses. That setback was offset by the fact that the faith appeared to help his volcanic temper. Recognizing that their disputes were often pointless, Serge hoped to end the fights with Lina. In one of his letters to Olga, a devout Catholic, he made the observation that "if you only knew the role Science has played in my relationship with Ptashka, you'd try to see greater value in it." One exception to the calming effect of the faith was an argument with Lina about her interest in singing again. Svyatoslav was cared for, and she felt good—back in full health. Though Lina realized that she would never have a major performing career, she hoped to become her husband's recital partner. Serge resisted, unwilling to share that part of his spotlight with her; plus, his standards eclipsed her abilities. Lina persisted, and her husband, hoping to avoid another fight, eventually capitulated. Now and then, he promised, they would perform together.

The efforts at self-healing dwindled, but their devotion to Christian Science increased. After moving from St. Gilles to Bellevue in the fall of 1924, the Prokofievs began to attend lectures in the faith. Serge preferred these to the actual church services in Paris, since he could not tolerate the singing. In his diary, he recalled an amateur soprano warbling behind a curtain of some sort. Her vibrato was as dreadful as the music, composed by an anonymous American. The psalms were better, since they were performed to archaic-sounding melodies borrowed from Joseph Haydn, but overall he felt that the music both distracted and detracted from the experience. Serge flirted with the idea of setting some of the religious texts himself, but nothing came of it.

The knowledge gleaned from the lectures had a lasting impact, informing his and Lina's personal and professional choices and helping them cope with the consequences. The tenets that most attracted them were moral rather than physical and could just as easily have been found in continental philosophies. Serge, who had steeped himself in idealist thought during his privileged youth, documented the connections in his diary. Eddy's contention that the world was but a representation that masked a richer experiential realm had derived from Immanuel Kant, he decided. And her consoling description of the essential falseness of death recalled Arthur Schopenhauer.

The most optimistic and seductive tenet of Christian Science was the eternal and infinite nature of love. By contrast, evil was a finite, temporal construct of material existence. Serge was tantalized by this proposition even if he found it paradoxical. If evil was a material construct created by man, but man was also a reflection of the divine, how and why did evil exist? It stemmed from man's rejection of the divine good in pursuit of freedom, Eddy proposed, with disconcerting succinctness. Material existence was but a phase in the eternal and infinite life of the spirit. Resisting the seductions of the flesh—from which evil arose—required constant consideration of the relationship between the human and the divine.

He found great inspiration in the postulate that if he, as an artist, was a reflection of the divine, then so too was his art. And while his music might be attached to images or words or be related to real-world events, it retained its abstract spiritual content. Often when starting a composition he would peruse his old sketchbooks for usable musical ideas. Context was unimportant, since his music, he boasted, existed outside time and space.

Some of his greatest melodies came to him when he was away from his desk and piano—while out strolling, playing bridge, haggling with Lina or Svyatoslav's nannies, hosting émigré Russian friends, or meeting with his agents or publishers. The music would form a distracting knot in his head until he jotted it down, at which point

the tension released and he could refocus and reconnect with his surroundings.

Musically, everything was positive about Serge's immersion in
Christian Science—except as it applied to *The Fiery Angel*. The opera
posed a real problem. It mixes events in the material world with supernatural happenings, and his faith did not recognize the latter. Also
problematic was the balance he had carefully struck in the score between the powers of good and evil. Serge agonized over the conflicts
as he completed revisions to the score in an effort to secure a contract
for a staging. He tried first for Paris; when that fell through he considered Berlin; and when that proved elusive, New York.

That he did not succeed in this quest after several years of head-
ache-inducing effort convinced him that *The Fiery Angel* might somehow be cursed. The opera's repeated rejection on artistic and practical grounds was also a devastating professional blow—one that
suggested to him that his time in the West might be up. Finishing the
draft had been a struggle, and working on the revisions was joyless.
He complained about the errors his beleaguered assistant, Georgiy
Gorchakov, introduced into the score, and failed to resolve the clash
between the opera and his religion. "Owing to Christian Science I've
completely lost interest in the subject, and fits of hysteria and devilry
no longer attract me," Serge lamented. He thought about torching it,
incinerating its demons and his, but Lina dissuaded him by reminding him of its musical novelties. So he kept at it, even reworking the
music as a symphony—his third.

At the same time another project consumed him, one entirely focused
on the material world—a ballet for Diaghilev on the subject of Soviet life. The goal was to celebrate the union of man and machine, the
kinship between the workings of the human body and those of Soviet
factories. While plans for a ballet imagining life in the Soviet Union
were taking shape, Serge became entangled with the Soviet government through its cultural representatives in Paris. Ever curious about
what was happening at home and desiring more information than
his friends provided in their letters, Serge reached out to Soviet diplomats, and they reached out to him. He became directly involved
in the 1920s with an organization called Vsesoyuznoye obshchestvo

kul'turnoy svyazi s zagranitsey, or VOKS. It was a cultural exchange organization, but it also engaged in low-level espionage.

In July 1925, while visiting the violinist Joseph Szigeti in his Paris apartment, Serge met Boris Krasin, newly arrived from Moscow. Krasin's presence in Paris was neither unusual nor particularly interesting, except for the fact that he served under Anatoliy Lunacharsky, the bureaucrat who had sanctioned Serge's departure from Russia to the West in 1918. Lunacharsky was appointed cultural commissar under Lenin and lingered in that position under Stalin, Lenin's successor. Lina later met him, his actress wife, and his daughter (from a previous marriage) in Moscow and Leningrad in 1927. Lunacharsky seemed to her like a sagging old-timer, a relic of the aristocratic intelligentsia. Stalin would dispense with him in 1933 by making him ambassador to Spain, but he died before assuming the position.

Serge's meeting with Krasin was not a chance encounter, but completely contrived. Krasin came to Paris on a mission, with orders from the highest levels of the Soviet government. In February 1925, Lunacharsky wrote to Stalin, requesting permission to travel abroad for the purposes of reestablishing cultural relationships in the West and also to engage those émigré Russian artists who had established an international reputation. The regime needed to reach out to Russian-born celebrities, Lunacharsky explained to the dictator, even if they harbored hostile feelings toward the Soviet Union as fueled by the capitalist press. Through such contact, misunderstandings could be cleared up, visits could be arranged, and perhaps some of these artists could even be convinced to return to their forsaken homeland.

Stalin's personal reaction to Lunacharsky's petition remains unrecorded, but that summer, the Central Executive Committee of the Communist Party resolved to invite Prokofiev, his rival Stravinsky, and the pianist Borovsky (Frou-Frou's husband) to the Soviet Union. Three days after the resolution was approved by the Central Executive Committee, Lunacharsky's deputy Krasin was in Paris, seeking audiences with the invitees. The recruitment effort began with astonishing swiftness, though Prokofiev knew nothing of the behind-the-scenes machinations. Neither, of course, did Lina.

Krasin did not travel alone. He had with him a youthful, self-assured assistant, Comrade Tutelman, who seemed to Serge to be the real

Communist of the two, the "eye of Moscow." Krasin had an amicably haggard face and spoke like a dolt—though in an effort to impress he tried to adopt a more eloquent tone. The strain of the effort caused him to wrinkle the bridge of his nose as though he had just bitten into something sour. He was a strident opponent of bourgeois composition, it emerged, and presented himself as a true champion of music for the masses, a concept that intrigued Serge, even if scores like *The Fiery Angel* did not fit the description.

It was high time for Prokofiev and his glamorous wife to travel to Moscow, Krasin announced. He presented the composer with a signed and sealed proposal from the Central Executive Committee. The precious document was revealed for a mere instant before being folded back into his large hands. Then, for dramatic effect, he began to read it aloud. The invitation came from the commission in charge of planning a jubilee celebration for the twentieth anniversary of the Russian Revolution of 1905, which, as Serge knew, was neither a revolution nor confined to 1905. It referred to a wave of social protests that had started in December 1904 in St. Petersburg and spread across other areas of Russia, eventually destabilizing the tsarist government and accelerating the enactment of liberalizing reforms. Since Soviets interpreted the event as a harbinger of the Russian Revolution of 1917, its jubilee merited lavish commemoration.

On behalf of the Central Executive Committee, Krasin asked Serge to compose a score for a blockbuster film about 1905. He assured the composer that if he found the notion of adjusting his music for a film difficult, an overture and one or two shorter pieces would suffice. Krasin added that the jubilee would be celebrated in the Bolshoy Theater in Moscow at an event attended by representatives from across Russia.

Although the offer was ludicrously attractive, Serge could not accept. "To agree would mean subscribing to Bolshevism, and then so long to my prospects in the lands of the bourgeoisie!" he thought to himself. He needed, however, to decline without causing offense. First he tried to dissuade Krasin by brashly stating, "It'll cost you dearly," to which Krasin replied, "Well of course we'll pay." Time to try another tactic. "And when do you need it to be finished?" "By New Year's." "Oh, then I'm afraid the offer has come too late: you see I've just agreed to a commission from Diaghilev. I can't do both, and

I can't turn down Diaghilev." Still, Krasin asked him to think it over, and they agreed to meet two days later.

Diplomatic relations were preserved, thanks to Tutelman, who unsmilingly extended an invitation to Serge for performances in Moscow, Leningrad, and two other cities—ten in all, at a price the composer could name. Serge deferred to them on the fee, at which point Tutelman proposed $200 per concert or, alternatively, $150 plus 25 percent of the receipts. Again, however, Serge felt he could not accept. His schedule was full through 1926, and besides, he needed written assurance that he would be permitted to leave the Soviet Union once the tour was completed. Krasin nodded and then asked, "So might we conclude that you are favorably disposed to the trip, and might we announce in the press that you are planning to come?" "Oh, of course," Serge answered.

He would continue to flirt with the idea without committing, sending Krasin a letter on July 28, 1925, to the effect that he was so tied up with contracts for other things that he did not have time to consider Soviet commissions. The seed had been planted, however, and news of his interest in a Soviet engagement, however vague, traveled quickly back to Moscow. In August, Serge received a letter from Nadezhda Bryusova, another of Lunacharsky's lieutenants, outlining the conditions under which he could travel to and from the Russian Soviet Federative Socialist Republic, otherwise known to Prokofiev as "Bolshevizia." Stravinsky received the same letter, as did the pianist Borovsky. "The government consents to your return to Russia," Bryusova deadpanned. "It agrees to grant you full amnesty for all prior offenses, if any such occurred. It stands to reason that the government cannot grant such amnesty for counter-revolutionary activities in the future. It likewise guarantees complete freedom of travel into and out of the RSFSR as you desire." The mechanical stiffness of the language could not help but insult Stravinsky and Borovsky, even though the latter agreed to a short visit. Prokofiev began seriously to weigh the pros and cons of the trip. Years later, Lina lamented about just how ignorant they both were at the time.

The offer to return to Russia soon worked its way into their lives, and it informed Serge's collaboration with Diaghilev and the constructivist artist Georgiy Yakulov on *Le pas d'acier* (*The Steel Step*), the new work for the Ballets Russes. Yakulov conceived the ballet as a fantastical construction with three overlapping spheres of action, each characterizing a separate feature of Bolshevism: a market on Sukharevskaya Square in Moscow, an NEP (new economic policy) enterprise, and either a factory or an agricultural exhibition symbolizing the remaking of Russian society. Set in the years following the Revolution and subsequent civil war, the ballet would narrate the creation of a brave new world.

Such, at any rate, was the plan. While Serge sketched the music, which he wanted to be tuneful despite the industrial whirling and twirling of the second act, Yakulov worked out detailed plans for the decor and choreography. The materials were then turned over to Diaghilev, who decided, after significant hesitation, that the subject matter might not impress his fickle audiences after all. He entrusted his newest protégé, Leonid Massine, with revising the scenario and creating the dances. When the ballet premiered (after much delay) in 1927, Serge was dumbfounded. Far from representing the dismantling and deformation of the old tsarist world in favor of a new, revolutionary order, the first act featured a parade of figures from Russian folklore, figures faintly reminiscent of secondary characters from Stravinsky's *The Firebird*, *Petrushka*, and other early Ballets Russes productions. The new sequence of episodes — "Baba Yaga and Crocodile," "Street Bazaar and Countesses," "Sailor and Three Devils," "Tomcat and Feline," "Legend of a Drunkard," and "Sailor and Worker Girl" — ended up baffling reviewers.

Le pas d'acier became a send-up of the very thing it was supposed to salute: collaborative artistic creation, the harmoniousness of the Soviet workplace, and the union of the individual and the collective. Massine's choreography depicted the factory as a prison, and technological utopianism as fraudulent. Most reviewers interpreted the ballet as a polemic against the Stalinist Five-Year Plans for rapid industrial development. For Serge, who feared offending his potential patrons in Soviet Russia, the anti-Soviet petitions were beyond imagining. The message of the work was meant to be ambiguous, but there was no way to leave anything open-ended, no chance at compromise. As Serge wrote in his diary: "To take a neutral stance, acceptable by one side and the other, is impossible, for contemporary Russia is specifically characterized by a struggle of red against white: a neutral stance does not reflect the times. 'You are either with us or against us,' thus a neutral stance will be rejected both here and there."

Political machinations—concrete ones about a possible visit, or even a move, to Moscow as well as creative ones with the ballet—engulfed Serge while Lina managed her first years of motherhood. Her husband indulged fantasies about navigating the East-West divide in music; she, meanwhile, was reduced to handling their frequent apartment changes and the hiring and firing of nannies. It also fell to her to fret about finances, though Serge promised her that, in the end, they would have more than enough to live on. Look at the potential earnings he might have in Russia, he consoled her. She had put her own musical career on hold long ago, so earned nothing herself, despite indulging her expensive Parisian tastes. Perhaps by touring with Serge, an idea that still caused him to flare up, she could exorcise the curse a voice coach in Milan had placed on her when she told him she was getting married: "Your career is finished. Don't you realize you're marrying *such* a musician, *un músico tremendo*, a tremendous composer." (She quoted her teacher in Spanish rather than Italian, less a testament to her flawed memory than the fact that, at first, she got by in Milan with Spanish.)

When Nina Koshetz came to Paris to sing Serge's *Five Songs Without Words*, competing with Vera Janacopoulos for attention in the salons, she encouraged Lina to return to singing. There was some mischief-making in the suggestion, since Lina had tried and failed to gain an invitation to the grand salon operated by Winnaretta Singer, otherwise known as the Princess de Polignac, heiress to the Singer sewing-machine estate. Serge, who had met Polignac in 1920, helped his wife choose some new songs by Debussy, Manuel de Falla, and the Moscow composer Nikolay Myaskovsky, his closest friend from childhood; in the end, her repertoire would include Myaskovsky's "Circles" ("Krugi"), from a symbolist poem by Zinaída Gippius, Musorgsky's "The Beetle" ("Zhuk") from his cycle *The Nursery* (*Detskaya*), Stravinsky's "The Pigeon" ("Golub'"), after Balmont, and a Rimsky-Korsakov lullaby. She resumed practicing, and after getting her voice back into shape Lina sang not in Paris, but rather during a tour with her husband in the United States. The trip was arranged by the founder of the American Pro Musica Society, the French-born pianist E. Robert Schmitz, and took up January and February of 1926.

Despite having pushed herself to perform again, Lina was reluctant about touring—afraid of the stage perhaps, or of leaving Svyatoslav for such a long stretch. She vented her unhappiness about cramming her life into cabin trunks to Serge as the French liner *De Grasse* approached New York Harbor on New Year's Eve. Upon arriving and clearing customs, their hostess, Schmitz's wife, Germaine, informed Lina that her expenses would be covered for those recitals she intended to perform with her husband. This mollified her, though Serge did not seem pleased. In his diary he signaled frustration with Lina's fussiness as a traveler by stressing that the success of the tour would depend on her mood as much as her singing. Just in case she could not perform, he prepared the piano version of Musorgsky's *Pictures at an Exhibition* to play as a substitute for her repertoire.

Serge's destinations included Boston, Chicago, Denver, Kansas City, New York, Portland, San Francisco, and St. Paul—a city "famous for its ugliness," in his opinion. Lina accompanied him only as far west as Denver, performing with "sincerity, charm and no little dramatic ability," according to a Kansas City reviewer. For her appearance in St. Paul, Lina dressed to resemble a "graceful, attractive type of American schoolgirl," with "certain subtle details of coloring and physiognomy" showing her "Spanish origin."

In newspaper interviews, Serge mocked the harsh reviews he had received in the United States, Germany, and France in the past, asserting that the critics tended to contradict themselves and each other. In an interview with the *Portland Telegram*, he amplified his thoughts about the provincialism of American musical life while battling to keep a cigarette in its holder. Upon declaring "I think there should be new things in music just as there are new styles in skirts," he permitted the cigarette to fall to the floor and "smolder on the Hotel Portland lobby floor."

The social obligations proved more taxing than the performances. The Mr. and Mrs. Smiths who chaired the regional branches of the society insisted on arranging elaborate receptions for them. Serge carped to a writer for the *Post-Standard* of Syracuse that "under the terms of his American contract he must shake hands with any person who approaches him," adding that in Kansas City, "280 strong Americans so greeted him and almost crippled his right hand piano digits." Lina deployed her formidable social skills to overcome his inability to make small talk over bad food. But she too found the experience exhausting, recalling in an interview that "the ritual was almost always the same: we arrived at a city and were met by a member of the club, a lady usually, then were taken on a ride round the city, then lunch at some club. We stayed at hotels and very often in people's houses." She added that she and Serge ended up suffering jaw pain "from so much smiling back and forth. 'Oh, how nice that you like it thank you very much.' Then, very often, they gave a dinner after that, and after the dinner we were put on the train for the next stop. We got fed up with it."

For Lina, the hardest part of the trip was in Denver at the Hotel Metropole (advertised on its stationery as "eminently fireproof"). A certain Mrs. Campbell ensured that she did not have a minute to herself, handing her a "horrifying" list of prearranged lunches, teas, dinners, and theater outings. The thin air further sapped her energy as well as her patience. "I realize that I'm still very worn out," she wrote to Serge on Friday, January 15, the day he arrived in Portland. "At times I think I'm having a colossal allergic reaction. But then I remember 'there is no action, inaction or diseased action' and I feel better." The quote comes from Christian Science. She found comfort and strength in her faith but could not help but feel tormented by a "stupid review" of her recital in Denver on January 12. After parsing it with Mrs. Campbell and the other local ladies in waiting, however, she concluded that it had a silver lining. The criticism centered not on her technique but on her choice of repertoire—too much inaccessible Russian music—though the reviewer also detected a lack of "assurance" in Lina's handling of the "ultra-modern tunes." For her next engagement, at a private residence in Denver on Sunday, Lina would stick to French works. "May God grant you success" in Portland, she teased her husband in a postscript, "and fewer receptions."

After wrapping up the American trip and returning to Europe, the couple embarked on another long-planned tour of Italy, including an orchestral and chamber concert in Rome followed by recitals in Siena, Genoa, Florence, and Naples. Their schedule did not permit much sightseeing, but Rome turned into an unexpected adventure. While they were there, an assassination attempt was made on Mussolini after he delivered a speech at a congress of surgeons. Two of the bullets struck his nose, shredding the tip, but he survived. Bandaged, he returned by motorcade to the Capitoline. Serge feared that the assailant might be a Soviet agent and worried that his performance of the Third Piano Concerto at San Martino ai Monti would either be canceled or subject to political protest. Following the rehearsal, however, he was relieved to hear that the gunman was a woman, Violet Gibson, from Ireland. She was in prison, having been almost beaten to death on the street. The performance was unaffected by the drama, save for the poor turnout (fewer than a thousand people in an auditorium holding four thousand).

The next morning, April 8, the Prokofievs received written notice from a messenger that they had been granted an audience with the pope, Pius XI. Serge had made the request for the audience the day before, at the encouragement of their local hosts. They scrambled to find an appropriately demure and unfashionable gown for Lina to wear; the mother of the composer Alfredo Casella came to the rescue with an oversized black frock. On the way to the Vatican, Serge and Lina teased each other about the awkward questions they might be asked about their faith and whether or not their son had been baptized. But the bespectacled, kind-faced pontiff neither asked nor entertained questions, offering only a prayer and a blessing. They kneeled to the side with the rest of the invited public. The pope paused before Lina, thinking her pregnant in her inflated gown and allowing her to kiss his emerald-and-pearl-encrusted ring. She and Serge were permitted to take in the view of the Vatican before being escorted out.

The following day, they rehearsed and then performed at the Accademia Nazionale di Santa Cecilia. Since the organizers had made a hash of the scheduling, instructing them to bring more casual matinee attire for a formal evening performance, they found themselves having to apologize to the audience for their appearance. Perhaps unnerved by the faux pas, Lina had a subpar outing and received tepid applause. The follow-up recital in Siena on April 11 also failed to impress. She sang better than she did in Rome, but it seemed to Serge that the audience could not grasp the music.

As in the United States, the tour tested their endurance. They went to sleep in the Grand Hotel in Siena at midnight on April 11, roused themselves at six in the morning, and left for Genoa at eight. The train pulled in at six in the evening for a concert at nine—another performance for which they did not have proper attire. The travel left Lina hoarse and unhappy. So Serge performed alone, explaining to the crowd that his wife was unwell and substituting the Second Piano Sonata for her scheduled French, Russian, and Spanish songs. Despite the onset of a cold, she managed to perform with him five days later in Florence and was pleased to receive an ovation along with a generous bouquet of roses for her rendition of the Myaskovsky songs.

The travel drained her strength, and her cold lingered, leaving her unable to perform the tacked-on recital in Naples. Plus her pride was injured when the organizers expressed indifference at her canceling, since Serge was the principal attraction. For him the performance would have been a non-event except for the unexpected appearance in the audience of the twice-exiled Russian writer and political agitator Maxim Gorky. He was living with his son and daughter-in-law in a large rented house in Sorrento, where the Mediterranean climate helped him cope with tuberculosis. He had once been close to the Bolshevik leader Lenin, but the two fell out in 1918. That year he publicly denounced Lenin for thwarting the ideals of the Revolution through his campaign of systematic, tyrannical repression. Gorky went into exile in Sorrento in October 1921—the catalyst being the arrest and execution in Petrograd of the pro-tsarist poet Nikolay Gumilyov, whom Gorky had petitioned Lenin to pardon. The pardon came too late.

Gorky invited Lina and Serge to his cliff-side house, a stack of unfurnished, uninviting rooms. During lunch, he insisted on drinking French rather than Italian wine, an ironic detail that Serge noted in his diary, together with the unpleasant particulars of Gorky's chronic hacking, which he likened to a yapping dog. The roughish, thickly mustachioed writer insisted on smoking despite his condition, which had left him with less than half a lung. Gorky seemed smitten with Lina and impressed her with accounts of the hospices he had established in southern Russia for orphans of the Revolution and civil war. He also spoke of the emotional and psychological counseling the facilities provided. The conversation reminded Lina of the philanthropist Catherine Breshko-Breshkovskaya, the "Grandmother of the Revolution," who had employed her part-time for a month in 1919 in New York. Eventually the discussion turned from general cultural matters to politics and economics. Gorky stood by his belief in the overarching importance of spiritual enlightenment in realizing socialist principles. Hearing that his guests were thinking of traveling to Soviet Russia, he asked sarcastic questions about Serge's supposed anti-Bolshevik activities in the past. There was some parting banter about the mass of publications and correspondence that Gorky received each week from Russia. He recommended recent Soviet fiction by Boris Pasternak and Leonid Leonov, among other talents. Then they bade farewell. Gorky's son walked them to the tram stop, regaling them with stories of the marvelous archaeological finds in the area.

There followed the long train ride back to Paris and a reunion with Svyatoslav, whom they had barely seen for several months. During the long tours through the United States and Italy, he had been entrusted to the care of Lina's mother. Olga had come to France in October 1925 and pledged to return in January 1927 to look after Svyatoslav again. It was then that Serge had agreed, after much negotiation, to travel to Russia — with Lina at his side. One of his Soviet hosts, Boleslav Yavorsky, had jokingly advised Serge to leave her behind in Paris. Her photograph was so fetching, he warned, that she might be abducted by one of his comrades. In lieu of an actual Soviet passport, Lina received the same Soviet travel permit as her husband and the same pledge of hassle-free border crossings.

The details of the Soviet tour would be settled not with the bureaucrats Serge had met before his long tours, Krasin or Tutelman, but with the pianist and musicologist Yavorsky, who visited him in Paris in May 1926. He behaved as though under surveillance — which he was, but Serge had known him since youth and enjoyed seeing him again. Through Lunacharsky, Yavorsky had gained enough political capital to be able to hire and fire professors at will at his home institution, the Moscow Conservatoire. He informed Serge that the Soviet government was interested in repatriating Russian émigré artists, no strings attached. Should Serge be inclined to accept Soviet citizenship, he could live in Moscow one month a year, the other eleven in Paris.

With the Soviet tour inked on their calendar—and the surprising possibility of a permanent move in the offing—the Prokofievs spent the summer in Samoreau, a township on the banks of the Seine near Fontainebleau. Though it lacked a piano, a problem soon resolved, the house was conducive to work and the surrounding garden an ideal play space for the hyper-energetic Svyatoslav, who had begun to speak a precocious admixture of French and Russian, although the rolling of the letter *r* eluded him.

Back in Paris that fall, the family settled in a six-room, top-floor apartment on rue Troyen near Place de l'Étoile, the center of a cluster of twelve outward-radiating avenues. Furnished in a tired bohemian style, at least it boasted a terrace on the mansard roof. Even so, Lina found the place dispiriting and for a week hesitated to sign the lease with the fourth of the agents she and her husband had enlisted. Ultimately she consented, with irritation, and blamed her husband for the choice. A neighborhood street served as a rendezvous for prostitutes and their clients. Serge impishly revealed this to Lina when they were out strolling one night. He darted ahead, greeted the women as they emerged from their doorways, and asked about their rates.

While tussling over their current situation and long-term prospects in Paris, the couple began to steel themselves for the journey to Soviet Russia, which would begin on the day their lease expired. They would travel to Moscow through Berlin and Riga on January 13, 1927, eventually returning to Paris and facing another apartment search at the end of March. Svyatoslav would not be left, as planned, in the care of Olga, since she did not make it back to France in time. Instead Lina arranged for her son to stay with trusted Christian Scientist friends in Sèvres.

As the tour neared, Serge sought reassurance from friends and acquaintances that Soviet Russia was not as fearsome as it seemed, and that he was not putting himself or his wife at risk. He avoided haggling over fees with Yavorsky and reminded himself that he needed to practice hard so as to make a civilized impression on stage. He had a hard time digesting the news from Russia that his cousin Shurik had been imprisoned as a counterrevolutionary. (He received word of the incarceration from his aunt Katya, who, to elude the censors, described the arrest in Aesopian language as an illness followed by a hospital stay.) Through Christian Science, he reminded himself that he was immune to any danger. Miss Crain, who had replaced Caroline Getty as his and Lina's Christian Science adviser, met with him the week before his departure to offer counsel, and bid him farewell by reasserting that as an artist, he was a reflection of the divine.

He took more practical comfort in a seductive last-minute offer he had received from Moscow for performances with the innovative Persimfans ensemble, an orchestra that performed without a conductor in accordance with progressive proletarian ideals. *Love for Three Oranges*, moreover, was set to be performed in Leningrad, though without Serge conducting. His colleagues urged him on.

Serge had not been to Russia since 1918, his wife not since early childhood. He described his relationship to his homeland to the French radio broadcaster Serge Moreux in an interview published in *Tempo*. "Foreign air does not suit my inspiration, because I'm Russian, and that is to say the least suited of men to be an exile, to remain myself in a psychological climate that isn't that of my race. My compatriots and I carry our country about with us . . . I've got to go back. I've got to move myself back into the atmosphere of my native soil. I've got to see real winters again, and Spring that bursts into being from one moment to the next. I've got to hear the Russian language echoing in my ears, I've got to talk to people who are of my own flesh and blood, so that they can give me back something I lack here—their songs—my songs. Here I'm getting enervated. I risk dying of academicism. Yes, my friend: I'm going back."

Prokofiev spoke sentimentally of Russia, but he was not a sentimental person. In essence, he returned to Russia because he had never left.

Chapter 6

LINA TOOK DETAILED notes throughout their trip to the Soviet Union in 1927, and these became part of her husband's diary, which he wrote up when he and Lina were back in Paris. During their nine weeks away, Svyatoslav turned three.

The Russian tour was a homecoming for Serge, who had left St. Petersburg in 1918, at the start of the civil war between the Reds and the Whites. Lina knew the language but little else beyond her mother's recollections and her own early childhood images of visits to Ukraine and the Caucasus. The Prokofievs sensed the seismic sociopolitical shift as they moved from West to East. A sign at the Soviet border commanded the toiling masses of the world to "Unite!" according to Karl Marx's famous dictum. Lenin was dead; a Georgian Bolshevik fighter who specialized in kidnappings and robberies had replaced him. He was born Iosif Vissarionovich Dzhugashvili, but he changed his last name to Stalin, meaning "man of steel." He seized control of the levers of power (the Central Committee of the Communist Party) even before Lenin's enfeebled death from his third stroke on January 21, 1924. Stalin thereafter removed his political opponents and installed genuflecting allies in their place. These allies would fall under suspicion of sabotage, and the cycle of purging and purifying would repeat. The true nature of his regime, however, would not reveal itself until the 1930s, following the catastrophic failure of Stalin's economic policies.

The touring Prokofievs were shown the best of what the Soviet

Union had to offer in 1927 and made to feel immune from what little they knew of the worst. Outside of Stalin's innermost circle, no one, least of all the pampered, privileged guests from abroad, had forewarning of the dreadfulness of the decade ahead: collectivization, militarization, the Great Famine, and the arrest and execution of Party officials, Red Army officers, the police, descendants of the nineteenth-century aristocracy, supposedly food-hoarding former landowners, Russian Orthodox priests, Jews, and average citizens, for crimes as trifling as gossip. These events would either go unreported or be justified, by Stalin's mind-numbing propaganda machine, as national self-defense.

On January 17, the Prokofievs gave a recital in Riga en route to Russia, performing the repertoire of their concerts in America and Italy the previous year; the occasion produced the sole surviving photograph of Lina on stage with her husband. As they reached the Latvian crossing into the USSR, they reassured themselves that they could still reverse course, end the trip there, and go back to Paris. But they purchased tickets to Russia and pressed on.

Having refused an offer of Soviet passports for the trip, they clung instead to their Nansen (League of Nations) documents, a decision that irritated their hosts but spared them future problems in France and the United States. Special travel papers were granted by Maksim Litvinov, Stalin's senior diplomat. They showed these at each border crossing while holding their breath, especially at the militarized Soviet checkpoint where the baggage of fellow passengers was confiscated. But they and their luggage arrived unmolested in Moscow's Belorusskiy-Baltiyskiy vokzal (Belarus-Baltic Station), which Serge referred to in his diary by its old name, Aleksandrovskiy. The huge shed, with its wooden platforms, pastel façades, and ornate spires, had a "provincial appearance," he commented. The lamp in their carriage had gone out, so he and Lina arrived in the predawn darkness by candlelight. Greeting them were the managers of Persimfans, the conductorless orchestra that had booked Serge for what seemed like an ever-increasing number of performances. One of its organizers, Lev Tseitlin, was the concertmaster of the ensemble; the other, Arnold Tsukker, was a dedicated Communist with a robust Party résumé who served as the liaison between Persimfans and the government.

Off to the side stood a ferret-faced musician Serge knew from youth, Vladimir Derzhanovsky, sporting an oversized *dublyonka* (sheepskin coat), *valenki* (felt boots), and ostentatious fur hat. His pince-nez trembled as he shouted his welcome. Lina tittered, though she allowed him to flirt with her. Derzhanovsky and his stout female assistant ran a music shop that stocked scores from Gosizdat muzsektor (the Music Division of the State Publisher). He offered use of a battered piano that Serge dismissed as worthless for practicing.

The couple was taken by taxi to the Metropole Hotel, which brochures for well-heeled travelers describe as a masterpiece of opulent art nouveau architecture dating from 1901. Built across from the Bolshoy Theater, the Metropole stands within walking distance of the present-day Duma (parliament) and the crenellated outer wall of the Kremlin. Its original financier, the railroad baron Savva Mamontov, had wanted the look to be decadent and the facilities modern. But in 1927 it was a mess, having endured successive half-finished renovations. Following the Bolshevik coup and the transfer of the Russian (Soviet) government from Petrograd to Moscow, the hotel was converted into cramped government offices. Now it was being refurbished as a hotel, but only a single floor had been finished. For all its grandeur, the suite assigned to Serge and Lina did not have a bathroom, and the restaurant was closed.

Their afternoon stroll along Tverskaya, an avenue extending northwest from the Kremlin to Sadovoye koltso (Garden Ring Road), revealed a city bursting at the seams, crammed with inadequate tramlines, buses (imported from England), and occasional taxis (Renaults from France). To accommodate the booming population, plans were being drawn up for a Metro system that would enable the former backwater of Moscow to grow into a proper seat of Soviet power, a true world capital. Already the churches that once defined Strastnaya Square had almost all vanished, abolished by decree to make way for the constructivist headquarters of the official government newspaper, *Izvestiya*. The monuments of imperial culture had also disappeared—one exception being the statue of the poet Alexander Pushkin, whose works were being scrutinized for prophesies of the Revolution.

That summer Tverskaya would be asphalted and the House of Communications (Central Telegraph) built across the street from the Moscow Art Theater. Its electronics came from foreign firms such as Siemens. Inside, citizens sent telegrams and mailed packages, their activities monitored by the enormous staff. The hulking granite building dominated an entire corner, competing for attention on the street with the gracious National Hotel, which, like the Metropole, housed government officials. Soon the smaller buildings lining Tverskaya would be razed to accommodate automobiles. Serge noted that people on the street seemed well fed, and the small shopkeeper co-ops did not lack for goods. These businesses, a vestige of Lenin's New Economic Policy, were soon to be replaced by government-run stores that had no need to invest in creative advertising. The bread store was named Bread, the fish and milk stores Fish and Milk.

But in 1927, before its most radical remaking under Stalin, Moscow was less a site of excavation pits and new construction than a landscape of inhabited but forlorn buildings with bedraggled exteriors, boarded façades, and unpleasant courtyard entrances. Tseitlin stressed the positive and, hoping to sway the sympathies of his foreign visitors, made invidious comparisons between Moscow and Paris. Most of his claims were ridiculous. Parroting *Pravda* (*Truth*), the newspaper of the Central Committee, he described a fictitious epidemic in the French capital and reported, bizarrely, that the Bolshoy Theater had been resurfaced with stone purloined from graveyards. The Prokofievs were not fooled.

Nor were they impressed to learn from Tseitlin that the government strictly controlled housing, with the result that assignments tended to be makeshift and requests for upgrades ignored. Tseitlin and his wife made their home in a basement office of the Conservatoire, living "behind a curtain" amid the files of Persimfans.

The composer Nikolay Myaskovsky, Serge's longtime friend, lived in an overstuffed room within a communal apartment. The outside of the building reflected the faded elegance of the seventeenth-century neighborhood, but not the inside, which had been awkwardly reshaped and resized. Owing more to the acute housing shortage than the principles of socialism, an apartment that had once accommodated a single aristocratic family had been turned into a dank dorm. Myaskovsky's sister lived beside him. So too did his niece, a devoted member of the Komsomol (Communist Youth League), who had taken to lambasting Myaskovsky for his bourgeois sensibilities. Her imprecations shielded the sound of his grand piano from the other families. He was in a sorry state, but others had it worse, including his own sister, whose husband had committed suicide. Lina and Serge later heard that in some of the converted mansions, the kitchens were the sites of terrible rows. "You can imagine the hellish scenes there," one of their escorts told them, "at the moment when the eighteen families living in this quiet mansion are cooking eighteen suppers on eighteen primus-stoves!"

Lunacharsky, in marked contrast, occupied an entire house suitable for chamber concerts, but it had fallen into disrepair. So too had the low-rise apartment building housing Nadya, the wife of Serge's imprisoned cousin, Shurik. They visited her and her children on Sunday, January 23, feeling ill at ease. Later they were able to relax at a birthday gathering for Derzhanovsky's wife. Some bureaucratic sleight of hand had allowed the Derzhanovskys to keep most of their apartment to themselves: the other rooms had been assigned to the housekeeper and a phantom resident.

Another confiscated mansion served as the gala reception hall for the Prokofievs after Serge's second performance in Moscow. There survives an image of the event, showing a beaming, flush-faced composer in three-piece suit and tie. Lina sits three seats away in a fur-trimmed coat, with a rope of pearls looped tightly around the neck, one end dangling down to her waist. Her hair is neatly styled in a fashionable bob. She sits to the right of the stern-looking, goateed Myaskovsky and to the left of Alexander Mosolov, the brash young composer of a sensational ballet score named *Stal'* (*Steel*). The table is littered with champagne bottles, and the balding, mustachioed Tseitlin looks from the distance into the camera. Several people, including Derzhanovsky, are standing, arrayed behind Prokofiev for the picture and posterity.

In another image from another day, Lina and Serge posed outside for the cameras, her leopard-skin coat and hat and his patterned suits contrasting with the generic grays and blacks of the Tseitlins and Tsukkers. A third photo—mislabeled "Moscow, 19 January 1927" (they had not yet arrived in Moscow on that day)—captures the casual elegance of Lina's Parisian wardrobe, if not the fragrances that went with it: she wears a cameo necklace, shawl-necked sweater, boldly patterned argyle tights, and a thin wedding band on her left hand, in the American style. To the right Serge slumps in a two-piece suit, buttoned sweater, starched shirt, and loosened tie. Both look tired. (As Lina recalled with brisk matter-of-factness in a 1982 interview with Harvey Sachs, "Serge was exhausted and so was I and we wanted to leave as soon as possible but they would keep us and they would drink.")

The drama surrounding the visit was such that Serge found himself besieged with requests for interviews and lessons with aspiring composers, as well as some sordid telephone solicitations. Little of his music suited the conservative tastes of the regime, but his international fame did. Having him back, if only for a few weeks, was a propaganda coup played up in the Soviet media.

For all the invective occasioned by his music in the United States, Serge was not, in fact, as radical as the generation of Russian composers who had come of age under Lenin. Reflecting the tumultuous, futuristic spirit of the Revolution, composers such as Mosolov, Alexander Kenel, Nikolay Roslavetz, and Vsevolod Zaderatsky had produced avant-garde quarter-tone scores, industrial symphonies, songs based on newspaper advertisements, and chance-based audience-interaction pieces. There also existed a proletarian musical organization whose members would be increasingly privileged by the regime for writing agitprop (agitational propaganda) choruses and marches. Mosolov, however, would be blacklisted as a bourgeois modernist, sent to prison in 1937 on charges of "hooliganism," and forced to repent by churning out ditties for folksy balalaika ensembles.

The twenty-year-old Dmitri Shostakovich had graduated from the Leningrad (formerly St. Petersburg) Conservatoire and produced his First Symphony, but Serge did not know his works beyond those that seemed similar to his own. The composers he met during his run of performances, and with whom he posed in group photographs, came instead from his own past.

On February 4, a newsreel was shot of Serge at the Moscow Conservatoire, focusing on his piano playing. He chose the allegro con brio final movement of his Fourth Piano Sonata but, he claimed, the noise of the hand-cranked camera and the lamps bothered him so much that he botched it. The shooting continued in the lobby, with Lina standing next to him in that spotted coat—the local cause célèbre. Part of the film survives, showing his hands flashing up and down the keyboard, but the absence of sound is disconcerting. Lina does not appear.

His concerts in Moscow were sensational. Serge received thunderous applause the moment he appeared on stage, and it did not matter that nerves prevented him from playing his best. Lina was asked to sing but declined on account of fatigue and a scratchy throat. Still, she too was courted and celebrated. On February 1 Tsukker invited her to see Rimsky-Korsakov's opera *Tsarskaya nevesta* (*The Tsar's Bride*) at the Stanislavsky Opera Studio. She found the singing superb, and Tsukker proposed that she join the theater, a startling overture, given that she no longer thought of herself as an opera singer. The shared recitals with her husband were taxing enough. In an interview much later in life, Lina remembered hearing other performances and claimed that the famed director Konstantin Stanislavsky himself asked her to sing with him. "But I said 'How can I? I have a family.' I could never leave my husband and family." This happened either on the 1927 trip or a later visit, or even after her permanent relocation to Moscow— she could not recall.

Serge and Lina dined at exclusive hotel restaurants offering hard-to-find Russian delicacies, avoiding the *obshchepit*, the graceless canteens serving the masses. He occasionally ate on the run, grabbing cabbage- or potato-stuffed *vareniki* (pierogies) from perspiring, bundled-up street vendors, and sometimes reverted to the staples of his student days: potato- and pickle-based soups, sweet wafers, raspberry-infused tea. Lina remembered the barrels of butter and herring for sale near the Metropole.

On February 5, the Prokofievs were invited to dine inside the Kremlin. The event was arranged by Olga Kameneva, the director of the Soviet cultural exchange organization VOKS. Her position had its privileges, including an apartment within the Kremlin's walls, but it was tenuous. Her high-ranking husband, Lev Kamenev, opposed Stalin's economic policies—the brutal, forced collectivization that followed Lenin's frantic embrace of free-market reforms. Even worse, Kameneva was the sister of Leon Trotsky, Stalin's nemesis. All three of them would meet a violent end in the purges. Although Kameneva put on the airs of a sophisticate, Lina found her crude, and Serge chafed at her demands that he entertain her and her daughter-in-law (a dancer) at the piano. Neither of them wanted to share their impressions of Russia over dinner, but they had no choice. They obliged her with sugarcoated vagueness. Lina enjoyed chatting with Ivy Low, the British wife of the statesman Maksim Litvinov. She had few official duties and spent most of her time translating and writing fiction; later she taught so-called Basic English. Lina was fascinated by her Soviet high life, and they made plans to meet up in Paris. The evening dragged on, and the food was merely palatable.

Three days after the unusual Saturday evening in the Kremlin, the Prokofievs left for the first of two visits to Leningrad. Serge's obligations there included two orchestral and two chamber concerts; appointments with student composers at his alma mater, the St. Petersburg (Leningrad) Conservatoire; numerous interviews; and attendance at a performance of *Love for Three Oranges.* The opera was to receive its stunning Leningrad premiere under the direction of Sergey Radlov, a force for iconoclastic innovation in the academic theaters. The performance on the tenth amazed the composer; here was a fast-paced, uproarious production of his opera like no other, with double- and triple-layered costumes and elaborate props (ladders, megaphones, mirrors, life-sized marionettes, and trapezes). The provincial Americans could not compete, nor could the self-involved French or Germans. Lunacharsky, who attended a follow-up performance specially arranged for him on the nineteenth, compared it, for Lina's benefit, to "a glass of champagne, all sparkling and frothing."

During downtime in Leningrad, Lina retreated to their hotel, the faded Grand Hotel Europe, still recovering from its conversion during World War I first into a hospital, then an orphanage. Serge's enraptured descriptions in his diary of Nevsky Prospect, the Hermitage and Winter Palace, the Peter and Paul Fortress, and the canals and embankments read like a hard-sell travel guide. He noted the boarded-up central market, Gostiniy dvor, and the sorrowful condition of the apartment of the former Conservatoire director Alexander Glazunov. Yet the rush of nostalgia prevailed. The theatrical city that Peter the Great had ordered into existence in the eighteenth century (on the backs of peasants and prisoners) retained its charm and grandeur for him.

Serge collected the stories of people from his past and of the transformation of Russia into the Soviet Union. The harpist Eleanor

Damskaya, for one, besieged him with tales of financial hardship and the barbarism of the Bolsheviks. She had rescued Serge's piano from his ransacked former apartment, along with letters and photographs, which she now proposed to sell back to him. Officials from the Commissariat of Enlightenment had tried to confiscate the piano from her, declaring that it belonged to the people. It was destined for the apartment of an apparatchik, but Damskaya was able to keep it after paying a bribe. Serge promised to look into the matter and wrote a letter of protest to Lunacharsky. Damskaya repeated the tale to Lina over tea in her hotel room in Leningrad while staring covetously at Lina's clothes.

The unscripted encounters gave her time in Leningrad substance and left a lasting impression, whereas the receptions and dinners hosted by flirtatious but ultimately tedious cultural officials did not. More than anything the trip was a shared adventure, and Serge's happiness brought them closer together, their hosts guaranteeing that their impressions of the Soviet Union were positive, fascinating rather than frightening. Lina's one scare was of an Old Russian sort: their sledge driver in Leningrad lost control of his horse while taking them across the frozen streets to Oktyabrskiy vokzal (October Station). No one was hurt.

They knew that they were under observation, their movements choreographed and conversations in public spaces transcribed. But this had also happened to Serge in Paris when, for example, he met Boleslav Yavorsky at Du Guesclin, a restaurant near their apartment in the fifteenth arrondissement. In Russia, Serge was bothered by just one thing — the fate of his cousin Shurik, a political prisoner. He asked Tsukker and others to intercede in the case but heard that the matter needed to be referred to someone else, or that it was too delicate, or that nothing could be done. The Red Cross helped to get the sentence reduced, but the case rested with the OGPU, the Obyedinyonnoye Gosudarstennoye Politicheskoye Upravleniye, Stalin's political police. Near the end of the trip, the eminent theater director Vsevolod Meyerhold, a longtime supporter of Serge's with stellar political credentials and powerful connections, promised to help. But he balked, and Shurik sat in prison. Lina did not dwell on the subject in her recollections of the trip, except to observe that her husband needed to be careful, to say the right things at the right time, and to heed his minders when they cautioned him. She had not been completely unaware in 1927, she concluded long after the fact, but she had certainly failed to take in the darker, grimmer implications of these constraints.

At 11 P.M. on March 6, the Prokofievs left Soviet Russia for Soviet Ukraine. They departed from Kursk train station, near their future Moscow apartment, in a building that would be assigned to politicians (members of the Council of People's Commissars) and artists. But the building had not yet been constructed in 1927, and the neighborhood retained its metal and textile industries.

Serge was scheduled to perform two recitals each in the three largest cities, Kharkov (or Kharkiv, in Ukrainian), Kiev, and Odessa. He also hoped to secure the Ukrainian premiere of *Love for Three Oranges*. When the train meandered past the village of his golden childhood, Sontsovka, he recorded the event in his diary but avoided mentioning that the village had been razed, obliterated by tanks during the civil war. Lina remembered either a peasant or a friend from Serge's childhood telling him the news. (She likely meant Vera Reberg, the daughter of the Sontsovka village doctor Albert Reberg, whom Lina and Serge visited in Kharkov.) Lina also thought, but was not sure, that the village had been rebuilt, with log houses replacing the original stucco—or maybe the opposite.

Kharkov was at the time the capital of the Ukrainian Soviet Socialist Republic and would remain so through 1934, after which Kiev became the capital. Serge performed his recitals at the Ukrainian State Central Opera, where he hoped *Love for Three Oranges* would be staged. (The future of the theater was grim, however. It would serve in 1930 as the venue for Stalinist show trials. Beginning that year, thousands of Ukrainian intellectuals would be targeted for arrest and execution.) Between his two recitals, Serge took a walk downtown, observing the dirty slush on the streets, the government-approved selling of bootleg copies of his piano pieces—a sign of some sort of acceptance—and the imposing unattractiveness of the architecture. Although he did not mention it by name, a massive building in a pseudo-constructivist style was being built at the time. This was

Derzhprom, the State Industry building, which featured corner towers of cement and granite, steel-encased windows, and germ-resistant
(or so it was advertised) copper fixtures in the offices.

He and Lina stayed just across the street at the Krasnaya (Red)
Hotel, another imposing structure made to last forever. Devoid of
ambiance, the hotel was short-staffed, their room lacked cold water,
and the telephone was tapped. As Serge wrote, "The telephone has
only an outside line, so to call room service I have to look the hotel up
in the directory and dial it through the local exchange." Though they
would have liked to bathe, they avoided doing so because the tub had
"a somewhat leprous appearance." It was acid-washed, the manage-
ment boasted.

On March 10, with their mud-stained luggage, they boarded the
train to Kiev. The effort to obtain a private compartment had been
botched, leaving Lina to sleep on the bunk above or across from a
female Ukrainian official who preferred babbling about her village
and family to sleeping. Lina and Serge awoke to find the ice-covered
Dnieper River under siege, shelled by soldiers to prevent flooding—a
"beautiful" sight, Serge declared. Once the train had crawled into the
station (on time as ever, Soviet trains having well-padded schedules),
they were taken by dilapidated car to the full-service Continental
Hotel at 5 Nikolayevskaya Street near Kreshchatik, Kiev's tram- and
tree-lined central avenue. At the time of their visit, the street bore
the name of a martyred Bolshevik, Vaclav Vorovsky. The buildings
had suffered extensive damage during the civil war, but the Continental Hotel survived intact. Following the German invasion of Kiev
in 1941, however, it would be detonated by Soviet forces, never to be
rebuilt.

After the first of Serge's recitals, a teacher from the Kiev Conservatoire burst into the green room to insist that he help adjudicate an
examination the next day, March 12. He thought he had politely declined but, according to Lina, he had done the opposite and rudely accepted. The teacher, surnamed Goldenberg, telephoned in the morning to confirm and arranged for a driver to take them to the building.
In his diary Serge described the magnificence of central Kiev, but also
the blown-out, grief-stricken ruins.

The morning with the students was pleasant. Several played excerpts from Serge's ballet *The Buffoon*, and a trio of girls offered their

thoughts on the form of the gavotte movement from his *Classical Symphony*. They clearly loved Goldenberg, who, according to Lina, "always had something up her sleeve." The examination was organized with the eminent composer's visit in mind, hence the insistence that he attend. Serge claimed in his diary that the students were nervous and failed to understand his music, but Lina remembered them as surprisingly, even stubbornly, self-assured. Serge leapt to the stage to challenge one girl's analysis of the gavotte. "Where do you see that? It never occurred to me it could be dissected that way." "Oh yes," said the girl. "This passage has a connection with that one." When Serge tried to correct her, she persisted, saying, "no, no," as she repeated the passage in question at the piano. He could only laugh. "Well, if you like." Later another group of students appeared at the door of their hotel room, clutching their incorrect analyses of the march from *Love for Three Oranges*.

The little hall was cold, and Lina sat in her fur coat throughout the examination. Serge insisted she perch on a windowsill for a better view, effectively banishing her after she had embarrassed him in front of Goldenberg. Her attention had drifted to the large framed pictures on the side wall, where she recognized the stern faces of Lenin and Stalin. But she had to ask about the third picture. "Who is that man?" Goldenberg was incredulous. "Don't you know? It's Karl Marx!" Lina tried to atone for the gaffe by saying that yes, of course, she knew the name but did not know Marx had such a big beard. "Why did you have to ask that?" her husband irritably whispered to her. She shrugged. "Well, how was I to know?"

From Kiev, the Prokofievs left for the Black Sea port of Odessa. Serge knew little of the place; Lina, in contrast, remembered being there with her grandfather, Vladislav Nemïssky, in her early childhood. She recognized the Russian baroque façade of their hotel, the Bristol Krasnaya, and the State Academic Theater of Opera and Ballet, recently renovated after a fire. She and her husband posed for a professional studio photograph. Ecstatic students all but mobbed Serge during his visit to the Odessa Conservatoire, and the response to his recitals was passionate. Here too the handpicked audiences made him feel needed, wanted.

The journey back to Moscow took two days, March 16 through 18, interrupted by a two-hour locomotive change in Kiev. It ended with Serge and Lina in the very same room in the very same hotel from which they had departed. A long tour of the Kremlin followed in frigid (minus fifteen degrees Celsius) temperatures. The day's political tutelage included witnessing the painstaking preservation of church frescoes and other remnants of the pre-enlightened tsarist past. Serge thought he had breached decorum by failing to remove his *shapka* before entering the Cathedral of the Assumption, only to be assured by the low-paid, selflessly dedicated restorer that the Soviet government had abolished religious services and turned the Kremlin churches, the glories of the nation, into museums. Besides, it was freezing. They also paid a social call to Serge's second cousin, Shura Sezhenskaya, who lauded the education her son was receiving in the Komsomol. Serge was skeptical: it sounded like brainwashing. The tsars also had their propaganda, Shura parried.

There followed his final two performances with Persimfans and another round of inquiries from cultural officials about Serge's stay in the USSR. Even Aleksey Rïkov, the powerful chairman of the Council of People's Commissars, asked if the tour had met his expectations. "My visit here has made one of the strongest impressions on me of my whole life," Serge answered, calculatedly noncommittal. Lina's response went unrecorded.

Their final two days in Moscow were consumed with collecting German and Polish transit visas for their Nansen passports and getting additional static for leaving through a hostile nation (Poland) rather than Latvia. The political overseer of Persimfans, Tsukker, took Lina to Gostorg, the State Trade Office, where he had elite access to goods meant for sale abroad, including fabulous coats. The headquarters was on Myasnitskaya Street, in a showcase constructivist building. But the massive building housing Komintern, the Communist International, was of greater interest to Lina. She never forgot her first sight of Komintern headquarters in the center of Moscow, describing it as "a kind of huge jar full of microbes destined for worldwide distribution." One of its thousands of employees placed an odd phone call to Serge, asking him to perform in a concert celebrating the presumed Communist Party of China (CPC) takeover of Shanghai, an event that Tsukker and his comrades greeted with a ludicrous amount of enthusiasm. The Komintern, Serge learned, bankrolled the CPC. He excused himself from the concert on account of the short notice.

The couple packed frantically and left on an international train from Belarus station. Prokofiev and Myaskovsky exchanged gifts during a tender farewell—shirts and ties from Paris, cartons of wrapped candies from a Moscow shop. "Those seeing us off looked at us not without envy because, of course, they knew that in two or three days we would be in Paris," Serge recalled, reflecting less on their plight than on the fact that, from start to finish, his tour had been a triumph. The reception accorded his performances in Moscow, Leningrad, and Ukraine exceeded his expectations—he had never felt as popular, as potentially influential, as he did on those occasions. Yet the skull in the garden was his failure to obtain the release of his cousin Shurik, who would later send Serge a letter pleading for an end to the efforts on his behalf. They only made things worse.

With the excitement behind them, the slow trip back to Paris blurred the images and eccentricities of the USSR. The days following their return were taken up with practical matters—the search for a furnished apartment and Serge's purchase of an automobile. His interest in driving predated the trip to the USSR but was only realized afterward, leaving his friends to speculate that the automobile was financed, in whole or in part, by the proceeds from his Soviet concerts. Serge obtained his *carte rose* (driver's license) in January; Lina passed her driving test in June, though she was unimpressed by her performance at the wheel. She found shopping for the car unpleasant, owing to the interference of Boris Bashkirov, who was now earning a partial living as a nighttime chauffeur. She dreamed of owning a Buick or a Lincoln, but Serge showed more interest in Hispano-Suizas and Delages. Their finances obliged them to settle on a used Ballot costing 27,000 francs rather than a new one for 80,000. It needed painting, which turned into an ordeal, and the insurance was more costly than they had expected.

Once these issues were settled, they took to the newer, wider roads of Paris and its environs. Serge drove most often, escaping his desk and piano for days at a time. Later he took his friends, including invited guests from Russia, on *tournées gastronomiques* in the south, the destinations determined by French gourmet guides and the location of Shell stations. He kept meticulous track of the kilometers traveled, the speeds attained (up to a reckless ninety kilometers an hour), and the gasoline burned. The fumes gave him headaches, which he tried to treat through Christian Science meditation, unwilling to surrender the wheel. Lina denounced his terrible driving. He dinged the roof and dented the fenders and wheel guards of the Ballot in the city and took the lives of innocent chickens in the country. Bicyclists also paid a serious price for crossing his path. In the spring of 1929, he collided with another car on the long drive back to Paris from Monte Carlo, receiving, according to a letter from Lina, "935 francs pour reparations de l'accident."

Six months after that, he yanked a muscle in his left hand, broke a tooth, and scuffed and scraped his nether regions in a rollover in the French Alpine town of Culoz. The Ballot had lost a rear wheel and flipped, jettisoning him and his family onto the pavement. Lina, who emerged from the wreckage with bruises around her eyes, remembered seeing glass and metal shards all around. Svyatoslav was, understandably, wailing. She also, to her disgust, heard her half-conscious husband fretting about his manuscripts, which had also been tossed from the car. They rented a hotel room in Culoz for five days of bed rest, after which Lina emerged to reassure her friends and sensation-seeking reporters that no one had been killed. (The newspapers described the accident in catastrophic terms.) Serge replaced the totaled automobile a year later with a comfier, stodgier Chevrolet, driving it much more slowly. Thus Svyatoslav remembered him as a boring, cautious driver. In Moscow in later years, the family would be driven around in a blue Ford from St. Louis, Missouri—an example of capitalist excess that made a shocking impression.

On April 7, 1927, Lina agreed to move into a furnished apartment at 5, avenue Frémiet in the sixteenth arrondissement. (Before that they were living in Paris at 18, rue Troyon in the seventeenth.) She moaned as she packed and unpacked but had to admit that the new apartment was pleasant, with two windows overlooking a garden and beyond that, the Seine. She and Serge retrieved Svyatoslav from his caregivers. One of them wept as she bade farewell to the toddler and watched him drive off with his parents.

• • •

For Serge, the return from Russia coincided with the beginning of preparations for the premiere of the ballet *Le pas d'acier*. It earned mediocre reviews that summer in Paris but positive ones in London, with critics on the political Left and Right scrutinizing its representation of the USSR for signs of political subversion. He did not appreciate the suppression of the well-thought-out original plot, replaced by episodes of gaudy choreographic display. Meanwhile, in the Soviet Union itself, *Love for Three Oranges* enjoyed another brilliant series of performances. Serge basked in sycophantic telegrams and letters from Moscow, which allowed both him and Lina to attribute the occasional complaints about him in the Soviet press to resentment from second-tier composers in the Russian Association of Proletarian Musicians. Royalties arrived from the State Music Publisher (paid by the Bolsheviks, Serge noted, in American dollars). There was talk of another Soviet visit, and perhaps another after that.

The task at hand in France, however, was grim: completing *The Fiery Angel* for a prospective performance under the direction of Bruno Walter in Berlin. Pressed for time, Serge worked on the opera with a professional orchestrator. This was the routinely unkempt, unshaven Georgiy Gorchakov, whom Svyatoslav called "Groggy."

Gorchakov was charged with realizing Serge's orchestrations based on the cryptic notational system that he had adopted as a time-saving method. He worked with the composer at home, where the atmosphere was oppressive. Lina, Svyatoslav, and the nannies were ordered to be silent while Serge was at his desk, especially in the mornings. From nine to noon he became "so absorbed in the progression and logic of his thinking," Gorchakov remembered with wonderment, "that any intervention from the external world would provoke a violent, even brutal, reaction." And if the toddler, then just three years old, "made too much noise in his bedroom which was remote from the study, Serge would open his door and call in Russian: 'Groggy, bring me the green ruler for a good smack on the bottom!' Svyatoslav would scream in French 'no, no!' and become silent."

Despite receiving regular tongue-lashings from Serge, Gorchakov was awestruck by him. In a fragmented account of his experience living with the family on 18, rue Troyon (before the move to 5, avenue Frémiet), he provided intimate details of Prokofiev's eccentricities and the horrendous pressure he placed on himself to meet competing deadlines. Gorchakov recalled Serge taking down the tunes that came to him out of the blue on scraps of paper, the relief he felt at getting his ideas on paper, and his habit of "twitching and tapping an imaginary keyboard" in social settings, losing track of the flow of conversation and staring into the distance.

Serge produced a tremendous racket on the piano in the otherwise quiet apartment, playing hundredfold repetitions of a single dissonant chord. The family would have been evicted were it not for the fact that the Russian neighbors were either hard of hearing or strangely well disposed to discord.

Gorchakov claimed that Serge, "shattered by the amount of work," would sometimes "lose all sense of time and space." Once, he "stopped working before the sacrosanct time of the 'five-o'clock tea' and, warning his wife that he would return around 5 P.M., he went out for a stroll on the Quai de Passy. Teatime arrived—no Prokofiev. Around 10 P.M. the door opens and Prokofiev appears—while walking he had started going through some passages of *The Fiery Angel* in his mind and without noticing, had walked all the way from Paris to Versailles, via the Bois de Meudon."

Groggy joined the Prokofievs periodically at the summer house they rented in Saint-Palais-sur-Mer, near Royan on the Atlantic Coast. They thought it would be a more tranquil setting than the resorts they had considered to the north, but the weather ended up being unpleasant. The dacha was enormous, a real find, with adequate furniture, clean floors and walls, a long balcony conducive to stargazing (an occasional hobby of Serge's), wildflowers on one side, and the water on the other. Serge continued with *The Fiery Angel*, assigning its premiere to the Fates. Ultimately, the provisional agreement for a performance was annulled, a devastating blow that he should have seen coming. But he did not want to, since he had been working without dividends on the score for eight years. Eventually, in the summer of 1928, he would hear selections from the second act in a Paris concert conducted by Serge Koussevitzky, but that was it. Nina Koshetz took the role of the fortuneteller. She was in the sixteenth year of her career and unable to perform the part of the heroine, Renata, her voice faded from too much cabaret singing. The performance went unnoticed in the press and did not interest the people Serge most wanted to impress.

The evenings in Saint-Palais-sur-Mer were quiet. Lina read, clipping articles from the *Christian Science Monitor.* Her husband played chess by letter with friends and reread the entries in his diaries from his St. Petersburg youth. During the day, while he worked, she ensured her son's French and Russian language absorption while suppressing her anxieties about the impending arrival of her parents.

They appeared on July 26. Olga seemed well, but Juan looked ghastly, green from a winter of angina pectoris. No sooner had he disembarked than he experienced harsh, radiating chest pains. They stayed with Lina and Serge in the beach house through the summer, at which point a decision needed to be made about child care and Juan's health. Olga resisted her daughter's advice about the benefits of Christian Science, treating her husband with medicine rather than meditation — not that it helped. Juan's condition worsened in August. He was constantly short of breath; the attacks grew more intense. Olga and Lina resumed their argument about his treatment, which made Olga even more resistant to the Science. Her incapacitated husband belied her daughter's pronouncements about the false nature of sickness.

Lina resumed singing, adding the title role of Rimsky-Korsakov's opera *Snegurochka* (*The Snow Maiden*) to her repertoire. In October, for her thirtieth birthday, Serge took her to a concert performance of the opera, but the evening was spoiled by an offhand remark she made about his complete ignorance of singing. The composer of four operas took serious offense. The dispute followed another late-night argument concerning his relationships with other women, including, on the benign side, Mariya Baranovskaya, also known as Frou-Frou, the onetime actress who had married the pianist Borovsky. She liked to taunt Lina with descriptions of her pampered lifestyle, which included professional manicures in Parisian department stores. The letters Serge had recently received from another female admirer came up. The fight was serious, and Lina decided to sleep on her own that night, though she eventually returned to her husband's side, spooked by something or someone she heard outside her window.

She struggled with her voice but kept planning to perform with her husband; the professional collaboration was sometimes more, sometimes less burdensome than their personal relationship. She received an invitation to sing with Serge in London. Her repertoire would include his Balmont songs from 1921, the texts translated from Russian into English for the benefit of the local audience. Serge noted an improvement in the timbre of his wife's voice but trouble with diction, even though her spoken English was flawless. The concert was arranged for broadcast on BBC Radio 1, with an audience of thirty invited to the studio to hear them in person. Serge would also perform selections from his *Fugitive Visions* for the piano.

The couple arrived in London by train and ferry on December 3, but they decided to return to Paris by plane. Imperial Airlines provided service from the Croydon aerodrome outside London to Le Bourget, Paris, using three-engine aircraft built by, among other firms, Armstrong Whitworth. These could hold up to twenty passengers in an enclosed cabin, one seat on either side of the cramped aisle. The two pilots, in contrast, enjoyed an open cockpit. On the Silver Wing route between the cities, two of the seats were removed to accommodate a bar and a steward, who offered the passengers tea and lunch service despite the considerable turbulence.

Excluding the purchase of tartan travel blankets, Lina suppressed her memories of the time in London, since for her it had been a distinct letdown. The London fog gave her a cold and forced her to cancel her performance. She broke down in tears of frustration, since she had been preparing for several nervous weeks. Serge consoled her, reminding her that a canceled performance was better than a subpar one and insisting, as he left their hotel for the broadcast studio, that they were still a team. But he too was frustrated, since he had counted on her to uphold her end of the contract and thus neglected practicing in late November and early December in order to compose. After battling through the recital, he returned to their suite at the Albemarle Court Hotel to find his wife in despair; another moment for recognition had passed unexploited. Lina would also, owing to another illness, have to forgo an invitation to perform with her husband in Barcelona in the spring of 1928.

Other singers she knew moved ahead. Vera Janacopoulos was still in circulation, and Serge received enthusiastic reports from the lyric soprano Zoya Lodiy about her success performing his *Ugly Duckling*, a chamber work for soprano and piano based on the Hans Christian Andersen tale, throughout the Soviet Union. Her audiences included Red Army soldiers and factory workers. Lina arranged for a coaching with Lodiy when she visited Paris on tour. There remained the overtures from the Soviet Union, but these were of course directed at Serge; the authorities felt obliged to court Lina as his wife.

Following the successful 1927 visit to Moscow, Leningrad, and Ukraine, a Soviet embassy counselor named Jean-Joseph Arens took the lead role in facilitating subsequent visits. He had a strong interest in music, having taken piano lessons throughout his youth, and he exhibited a gift for languages, which allowed him to serve the Stalinist regime both in Paris and, later, Ottawa and New York. (Upon being recalled to Moscow in 1937, he would, in a perverse turn of events, be arrested and shot for his treasonous embrace of foreign influence.) For Serge, Arens displayed the pile of scores by Soviet composers he had with him in his office at 79, rue de Grenelle, and asked him to select the finest for potential Paris premieres. He flattered Lina when he met her at a Russian restaurant, bending low in his elegant suit to kiss her hand after their formal introduction. He invited the couple to an official reception, an invitation they could not refuse, since to do so would have been an insult. And Serge feared the impression he had made by allowing his Soviet travel papers (those that he had used on the tour in 1927) to expire. Arens arranged for new ones to be issued for a steep fee of nine hundred francs, while also encouraging Serge to use the rubles he had earned in Moscow to secure an apartment there.

They first made contact with Arens at the end of the summer of 1928, during which time Lina and Serge escaped Paris on vacation. They took the Ballot to the French Alps, first renting a chateau that pleased Serge but not Lina, then parting company on separate walking tours —his more vigorous, owing to the fact that she was now pregnant with their second child. At some point on the trip, their car had to be pulled from a ditch by a horse.

Lina did not sleep well in her condition, and the mountain thunderstorms startled her awake and provoked nightmares. She reunited with her husband in Chamonix, staying at the summer residence of Serge Koussevitzky and his wife, Natalie, who adored Lina and Svyatoslav. A sunny image survives of the four of them at the house, the ladies in print dresses, the celebrated (if undisciplined) conductor and Lina's son in walking shorts. Stravinsky turned up, as did Serge and a colleague from Leningrad, the music critic and composer Boris Asafyev. They drank wine and ate shish kebab. The talk of Russia was about the imperial past; Stravinsky had an allergic reaction to all things Soviet, owing to his Russian Orthodox faith and right-wing politics. That night Natalie awoke to the sound of someone vomiting —Lina, she thought, was experiencing morning sickness. But it was Stravinsky with food poisoning.

Lina recalled spending part of that summer with two Russian émigré composers: Vladimir Dukelsky, also known as Vernon Duke, and Nicolas Nabokov, cousin of the famous author Vladimir Nabokov. Duke was a composer of both popular and serious music, and Serge liked to tease him for selling out. Lina remembered his struggles composing the music to the 1925 ballet *Zéphyr et Flore* and how much he relied on Serge for help. She also remembered his mischievousness and the jokes he made at her husband's expense, even though he worshiped him.

Lina was due in the first week of December 1928, and the birth was to occur in Paris at Hôpital Saint-Antoine, where she had delivered Svyatoslav. She and her husband, desiring a girl, mulled over possible names: two of Russian vintage, Svetlana and Lyudmila, and two more cosmopolitan, Lydia and Natalie. Lina rejected a fifth choice, Galina, because it would sound awful in Italian. If the baby turned out to be another boy, Serge proposed his longtime favorite, Askold. Lina reminded him of its potential for ridicule in English.

She felt mild discomfort on December 3 but was advised that it was too soon to enter the hospital. Serge proposed an afternoon at the cinematograph, but none of the billboards appealed. The discomfort eased; her due date came and went. Finally, on December 13 — four years to the day since the death of Serge's mother — Lina began experiencing contractions. She entered the hospital in the morning, suspecting that her labor would extend far into the evening. Serge left her in the care of Caroline Getty, matron of the Christian Science Committee on Publications. He returned in the early evening to hear the periodic moans of his wife from the room he was assigned a floor below her. She delivered at 5 A.M. on the fourteenth. Knowing that he would be barred from witnessing the birth, he listened outside the delivery room as his wife's doctor yelled, "Respirez tranquillement! Poussez! Ne poussez pas! Poussez encore!" (Breathe calmly! Push! Don't push! Push again!) His daughter would enter the world at any moment. Then he heard the doctor's declaration: "Un garçon!" (A boy!)

The disappointment did not last. Serge giddily telephoned Lina's mother with the news, then stopped at a cafe, curious as to who would be up and about before dawn besides letter carriers and insomniacs. He saw both. He tossed and turned for two hours at home, then returned to the hospital to find his wife in a wonderful mood, though the "freakish" sight of the baby shocked him, resembling, he vulgarly declared, the Jewish Ukrainian violinist "Mischa Elman—what could be worse!" Cuteness prevailed, however, and his heart melted. The next day Serge brought Svyatoslav to see his mother and the baby, who was described to Svyatoslav as his store-bought Christmas present. "A little sister would have been better," he declared, to which his parents replied that little brothers cost less than little sisters.

A debate about the child's name ensued. December 17 was the deadline for registering the birth. Serge returned to his obsession with Askold; Lina rejected it anew, as did a doctor on the ward, who told him that the name was not canonized. Since Prokofiev's father also had the first name Serge (Sergey), the new arrival could not take the same first name. That would have made three of them in the one family. Oleg came to mind at the last minute. It had a glorious historical precedent: Oleg the Seer had reportedly established the capital of ancient Russia (Rus') in Kiev. Pushkin wrote a ballad about him.

The new arrival meant that Lina could not travel with her husband on his next trip to the Soviet Union. They had planned on going together earlier, but the trip was delayed for financial and political reasons, the former bound up with the latter. Derzhanovsky, one of his contacts in Moscow, advised him by telegram on December 19, 1928, that problems obtaining hard currency as payment meant pushing back a visit to February or March. The new father felt blue: "Walking home, I thought about Russia and my terrible yearning to be there. Why the devil am I here and not there, where people want to see me and where it's much more interesting? Christian Science calmed me. Neither place nor surroundings constitute happiness. The kingdom of God is within us."

Chapter 7

Relocating to the Soviet Union was a protracted process and, for Lina, a lonely one. Its showcase capital, Moscow, was intimidating. The city possessed an aberrant splendor—the buildings, avenues, and squares of the capital serving as monuments to power, not places the Soviet people could call home. Life in the USSR focused on groups: pioneers, the Communist Youth League, the All-Union Communist Party of Bolsheviks, trade unions, collective farms, work brigades, and labor camps. Moscow's streets had been widened and smoothed to accommodate marching soldiers. Red and black banners in stark, constructivist style aestheticized the hard angles of Cyrillic lettering. The sarcophagus of Lenin lay at the city's heart, autopsies of his brain attesting to a colossal intellect.

In the months before the move, from October 1935 to February 1936, Lina lived in a hotel in central Moscow. Ironically, Serge spent part of this time on tour in her native Spain. She found herself having to navigate the bureaucratic maze of the Stalinist regime and make crucial decisions, on her own, about her family and its future. The experience was at best trying and at worst humiliating, but it was too late to change course. The magnetic pull of the Soviet Union increased even as the wisdom of the decision came into question. Ultimately she, rather than her husband, put the final pieces into place.

Of course Serge had begun the process. His 1927 homecoming

tour was a success for all concerned: the administrators of the theaters and concert halls where he performed, his old friends from the St. Petersburg Conservatoire, the self-proclaimed admirers of his fashionable wife, and the bureaucrats at the top of the Stalinist power structure. The positive memories of the trip, on top of his childhood nostalgia and the frustrations with his career in the West, erased what he knew of the defects of the Soviet system—he continued to think he was immune to them.

He was deceived, but he also deceived himself. Proof comes from the letters he exchanged with the composer Nicolas Nabokov, whom he mentored. The two met through Serge Diaghilev and the Ballets Russes and remained in regular contact in the early 1930s, prior to Nabokov's move from France to the United States.

Most of the time they gossiped about rival Russians in Paris (Stravinsky was the subject of jealous anecdotes), but on one occasion they exchanged views on Lenin and Stalin. In 1931, Serge offered his friend a rambling account of the life and imminent death of the Russian Association of Proletarian Musicians, his chief Soviet antagonist in the late 1920s. He offered his comments in response to Nabokov's overview of musical life in Russia since Stalin's rise to power and the introduction of the Five-Year Plans for rapid industrial development. Nabokov despaired that "the music that's needed" in Russia "is not our music, but something cruder, simpler." While he and Serge might "sympathize" with the "inevitable political process," living there was impractical. "If I weren't a musician," Nabokov continued, "I think that I'd make haste to the USSR. And this is not a throwaway line, but serious; I've thought a lot about this recently." Instead, Nabokov rushed to the United States, eventually working for a division of the CIA.

Serge waxed poetic about his 1927 trip and predicted that the Soviet cultural scene would flourish under Stalin, rather than decline. In contrast to Nabokov, he believed that Stalin's attitude toward culture was becoming more rather than less liberal. For this reason, he advised Nabokov, "I think that matters on the musical front are not so bad, and I hope that if I'm successful in going to Moscow soon, it will be precisely because I'm a musician." The formal effort to bring him back, which was motivated by a Central Committee decree in 1925, took time to succeed. Lina also needed to be targeted, but the specific overtures to her did not begin until much later. She could resist the pressure; Serge could not.

Nevertheless, he hesitated about permanently relocating to the USSR until it became obvious that he could not expect to receive commission after commission for Soviet-themed operas, ballets, film scores, and theater music without a change of address. Yet there was reason to be skeptical of the apparent benevolence. Serge's second visit to the USSR dampened his enthusiasm about moving to Moscow because his ballet *Le pas d'acier* was hostilely criticized. It seemed to the Soviets that in its second act, Serge had mocked Stalinist industri- alization policies by representing the worker as a slave to factory ma- chines. Either he had done so intentionally or, equally damning, be- cause he did not appreciate the progress made by the proletariat under Lenin and Stalin. The critique followed a hearing of the score at the Bolshoy Theater and came from representatives of the Russian Asso- ciation of Proletarian Musicians. The tin-eared criticism of his music galled Serge, so he pointed out the fact that there was no relationship between his creative process and their blather about politics. By this time he had to know that in the USSR, music—like all the arts—was political capital.

But by 1934, he would have convinced Lina that to rescue his ca- reer as a theatrical composer, he needed to shift his sphere of op- erations from Paris to Moscow. She would benefit as a singer in the USSR, he assured her, and their children would receive a proper ed- ucation in Russian as well as English (they were promised admission into a special English-language school for the children of parents in- volved in foreign trade). The Soviet cultural scene was flourishing. With the restructuring of the curricula of the conservatories and repertoires of the theaters along ideological lines, musical standards had improved. The Russian Association of Proletarian Musicians had been mercifully disbanded, and a professional union had taken its place. Serge's interest in reaching a broader audience and his recently simplified melodic and harmonic language would, he believed, win the hearts of Party bosses. He would not repeat the miscalculation of raucous scores like *The Fiery Angel;* rather, he would re-immerse him- self in those Russian musical traditions that the Soviets sought to pre- serve.

France and the United States, in contrast, seemed to offer fewer opportunities for creative enrichment. Diaghilev, the impresario of the Ballets Russes and Serge's mentor in dance, succumbed in 1929 to furunculosis, a complication of diabetes. The loss was devastating to all who had known Diaghilev's genius. Serge had also learned the hard way that he could not rival Stravinsky—even if, as Serge liked to tease him, Stravinsky was eight years his senior. And although he arguably surpassed Rachmaninoff as a virtuoso, his music remained less popular than Rachmaninoff's (and less respected than Stravinsky's) in the West. Prokofiev's ambitions cast the die.

He was also the target of a relentless recruitment effort, in Paris as well as the USSR, by the agents of the NKID, or Narodnïy Komissariat Inostrannïkh Del (People's Commissariat of External Affairs). One of these agents was a dashing, roguish part-time cellist and part-time bureaucrat named Levon Atovmyan. In his memoirs, which he typed up in retirement, Atovmyan described being summoned to the NKID in 1932 and enlisted to convince Serge, among other leading Russian artists abroad, "of the merits of moving to the Soviet Union." Atovmyan recalled him responding to the appeal "very positively, but with the qualification that he was overloaded with concerts and would thus provide the date of his arrival a little later." There ensued an intense correspondence leading to a series of performances in the USSR. There was even, according to Atovmyan, the possibility of a private house in Moscow. Serge claimed he could not afford it.

At the same time, Serge's music began to be heard in Moscow more and more often—a seductive counterpoint to the declining interest he perceived in the West. In 1933, he composed his first film score, *Lieutenant Kizhe*, for a studio in Leningrad, and beginning in 1934, he found himself awash in commissions for theatrical compositions. These were accompanied by promises of opera and ballet stagings, though his friends cautioned him not to get his hopes up, since the situation in the Moscow and Leningrad theaters was fraught. He gushed about the friendliness and general success of his visits in 1933 and 1934 to Lina back in Paris. She shared his excitement: "Your letter is so interesting that I read it over and over again; the USSR tugs at me; here everything seems so listless." She wrote back with accounts of the marvelous treatment she had received at the Soviet embassy in Paris from Vladimir Potyomkin, the new ambassador.

Their specific thoughts about relocating are not preserved in their letters. They discussed the matter in person and sometimes—futilely —on the telephone. Twice in 1934 Serge called Lina from Leningrad, but the line was deliberately disconnected in the middle of the conversation. Operators made a point of allowing them to talk when the connection was poor, but interrupted them when it became clearer. Serge's words were drowned out by cackles of laughter from those listening in. When Lina caught on to the ruse, she resorted to subterfuge, talking around sensitive subjects and sprinkling her sentences with metaphors. Still she felt a chill when, on November 19, Serge telephoned her unexpectedly, only to hear the line go dead when he said, "V. F. asks why you . . ." "I can't hear you!" she yelled into the receiver, at which point the eavesdropper announced, "You were perfectly audible, I just decided to cut you off."

Such experiences made Lina uneasy, but Serge felt secure, extremely so. Perhaps he could musically bridge the West and the East; perhaps fame in the USSR—where Stravinsky and Rachmaninoff feared to tread—would enhance his celebrity in France and the United States. While Serge had Lina on the line, he managed to tell her that he had been feted at the Kremlin. Earlier, he heard secondhand that Stalin had referred to him as "*our* Prokofiev," meaning that he was a supporter of the Soviet cause, in solidarity with the people.

The endorsement engendered tragic confidence. Serge sold his wife on the future that had been sold to him, and she became a dutiful student of Soviet politics, reading transcripts of Stalin's speeches, the biography of the ruler published in 1931 by Sergey Dmitriyevsky (which she found "very lively and interesting, but it didn't entirely make sense, contradicting itself"), and the culture section of the Russian émigré newspaper *Posledniye novosti* (*Latest News*), to which she and Serge subscribed. These sources were balanced by reports about the menace of Adolf Hitler and the National Socialists in *Nouvelle Revue Française*. Lina read critically but quickly adopted a Soviet perspective, dismissing the grimmer news reports from the USSR as reflecting a Western bias. When word broke of the assassination of the Leningrad Communist Party boss Sergey Kirov and the mass arrests that followed, Lina seemed more sympathetic than fearful. "How sorrowful it's all become in the USSR. Here the emigrant papers write the devil knows what. If only it quickly resolves for the better."

Lina became a regular visitor at the Soviet embassy in Paris, taking in concerts of Russian and Soviet music, lectures, and films. She saw the musical comedy *Vesyolïye rebyata* (*The Happy-Go-Lucky Guys*) but found the antics a little too banal, and she watched pseudo-propagandistic fare about winter sports in Leningrad and a Stalin-hosted reception of representatives from the Turkmen Republic on the tenth anniversary of its absorption into the USSR. The receptions held on the anniversaries of the Revolution glittered beyond compare. She raised her glass in exclusive company: the industrialist André-Gustave Citroën, the French socialist politician Pierre Cot, the *grand écrivain* André Gide, Sigmund Freud's English nephew Sam, and leftist Americans were all there. Iconoclastic French artists turned up, as did the Soviet theater directors Alexander Tairov and Vsevolod Meyerhold (Serge collaborated with both of them and lauded their talent; Lina recognized their rivalry). Hundreds of people attended these gatherings, eager to share in an atmosphere of intense political intrigue.

The ambassador's wife, Mariya Potyomkina, summoned Lina to teas and luncheons, seating her beside the ambassador himself and reacquainting her with Jacques Sadoul, the French correspondent for *Pravda*, and the new VOKS director Alexander Arosev, whom she and Serge had met before at the opera in Prague. (That Arosev, a politician of impeccable credentials, felt the post was beneath him did not come across in the encounter.) The lower-level officials Lina met at the embassy made a less positive impression, with their dull eyes, pallid faces, and stiff mannerisms. Some of the people she met expressed affection for old-world Paris, but most were keen to present themselves as bona fide revolutionaries. Topics of conversation included the heroic reconstruction of Moscow, the glories of collectivism, and the need for the global defense of socialism in response to Hitler. The rise of the Popular Front in Spain came up. Lina relished it all.

She was glad to be rescued from the domestic routines that had drained her life of glamour. Tending to Serge's affairs and to their two boys was, Lina pretended to believe, the reason her career had stalled. Her performances at the American Women's Club in Paris could not compete with what Vera Janacopoulos and Nina Koshetz had achieved, and she suffered from professional jealousy if not personal regret. She toured with her husband in 1931, appearing in Paris,

Vienna, Budapest, and Bucharest. Her appearance on March 27 of that year, in the ornate domed Atenelui Român (Romanian Athenaeum), featured her entire current repertoire—from a Spanish folksong her father had taught her to the Russian folksongs Serge arranged, bundled with selections by Glinka, Musorgsky, and Stravinsky. To her dismay, the positive reviews focused only on her husband. She was panned. "The thing about last night's concert that defies understanding," one critic fumed, "is why the famous guest burdened such an extensive program with the lamentable vocal divertissement of Madame Llubera, who ruined dozens of beautiful tunes, managing to sing them not only without any voice but a quarter-tone low as well." The reviewer allowed that Serge's fame was such that he could transcend "such an astonishing whim."

Lina declined to remember the critique, recalling, to the contrary, that "the concert was such a success" that she was invited to dinner at the Bucharest Military Club, "and I had such success with all those military men that Serge was very much annoyed." In this context, she elaborated, he could become as disagreeable as the mythological three-headed beast Cerberus. One of the officers who danced with her promised to send some Romanian folksongs to Paris. Serge stuffed them in a closet, refusing to even look at them. "Those are from your military admirer," he said, clearly chafed.

Despite the woeful reviews and flirtatious behavior, Serge continued to arrange joint performances with his wife. Perhaps he wanted to express his devotion to her, perhaps keep her occupied. The programs often included the French-language version of his 1914 narrative song *The Ugly Duckling*. He orchestrated the same work in 1932, and Lina wanted to be the first to perform it in the major cities of Europe. (The piano-vocal version had long been championed by Janacopoulos, Koshetz, Zoya Lodiy, and others.) Serge secured the Paris premiere for his wife with a small orchestra called La Serenade. The dress rehearsal went well, but during the actual premiere, on the evening of May 19, 1932, Lina suffered an attack of nerves and lost her confidence, her voice dropping below the threshold of audibility. Her husband noted the snickering of Parisian snobs in the audience; the best he could say of the performance was that Lina looked radiant on stage, her white dress matching the lilies she was brought at the end.

Broadcasts of her performances were heard in Warsaw and

Prague, the former a success (despite a doddering accompanist), the latter a disappointment that she hoped had not been transmitted to the USSR. Her latest teacher in Paris, the Basque transplant Alberti de Gorostiaga, complimented her technique but questioned her overall commitment and tested her patience. He assigned her an aria from Puccini's *La bohème*, working on her breathing and phonation for several months in 1934. She tired of the aria, even though she recognized that Gorostiaga's perfectionism would prepare her well for the audition for a staging of *La bohème* in Bordeaux. Domestic affairs and the usual spate of colds forced her to change her mind about the audition. Lessons were thereafter intermittent, and Lina felt abandoned when, in the spring of 1935, Gorostiaga relocated to Hollywood. There he worked with his prize pupil, the remarkably gifted French-American coloratura Lily Pons, on the film *I Dream Too Much*. Later, Pons would appear in two other films, *That Girl from Paris* and *Hitting a New High*. She would sing before huge crowds (175,000 in Chicago's Grant Park in 1937) and break the hearts of well-heeled suitors, and her image would be splashed across the pages of fashion magazines. Lina had once imagined such a life for herself.

She was now bathetically counting on performance opportunities in Moscow, and struggled to learn the kind of folksong-derived repertoire that, Serge assured her, would meet with approval from Stalinist cultural officials. She would have preferred to concentrate on arias by Musorgsky, Tchaikovsky, and Rimsky-Korsakov, but her Russian diction needed to improve. And the Soviet arias she asked Serge to send were slow to arrive. Deferring to her husband, she began to learn a suite of folksongs gathered in the Kirghiz Soviet Socialist Republic by Alexander Zatayevich, who made a name for himself as an ethnographer, arranging fifteen hundred tunes from Kirghizstan and Kazakhstan. Some of the melodies lacked texts and needed to be vocalized on a single vowel. Lina found them nettlesome, but Serge, thinking ahead, encouraged her to persevere. Lina complained that the harmonies sounded dumb. Flummoxed, she defaulted to two easier works: "Shepherd's Song of Georgia," by the Georgian composer Azmaiparachvili, and "Lullaby of Bashkiria," by Léon Schwarz, a twenty-two-year-old recent graduate of the Moscow Conservatoire. Serge had met both composers in the fall of 1933 in Moscow, and as a comradely service to the head of the composition division of the Conservatoire had given them and a few other students lessons. Now he was encouraging his wife to promote their works. Lina's debut as a supposed folk-music specialist came on January 5, 1934, in Rome, in a recital at the Accademia Nazionale di Santa Cecilia, with her husband accompanying. The primarily French-language program was a great success, as was a related program broadcast on the radio four months later, though the unidentified announcer on the unidentified station bungled his descriptions of the folksongs and mispronounced Lina's husband's name as "Protopief."

As part of the now two-pronged recruitment effort, Serge was invited to the USSR in March 1935 to present seven concerts in eight days on the far side of the Urals in Siberia. He performed in factories as part of educational outreach programs for laborers. The schedule was "a little too much," he deadpanned in a letter to the Christian Scientist Lawrence Creath Ammons, though he admitted that "there are many interesting things to be seen." Serge admired the massive smelting furnaces and housing developments that featured "large buildings trying to scrape the skies," obliterating the "squat and squalid" structures of the past.

Lina heard little from him during this period and suffered through his silence that summer, which he spent on the grounds of the estate of Polenovo, the summer retreat of the artists of the Bolshoy Theater. The private accommodations at Polenovo had been offered to him by the Bolshoy's business manager, a former Red Army official named Vladimir Mutnïkh, who had contracted Serge to compose the ballet *Romeo and Juliet.* The surrounding fields, forest, and river proved inspiring, and the recreation—morning swimming and raft diving in the Oka, tennis and occasional games of catch with the dancers staying at the estate, a chess match or stroll in the evening—calmed the composer's nerves.

The soup and meat on the menu were dubious, however, and salads and vegetables were scarce. Though he was pampered, elsewhere on the grounds up to three adults slept in a single room, and children ran around unsupervised. In his letters to Lina, Serge praised the local berries, along with the milk and curds that could be obtained from the cleaning lady. He reassured her that the crowds would thin by the time she and the children arrived in September and advertised the therapeutic benefits of the glass-enclosed bathhouse, which had just been refurbished. And there were two accompanists in residence who would be pleased to work with her, he promised.

Work on *Romeo and Juliet* proceeded at a Mozartean clip. Serge pushed into the third of the four acts of the ballet while also working on a violin concerto, a cycle of piano pieces for children, and an Olympic-style march for Soviet athletes. He was amazed at his own powers of invention. Each day, his muse would find him working at a Blüthner piano in a log hut at the end of the forest, overlooking the river. Besides Mutnïkh and the artists of the Bolshoy, his neighbors included Dmitri Shostakovich, who was now the leading Soviet composer, a virtuoso at mixing popular and serious musical styles and a brilliant musical satirist. He had three propagandistic symphonies to his credit and three ballets on subjects ripped from the Soviet headlines. The sheer macabre daring of his two completed operas (*The Nose* and *The Lady Macbeth of the Mtsensk District*) suggested a future in that genre on a par with Richard Strauss. Shostakovich might not have had Serge's melodic talent, but he had greater stylistic breadth and an even more capacious imagination. He was a force to be reckoned with, but Serge did not perceive him as a rival, since they came from such different worlds and, at the time, had opposing creative methods. Compared to the twenty-eight-year-old Shostakovich, an iconoclast who theatricalized symphonies and cinematized operas, the forty-four-year-old Prokofiev was a captive of tradition. At Polenovo, they did not talk shop but played volleyball together.

Lina remained in Paris, dealing with her mother and children; the renewal and extension of her French residence permit, or *carte d'identité*; the search for another, less expensive apartment that could both house her mother and serve as an anchor in Paris after the relocation to Moscow; the selling of Serge's latest automobile (the Chevrolet); the termination of the lease on its garage; and taxes. She found it enervating to socialize; her friends and acquaintances who had decided to remain in Paris for the summer were obsessed with the gravely depressed economy and political instability. Her mother's mood swings exhausted her at home. Lina lost her spiritual counsel when Ammons went for the summer to Lugano. The departure of her teacher and accompanist, moreover, deprived her of the chance to prepare for the promised engagements in Moscow. Not that there was any time to practice. Worst of all, her body had once again let her down. Her ears and nose were blocked, a condition that a specialist attributed to swollen glands and poor diet. He recommended a minor operation, to be followed by a protracted convalescence. Lina mulled it over but ultimately declined the surgery.

Her frustration was compounded by Serge's delay in sending directions to Polenovo. If she traveled as she planned, with "acquaintances of acquaintances" by steamer across the Baltic Sea, how would she get from Leningrad to Moscow? Could Serge arrange a train coupe for her and the children? And how would she get from Moscow to Tarusa, the village across the river from Polenovo? Instead of providing the crucial details, he reported that he was leaving for another tour—this time to the Caucasus (Baku and Tbilisi).

"I can't tell you how lonesome I am for you," she wrote to him despairingly on July 25, 1935, in both English and Russian. "I can't express my keen desire to see you." Her entreaty worked, at least this time. Two days later, Serge wrote a detailed letter containing the necessary information, with the options worked out for travel either through Finland or Poland into the USSR, along with the names of whom to contact where for accommodation, if need be, and assistance with the children and the luggage. He advised her to travel to Moscow by train (Svyatoslav, then eleven, remembered pillow fights and games of hide-and-seek with his brother, age seven, in a deserted first-class carriage), then head to the Bolshoy Theater administrative offices to obtain a travel permit to Polenovo. He would also leave a check for local expenses at the offices of the All-Union Radio Committee at 17 Gorky Street. She should insist on chauffeured transport by car, not bus or truck, to Tarusa.

Before she packed for the trip, Lina was hosted one last time at the Soviet embassy in Paris by Ambassador Potyomkin and his wife. Other guests included the director Tairov, the actress Alicia Koonen (Tairov's leading lady and also his wife), and the writer and journalist Ilya Ehrenburg—all persistent, longtime advocates of the Prokofievs' permanent relocation to the USSR. On July 31, she left, tucking into a suitcase the opera arias that she planned to perform on Soviet radio. She also brought along the orchestral score of *The Ugly Duck-ling*. After her arrival, the family spent just thirty-six hours together before Serge left for the Caucasus for three weeks. Lina's mood was understandably sour; they had been apart for three months, and now here she was in Russia, on her own again. She complained in a tele-gram sent to her husband in Baku, Azerbaijan. "Bath house a prison cell. Children out of control. Exhausted. Kisses. Hurry back."

She made it through the summer and, with the promise of being able to perform on Soviet radio, remained in Russia deep into the winter. While Serge's schedule required him to travel back to Paris with the children at the end of October, she checked into the Hotel National in the center of Moscow and entered the maelstrom of So-viet life. She wrote to him about her upcoming broadcasts and reper-toire, the first of them a month after her thirty-eighth birthday. On November 21 at 8:20 P.M., she was asked to sing various folksong ar-rangements on the domestic- and foreign-broadcast Komintern sta-tion, one of the most powerful frequencies in the world; on Novem-ber 30 at 12:15 P.M. on the same station, she was assigned the dreaded textless Kirghiz melodies. Lina resisted, fretting that the music was not serious enough—it was beneath her operatic training—but she had no choice in the matter. The Radio Committee expected her to demonstrate a commitment to folklore-inspired populism, the diktat of the day, and thus to show that the stylish socialite from Paris could be a good Communist.

To make matters worse, the program she herself wanted to sing on a concert scheduled for November 23 (on another, weaker station) came in for withering critique. Lina learned that her choice of rep-ertoire, which included selections from Wagner's *Lohengrin* and Puc-cini's *Turandot*, had been judged uninteresting—a crashing bore, in fact. She offered to revamp it. The Wagner could go, and the Puccini could be performed between arias by Manuel de Falla (a composer from her Spanish "homeland") and Gabriel Fauré. There was also room for Stravinsky's "Rosyanka" ("The Dew Song"), but she felt that the range was too high. In the run-up to the broadcasts she gave a private Moscow recital of excerpts from Mozart's *Marriage of Figaro* and Debussy's *Martyrdom of St. Sebastian*. The latter, she informed Serge, "had big success with the ladies."

But the broadcasts themselves were disappointing, a serious professional setback that left her feeling foolish. A lot had gone wrong: The logistical arrangements with the Radio Committee were erratic, subject to sudden change; furthermore, the contract came late and the payment was only half of what she had been promised—something she learned only when she turned up at the Sberkassa (Savings Bank) to collect it. The piano she needed also arrived at the last minute, and she had to change hotel rooms to accommodate it. Her first accompanist abandoned her, and his replacement had struggled with sight-reading. The conductor of the orchestra, Alexander Gauk, had neither the desire nor the time to rehearse.

Succumbing to the stress of the situation, Lina took ill with a head cold, but there were no homeopathic remedies (the only kind allowed by Christian Science) to be found to treat it. She pulled herself together as best she could since postponing the performance was out of the question. But her singing fell short of her own expectations. Sympathizers blamed the Radio Committee for the fiasco—"who needs folklore, especially that kind?"—but admitted, painfully, that she sang better in rehearsal. It was also regrettable that she had not been able to perform *The Ugly Duckling*.

Her second outing was no more successful. Perhaps to her benefit, the broadcast signal was weak, compromised by a high-pitched whine, so that even those people with good sets had trouble hearing her. For obvious reasons, the broadcast at the end of November was hurriedly canceled, bumped from the schedule. Perhaps it would happen in January, Lina was told. Contact with the staff of the Radio Committee thereafter ceased—she was even refused a pass into the Gorky Street building—and when she ran into Gauk he avoided her gaze. Her plan to perform *The Ugly Duckling* under his baton went nowhere. Over the phone she talked with Serge about the fiasco, but their conversation was cut short by terrible reception and the overworked Moscow telephone eavesdroppers. She wrote excruciating, belabored letters to him, detailing her disappointment in herself, Gauk, and the Radio Committee. "Well that's it then," she declared with wounded pride, "*basta!*"

Serge wrote to her from Casablanca on December 5: "It'd been so long since I'd heard from you and I was concerned," he offered, having deduced the worst about her experiences with Soviet radio. Of the cancellation of the November 30 broadcast and the fiasco of the one before, he gently suggested that "it does happen, and it's insulting." He thought it a great shame that she missed the chance to display her "superior vocal technique" for the locals. (She did indeed have strong technique, but the quality of her voice evidently did not match it and stage fright continued to get the best of her.) "But concerning Radio, the people there are remarkable, good-hearted in one sense, absurd in another," he concluded. Lina was flabbergasted. "They're not remarkable people but detestable," she protested, "not absurd but uncouth, and everyone knows it's a madhouse in total chaos." She was right.

It remains unclear whether any of her performances were recorded. If so, the tapes would have been destroyed after her arrest in 1948, an act of official amnesia.

Though Lina would be unable to make a name for herself as a Soviet musician, she felt she could help her husband make his. His talent was writing a score, hers was working a room. Lina took pride in her ability to read a situation and could always count on her cosmopolitan charm. Her disappointment over the Radio Committee debacle was eased by the high-profile diplomatic receptions where she not only assumed the role of her husband's attaché, but also effortlessly held her own.

Among the more memorable events was a "cocktail" hosted by Americans and attended by, among others, the eminent Soviet writers Mikhaíl Bulgakov and Leonid Leonov—the latter greatly admired by Serge. Lina was also privy to the backstage and entr'acte intrigues of the Bolshoy Theater. She learned, for example, that Shostakovich's ballet *Svetlïy ruchey* (*The Limpid Stream*) had disappointed cultural officials. Everyone expected more from the composer, though what "more" meant was never quite articulated. She confined her own critique to the antics-filled plot—a comedy of collective farm life, with a dancing harvester machine, a bumbling crop inspector, a dog on a bicycle, and amorous intrigues—and what she considered a tasteless excess of musical reprises.

Lina also picked up on the tension between Mutnïkh, the official who had commissioned *Romeo and Juliet* for the Bolshoy, and Sergey Radlov, the iconoclastic director with whom Serge had drafted the scenario. (Radlov's wife, Anna, noted snags in getting contracts signed.) Mutnïkh, however, reassured her that Serge's ballet, when performed, would be a great cause for celebration.

With her performances canceled, Lina had more time on her hands than she would have liked, but still she was busy running errands for her husband's benefit. (At the time, he was on an exhausting tour with the violinist Robert Soëtens, in Spain, Portugal, and Northern Africa — thirteen concerts in as many days.) She was asked by students at the Moscow Conservatoire to sing at a benefit; she wanted to decline, but Serge advised her that the tradition in Moscow among professionals was never to refuse an invitation from students. Besides, she needed the boost. Those English-language novels she managed to acquire might keep her company at night, he gently chided her, but they did nothing to improve her spirits.

Also heeding Serge's counsel, she kept up the pressure on his contacts for an apartment and was promised that she would soon be able to consider the options. Lina later incoherently remembered befriending someone whose husband worked in the upper ranks of the government, a woman with an "enticing voice, feline, purring people into agreement." She promised to secure housing for the Prokofievs. In exchange, and at the woman's repeated request, Lina gave her the 78s that she had with her, a collection of recordings of Italian opera arias. Lina was later told that these went to the woman's husband, who passed them on to the supreme Soviet leader, Stalin himself, purportedly a great opera lover. The 78s were never returned, and her friend's husband ended up in prison.

At first, it seemed that the Prokofievs would be given a flat on the Arbat, now a cluttered pedestrian street in the city. But the offer was rescinded as soon as it was made. Instead Lina heard through her persuasive friend about an apartment in a soon-to-be-finished building intended for luminaries in the arts and sciences. She began shopping for furniture, which proved frustrating, a modest lesson in the challenges that average Soviets confronted. Apartments were scarce, and likewise the goods to fill them.

No expense, however, was spared on the marble pillars and gilt embellishments of the Moscow Metro, whose first thirteen stations had just opened. The government similarly lavished funds on celebrating the anniversary of the Revolution on November 7. At the

National Hotel, Lina enjoyed a front-row seat. The central avenue, Gorky Street, had been asphalted just in time for the festivities, and since the National stood across from the Kremlin and the newly paved Manezh (Equestrian) Square, she could not avoid being swept up in the holiday. "I saw part of the parade, which was much smaller than the one on the 1st of May. But even so, after the marchers I saw endless echelons. They passed by from 12 to 5, each with its own band and all right in front of my eyes. The illuminations this year were amazing, the new buildings all lit up, the procession to Sverd-lov Square—home to the Bolshoy—like an electrified waterfall, the stars on the Kremlin towers, Red Square, in general the city all splen-didly decked out."

After the parade, and once the streets around the hotel had been reopened, Lina made coffee in her room for Alexander Afinogenov and his American Communist wife, Jenny Marling. The two of them were almost frozen from standing outside all day. That evening, Lina attended a large party in a smoke-filled room hosted by the recently appointed people's commissar (minister) of foreign affairs, Maksim Litvinov. His British wife, Ivy Low, asked about Serge; Lina brought up the matter of the apartment. It looked as if they would finally be given a home in early February, and Serge advised Lina to stay in the city to attend to logistics. He joined her in Moscow to ring in the New Year but then left on another tour, this time in northern Europe. As January 1936 passed into February, the apartment did not materi-alize. Lina returned to Paris, her children, and her mother, bearing the Soviet passport that had been issued to her on January 26.

Meanwhile, the entire Soviet musical world was thrown into tur-moil by a pair of unsigned editorials in *Pravda*, the newspaper of the Communist Central Committee. The first of these editorials attacked Shostakovich's opera *The Lady Macbeth of the Mtsensk District*, which had enjoyed enormous success both in Russia and abroad, but which had been seen—and rejected—by Stalin. He neither took to its musi-cal representations of rape and murder, nor to the outrageous produc-tion that had been mounted at a branch theater of the Bolshoy. The second editorial upbraided Shostakovich for the ideological deficien-cies of his ballet *The Limpid Stream*. The scandal, an infamous episode in the annals of Soviet music, did not directly affect Serge, but it cast a pall over musical life that he should have recognized as a grave threat to his career plans. Shostakovich's ideological correction stemmed from a top-down reconfiguring of the Stalinist cultural establishment and the imposition of oppressive ideological guidelines on the arts. Music needed to be drained of discord, the harmonies brightened, and melodies made cheerier. The classics of the Russian tradition needed to be honored, not satirized. Insofar as Serge understood the conservative new regulations, he imagined that his self-imposed aesthetic of "New Simplicity"—the sophisticated tunefulness to which he began to aspire in the mid-1920s—would accord with them.

Serge's specific reaction to Shostakovich's troubles remains unclear; Lina, however, documented hers in letters sent from Paris to her husband, who was concertizing in Budapest, Prague, Sofia, and Warsaw. She blanched at what she read in *Pravda*, and expressed her alarm—knowing all the while that it was too late to reconsider their plans. Of the ongoing turmoil in the Soviet press, Lina declared, "The musical idiots and cretins" in Moscow "have suddenly used the opportunity to put forth their unwanted opinions . . . while everyone else is silent." The antimodern, anti-Western Soviet rabble who had given Serge such grief over *Le pas d'acier* remained in control of cultural affairs—even though, just months before, it seemed that they had been silenced. The establishment of the professional Union of Soviet Composers had not, in the end, removed the crass aesthetic police from the scene. To the contrary, it had given them stable employment. Ideologues and second-tier composers with axes to grind had declared war on the cultural elite, and no composer was, in their book, more elite, and more elitist, than the cosmopolitan Prokofiev. The fight among the lesser musicians in Moscow, Lina wrote to her husband, "to be the one who is showing the new way" only reflected their ignorance. The cabal that had once attacked him—and that now had its sights trained on the younger Shostakovich—evinced amazing rhetorical skills (the language of the *Pravda* editorials is nothing if not colorful) but showed no creative insight.

Since Lina did not find the reports in the newspapers altogether credible, she counted on her husband to form his own opinion of the situation when his tour had ended and he was back in Moscow. But she was worried. "Be a little more careful," she warned him before adding, in English, "Perhaps you better destroy this letter." Once again Lina was right. She had a dark intuition about the people running cultural affairs in Moscow and was not alone in her concerns. An émigré Russian friend, the publisher Pierre Souvtchinsky, articulated his resistance to all things Soviet by advising her to rethink the decision to relocate. "Don't rush with the furniture," he said, with reference to her domestic shopping spree. It was a huge problem that she and Serge were trying to solve the most important matters in their lives by mail and telephone rather than in person.

Going against her instincts, she allowed herself to be convinced by the Soviet operatives who surrounded her that the crisis would not trouble them in the slightest; it was all just a matter of complex internal politics. Her anxieties were further assuaged by an evening spent with the Soviet ambassador to Paris and his charming wife, the Potyomkins. Somehow she left the encounter convinced that if the glow was momentarily dampened, the future remained bright. She even imagined that the scandal was not a threat to Serge, but an opportunity. Now it was her turn to be delusional: "It seems to me that in all of this drama you can play a very important role, but only, of course, with great tact, and without creating any unnecessary enemies." But from personal experience, Lina knew that for all his phenomenal skill in music, her husband altogether lacked that tact.

Things were now moving very fast. Lina's *carte d'identité* was set to expire, the lease at their current Paris abode (5, rue Valentin Haüy) was up, and decisions needed to be made about the schooling of Svyatoslav and Oleg. Would Svyatoslav remain behind in Paris through the summer, or would he travel to Moscow in the spring? And how would she handle the unexpected offer, from Serge Moreux, of a pair of broadcasts on Parisian Radio Cité, one including *The Ugly Duckling*? For that, she would need vocal coaching from Gorostiaga, but how? And when? Her mother was in hysterics, and she didn't have a minute to herself in the apartment. As a temporary escape, she took her sons to the movies. They saw *The Personal History, Adventures, Experience, and Observation of David Copperfield the Younger* on Svyatoslav's birthday. But the tale of the plucky itinerant orphan frightened Oleg, and he closed his eyes, asking his mother, "When's it over?"

To alleviate her stress Lina visited Ammons for spiritual counseling. Then she started to pack, obsessively listing and relisting the designer clothes and cosmetics that she planned to ship to Moscow, types of furniture she wanted Serge to acquire in or en route to Moscow, and the material she thought she should store. Curtains were needed, but she didn't know the width and height of the windows in the apartment, since it had yet to be assigned or even, she knew, fully built.

Still she tried to prepare, tried to shake off her worries by cleaning and packing. Her mother and the boys were shooed off to see an arctic adventure movie (*L'Expédition Byrd au Pôle Sud*) as she sorted through the stacks of books and papers in the living room, dining room, and what she called the "flirting corner" of the Valentin Haüy apartment. She struggled with decisions to store or ship the French novels by Colette, Farrère, Maurois, and others; the English detective tales and the children's old textbooks; the bridge table; the city maps and travel guides; the postcards and publicity photographs—and on and on. She could not, as she hoped, go through the drawers in his desk because he forgot to leave her the key. "How many evening dresses do I have a right to take with me when I go?" she asked him —more than once—in English.

Lina wanted to ship their sofa to Moscow, but not before having it reupholstered. Her tut-tutting about its condition suggested, on the one hand, the delicate concerns of a Parisian woman of taste, and on the other, an unwillingness to come to terms with the place to which she was relocating. She would need ten meters of fabric in *style rustique* for the divan. If reupholstering was impractical, then *une autre suite d'ameublement* would have to be shipped east. Of course she wasn't really concerned about the divan. She wanted to banish her worries, and they ended up settling on the sofa.

Serge was fundamentally uninterested in domestic issues and swatted away Lina's questions about the move—even the critical ones —during his tour in eastern Europe. She longed for him, needed his help, tried to convince him to respond with some words of advice or just plain comfort. "I wish I had thought of all this while you were here," she lamented. "It would have been so simple to ask you in person—but there was so little time. I wish I had someone to help me with some things. Mémé is here, of course. I don't pay attention to her grumbling, but sometimes she drives me nearly crazy—a lesson in patience."

Then, with a vague reference to Ammons's counseling not to

give in to such negative thoughts and feelings, she added, "Every day something new with the children: They have worms, nerves, bad eyes and what not, so I must deny and deny." Serge told her to live in the present—each hour is precious, he wrote—but she could not help thinking ahead, especially when her entire family depended on her to make decisions about a future she could not imagine. She had visited, developed friendships, enjoyed the attention lavished on her on her husband's behalf, but she had just been a guest of the Soviet Union, not a resident. Being on stage, she knew, was much different than sitting in the audience.

Olga had entertained the idea of traveling to the USSR just before Juan's death from a stroke in the spring of 1935, both to visit her daughter and grandchildren in the capital and to seek out distant relatives elsewhere in Russia and Ukraine. For months Juan had been confined to bed, partially paralyzed and as helpless as a baby; his death was not unexpected but went unreported in Lina's extremely fragmented recollections of that year. Serge felt that it would be "much more interesting" for Olga to visit Moscow than return to friends in New York or linger in Paris. Actually he was motivated by self-interest: the children would need a nanny in Moscow, especially if Lina somehow managed to establish herself as a singer there. (He pledged to secure additional engagements for her through the Radio Committee.) The idea of bringing Olga went unrealized, however, because the Soviet embassy in Paris made securing the required travel papers too onerous. Olga carried a Spanish passport, and Spain had not established diplomatic relations with the USSR.

Olga would remain in Paris, which meant that her daughter needed to secure housing for her. Lina also thought to preserve a place for herself there, keeping a foot in western Europe irrespective of the ever-increasing political uncertainties. She struck a bargain with her husband: if things did not succeed for either of them in Moscow, if, for whatever reason, they soured on it, they would return to France. He agreed. And so, after a taxing search in unglamorous neighborhoods, she signed an agreement for a small apartment at 14, rue du Dr. Roux, in the same arrondissement—the fifteenth—as their home on Valentin Haüy.

Meanwhile, Serge was commissioned for one prestigious score after another. Besides the *Romeo and Juliet* project for the Bolshoy Theater and Mutnïkh, there was the massive *Cantata for the Twentieth Anniversary of October* for the Radio Committee, *Peter and the Wolf* for the Moscow Children's Theater, incidental music to theatrical productions of the Pushkin classics *Boris Godunov* and *Eugene Onegin*, and the score for a partially colored film version of the same writer's *Queen of Spades*. These projects made Serge feel euphoric, as if he could conquer time and space.

That feeling did not provide him with a place to live in Moscow, however. The apartment had not materialized, and like Lina before him, he grew tired of life at the National Hotel. He was offered a generous residence in the center of Moscow at Dom kompozitorov (House of Composers), but he decided that he did not want to live with other, lesser composers as neighbors. The building had not been soundproofed, he learned, and he couldn't imagine trying to compose a melody while hearing a different one from the adjacent flat. He instead petitioned for housing in a building partly operated by the Komitet po delam iskusstv (Committee on Arts Affairs), in a neighborhood under rapid development near the Kursk train station. The prestige of *Romeo and Juliet* would give him some leverage, he assumed, and his international reputation much more.

On April 8, 1936, Serge expressed his frustration about the apartment runaround in a postcard to his mother-in-law—one that featured an image of an imposing neo-constructivist edifice similar to the one in which he expected to live. "Each morning I sit by the telephone waiting word that I've received my apartment, but each time the pleasure is put off." Olga did not respond, having chosen silence and the occasional life-threatening illness as forms of protest against the move.

But by this point it was inevitable, and the Prokofievs had filed their intention of leaving Paris with the Préfecture de Police. Lina arrived in Moscow with Svyatoslav and Oleg in the middle of May, expecting that the apartment would be ready. It was not. Serge dispatched an indignant letter of complaint to the chairman of the Executive Committee of Mossovet, the Office of the Mayor. Finally, in late June, the family was assigned an apartment at 14/16 Zemlyanoy val, an eight-story building with thirteen entrances, an inner courtyard, thick stucco-on-brick walls, narrow recessed windows, and angular parquet flooring. (In 1938, the street would be renamed

Chkalov, in honor of a pilot, Valeriy Chkalov, who completed a re-cord-breaking flight from the Soviet Union to the United States over the North Pole.) Two apartments occupied each landing, one bigger than the other. Anyone who was anyone wanted to be in the build-ing, Lina recalled—prominent Soviet actors and writers, people con-nected to the People's Commissars, foreign engineers helping to build hydroelectric dams. She was told that their apartment would be on the fourth floor, but then it was taken away, given instead to the string-pulling daughter of a senior military officer, "some big hero."

The family ended up in apartment 14, on the third floor of the tenth entrance. It was available as of July 1, 1936. On that Wednesday, the newspapers announced a new train service from Belarus Station. It reduced the travel time from Moscow to Paris from fifty-seven to forty-three hours. The square in front of the station was being as-phalted. There was also an announcement of a public meeting on the pace of the construction of housing and schools in the city, and front-page letters selected from children describing their excitement at the opening of the Moscow City House of Pioneers named after Stalin. The advertised amusements at Gorky Park included roller-coaster rides and 150-kilometer-per-hour motorcycle races.

The apartment had four rooms, totaling sixty square meters; the two biggest served as the living room and children's bedroom. While not as large as 5, Valentin Haüy, it was impressive enough to be show-cased to tourists from England, whom the Prokofievs invited inside to observe the inadequate cupboard space. Construction around the Kursk train station made the neighborhood unbearably noisy and dusty at first. (Happily, Polenovo would provide the children with another tranquil summer.) Outfitting the apartment with fuses, taps, and doorknobs took several months, eclipsing worries about the con-dition of the imported sofa. Lina had arranged for eleven crates of clothes and small household items to be shipped in June from Paris and fretted about the levies that might be imposed on them at the So-viet border. Serge received a piano as a gift from the August Förster firm of Löbau, Saxony, in hopes that he would advertise the instru-ment to colleagues in the Soviet Union. It fell to Lina to schedule its transport from Paris to Moscow, an additional headache.

To Serge's Soviet handlers, Lina was enticingly attractive but ir-ritatingly demanding, perhaps overindulged by Paris and altogether unprepared for the relative primitiveness of the Soviet system, which did not prioritize material comfort. She did not cook, and she certainly had no intention of maintaining the apartment on her own. Hiring a *domrabotnitsa* (female domestic worker) from a local *profsoyuz* (trade union) became a pressing concern—so much so that Lina recalled inviting a stranger, a homeless woman she met on a train who asked her if she could sleep in the corridor of their building, to do the job.

The word *servant* was outlawed in the Soviet Union, which, rhetorically at least, aspired to classlessness. Bewildered by the baroque intricacies of everything associated with the apartment, Serge arranged to hire a housekeeper named Ustina Bazhan from Sontsovka, Ukraine, the village where he was born. He remembered her from his paradisiacal childhood, and it appears that she was with the family in Moscow for a year or so, perhaps semi-legally registering with the authorities as a distant relative. There were several other nannies, remembered only by their abbreviated first names or patronymics: Nika was one of them; a much-maligned Stepanovna another. And there was a good-humored older woman from Siberia who went back to her village during the war, but not before helping herself to the pantry. Lina did not mind. Oleg only remembered his mother being helped by a young woman from western Russia, the area around Smolensk and the Dnieper River. Her name was Frosya. The authorities mobilized her for the Metrostroy, the construction of the subway system, but still she came to clean. Oleg recalled Frosya having a very hard time pronouncing the word *composer*—it came out nasally as "cam-pan-zer." Here and at school, where his teachers liked to refer to him not by name but as the cam-pan-zer's son, Oleg sensed disdain for the family's foreignness.

As of the extremely hot, parched summer of 1936 (August broke a record), the Prokofievs had some semblance of a home in Moscow. They assembled most, if not all, of the comforts of life in Paris—though that life, like the city itself, had never had the radiance the composer's career implied it should.

Now that they were together, no longer crossing paths intermittently, an unavoidable question arose: whether Lina and Serge's marriage could survive each other's constant presence. It took some time to answer, since for the first two years as a permanent Moscow resident, Serge maintained his international career, concertizing throughout Europe, the United States, and the USSR. Moscow had simply taken the place of Paris as a mailing address. Yet foreign travel became more and more problematic, and after a final tour abroad in 1938, it proved impossible. Now bonded to a single place—an unforgiving place—as much as to each other, Lina and Serge's relationship began to unravel.

Serge Prokofiev at the Hotel Wellington, New York City, October or November 1918, before his major American debut at Aeolian Hall. The composer had arrived in the United States from Russia the previous August and was scrambling to secure performance opportunities.

The future Mrs. Prokofiev, convalescing from appendicitis at a small clinic in Paris, March 1921. Her voice teacher, the famous dramatic soprano Félia Litvinne, brought her one of these bouquets; another came from Serge.

Lina with her son, Svyatoslav, at the apartment the Prokofievs rented on 5, rue Charles Dickens, two or three weeks after his birth on February 27, 1924.

The elegant Parisian in a photograph taken by Pyotr Shumov at his Montparnasse studio, 1924.

Lina and Serge, during the composer's homecoming tour of Soviet Russia and Ukraine, late January through late March 1927. The photograph was taken in Moscow toward the end of the trip, which the couple found stimulating but exhausting.

Lina, Serge, and Svyatoslav Prokofiev in the French Alps, September 1928. Lina is expecting their second child, Oleg.

Svyatoslav and Oleg returning to Paris from Moscow, October 1935. A companion photograph shows Serge with the two boys; he, rather than his wife, accompanied them home. Lina stayed in Moscow in hopes of furthering her career as a singer.

A parade celebrating the Russian Revolution, as photographed by Lina from her room at the National Hotel in Moscow, November 7, 1935. She was living apart from her family at the time, preparing recitals for broadcast on Soviet radio.

The composer and his sons, 1935.

The newly constructed apartment building on Chkalov Street (Zemlyanoy val), where Lina, Serge, and their two boys settled in July 1936 as permanent residents of the Soviet Union. Their neighbors included artists, engineers, and politicians.

Lina with her younger friend and neighbor Anne-Marie Lotte at the French embassy in Moscow, 1946. Both women sought to escape the Soviet Union by means of diplomatic connections. In June of this year, Anne-Marie received a French passport and a ticket for a special flight to Paris. The dress she wears came from Lina.

Lina with Oleg, age eighteen, in Moscow, 1946.

Lina sewing in the apartment on Chkalov Street during wartime, in a photo taken by Svyatoslav, 1943. By this time Lina and Serge had been separated for three years.

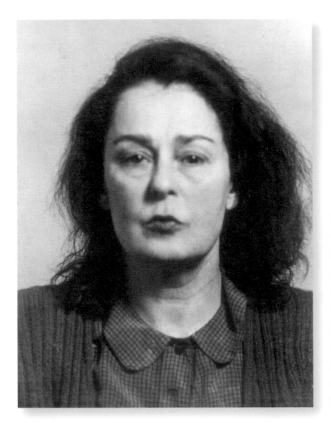

Lina's arrest photograph, taken at Lubyanka prison, February 20, 1948. She was held and interrogated in Moscow for nine months. During her trial, on November 1, 1948, she was within minutes found guilty on four counts of treason and sentenced to twenty years in the Soviet prison camps.

The looted apartment on Chkalov Street on February 21 or 22, 1948—a day or two after Lina's arrest. The photograph, taken by Svyatoslav, shows Oleg seated on a kitchen footstool, staring at a scrap of paper left behind by MGB agents. The boys witnessed the confiscation of their mother's possessions, but not her actual arrest.

The burlap sack that held Lina's belongings, including the music her sons sent to her, at the Soviet prison camp of Abez near the Arctic Circle. She stitched and embroidered it herself.

The single known photograph of Lina in the gulag, perhaps taken at the Abez House of Culture, where prisoners mounted agit-prop spectacles for the guards. It was found among Svyatoslav Prokofiev's possessions after his death on December 7, 2010.

Lina, her daughter-in-law Nadezhda, and her grandson Sergey northwest of Moscow in Povarovka, 1956. The photograph was taken by Svyatoslav at his rented dacha, just after Lina's release from eight years in the gulag.

Celebrating Lina's last birthday, in Bonn, Germany, October 21, 1988. She died in London on January 3, 1989, at age ninety-one. Svyatoslav is on the left, Oleg on the right.

Chapter 8

L INA NEVER MET Stalin. But she saw him once at the Moscow
Conservatoire. The occasion was the First All Soviet Union
Competition for gifted young musicians, won by a sixteen-
year-old pianist named Emil Gilels—"a red-headed timid boy," in
Lina's recollection. She and Serge were sitting in the fifth row on the
left of the Grand Hall, near the loge reserved for officials. Usually it
was vacant, but that evening, May 25, 1933, it was crammed. A woman
sitting next to Lina cautioned her, under her breath, not to look at
the loge "because Stalin is there." Of course Lina looked, and according to Serge's diary, she "locked eyes with Stalin, who had just then
entered. His look was so piercing that she flinched." The menace of
that stare, seen three years before the Prokofievs' relocation, contributed to stressful conversations between husband and wife about the
wisdom of living in the Soviet Union. Lina felt she had no choice but
to agree to the move; if she refused, Serge would blame her for com-
promising his career. She had been trapped by his ambition, which
had inured him to the risk they were taking in moving to Moscow;
though she longed to finally settle down with him, this no longer
seemed like the right context. "You don't know what you're getting
into," she had said, hoping to convince Serge to care about more than
his music. If he would not consider her feelings, perhaps he might at
least think about the family. "Your children will not get the education
they need," she warned.

Lina recalled these details near the end of her life, in the bleak light of hindsight. Much of what happened in the anti-Fascist French court of the Soviet embassy in Paris and the never-ending construction at the Moscow apartment appeared, in her dotage, as a dull blur. So she gilded her experiences in Paris with accounts of the theater scene and purposely forgot that at the time, she was much more willing to commit to the move than she wanted to admit. Its dreadful consequences inspired a willful amnesia, a conscious rewriting of her own life.

Lina did not directly experience the repressions that began in 1936 and peaked in 1938—the year of the Great Terror—but she was aware of the plague in the land: the arrests, blacklistings, deportations, and executions. Their exact cause continues to be mooted by political historians, but Stalin's psychopathic megalomania remains the obvious one. The Kremlin launched a massive propaganda campaign dedicated to eradicating the threat posed by "enemies of the people," and the newspapers and radio reported the confessions that came from the hysterical show trials of supposed traitors. Lina read these reports and indulged the fiction, the psychotic belief, that the repressions were justified. The alternative was too heinous to contemplate.

Serge took basic precautions, knowing from the start that the Soviet Union was not free, that whatever liberties he enjoyed were a reflection of his elite status. He stopped keeping a diary in Moscow, with the exception of lists of errands to run and chores to complete, and he stored sensitive letters and documents—those dating from before 1936—in Paris and New York. He spoke his mind about musical matters at meetings of the Union of Soviet Composers but resented the required ideological discussions. Lina believed that their position of privilege protected them, but by the end of 1937 she no longer felt immune. She suspected that her husband's minders wanted to confine her to the apartment, to remove her from circulation, because "they didn't like me speaking so many languages and becoming popular in diplomatic circles." Serge declined the invitations he received to soirees at the French, British, and American embassies in Moscow and advised his wife to do the same.

In the first months of their relocation, before the fear became palpable, Lina endured Soviet existence while Serge seemed invigorated by it. She remembered him telling her how happy he was to be back.

Socializing with the innovative, iconoclastic artists in her husband's circle (who now sought to create work in accord with an amorphous doctrine called Socialist Realism), accepting invitations to the directors' loges in the theaters, and attending diplomatic receptions distracted her from the grim streets. Despite her concerns about Svyatoslav's and Oleg's schooling, the boys were well educated. Svyatoslav attended an English-language school while also taking Russian lessons and, on Lina's insistence, speaking French at home; she had similar plans for Oleg. Her days were filled with humdrum domesticity, since it was difficult to find and keep housekeepers, and she continued with her singing until it became pointless.

The highlights of her musical career after the move were a performance of *The Ugly Duckling* at the Moscow Conservatoire on November 20, 1937, with Serge conducting. In the United States four months later, on March 21, 1938, Lina sang a recital at the Soviet embassy in Washington, D.C., with her husband at the piano. There were other performances before, after, and between, but these two had the greatest personal meaning for her: they marked the end of the imagined happy future and the beginning of the bitter present.

In the spring of 1938 both she and Serge suffered professional disappointments. Her work for the Radio Committee had been limited to a broadcast on April 20, 1937, featuring her husband's three songs based on poems by Pushkin—the smallest of the commissions that Serge received to mark the centennial of the poet's death, yet also, for political reasons, the most successful. Lina had a fraught relationship with the Radio Committee, but their association ended through no fault of her own. Boris Gusman, the official who arranged the contracts for her, lost his job. Though she could not have known it, he was then arrested.

In Paris, practical matters had exasperated her; in Moscow, she found herself overwhelmed by overlapping bureaucracies and an opaque patronage system. In an affront to socialist principle, the *nomenklatura* (people holding senior positions in the Communist Party and the government) received numerous perks for themselves and their families—from choice apartments and summer houses to special hospitals and exclusive spas. These advantages existed before, during, and after the purges—until one fell victim or knew someone who had. Foreign travel was the greatest liberty but also posed the biggest risk; contacts with foreigners were monitored, transcribed, and scrutinized by the NKID. Other privileges included automobiles and chauffeurs.

For Serge, a dedicated but dangerous motorist, obtaining a driver's license and a vehicle was a bureaucratic challenge that he was determined to overcome. In a stunning coup, he arranged for an eight-cylinder blue Ford to be imported from the United States to Moscow. Permission was prearranged with Narkomvneshtorg, the People's Commissariat for External Trade, in January 1937. Later, when the pistons wore down, he arranged permission to import new ones, paying for them in dollars from foreign royalties. His driver, Fyodor Mikhaylov, received fuel coupons as needed. This demonstration of extravagance was compounded by Serge's collection of tailored three-piece suits, colored ties, and designer shoes. He overdressed to make a point to his shabbier colleagues and ensured that Lina also looked her best, arranging for *Vogue Paris* to be sent to her. She enlisted a dressmaker and furrier to create a chic Franco-Russian look.

The fortunate few also had access to imported fruits, meats, and wines through special distribution systems. Lina shopped at the former Eliseyev gourmet shop, renamed Gastronom No. 1 by the Soviets, on Gorky Street, placing advance orders for the goods that, she was told, made the best gifts. Even as a person of means, supported by her husband's recent commissions, Soviet and non-Soviet performance fees, and Soviet and non-Soviet royalties, she was told by a housekeeper to stock up on staples — cereal, flour, sugar, and soap — and so turned the space between the entrance to the apartment and the kitchen into a cluttered pantry. As the wife of a prized cultural asset, Lina was invited to clubs affiliated with the guilds for composers, filmmakers, artists, and writers. Members enjoyed generous meals at discounted prices. Access to the cafeteria of the Union of Soviet Composers was essential to Lina during World War II, when food was rationed and, as she recalled, "people would sell a diamond ring for a bag of flour."

The club affiliated with the Union of Soviet Writers, which operated out of a former nobleman's mansion, had the most interesting gatherings and lavish banquets, since it was crucial to the regime in terms of (to adapt a phrase coined by the Soviet novelist Yuriy Olesha) the ideological engineering of human souls. Lina also remembered frequenting dance halls—without her husband. Though Serge disliked dancing and had avoided it in Paris, in the Soviet Union he tried with limited success to learn the fox trot, tango, and waltz from an illustrated brochure. Sometimes the couple enjoyed seeing foreign films at VOKS, but the screenings were infrequent and off-limits to the general public. Serge was so busy working that Lina often went out alone.

She also received invitations to receptions at the American, British, and French embassies. These could be stunning affairs. William C. Bullitt, the well-heeled first U.S. ambassador to the Soviet Union, arranged an extraordinary overnight ball in the spring of 1935 at his own expense, costing some $7,000. Over four hundred guests crammed the official residence, among them Mikhaíl Tukhachevsky, marshal of the Soviet Union; the Komintern secretary, Karl Radek; and the ballerina Lolya Lepishinskaya. (Although Stalin thought it useful to maintain good relations with Bullitt, he did not attend.) The wife of the commissar of foreign affairs, Madame Litvinov, an acquaintance of Lina's, appeared but was appalled by the spectacle: brightly colored pheasants and parakeets squawked in their cages; a cloud of a hundred zebra finches circled behind netting illuminated by colored lights; baby bears, goats, and lambs were on loan from the Moscow Zoo; white roosters crowed on cue at dawn. There was a forest of birch trees, a thousand tulips had been imported from Helsinki, a Swedish orchestra performed, and the dining room featured a mockup of a collective farm. Sometime during the accordion-accompanied Georgian folk dances and Russian folksongs, Radek got one of the bears drunk by funneling champagne through a baby bottle. An escaped rooster crashed into the pâté. The decadence of the event affirmed the vacuous state of U.S.-Soviet relations during a delicate period of negotiations over (among other things) intensified Komintern involvement in U.S. policy.

The Soviet writer Mikhaíl Bulgakov immortalized the spectacle in his novel *The Master and Margarita*, nicknaming it "The Spring Ball of the Full Moon." Lina later claimed to have attended, but actually she was in Paris at the time. It seems instead that she had read about the ball in Bulgakov's book and placed herself at the scene. She did meet the American ambassador in 1936, just after she and Serge moved into their apartment. Bullitt, a rakish figure with an eye for the ladies, lasted in Moscow until October of that year, after which he was posted in Paris, where his staff continued to organize grand receptions, now complete with horseracing and tennis.

Likewise Lina had hazy memories of invitations to the Kremlin and encounters with Litvinov and his wife. She kept exclusive company at such events, circulating among the most fearsome members of the Soviet government. Stalin himself never appeared at official Soviet receptions, however, except for those on the anniversary of the Revolution. Vyacheslav Molotov, the chairman of the Council of People's Commissars, attended in his stead. During the period when Molotov was negotiating the Nazi-Soviet non-aggression pact with his counterpart Joachim von Ribbentrop, Lina attended a reception with representatives of the German government. One of Ribbentrop's aides asked her to dance. Serge was irritated by her indiscretion—he had learned to avoid extraneous fraternizing with foreigners—and insisted they go home. Before she left, the aide, a marvelous dancer, asked her to look him up the next time she was in Berlin. Her recollection of the man collided with memories of the soldiers in Bucharest with whom she had waltzed in 1931.

Serge had several old friends in Moscow, and Lina made new ones —some Russian, some visiting workers from other countries. Few of their acquaintances from New York and Paris made it to Moscow, for obvious reasons, with the notable exception of Serge's old flame, the actress Stella Adler. She had traveled to Moscow from Paris in the late spring of 1934 to study with the director Konstantin Stanislavsky, the pioneer of Method acting. Serge agreed to see her, and as always, she teased him—giving him a note from another of her admirers, the film scholar Jay Leyda, in hopes of inspiring some jealousy. Adler's time in Moscow was a bustle of decadent enchantments: all-night dinners, horseback rides, drives through the new streets in imported Lincolns. Such, at least, was what Leyda accused her of doing in her spare time.

One of Lina's closest female friends—and most hazardous, given her connections to the regime—was a fresh-faced, energetic young woman named Jenny Marling (Schwartz), a native Californian who had moved to the Soviet Union just before the Prokofievs. Lina recalled her as "a very convinced Communist" whose "life began after she read Lenin's speeches, that is to say his directions." They spent a good deal of time together in Moscow, which might have been unwise. Jenny was rumored to be a low-level agent of the People's Commissariat of Internal Affairs (NKVD), tasked with reporting anti-Soviet behavior to the authorities, and the American embassy in Moscow warned Lina against seeing her. (For the record, Jenny's surviving daughter, Alexandra, doubts that her mother was deeply engaged in spycraft, believing that her activities on behalf of the regime were confined to matters of cultural exchange.) Serge, for his part, preferred the company of Jenny's husband, the Soviet writer Alexander Afinogenov, whom he had befriended in Paris in 1932. Serge briefly considered composing incidental music for Afinogenov's successful, long-running play *Strakh* (*Fear*).

Afinogenov was no less connected than his wife; he had been among those involved in recruiting Serge back to his homeland. His relationship to the regime was by no means unproblematic, however, and the way he managed to recover from official rebuke provided an important lesson for Serge, if not Lina. In 1937, he responded to the criticism of supposed ideological deficiencies in one of his plays first with depressed self-defense, then with sincere soul-searching. The play was called *Lozh'* (*The Lie*), and the intrigue surrounding Stalin's editorial correction of the original version and rejection of the revised version resulted in Afinogenov's expulsion from the Union of Soviet Writers, the Communist Party, and even from his apartment. Despite the humiliation, Afinogenov's commitment to the Soviet system was such that he found wisdom in its mercilessness. He scripted his own ideological rebirth and would have a perfect sacrificial demise, dying during a bomb raid on Moscow in 1941.

His wife, Jenny, was likewise prepared for self-sacrifice. Known to Russians fascinated by her embrace of Engels, Marx, Lenin, and Stalin as the "American Bolshevik," she had first visited the Soviet Union in 1930 on the arm of her then-husband, John Bovingdon. The occasion was a theater festival. A reception for the foreign guests in attendance was hosted by Afinogenov. Bovingdon had abandoned a career in finance, having graduated with honors from Harvard with a degree in economics, to pursue a passion for conceptual dance. Jenny also danced, barefoot and half-clad, in the style of Isadora Duncan—

which is how they met. Bovingdon's career peaked in the late 1920s, but he continued to perform long after the festival in Moscow and his return to the United States a year and a half later.

Jenny decided to take up residence in Moscow: her marriage to Bovingdon ended almost as soon as she laid eyes on Afinogenov, and they began a torrid affair in 1932. He had affairs with several other women as well, causing Jenny to leave him and return to the United States. But after working in New York in 1934 with the Workers Dance League and other left-leaning cultural organizations, she decided to return to Moscow and reconcile with Afinogenov. They married. Jenny stopped dancing, learned Russian, and assisted Afinogenov with his work. When he came under attack in 1937, she wrote an eight-page letter (in English) in his defense to Stalin and renounced her American citizenship.

Traveling with Jenny through Italy and France in the summer of 1932, Afinogenov purchased a Ford automobile. They gamely decided to drive it all the way back to the Soviet Union. The trip home was not without its "particularities," as Afinogenov related to both Lina and Serge in a letter to them in Paris. Pouring rain, wind, and terrible Latvian roads led to an all-night wait at the Soviet border. "The concerned Latvians didn't allow us into the Soviet side," he wrote, "saying 'The Bolsheviks will shoot you.'" By the time he and Jenny reached Leningrad, the car needed repairs, though "nothing serious, just tightening a few screws, springs." They lazed in a hotel for three days, unwilling to venture out in the late-summer heat, content to postpone their return to Moscow. Eventually they retrieved the Ford from the garage and drove the remaining seven hundred kilometers to the capital. A year later they were living together in a four-room apartment in the center of Moscow on Krivokolennïy pereulok, bought for twenty thousand rubles. It had chandeliers, silk rugs, and was in a prestigious building managed by the NKDV.

The tale of Jenny's move to Moscow astonished Lina, not least of all because of its points in common with her own, and the Prokofievs harbored no small amount of jealousy toward the Afinogenovs. Living outside the center of Moscow, Lina coveted their apartment, while Serge envied their car, which explains why he himself arranged to import a Ford.

For her service to the state, Jenny had earned a pass to the Metropole Hotel, otherwise off-limits to locals, and the chance to enjoy salad vegetables. She and Lina met there on occasion in the late 1930s, with Lina indulging Jenny's cant about the glories of the Soviet system and life under Stalin. Her friend seemed to revel in the intricacies of the Soviet bureaucracies: the Central Committee, the Central Control Commission, the Communist International, the Council of People's Commissars—these bored Lina, but fascinated Jenny. They chatted in English, which on one occasion attracted the attention of a foreigner at another table. "At last I can speak some English," he leaned over to whisper, then confessed, "My goodness, I can't wait to get out of this awful place." He turned to Jenny, who looked patently Californian, and asked what she was doing in Moscow. Her response stunned him: "I like it here." "You should have your head examined," he muttered.

For general advice on how to conduct himself in the Soviet Union, Serge relied most extensively on the composer Nikolay Myaskovsky, his friend from the St. Petersburg (Leningrad) Conservatoire. On Myaskovsky's counsel, he wrote patriotic choruses and marches and granted interviews abroad with boilerplate statements about Soviet music and the tremendous support he enjoyed. For his foreign tours, VOKS issued him a press kit that emphasized his commitment to "the musical advancement of the large masses of Russian people who are now flocking to the concert halls." The *New York Times* titled one of the interviews "Prokofieff Hails Life of Artist in Soviet." The composer described receiving three sources of income—commissions, performances, and publications—as well as a modest stipend from the Union of Soviet Composers. His Soviet colleagues lived better than Wall Street traders, he claimed, failing to add that there was little for them to buy in Moscow with their excess rubles.

(He made this point to his younger son when, one day, the boy came home with torn trousers. New ones were much harder to acquire in Moscow than in Paris, he lectured Oleg, and the "unpleasant seriousness of the talk" lingered in the boy's memory. There the problem was a shortage of money; here it was a shortage of goods.)

As a Soviet citizen traveling on a Soviet passport in the West, he read from the script provided to him by VOKS. Back in Russia, the interviews he gave to journalists were vetted, making it appear that he had converted wholesale to the cause. The extent to which Serge believed, or wanted to believe, his public statements is unclear. He was accustomed to speaking his mind and resented curbing his tongue, especially after the promises that had been made to him began to be broken and his various salaries reduced. Royalties for performances were the first to be trimmed, since these added up to huge amounts, and instead the composer was paid just for premieres. If the premiere did not happen, he received only the 25 percent advance on the contract.

He was able to speak his mind to his colleagues at the Union of Soviet Composers, but he despised wasting time in meetings and refused nominations for committee work. He turned up at the meetings only when his music was under discussion, acting incredulous at any suggestion that his melodies and harmonies evinced anti-Soviet tendencies. After 1938, when it became clear that he would never leave the USSR again—when, that is, the arrangements made on his behalf by the Committee on Arts Affairs for foreign travel were suspended —he just said what was required. The censors did not need to adjust his words. He had been badgered into submission.

For a few months, the promises that had lured the Prokofievs to Moscow were kept, but then, inexorably, they began to be broken. One of the setbacks consigned his *Cantata for the Twentieth Anniversary of October* to the dustbin. A massive work commemorating the Bolshevik Revolution, the *Cantata* was conceived in 1932 during a halcyon vacation in the south of France at the summer home of Jacques Sadoul, the French correspondent for the Soviet newspaper *Pravda*. A contract was signed in 1935, for a large fee. Seeking to establish his political credentials, Serge pulled out all of the stops. He composed a score featuring double mixed chorus, orchestra, accordion band, military band, and *musique concrète* (a siren, an alarm bell, recorded speech, and marching feet). The work started out as a tribute to Lenin but evolved over time into a ten-movement narrative about the Revolution, the civil war, Stalin's posthumous pledge to Lenin, and the writing of the Soviet Constitution. It was the composer's transparent high-stakes attempt to burnish his standing with the regime.

But the work had no chance of success because Serge decided, for musical reasons, to alter the political speeches at the heart of the libretto. Tampering with Lenin's words was akin to burning the Bible—absolutely taboo. The composer also erred, fatefully, in setting Stalin's 1936 "On the Design of the Constitution," a speech that revealed the ruler's poor command of Russian grammar.

Because Serge had allowed musical concerns to trump political priorities, the cantata was doomed. The run-through of the score at the offices of the Committee on Arts Affairs (essentially a board of censors) on June 19, 1937, was a disaster. Even if Lenin and Stalin had been left out of it, the cantata had no chance of being performed. The chairman of the committee, Platon Kerzhentsev, tore into Prokofiev. "Just what do you think you're doing, Sergey Sergeyevich," he demanded, "taking texts that belong to the people and setting them to such incomprehensible music?" The work was banned. The artistic freedoms promised by officials who preceded Kerzhentsev had been revoked by him. In recognition of the new conditions and his need to adapt, Serge composed a paean to Stalin for his sixtieth birthday in 1939, for a trifling sum. It contains some of his finest vocal writing and was a favorite of Lina's.

The utter waste of the *Cantata for the Twentieth Anniversary of October* was heartbreaking, as were the endless demands to revise his ballet *Romeo and Juliet*. The latter eventually became the greatest success of his career in the Soviet Union, but not until it had endured five years of tampering. The scenario of the first draft, completed at Polenovo in the summer of 1935, revised Shakespeare's famous ending. Instead of committing accidental double suicide, the two lovers escape into a star-filled elsewhere to live out their love. The change was inspired by Christian Science, which speaks of the immortality of the spirit. Serge left the last movement of the ballet untitled, because, according to Christian Science, "no form or physical combination is adequate to represent infinite love." Only music, not dance or decor, could capture that spiritual energy.

Yet even before the music was complete, forces had begun to align themselves against *Romeo and Juliet*. The run-through of the piano score at the Bolshoy Theater on October 4, 1935, did not impress the audience. The rhythmic writing was criticized for its irregularity, the harmonic and melodic writing for its anti-Romantic rationalism. The premiere was put off for one year, from the 1935–1936 season to the following one, then indefinitely postponed. A partial premiere took place in Brno, Czechoslovakia, on December 30, 1938, but Serge did not attend; by that point, he was not allowed to leave the Soviet Union. The choreographer Leonid Lavrovsky received permission to stage *Romeo and Juliet* in Leningrad in the 1939–1940 season, but he demanded so many changes from the composer that the two nearly came to blows. Serge defended his ballet, but lost. The happy ending was sacrificed for the familiar tragic one, solo variations and group dances were added, and the orchestration thickened by hack composers without Serge's permission.

Had *Romeo and Juliet* been composed in the mid-1920s, as opposed to the mid-1930s, it might have survived some of these changes. Instead it was completed during a period of intense ideological control of the arts. Shostakovich's experience with his opera *The Lady Macbeth of the Mtsensk District* became Serge's with his ballet; both composers were censured by the regime. The official reprimand that Shostakovich received did nothing to boost Serge's career, as Lina had imagined it might. He did not become the new favorite of the Committee on Arts Affairs but, like Shostakovich, was placed on a list of composers requiring ideological correction. And while some of his colleagues supported the happy ending, others mocked it. Afinogenov, for one, privately derided its unnaturalness in his diary, quoting the very last lines of Shakespeare's own ending as true of the original tale—and of Serge's own saga: "For never was a story of more woe / Than this of Juliet and her Romeo."

The criticism of the plot actually proved trifling, however, and Serge soon had much more to contend with beyond complaints about the problems his rhythms presented to dancers. On April 20, 1937, Vladimir Mutnïkh, the official who had commissioned the ballet, was arrested as part of a purge within cultural circles. His name had appeared on an incarceration and interrogation list initialed by Stalin. He was executed by firing squad on November 11.

The awful chain of events associated with the ballet marked, for Lina, a moment of realization. They had been deceived; the move had been a mistake. For Serge, frustration became despair, then devastation. By the time *Romeo and Juliet* was premiered, in 1940 in Leningrad during the brief Soviet-Finnish Winter War, his spirit had been broken.

Serge would continue to compose, brilliantly, but only in a way mind-ful of political imperatives. Lina knew he had been forever changed, that a fog of fear hung over their lives. They could take nothing for granted; everything was suspect. Serge hesitated about being in Leningrad for the premiere because he wanted to avoid the foreign reporters who smuggled themselves into the Soviet Union aboard freighters. To keep the madness at bay, he secluded himself in his study.

The purges had begun to touch the lives of the Prokofievs. Ac-quaintances on the first floor of their building were taken into cus-tody. The arrest would have gone unnoticed except for the sound of footsteps and muffled shouting in the corridor. And a car door slam-ming shut. Lina suffered insomnia. "Why don't you sleep?" Serge asked; she whispered, "I'm frightened." He spoke with naive opti-mism, proposing that the arrests would end, things would calm down. After learning that another neighbor in the building had van-ished, Lina panicked: "I want to go back to my mother." Serge tried to reassure her, but she insisted, reminding him that he had promised they could leave if need be. His answer: "What I promised then can't be done now."

They were still able to travel, at least for the first two years of their relocation, but the process of arranging for permission through the Committee on Arts Affairs was exasperating. Tour dates had to be re-scheduled to accommodate the purposely slow-moving bureaucracy. And Serge found himself taking the Soviet Union with him when he left.

He undertook two tours to the West during the purges, the first extending from late November 1936 into February 1937. He traveled to Belgium, France, and the United States. Lina wanted to join him, but she was delayed in leaving and was not reunited with him until Christmas Eve in Paris. In early December, she wrote a desperate let-ter to her absent husband, making light of the fact that, counter to his belief, his departure had not lessened the "nervous atmosphere" in the Moscow apartment.

Actually his leaving had been the cause of it. Lina was over-whelmed, left alone again to make arrangements and manage their affairs. Not only was she expected to care for the children, but she was also required to supervise the workers who were redoing one of the walls in Serge's room—perhaps with the aim of soundproofing it. One group of plasterers had been replaced by another, who had generated no end of dirt and blocked access to the piano. Plywood and tarpaper had been put up, but mortar needed to be mixed and applied. Lina had had enough: "If it were up to me I'd put a stop to it all." They were not able to finish on time for her planned departure.

She also had to secure an exit permit and external (travel) passport, and in doing so wasted a whole day on the telephone, hearing from one bureaucrat that he had received no instructions regarding her departure, then from another that he knew nothing about it. Ultimately she was told to write a letter petitioning for the visa so that the information could be relayed to the chairman of the Committee on Arts Affairs, Kerzhentsev. The runaround was intentional, pointed in its pointlessness, and Lina lashed out at her husband for not helping her. Had Serge written on her behalf to the committee before he left, everything would have been simple. But he failed again to consider her, neglected her needs because he was too busy with his own.

Now she was obliged to turn down a potential engagement in France. "I completely understand your situation, that it's not up to you," she wrote, trying to avoid his ire by offering her sympathy. "But despite this you haven't made anything easy for me and it's difficult for me on my own, since I'm hardly you." Then, feeling as if the walls were coming down around her, Lina took on the unhappy task of reporting that she had just received a telegram instructing Serge to immediately halt work on the incidental music he was orchestrating for the Moscow Chamber Theater. It was intended for an innovative adaptation of Pushkin's novel *Eugene Onegin* for the stage, but the script, by the phantasmagorical writer Sigizmund Krzhizhanovsky, had been banned. Another broken promise. By way of an incongruous and perhaps embittered conclusion to a letter full of woe, Lina added that "today there was a demonstration in honor of the ratification of the Soviet Constitution. A big celebration with a ceremonial procession!"

The letter was written in frantic segments throughout a disordered day, a diary of one exasperating interruption after another. In the end, Lina decided not to mail it; the complaints were too sensitive, anti-Soviet. Instead, she seems to have hand-delivered it to her husband in Paris, perhaps as testament to how hard it was for her to take care of everything while he was away, but certainly because it included the telegram about *Eugene Onegin*.

She joined him on the journey from Paris to the United States in December, but did not tour with him. She returned to Moscow on her own, refusing to write to him as a form of protest, and settled back into domestic life.

Her time in New York, with and without her husband, comes into sharp focus in a charming memoir by Alice Berezowsky, the wife of the Russian émigré violinist and composer Nikolay (Nicky) Berezowsky. She met Lina at the Savoy Plaza Hotel in midtown Manhattan on January 6, 1937, at the invitation of Serge Koussevitzky, who was staying at the hotel with his wife and valet. Alice expected to encounter a dour, drab Soviet; she was astonished by Lina's luxurious attire and the select details she heard about her privileged existence in Moscow.

Lina assumed the role of the grande dame, mentioning the English-language school Svyatoslav attended and how difficult it was to find good help. Her last cook was expensive, she complained, a pre-revolutionary type who needed to be driven to church by Serge's chauffeur. Alice complimented her on her "stunning" attire, which comprised a burgundy suit and heels, emerald-encrusted gold orbs that she wore on her collar and toque, translucent stockings that brought out the best in her fine legs, a stylish "upswept" coiffure, and furs galore. (Prokofiev's Soviet income had not been compromised by his battles with the censors, and his engagements in Europe and the United States earned hard currency at favorable exchange rates.) Lina replied, "Thank you, I rather like it. I bought the material in Paris but had the suit made at home. I have such a good dressmaker in Moscow, and besides, no one understands and handles furs so well as a Russian furrier."

The fashion show continued the next night at Carnegie Hall, where Koussevitzky was conducting the Boston Symphony in a program featuring Brahms, Clementi, and Ravel. "When Madame Prokofieff took her seat in the Koussevitzkys' box," Alice said, "everyone within lorgnette range gazed at her. As she let a magnificent sable cape slip from her shoulders, she revealed her exquisitely cut, shimmering lamé evening dress. In her hair, around her neck, and on her arms and fingers she wore a set of enormous antique topazes. The stones were mounted in massive ultra-modern gold settings that she told me had been designed by a jeweler in Paris." Serge did not impress Alice, who found his dress and demeanor, specifically his "poker-face expression," unappealing.

As he left for his tour in the Midwest, Lina remained behind, and Alice invited her to her and her husband's home. There they relaxed, with Lina noting how greatly she missed Svyatoslav and Oleg, especially since it was the holidays. (Alice and Nicky had a son of their own.) When the subject shifted to Soviet cultural politics, Lina stressed the benefits afforded to Russian artists while also downplaying the 1936 denunciation of Shostakovich in *Pravda*. "The government hasn't done anything to Shostakovich," Lina emphasized. "We saw him just before we left home. He's working hard, living quietly with his family, and getting along fine. Just because he wrote a work —the opera *The Lady Macbeth of the Mtsensk District*—which didn't meet with success doesn't mean that he's in disgrace . . . You'll see, Shostakovich will write new works and have greater success than ever before."

It was all sables and jewels, except for the mention of some mutual acquaintances who had been dispatched to the labor camps. "You know, it's too bad but I think he must have been a little indiscreet. I heard they were both in Siberia," said Lina nonchalantly. There was no mention of the neighbors who had disappeared, no reference to the challenges her husband faced as a Soviet composer, the difficulties obtaining an apartment, and the hassles securing permission to travel.

Serge traveled to Chicago in January, where he was received enthusiastically by musicians, critics, and the public, and where he confronted a bitter irony: the selections from the ballet *Romeo and Juliet* that he had brought with him were performed better by the Chicago Symphony Orchestra than they had been by the Bolshoy Theater in Moscow. (Naturally, it helped that he was conducting.) Nonetheless, to a reporter for the *Chicago Tribune* he boasted of the Soviet patronage system and its beneficial effect on his music, all the while wolfing down a slab of apple pie at a downtown diner. In St. Louis in February, he paused between performances to buy the car he planned to ship back to the Soviet Union. As in Chicago, he was received graciously, thanks to the efforts of his unofficial Midwest representative, Ephraim F. Gottlieb. An insurance agent by profession, Gottlieb was an intense admirer and advocate of Serge's music. The two had met in 1920 and maintained an English-language correspondence for more than twenty-five years. Serge relied on Gottlieb to negotiate favorable fees for his American appearances. Lina did not take to him when they first met—she found him boring—but he won her over by sending her leather-clad desk calendars embossed with her name. The covers of the 1937 and 1938 calendars survive intact, but most of the pages are missing, torn out. Only the blank ones remain.

On the return leg of his American tour, Serge met in New York with another Russian émigré composer, Vernon Duke. (Lina had already left for Moscow.) Duke was a close friend who had found success on Broadway; Serge liked to tease him about prostituting himself on the Great White Way. The pair visited Duke's mother, Anna, an admirer who wanted to hear details about Serge's life in Moscow. Duke recalled the conversation in his colorful memoir. "Sergey Sergeyevich, do you mean to tell me that the Communists let you out —just like that?" "Just like that, Anna Alekseyevna," he assured her. "Here I am all in one piece, as you see."

Then Duke's mother asked after Lina. Serge told her that she would be traveling with him to the United States in the fall, since he had additional engagements at that time. Another question, more probing: "What about your boys?" Serge demurred, wanting to talk about something else. Duke claims that he "later learned" that Svyatoslav and Oleg had been denied permission to travel abroad—"in other words, they were forcibly left behind in Russia, as hostages."

Afraid to say anything critical of life in the Soviet Union, even in private, Serge brightened the conversation by boasting about the amount of music he had been asked to compose, his apartment, the dacha he was able to rent outside Moscow in the summer, and the English-language school that Svyatoslav now attended. (Oleg, in contrast, had an English tutor who worked on his written and verbal skills with him as well as teaching him arithmetic.) The price of a travel permit was jingoism, so of course there was no mention of the cancellations and prohibitions. Of Lina, he informed Duke only that she "whimpers now and then—but you know her." Then a true confession: "Being a composer's wife isn't easy."

For a while in the spring of 1937, Serge and Lina were at home together in Moscow, but they parted company again that summer, taking separate vacations in the North Caucasus. He liked the spas of the mountains where it was cooler, while she preferred the sea and the heat of the Crimea. After finishing the *Cantata for the Twentieth Anniversary of October*, Serge traveled for a month to Kislovodsk for a month's rest, checking into the Ten Years of October sanatorium in a mountain-ringed oasis outside town. (The Great October Socialist Revolution could not be escaped, even while on vacation.) Kislovodsk boasted mineral springs, hikes in the mountains, chess, tennis, and volleyball matches, and a room with a piano where Serge could check over the proofs of recent scores and attend to revisions. The evening's entertainment, or "cultural diversion," took the form of open-air group dances to the accompaniment of the Kislovodsk Philharmonic. Serge learned some leaden steps from the brochure *Pamyatka po sovremennomu tantsu dlya uchashchikhsya dansinga na KMV s risunkami i diagrammami* (*Manual on Modern Dance for Students of Dancing at the Mineral Water Spas of the Caucasus, with Pictures and Diagrams*). Later on he took to the dance floor with Lina, but she found him an awkward partner—jerky, stiff, and tense. Given his acute rhythmic sense, the composer's lack of coordination puzzled her. He was also a terrible swimmer.

Serge encouraged Lina to join him at the Ten Years of October, but she did not have permission to stay there (the benefit was granted to individuals, not families, based on rank and merit). Instead, she braved a ten-hour trip on three separate planes down to the Black Sea resort of Sochi, where the water was warm and the waves high. "Cultural diversion" there took the form of hoarse-throated hymns to Lenin and Stalin. She found little relief for her frayed nerves and insomnia, and she longed to be with her husband. Her fellow lodgers at Sochi were "exceptionally uninteresting" and inconsiderate, banging their doors at all hours and talking in loud voices. Processing the complaint, Serge proposed that she travel to Kislovodsk and stay at the Intourist Hotel. She came but soon left, limiting her stay to less than a week. Serge chastised her for being so fickle: "I can well imagine the mood you're in. First you didn't like Kislovodsk, then you did, but you've taken to the élan of Moscow, but when you woke up after Rostov—on the train back—and you saw drizzly Moscow in front of you and its tediousness, you had a change of heart." She simply did not know where she wanted to be, could not find a place she was comfortable, and again felt neglected, alone. Serge was, as usual, immersed in his own affairs, though he did take the trouble to arrange a performance of *The Ugly Duckling* for Lina in Kharkov for the fall.

He treated her as he treated his sons: as someone to be kept busy and at bay, a problem to be solved. In general, he seemed better at consoling the children's nannies than soothing her. The children's caregivers, Nika and Stepanovna, groused about being overworked, and Serge had to bribe them to remain with Svyatoslav and Oleg during his and Lina's summer getaways from Moscow. He told Lina to go easy on the two women, lest they bolt. Child care, in his opinion, was about disciplined education, and he was pleased to know that Svyatoslav and Oleg were up at eight in the morning and in bed by nine or ten at night, and that they spent the bulk of the day practicing their sums and their English, French, and Russian grammar. Claiming illness became their way of demanding attention, but one time Serge overreacted when Oleg became truly feverish after eating too much melon and drinking too much milk. The doctors he summoned scrutinized the boy's mucus and quarantined him for a day for diphtheria. His fever, however, lifted within hours.

When, in the fall of 1937, it came time for Serge to arrange his next tour abroad, Lina insisted on joining him. They could not know it, but this would be their last time together in the West. Permission to leave came late, and would not come again. (As before, the children once again remained behind in Moscow, thus ensuring their parents' return at the end of the tour.) A series of recitals and guest appearances with orchestras were arranged along with official embassy events that included Lina; unofficial ones did not. Serge visited Prague, Paris, London, and various cities in the United States, including Boston, Boulder, Colorado Springs, Denver, Detroit, Los Angeles, New York, and Washington, D.C. Regular reports on his activities were submitted to Moscow from the Soviet embassies in Paris, London, and Washington.

They were no longer free, either at home or abroad. Reports on their activities were exchanged between various VOKS offices. The Soviet ambassador to the United Kingdom, Ivan Maysky, submitted an account of Serge's time there to the new chairman of the Committee on Arts Affairs. And in Los Angeles, he was hosted by Boris Morros, music director at the Paramount studios as well as a Soviet agent. Morros made a huge fuss over him, taking him through the *Tin Pan Alley* set, where, according to a syndicated newspaper article, "The composer got it in the raw, from Indian tom-toms to jitter-bug swing." Lina took part in the tour as well and chafed at the assumption that she could not speak English. "Well, our slang may not be very up-to-date, but we certainly do speak English," she said. She was serenaded by a cowboy song (which she described as a "cow lullaby") from the film musical *The Texans*.

The trip was otherwise often tense, and Lina and Serge knew they had to be careful. But whereas Serge exercised restraint, Lina allowed her feelings to emerge in a postcard to her mother. "The three days in London were most tiresome," she wrote. "In the first place the sea was very rough crossing the channel from France and almost everyone was seasick except me. The concert in London was a big success for—or irrespective of—the cold English people. The next evening a concert at the Soviet Embassy and yesterday at a society—VOKS —for cultural relations with the USSR."

Then the grim news from Moscow. "We received a letter from the children. It seems that the English school was closed down unexpectedly—it is most annoying and I feel rather upset about it. Now they will have to go to a Russian one." Though Svyatoslav's letter to Lina did not provide the details of the school's closing, in his later recollections he explained that several of his classmates' parents had been branded as enemies of the people. Some were arrested; others were sent abroad. The school was padlocked and the students were ordered into common Russian schools, which, Svyatoslav remembered, were desperately overcrowded. At least School N336, named after the martyred eighteenth-century social critic Alexander Radishchev, was only a fifteen-minute walk from home. (Oleg remembered only the teasing he endured, especially when his father agreed to play for his classmates "in connection with some revolutionary festivities.") One of the nannies looking after the boys in his parents' absence, either Nika or Stepanovna, sent Lina a panicked telegram about how difficult it was to find a new school for Svyatoslav.

After arriving in New York, Lina and Serge parted company. She stayed behind in the city, reconnecting with old acquaintances, while he headed west for a series of engagements. In the absence of people to do it for him, the traveling Soviet composer was obliged to report on himself. Serge sent digests to Vladimir Potyomkin, the diplomat who had played such a crucial role in luring him to Moscow in 1936, and who, in his new job as deputy people's commissar for foreign affairs, had helped him arrange this last tour abroad. The most revealing of the digests was sent from 200 Cherry Street in Denver, Colorado—home of the philanthropist Jean Cranmer. Cranmer found Serge a miserable guest, sullen and intemperate, until they went to see the Disney film *Snow White and the Seven Dwarfs*. That he enjoyed —so much so that he asked to see it again.

In a cravenly cheerful dispatch to Potyomkin, dated February 21, 1938, Serge reassured the diplomat that despite the wonderful treatment he received in the United States, "I'm not getting a swelled head and, amid the concerts, continue to work on Soviet topics." One of these was a mass song in honor of the people's commissar for defense, Marshal Kliment Voroshilov. Although Prokofiev could not have known it, Voroshilov was an architect of the purges, which meant that he composed a work in honor of a mass murderer. And it would not be the last time.

The digest to Potyomkin ends with pleasantries: "I send your wife and you my heartfelt greetings, and undoubtedly so does Lina Ivanovna. I say 'undoubtedly' because she's not with me here. I'm in Denver, in the Rocky Mountains, and she's staying in New York."

Eventually Lina headed to Los Angeles, her arrival delayed by flooding and washed-out train tracks in Colorado. She arrived on March 7, spending a night at the home of Carita Daniell (née Spencer), one of the well-educated, well-traveled ladies who had looked after her in her youth in Paris.

Meanwhile, Serge had received an offer to write film music for

Paramount. While waiting for Lina's arrival, he shared the news with her mother. The offer was enticing, a seductive bauble, but he could not accept it. To do so, he stoically advised Olga, would mean lingering in California until June 1, which was "inconvenient." In other words, he could not exceed his Soviet curfew—March 15 was his California cutoff—so he had to say no.

Lina's reaction to his decision could not have been positive, especially since, on March 13, she enjoyed the kind of evening that she had at one time imagined would fill her entire life—the kind of evening that Lily Pons and her former teacher Alberti de Gorostiaga were now enjoying in Hollywood as a matter of course. On March 13, the director Rouben Mamoulian hosted a dinner for them at the Victor Hugo Restaurant in Beverly Hills, after which they and the other guests returned to Mamoulian's mansion for an impromptu recital. Lina mingled with the stars: Mary Pickford, Marlene Dietrich, Gloria Swanson, Douglas Fairbanks Jr.—some at the Mamoulian gathering, others at the Academy Awards at the Biltmore Hotel on March 10.

But as Serge had turned down the Hollywood offer, it was back to Moscow.

Before boarding the steamer for Europe, Serge paid another call on Vernon Duke in New York, who tried to convince the Prokofievs to stay. He had in his hand a telegram from an artist's agent named Rudolph Polk. It contained a onetime offer of $1,500 from Walt Disney for the rights to a cartoon version of *Peter and the Wolf*. Duke misremembered the details, but his recollection of the conversation with his friend is, on balance, accurate—movingly so. "There was a flicker of interest for a mere instant, then, his face set, his oversize lips petulant, he said gruffly: 'That's nice bait, but I won't swallow it. I've got to go back to Moscow, to my music and my children. And now that that's settled, will you come to Macy's with me? I've got to buy a whole roomful of things you can't get in Russia—just look at Lina's list.'"

Then, Duke continues, Serge's mood softened. He became strangely and uncharacteristically emotional. "'You know, Dima, it occurred to me that I may not be back for quite some time . . . I don't suppose it would be wise for you to come to Russia, would it?' 'No, I don't suppose it would.'" Although Duke lived until 1969 and Prokofiev until 1953, that day in Macy's department store was the last time that they saw each other.

In New York, as in Los Angeles, Lina reached out to friends and acquaintances for support. On April 3, 1938, just before the long trip back to Moscow, she sent a note expressing gratitude to Warren Charles Klein, a Christian Scientist who worked out of a midtown Manhattan office. "I want to tell you once more how much it meant to me to have seen you again after all these years and heard all your good words, they are so substantial — now I must use all that constantly and especially at very necessary moments, when being back there." Then, both obliquely and poignantly, she wrote, "It was a relief to know that you understand some of my problems." She was also in touch with Lawrence Creath Ammons, the Christian Scientist whom both she and Serge had consulted in Paris. She heard from him on the Ides of March. He assigned her some readings to help her overcome stress and encouraged her to keep her eyes, both "spiritual and human," trained on "all the good" that exists in life, should one accept its "divine outline." The "good" was a fantasy. Lina imagined leaving Moscow for Los Angeles, at least for a few years, with or without her husband. Ammons approved. "Hollywood sounds promising," he wrote, "and if it opens as you both hope I trust that that heaven planned place may be your quiet abode with the children for a few years. It has so much of the real Science about it there even if there is another artificial side in the movie life. Ideal American atmosphere for raising children!"

But the cage door was closing on them. Having moved to Moscow together, they soon started moving farther and farther apart, each suffering the peculiar stresses of life in the Soviet Union. Whenever they were in the same place, they argued and fought, and Lina was often in tears. Duke reported Lina's weepiness, along with the deficiencies in her singing, with cold-hearted élan in his memoir.

The final trace of Serge's existence in the West is a filing with the Préfecture de Police in Paris for a stay from April 6 to May 7, 1938. He and Lina had arranged to spend that month together there. Yet he left for the Soviet Union long before her. After crossing the border at Negoreloye and arriving in Moscow, he exchanged his external passport for his internal one. The internationally acclaimed composer was then declared *nevïyezdnoy*—ineligible for travel—by the NKID. So too was his wife. Planned tours abroad in 1939 and 1940 were postponed and then canceled, the war serving as the obvious excuse. Stravinsky substituted for Prokofiev at one of his planned New York engagements. Painfully conscious of his change in status, Serge never again requested permission to leave. "He didn't ask," Lina remembered, "because he was afraid of being refused."

In anticipation of her own entrapment, Lina extended her 1938 trip to the West as long as she could, spending April 6 to May 8 at the Hotel Astor Saint-Honoré, a boutique hotel in an exclusive part of Paris, between the Champs Élysées and the Opera. Her mother had left the apartment at 14, du Dr. Roux for a room on rue d'Assas, near the Jardin du Luxembourg. Olga felt abandoned, and Lina grieved for her as she did for herself.

Chapter 9

THE RATIFICATION OF the non-aggression pact between the Soviet Union and Nazi Germany, a conspiratorial collusion between Stalin and Hitler, segmented eastern Europe. Just a month after the pact was signed, the Second World War started, as Soviet and German troops ravaged Poland in September 1939. Hitler invaded Denmark and Norway, moving from there down into Belgium and the Netherlands. Stalin responded by enslaving the three Baltic states, turning Estonia, Latvia, and Lithuania into Soviet Socialist Republics—forced comrades of the peoples of the eleven other Republics. Bessarabia (Moldavia) was the next rook to be castled in the totalitarian chess match; the Moldavian Soviet Socialist Republic came into being in August 1940.

France capitulated to German forces in June 1940. In the early morning of the twenty-third, Hitler slunk through a shuttered Paris, insisting on seeing the Opera and posing in front of the Eiffel Tower. Rumors that the elevator cables had been severed dissuaded him from ascending to the top. His forces occupied the north of France, and a puppet regime, a collaborative French-German government, was established in Vichy.

Great Britain resisted conquest despite months of assault by the Luftwaffe. The setback did nothing to prevent Hitler from launching Operation Barbarossa, the gigantic multi-pronged invasion of the Soviet Union, in June 1941, with the support of Mussolini and anti-Bolshevik forces in Europe and Asia. Stalin anticipated this ultimate conflict, but it came earlier than expected—before the Red Army had been mobilized, and before he, rather than Hitler, could shred the non-aggression pact.

The official Soviet perspective on the unfolding cataclysm was published in *Pravda*, the mouthpiece of the Central Committee. The Prokofievs absorbed the coverage along with the fragments of information that leaked into their apartment from the bourgeois capitalist world. Meanwhile their marriage deteriorated. It ended, according to Lina, at the start of the war, when Serge was evacuated from Moscow.

In truth, he left her in March 1941, three months before the invasion. In anguish Lina confined herself to bed, so Serge called a doctor for her from the Leningrad train station. Prokofiev told his older son that one day he would understand his decision to go. But Svyatoslav never did, and his father's parting words haunted him until the end of his life. Serge believed, falsely, that Oleg would forget him. Searching for an explanation besides the obvious one—that he had fallen in love with another, much younger woman—Lina concluded that her husband had suffered a moral lapse, succumbing, in opposition to the teachings of their shared faith, to the evil of life under Stalin.

The distance between them had grown immeasurably since their move to Moscow. Though they spent a great deal of time apart, Lina had always known her husband's schedule and general whereabouts, even when he was on extended tours. That began to change—through no fault of his or hers, at least at first. By the time he walked out, they had long since ceased speaking to each other, except in staccato outbursts.

She tried to keep up with him, to remain a part of his life, but she was boxed in. In the spring of 1938, Lina planned to attend the premiere of Serge's incidental music for a production of *Hamlet* in Leningrad. Officialdom intervened, however, and she was prohibited from taking the overnight train from Moscow—the worst signal yet that she no longer enjoyed elite status in the Soviet Union. She faced the bureaucratic hindrances and restrictions that average citizens did. Foreign travel was already out of the question, but now local travel was encumbered. On May 14, when Lina went to the NKID to exchange her external passport for an internal one, she was told that the latter had expired on May 5. She needed to obtain a new one at the passport desk of her local police station. There she was informed that the passport would take several days to be issued and, adding insult to injury, that her passport photographs were the wrong size.

The humiliation compounded her irritation with the rules and regulations governing travel by train or plane. In frustration, she hurled invective at her husband. "So tomorrow I have to stand in line with the kind-hearted citizens of Moscow for who knows how many hours and go through the entire procedure," she complained, "and, what's more, justify an expiration for which I'm not at fault." Then a plea for companionship: "I kiss and hug you and regret that I've been deprived of the chance to be at the premiere. Greetings to all our friends. If you leave on tour in June I'll hopefully be able to travel with you to Leningrad. Perhaps we can see *Hamlet* then?"

While *Hamlet* was being produced, Serge accepted an important commission to write music for the film *Alexander Nevsky*, a piece of chest-beating propaganda about the heroic exploits of a thirteenth-century warrior who defeated the invading Teutonic Knights. The scenario called for protracted battle scenes, including one on the frozen surface of Lake Peipus, along with images of self-sacrifice for the nationalist cause and touches of Gogolian folk humor.

The commission presented an obvious opportunity for the composer to curry favor with cultural officials. Since the film was meant to prepare the Soviet people for a potential conflict with the Nazis, Nevsky needed to appear as an allegory of Stalin—focused and resolute. The Teutonic Knights, in contrast, became the Wehrmacht. The film was shot by the pioneering director Sergey Eisenstein, who was himself in need of official reprieve, since his previous film had been banned by the censors before its completion. Eisenstein and Serge enjoyed a harmonious working relationship, but the editing of the film proved arduous, both for logistical and technical reasons. Serge had to turn up at Mosfilm, the Moscow film studio, at odd hours and sit with stopwatch in hand, reviewing reels and reels of battle footage shot in the heat of summer on cardboard "ice." Lina had no idea when to expect her husband home and worried about his poor diet. At least she had a marvelous *domrabotnitsa* who cooked for her.

It was a showcase score. Serge composed spectacular music for the battle scene and a moving aria, "Ya poidu po polyu" ("I Shall Go out Across the Snow-Covered Field") for the scene mourning dead Russian soldiers. Years later Lina asked her sons, from prison, to send her that song.

In between the shooting and editing of *Alexander Nevsky*, Serge left for vacation—without Lina—in the North Caucasus. This was his second summer there since their move to Russia. He stayed first at a new rest home in Teberda, taking a room with a view in one of the quieter buildings in the valley, then moved to the Gorky Sanatorium in Kislovodsk. There, in late August 1938, he noticed that he had an admirer, an unprepossessing young woman named Mira.

Lina recalled making other plans for the summer because Svyatoslav and Oleg were not permitted to stay at the sanatorium, since passes to its services and recreational opportunities were reserved for the well connected. Lina did, however, manage to visit Kislovodsk for a brief time in August, after two weeks in the Crimea. She was not able to stay with her husband—he did not pull the right strings for her—and the boorish staff at the second-tier sanatorium, the Bataliman, upset her, fraying her nerves anew. She received none of the pampering she expected and begged off the mud-curing ward, along with the array of tests on offer for blood, nervous system, and breathing disorders. For the children's sake, she returned to Moscow, making the long trip back on an overheated, much-delayed train. But for the rest of her life she rued her decision to leave Kislovodsk when she did. What happened in her absence confirmed her growing suspicion that, in Serge's dealings with others, he had begun to exhibit *laissez-aller*, a lack of restraint.

With Lina back in Moscow, Serge could spend his free time, such as it was, as he liked. Depending on the source, his relationship with Mira began either by innocent accident or calculation. The innocent accident version is Mira's. She first met Serge, she claimed in a short memoir, on August 26, 1938, when she deferentially introduced herself in the sanatorium dining room. They became friends and spent as much time as possible together. One of them asked the other to take a trip to the Adïl-Su gorge, a natural wonder. Lina heard from a friend of a friend that Mira had tried to visit Serge's room during the siesta at the sanatorium, the silent period in the afternoon intended for napping. Mira screwed up her courage to sneak up to his quarters, only to be shooed away by the head nurse.

The tattle among the diplomatic corps in 1941 was that the Soviet authorities had set a beguiling agent onto Serge, with a view to keeping tabs on him. The talk had no basis in fact, but neither did most of the speculation about the composer's relationship to the regime. He said nothing about Adïl-Su or the other trysts to his wife, instead filling letters with idle chatter about the weather, his exercise regime, the comings and goings of the other guests, and his workload.

Mira (Mariya) Abramovna Mendelson was just twenty-three when she met Serge, then forty-seven. She was a student at the Gorky Literary Institute in Moscow, seeking, with the support of her well-connected parents, to become a translator and writer. She was allowed to stay at the sanatorium that summer thanks to their credentials. Her father, Abram Solomonovich Mendelson, was an economist and statistician who had worked for Gosplan, the State Planning Commission, before settling into a teaching career. A devoted servant of the regime, he avoided arrest during the purges. Mira's mother, Vera (Dora) Natanovna, was an active member of the Communist Party, twice receiving diplomas for her contribution to socialist construction and Stalin's Five-Year Plans for rapid industrial development. The family lived together in two rooms of a communal apartment in the heart of Moscow, across from the Moscow Art Theater. Mira had started her advanced education at the Energy Sector of the Moscow Planning Institute before moving to the Chernïshevsky Institute of History, Philosophy, and Literature, and finally enrolling at the Gorky Institute.

She wrote talentless poems, as she herself realized, and imagined that she might become a librettist. Doubtless she influenced Serge's creative work in his later years, and she assisted him with the insipid political articles that he had to write for the Soviet press. As a member of the Komsomol (Communist Youth League), she was on her way to joining the Communist Party. (Membership was a mark of distinction not available to everyone.) Mira was much more ambitious than she imagined herself to be, and her desires had a dark edge: the potential to be destructive in pursuit of what she wanted. Such, at least, was what Lina claimed to have heard from her masseuse, whose daughter had overheard Mira at school declaring her intent to catch a big fish — or as Lina put it in French, a "*grand légume*." Returning to Moscow from Kislovodsk and her first meetings with Serge, she boasted to her incredulous classmates that she had succeeded. They chided her: "You're insane—he has a wife, an attractive wife, and children." To which Mira replied, "Well, what of it? She's had a good life and I also want to have a good life."

As a template product of the Soviet system, Mira knew nothing beyond the precepts of her true-believing parents and the dogma of her education. She had imagined nothing more for herself than a dull-gray existence in the service of the state before the colorful Serge entered her life. She was the antithesis of Lina, who, for obvious reasons, denounced Mira in her recollections, stressing over and over again her lack of grace. Mira was unfeminine, walked without bending her knees, frowned, spoke in a monotone nasal voice, wore her hair boringly pulled back or piled up, and liked unflattering frocks. She did not like being out in public—an unfortunate trait for the would-be companion of an eminent composer. Mira's Jewishness damned her yet further; Lina had never overcome the anti-Semitism inherited from her father.

For the sacrifice of her youth, health, and safety, Lina felt she deserved better from her husband than neglect, and now, betrayal. The question of Mira's attractiveness, she recognized, was trivial; what devastated her was Serge's recognition that Mira could help him in his art—his one true satisfaction—whereas Lina could not.

For every negative account of Mira's character, there was a positive one. It is impossible to get at the objective truth of the situation, since the various first- and secondhand sources are at odds with one another. The cellist Mstislav Rostropovich, among others, found Mira appealing, her voice a gentle burr, her slim figure less brittle than elegant. That she resisted wearing her hair in the fashion of the day was to her credit. And paramount was Mira's selfless devotion to Serge. She existed from the start for him and him alone. Unlike Lina, who sought attention, especially from her distracted husband, Mira just wanted to be useful, of service. The modest black bodices and collars, and the dull poems that went with them, confirmed this point.

Mira recalled the burgeoning relationship in gentle, innocent terms. There were visits to the Honey Waterfall in Kislovodsk (named after the surrounding honeysuckles), the Valley of Roses, and, seven kilometers away, the Castle of Wile and Love. She would have known the legend of the prince who once lived at the site. A bitter and cruel man, he prohibits his starry-eyed daughter from marrying her beloved, the son of a herder. In despair the thwarted groom throws himself off a cliff. She thinks better of joining him in the abyss, however, and is rewarded with an even greater love. (The expensive, faux medieval restaurant that has operated at the site in recent years trades on the tale.)

Besides the local attractions, the couple visited other resorts in the region, indiscreetly as part of group tours. Later in Moscow, there were strolls along the river, gifts (Serge gave Mira flowers and a photograph inscribed "to a blossoming poet from a modest admirer"), and since Serge had somewhat improved his skills as a dancer, social events at the Union of Soviet Writers club. Mira's recollections are self-aware in that they avoid any suggestion that her flirtation with the composer was planned, as Lina believed it was. She slipped only in stressing the power of Serge's presence and graveness of his demeanor. To win such a person over, Mira recalled thinking at the time, would be a great challenge.

Whatever the pretext, their romance developed during a nightmarish period in Serge's career, when another of his compositions was banned: his innocuous twenty-five-minute suite of "music for athletic display." At the same time he learned that his first opera on a Soviet theme, *Semyon Kotko*, had to be adjusted to reflect current political realities. The foreign ministers of the Soviet Union and Nazi Germany, Vyacheslav Molotov and Joachim von Ribbentrop, had just signed the non-aggression pact. With its ratification, anti-German art suddenly became taboo. Like the agitprop film *Alexander Nevsky*, the opera *Semyon Kotko* set goodhearted, folksong-loving Slavs against the loutish Germans. It was suitable entertainment for Soviet audiences in 1938 — but not in 1939, the year of the pact.

Molotov himself advised Serge to reconfigure his opera, as did one of Molotov's deputies at the People's Commissariat of External Affairs. So instead of having the operatic hero, the Ukrainian pig farmer Semyon Kotko, assemble a ragtag militia to defeat invading Nazis (thus ensuring marriage to his true love and an invitation to a May Day celebration on Red Square), Serge changed the libretto to force Semyon into conflict with nondescript Austrians. Later the enemies were made into anti-Soviet Ukrainian nationalists, which rendered all of the sarcastic German march music in the score suddenly inapposite. Oleg remembered playing dress-up at home with the ever-changing cast of characters; his father could not have been amused.

Most of the adjustments were demanded after the score was finished. Serge had composed *Semyon Kotko* quickly—in just four and a half months—because the eminent director with whom he was working, Vsevolod Meyerhold, was under extreme political pressure to salvage his reputation following a series of official attacks. For all his efforts, however, Serge could not save his longtime colleague. Meyerhold disappeared in the summer of 1939, just after beginning work on an outdoor event in Leningrad intended to showcase Soviet fitness. It was for this event that Serge wrote his music for athletic display. That score was banned as soon as Meyerhold was imprisoned. The director, the pride of the cultural revolution of the 1920s, would be savagely beaten for months, the rubber truncheons lacerating his legs and leaving him unable to stand. The torture broke him. He signed a fictional confession of treason while also scrawling abject, futile protestations of his innocence on scraps of paper. It is now known that on February 1, 1940, he was executed by firing squad. Serge never learned what happened to him.

Given the stakes, he had no choice but to continue work on *Semyon Kotko*. He disdained the new director assigned to the project, Serafima Birman, but forced himself to be collegial. Yet no sooner had they come to an agreement on the staging than Serge learned, from the NKID, that more changes needed to be made to the score. He revised the opera, but it still proved unsatisfactory. The delayed premiere would be panned, with official encouragement, by the critics.

The pressure on Serge was immense, but his concerns were wholly professional. Personal and practical matters fell, as always, on Lina's slight shoulders. In the early summer of 1939, while Serge was away, she remained in Moscow to explore the possibility of exchanging their apartment for another with an extra room. He also wanted to rent a dacha in the suburban Moscow enclave of Nikolina gora, where several leading Soviet artists, including his friend Nikolay Myaskovsky, spent summers and weekends.

On December 26, 1938, Serge had sent a letter full of naive hubris to the Moscow housing administration, arguing for a larger apartment—eighty square meters instead of sixty—in a new building not far from them on the Bolshoy Kazyonnïy side-street. He and Lina were both musicians, he argued, and needed studio space. Irrespective of the critical housing shortage in the city, he somehow thought that he could convince the directorate to assign him one full apartment and a portion of another. The added space, he proposed, would speed "the composition of new works of Soviet music."

More moving. In her husband's absence, Lina faced a long list of phone calls to make and people to meet. She was now frustrated and irritated not only by the logistics of the prospective move but also by Serge's apparent inability to settle down. Wasn't the entire point of relocating to Moscow to have a stable home? To travel less? To live together as a family? Lina resentfully supported his plan so long as she could also make use of the extra twenty square meters for her singing. But she perceived that something was wrong, that he wanted more than just a quiet place to work. Even before Lina knew about Mira, she sensed that her husband was seeking an escape.

Nothing would come of the proposed apartment swap except aggravation. "Alas, I have nothing special to use my activity on," she lamented in English before switching to Russian, "since the business with the apartment has come to an absolute standstill." She exhorted Serge by telegram to become involved in the process, but he claimed not to have received her message. Her unhappiness metastasized. The fracas with the All Union Radio Committee in 1935 had cast a shadow on her hopes of future performances; her doctor could not help her with her exhaustion and loss of appetite; even her tennis instructor could not be reached (she had had just one lesson with him before falling ill).

Later in the summer of 1939, Serge returned to the mountains and gorges of Kislovodsk, this time at the invitation of the Stanislavsky Theater. It would be a working vacation, dedicated to the completion of the opera. He encouraged Lina to visit, but travel papers into Ukraine could not be arranged in time to secure accommodation. Perhaps, contingent on those same papers, she would instead travel to the Crimean Black Sea. Or she might visit her sons, who were fishing, swimming, and playing volleyball at a camp between Moscow and Leningrad. There was also the chance that she would do nothing at all, paralyzed by her own bleak mood.

Lina expressed her exhaustion to her husband in a letter dated July

16, which she began in the morning and continued later that afternoon. In the interim, she learned something horrible. The Odessa-
born theatrical actress Zinaída Raykh, beloved wife of director
Vsevolod Meyerhold, was dead. She had been attacked by thieves in
her apartment and arrived by ambulance at the hospital too late to
be saved. She had corresponded with Lina intermittently in the late
1920s and early 1930s, about both artistic and personal matters, and
they had seen each other in Paris and in Moscow. They were not close
friends, but they knew each other well.

Lina learned the news from the director of the Stanislavsky Theater, where she went at midday to collect Serge's advance for *Semyon
Kotko*. She immediately wrote to her husband. "It seems that two
days ago burglars broke into Z. Raykh's apartment, first bludgeoned
her housekeeper and then stabbed her—the actress—twelve times.
She died in the hospital an hour and a half later—what a tragedy!"
Since letters, even those hand-delivered, were not private, Lina could
not express her candid opinion of the news. "I still can't get my head
around this," she admitted, before adding that she decided not to tell
her own housekeeper "since she's so afraid." She may or may not have
sensed that Zinaída's death came at the hands of the NKVD. It was
not the work of jewelry thieves, as officially claimed. Neighbors in the
building heard but did not respond to the actress's screams, and she
was found with her eyes and face disfigured. Had she been the victim
of a theft, she might have been given an official burial, and her neighbors would not have been sent to the north—to the labor camps.

Quickly changing the subject, Lina wrote with disappointing news
about her efforts to sing again. Georgiy Kreytner, the artistic director of the Moscow Philharmonic, had promised her a contract for a
recital of French and Italian songs, she reminded Serge. The performance required membership in the Rabis (Arts Workers) trade union,
however, which had earlier been denied to her, owing to the "spasmodicism" of her performances. Without membership, a fee could
not be established for the recital. There was almost no chance, moreover, of a radio appearance. The director of the programming division informed her that her performances in 1935 had received such a
negative evaluation that the proposed foreign-language recital, for all
its possible interest, could not be scheduled. Lina protested the matter to Kreytner, insisting that she hadn't sung badly in 1935; the prob-

lem, as everyone knew at the time, was the static-filled broadcast. Besides, she had performed with her husband in November 1937 without the slightest complaint. Kreytner sympathized, pointing out that the staff of the Radio Committee had turned over and that she needed to try to "rehabilitate" herself with the new administration, albeit cautiously.

Serge responded from Kislovodsk by hand-delivered letter three days later. "What a horror about Zinaída!" he exclaimed, having himself heard that the housekeeper had survived. "Poor V. E.!" he added in vague reference to Meyerhold's arrest. Serge had lost one of his closest friends, the mentor who had encouraged the composition of three of his operas, but he wrote only the initials of his first name and patronymic. The official rebuke preceding the director's arrest had made him persona non grata among his peers, and now he could not even be mentioned outright. As for Raykh, her ghastly demise was attributed to "a tragic romantic fate," a reference to the mysterious end of her first marriage. Meyerhold was Raykh's second husband; her first, the poet Sergey Esenin, had committed suicide in dramatic fashion in 1925, following a nervous breakdown. He supposedly hanged himself from a pipe, after writing a poem in his own blood. Meyerhold adopted Raykh's two children by Esenin and raised them lovingly as his own. Now all three parents were gone. Serge would later summarize the series of events in a single word: "perverse."

Feeling abandoned and besieged, Lina sought a summer distraction. She hoped to leave Moscow for the Crimea in the first week of August, using her husband's connections to arrange a stay at the Gaspra sanatorium in the Yalta region. It was a former palace that had been converted into a sort of medical spa for special Soviet citizens; she sought to alleviate her anemia there. She was delayed in arriving at the sanatorium until the eighth and had to plead to keep her reservation.

At the Gaspra she remained in regular contact with her husband but heard little from the children back in Moscow, which added to her worries. Lina's only companions consisted of the guests who shared her table in the dining room, chief among them an unnamed, wisecracking "metallurgist." Another guest, an acquaintance of Lina's from Kiev, commented on her drastic weight loss, but during her stay she actually managed to add half a kilo to the 51.5 kilos she now weighed, thanks to the simple good food at the sanatorium. Sugar was not in short supply, as it had been in Kislovodsk (Serge, who had a sweet tooth, told her to pack some of her own to bring to the Gaspra). Still, she struggled. Everything felt off balance. Though she was given a decent-sized room with a view of the beachside cliffs, and swam when she had the energy, the weather was poor, with unseasonable rain and wind. The chatter of the other guests on her floor was even more irritating than the mosquitoes, and just two couples participated in a dance arranged one evening, so there would not be other such occasions. *Alexander Nevsky* was screened, as it was at numerous theaters in the Soviet Union, but the music was marred by the dreadful recording.

Lina asked about her husband's routine in Kislovodsk, expressing her sincere hope that his work had progressed with the aid of his beautiful, temperate surroundings. She doubted he found time to relax; he joked about being asked to be a judge for a Viennese waltz competition in the central wing of his sanatorium. That, along with the steam room (as scalding as "a branch stuck up your navel"), absorbed his evenings. The famed Narzan mineral waters, one of the principal attractions of Kislovodsk, upended his stomach, and he learned the hard way that the bacteria took ten days to die once absorbed. Others had also taken ill after their visit to the Narzan Gallery, and he should have known that the liquid bubbling up through the fountains in the marble-floored, chandeliered hall would cause him intestinal discomfort. It smelled rancid. Nonetheless the folksy doctor at the sanatorium gave him a clean bill of health: "You'll be manning the plow for a long time yet."

Serge didn't volunteer information about Mira, but Lina couldn't help asking: had his admirer, the petite "poetess," returned to Kislovodsk for another vacation with her parents? He declined to answer. She was unaware of how serious the relationship had become.

Mira did in fact return. Indeed, Serge tried to assist with her travel —the first explicit betrayal of his wife. In July he sent a jocular note to Mira, asking her to "subordinate home and hearth" and travel to Kislovodsk "10 days" before her mother and father did. He urged her to book a train ticket and recommended that she take a room at the Grand Hotel. It was crowded, a "horrible bazaar," and she would have to stroke the ego of the proprietress for a chance at decent quarters. Ultimately the plan collapsed; she would travel to Kislovodsk at the same time as her parents.

Meantime, Mira asked how Serge was spending his days. He offered a saccharine variation of what he had described to Lina. He also flattered Mira, writing that he was reminiscing about their previous times together and anticipating new ones, all while feverishly composing. From morning to 6 P.M. he did not rise from his desk, interrupting "the scratching of the pencil only for the pine wood sauna, lunch, or a hundred paces or so around the room." He allowed himself to relax for just two hours most days, playing tennis or chess with colleagues at the neighboring Ten Years of October sanatorium between 6 and 8 P.M. Mira's presence (in place of his wife's) would provide a welcome diversion from his labors, even if her mother and father would be hovering. "I haven't danced," he teased, "for which I curse you." He closed his letter with an uncharacteristic romantic flourish. "Even the heavens wept today from grief at your absence. Bon Voyage!"

Mira's notes to him were no less impatient—"Each passing day brings me closer to sunny Kislovodsk. If only the time passed more quickly!"—while also reflecting the enormous difference in their ages. She was absorbed in her end-of-year exams and the foreign-language books she was reading, he with the pressures of an official commission in fraught circumstances.

His correspondence with Mira was light and affectionate, almost boyish, but Lina pressed her husband to respond to the menace in the news and its potential impact on their lives. That he did so in an offhand, abstract manner troubled her now more than ever. He seemed less and less able to connect, to exhibit any feeling—whether about her or the world around them. In one of his more cerebral dispatches from Kislovodsk, he itemized Meyerhold's unexpected disappearance, Raykh's murder, the rehabilitation of his colleague Levon Atovmyan after an unexplained incarceration, and the sentencing of a writer both he and Lina knew to six years in prison on charges of raping a twelve-year-old girl. The list underscored the moral decay in Stalin's Russia.

Serge also wrote about Hitler and the war that was still far away in Europe, but his tone remained that of a disinterested accountant. He noted the mobilization of Great Britain (he acted surprised that the "British lion" hadn't kept a grip on its own tail), the Nazi invasion of Poland, and the destruction of cities he had once visited. With a flash of concern for Lina, Serge asked after her mother. Was Olga still at her dacha outside Paris? Then he immediately turned back to his own affairs. He wondered about the atmosphere in the French capital and whether or not his representative there would be conscripted. Was his publisher still operating? And what had happened to the manuscript of his Cello Concerto? he wondered.

His other comments parrot the biases in *Pravda*, expressing hope that Italy wouldn't "inject itself" into the hostilities. He was "certain," moreover, that the "English were already sitting at the gates of Rome with bags of gold." It is unlikely that he believed what he was reading in the Soviet newspapers, and more likely that he no longer believed in anything.

Finally, in his postscript to the news of the day, something serious: Serge noted the new Soviet law that would require Svyatoslav to join the army in just two years, at age seventeen. If his son entered the Red Army, he would serve for two years; if the officer corps, for three.

That September, Serge returned to Moscow before Lina, their communications en route confined to sentence-long telegrams about train times. It soon became obvious that he intended to continue his dalliance with Mira. The pretext for seeing her was his search for a new libretto. In an effort to forget the nightmare of *Semyon Kotko*, he had decided—impulsively—to compose another opera, this one on a benign comic theme unrelated to politics. Mira encouraged Serge along these lines, offering her services as co-librettist.

Serge had always prided himself on writing his own opera scripts, so Lina thought it strange that he now wanted to collaborate with someone he had met by chance two summers ago in Kislovodsk. Mira proposed that they collaborate on an adaptation of *The Duenna*, a popular eighteenth-century play by Richard Brinsley Sheridan, and Serge quickly agreed. The plot is cheerfully amorous. Lina was not fooled, especially after she saw some of Mira's awful efforts at verse. As the project developed, Mira began to telephone the apartment. Lina would tell her as a matter of course that Serge was out, at which point Mira began to leave notes for him in the mailbox. He answered them, pretending that it was all perfectly innocent. She was "just some girl who wants to show me her bad poems," he told Lina. When her attentions threatened to break decorum, however, he mocked frustration, disingenuously asking Lina to help him to "get rid of her."

Since she could not broach the subject directly, Lina offered pointed remarks about the relationship: "Well, go ahead and see her," she said acerbically. "I won't object; but that doesn't mean you have to live with her!" The affair became public, the subject of gossip; Lina lost her dignity and her ability to control the narrative of her life. According to an interview she provided in 1982 to Harvey Sachs, she heard the details through the grapevine. "I'm telling you this not to pain you," an acquaintance reported, "but before it's too late to do something about it." Lina responded plaintively: "I don't know what I can do — I can't beat her about or forbid him from seeing her." As she realized the implications of the situation, she sank into depression.

Things worsened. The winter of 1939–1940 was brutal, with a record low for Moscow in January: −42.2 Celsius. Serge was roped into the orgiastic celebrations of Stalin's sixtieth birthday, for which he was obliged, like his colleagues, to compose a tribute. The resulting score, a gorgeous thirteen-minute cantata titled *Zdravitsa* (*A Toast*), was composed and performed for a sum that Serge could not refuse. On December 21, 1939, the shortest day and longest night of the year, Stalin celebrated his sixtieth in secret. *Pravda* nonetheless noted the flood of congratulations that the Great Leader and Teacher of the Soviet people had received from Berlin, Rome, and the proletarians of the world. Cultural officials decreed it time to gift Prokofiev with a success, and *Zdravitsa* made it past the censors. Reporters covering the festivities mentioned the cantata in passing, but positively. Its lilting paeans to Stalin's benevolence were blasted through loudspeakers on the streets of the city. Oleg recalled how "incredibly lonely it seemed as it resounded through the deserted Chkalov Street . . . Winter, the wind whirls snowflakes over the dark, gloomy asphalt, and the national choir booms out these strange harmonies. I was used to them, though, and that calmed me down. I ran home to tell the big news: 'Daddy! They are playing you outside.'" But his father did not respond.

From Lina's shattered perspective, there were two explanations for her husband's silence and the atmosphere it created in the apartment that winter and beyond. Both were disquieting: a true May-December romance with Mira, meaning that their summertime fling in Kislovodsk had evolved into something potentially permanent; or, as the gossipers suggested, an attempt by Mira to improve her modest lot by snagging an eminence, irrespective of his obligations to his foreign-born family. In either case, Lina suspected that they were all being watched from above. She believed that Mira's parents were against the relationship, which meant that it was not politically motivated. But at the same time, in a society that could have easily intervened in the seemingly private affairs of a very public figure, no one put a stop to it. Lina had no allies.

One rain-soaked evening in the summer of 1940, Lina saw Mira at a concert (perhaps the delayed June 23 premiere of *Semyon Kotko*) sitting with her father a little farther down the row. Serge was there as well, sitting near but not beside Lina, which led to awkward glances all around. Mira attended as many concerts and theatrical productions as she could and had evidently asked Serge to reserve tickets for this one. Lina turned now and again to stare at Mira, at "the little girl with her daddy," but Mira kept her head down. During the entr'acte, Lina pointedly asked Serge for an introduction, but he became flustered, strangely claiming that they had already met. Afterward, while waiting for their car and driver to appear, they all ended up bunched together, and Serge was forced to make curt introductions. Mira's father had disappeared for some reason, perhaps fearing a contretemps. As the rain intensified, Lina tried to assert herself in a situation that otherwise left her powerless; her fear mixed with anger to become provocation. Perhaps to shame her husband, she suggested that they offer Mira a ride home. "She lives very near the theater, and we have a car. Why not?" He resisted.

Following the performance, Lina had organized a celebration for her husband: champagne, caviar, vodka, hors d'oeuvres. But he did not want a celebration, did not want to be feted or entertain his colleagues in the apartment. "Probably some had already heard the rumors and he thought I was doing it to confirm the opposite," Lina remembered. "But I didn't want to confirm anything." It was a cheerless evening during which Serge appeared intent on starting an argument with her.

Lina pressed further, pushed Serge on the subject of Mira, purposely made him uncomfortable. Knowing that the two were talking about collaborating on a libretto, she proposed that he invite Mira to the apartment. She would serve tea and then slip out gracefully so that the two of them could talk about their project. Serge was furious. How could she think of such a thing? His rage revealed the depth of his feeling, which Lina had sensed long before. She recognized her diminished role in his life. Once lovely muse, she was now a former singer and cast-off wife. Stoic victimhood loomed.

Serge began to leave the apartment without explanation, and Lina sat awaiting his return. Feeling guilty without being remorseful, he changed his behavior and offered small tokens of affection—or apology. Once he gave her a box of ten grapefruits, a luxury in Moscow. Lina tried to learn more about the relationship, to track her husband down. She asked the driver, Fyodor Mikhaylov, whether or not he had used the car for meetings with Mira. Mikhaylov acted incredulous, refusing to believe her: "He's never used the car with anyone besides you." Lina thought about having him (or her) followed, but in the end she did not need to. Over time, all of the details of the affair were leaked to her.

Her husband recognized that she was devastated. His behavior was childish, in Lina's opinion, since he could not bear her grief on the one hand, but did nothing about it on the other. Myaskovsky took his side, reminding him that someone always suffers in such situations—though he knew little of these things himself, living as he was with his sister and tempering the unhappiness in his own life with cognac. As a result, Myaskovsky became a traitor in Lina's eyes, as did those of Serge's cousins who did not come to her defense but stayed on the sidelines to see which woman would triumph in the sordid drama.

Serge hesitated—realizing, before he suppressed the feeling, that the emotional and psychological consequences of ending his marriage would be grave. Mira became anxious; she reminded Serge of his isolation at home, of Lina's dissatisfaction with him and herself. His conscience got the better of him, his resolve faltered, and at a climactic moment he decided to reconcile with his wife. The decision, which lasted just ten days, provoked veiled suicide threats from Mira, pitiably and selfishly motivated. Lina was not fooled, but Serge indulged the threats, even using them as a pretext for his final decision to leave. "The life of somebody depends on it," he told Svyatoslav. "How about Mother's life?" Svyatoslav pleaded.

On March 15, 1941, nearly three years after he first met Mira, Serge walked out the door with a suitcase. He had arranged to meet her in Leningrad, where the couple would stay for a few days with a trusted friend from his childhood while trying to decide what to do with their lives. (They spent the next few months partly with Mira's parents, with whom Serge developed an adequate relationship, and partly at her family's dacha.) He thought enough of his wife to summon a physician, to ensure that she was cared for.

Before that abrupt and radical move, he and Lina had exchanged final pleas, hers for reconciliation and his for immediate, unconditional release. In June 1940, letters replaced conversation, despite the fact that they generally remained under the same roof. (He rented a dacha for the family in Nikolina gora in the summer of 1940 but, according to Svyatoslav, he did not spend much time with them.) References to Christian Science and Tolstoy crowd the pages of Lina's entreaty, which she left for him with a cover note: "Please read through this, don't set it aside." Remarkably, she voices much less anger than compassion for her husband, but protests the torment she had endured over "the past eight months, the last five in particular." His features had hardened, Lina noted, and his demeanor was sullen. In the apartment, he moped about in his housecoat, and for the past eight months he had confined himself to his room, isolating himself from his wife and children. The self-imposed alienation amounted to "spiritual suicide."

As in the tender letters of her youth, she made her points in a mixture of circumspect Russian, emotional French, and pragmatic English. She dwelled on her disappointment and sense of betrayal. He had become cold, even hostile, yet she always thought he would be her best friend. Lina confessed to being on the edge of a complete collapse, feeling hysterical and looking a wreck. Though she nursed her own resentments and suffered true heartbreak, her main concern was for their children. Svyatoslav understood everything, and she did not know what kind of life he would have without the support of his father. (His conscription was imminent.) The trauma would, she antic-

ipated, leave a lifelong imprint on Oleg. And she worried about their
future. Why had Serge not allowed her to leave with the children, to
go back to her mother and friends in France? "Even though it's difficult there," she explained in reference to the war, "it would nonetheless be better than living in the situation you've created for me."
Without him in Moscow, she would be defenseless.

In response, he accused her in degrading fashion of being manip-
ulative, of "machinations" in her attempts over the years to preserve
their troubled marriage. Their problems were long-standing, their
differences irreconcilable, he announced. Stunned by his accusations,
she posed a simple question in her defense: "Could you possibly believe that I moved here with the children out of pride?" By pride Lina
meant undamaged self-respect. She had overlooked his past flirtations, forgiven previous arguments, and remained steadfast while he
reeled from the disappointments of his Soviet career—*Semyon Kotko*
being just the latest, grimmest example. And if his leaving was so
long-planned and premeditated, why had he left her in the dark?

Yet even as he so cruelly rejected her, she still fought for him, tried
to help him—and not out of pure self-interest. Serge's idealization
of Mira was delusional, she believed; he didn't understand the mo-
tivations of the ambitious young woman who had latched on to him
in Kislovodsk. Falling under Mira's influence, imagining a life with
her like something from an eighteenth-century novel she had foisted
upon him, had made him a laughingstock in the eyes of his friends
and colleagues. Serge needed to realize that he had fundamentally
lost perspective on his own life and lacked self-awareness. Lina tried
to show him the truth, at least as she saw it. She wanted to rescue him,
to be the one who would return him to his former, pre-Soviet self, his
true self.

Her assessment of Mira's character was couched in the knowledge
of her own bias, but for his sake she had to comment on her motives
and to suspect something other than true love. "Remember what you
wrote after the first time you met her: It wasn't you who chose them
—Mira and the people presumably motivating her—but they who
'chose' you. And at a summer resort. You—not some speck of sand on
the beach, but Sergey Sergeyevich Prokofiev, the leading composer in
the land, a famous person with the aura of a family-man, and twice as
old. And it wasn't incognito. You might be able to claim 'love at first

sight,' but who will believe you? There were sufficient witnesses in Kislovodsk to the fact that she followed you everywhere." Long ago Serge had accused Lina of merely wanting to be on the arm of a famous composer, to pose before the world; that wasn't true of her at all, as she had proved through the years of benign neglect. It was, however, true of the more vulnerable, but also more calculating, Mira.

Lina reminded Serge of the Soviet catch phrase "Never travel to the south alone," meaning that what happens there does not remain there, so it was best to have a friend keeping watch. She was trying to do that now for him. But she was exhausted. She could not continue, except to reassert her belief that his judgment was clouded. Paraphrasing Christian Science, she ended her four-page letter by writing, in English, that the "despotism" of Mira's "hypnotism" of her husband was "but a phase of self-deception, therefore of nothingness." In the end, she could not force him to alter his drastic course, meditate on the flaws in his own character, and take responsibility for them. She could neither save him nor their marriage.

Serge felt his wife's suffering—how could he not?—but insisted that she did not appreciate the depth of his feelings for Mira. "It's only now," he declared, brutally, "that I recognize the barrenness of my life, excluding my work, over the last few years." There had been wonderful times with Lina, he implied, but he could no longer remember them. He accused her of the very same things she said of him to justify the impending separation: antagonism, frostiness, indifference. They had become so estranged from each other, he emphasized, that when Lina last emboldened herself to kiss him, he felt like an adulterer, betraying the person he truly loved—Mira. He hadn't admitted this love for another because he knew that it exposed him to ridicule, given the gap between his and Mira's ages and his elite status versus her lowly one. For two years he had been mulling over his predicament, and matters had now come to a head. Mira could not remain in the shadows forever. He had made his choice.

That was all he said, three hundred words in response to her fifteen hundred. He imagined Svyatoslav forgetting him in a year or two, and the little one having no memory of his chaotic pre-teen years. He was wrong—Oleg was eleven at the time and would of course remember—and was likewise mistaken about Lina's level of commitment to him. In the end, he was correct about just one thing:

his belief that the bond he had forged with Lina could not be broken. This bond, he predicted, would remain forever intact, "for it cannot be otherwise."

On June 22, 1941, Hitler authorized his long-planned invasion of the Soviet Union. Stalin had been deceived, and it was left to Vyacheslav Molotov, the co-signer of the pact with Germany, to report by radio the early-morning attack to the Soviet people. There followed the disorganized evacuations of high-level officials and other state assets—including great artists—to points southeast. In the chaos, the Moscow train stations were transformed into Sodom and Gomorrah, with husbands and mistresses sent in one direction, wives and children in another.

Serge would be away for two years. When he returned to Moscow with Mira in 1943, he looked dejected, miserable. The unmarried couple arranged what Lina called "disgraceful" accommodation in downtown hotels, while Serge immersed himself in revisions to his latest opera, a patriotic adaptation of Leo Tolstoy's novel *War and Peace*. He had little to say to his wife and even less to his sons, who, on their mother's counsel, neither demanded nor expected explanations of him. Svyatoslav and Oleg remained with Lina in their Moscow apartment throughout the war, protecting her as much as she protected them.

Chapter 10

I N   T H E   E N D,   S V Y A T O S L A V did not serve in the Red Army, but received an exemption owing to bad eyesight and, later, tuberculosis. His *voyennïy bilet*, or military service record, listed him as "unfit" for combat. Even so, he contributed to the Soviet defense during the Nazi siege of Moscow from the fall of 1941 to the spring of 1942. Svyatoslav was among thousands of citizens mobilized to keep watch on the roofs of apartment buildings during nighttime air raids. Hundreds of small, crude firebombs would rain down, igniting upon contact. They lacked the power of the massive five-hundred- and thousand-pound explosive bombs in the Luftwaffe arsenal, but they could cause intense fires that burned through walls. Residents wearing asbestos gloves scrambled across the rooftops to hurl the firebombs to the ground. Neighbors in the courtyards then extinguished them with sand or water. Footage survives of women in gas masks shoveling the flaming projectiles into buckets. Lina was on the roof just once during the raids, but the all-clear alarm had sounded before she got there. She could see distant fires, rooftop cannons, and the beams of massive searchlights ringing the city and its four million inhabitants. Within the city center, Moscow fell silent. She often recalled the eeriness of that calm when describing the war.

When Hitler's intense bombardment of Moscow began in July 1941, Lina and her sons took shelter in the Metro station nearest their apartment—Kurskaya. On the first, most severe night of attacks, two hundred aircraft dropped huge explosive bombs in half-hour waves for well over five hours. The order to take cover was relayed through pairs of speakers hanging from the sides of buildings —the same ones that had broadcast Prokofiev's musical toast to Stalin to the masses in 1939. The Sovinformbyuro (Soviet Information Bureau) radio announcer Yuriy Levitan issued directives on behalf of the government in a funereal monotone. (Even when announcing positive developments, his voice never lost its deadness.) Between 11 P.M. and midnight, thousands of people, primarily women and children, descended the long, fast-moving escalators into the Metro stations, bringing enough clothing and bedding to keep them warm through the night. People slept on plank beds on either side of the cathedral-like center halls as well as on the tracks, since train service had been suspended. Women in uniforms of the Soviet Red Cross patrolled the center aisle, dispensing bandages, water, and vitamins. Board and card games provided distraction for adults, while children wandered the tunnels between stations. The bomb shelters became second homes; one station offered milk for sale, another housed a makeshift library.

To protect herself and her children in the absence of her estranged husband, Lina cobbled together a network of supportive friends, trusted and not-so-trusted acquaintances, sympathetic neighbors, and Westerners she met at the embassies. She was no more or less heroic than the other women she knew, and she did not register to receive one of the medals handed out to those who survived the war in the capital. (Over a million *Za oboronu Moskvï*—For the defense of Moscow—medals were distributed to civilians and soldiers who defended the city from October 1941 to January 1942.) But she was brave in ways great and small. She saw to it, for example, that Oleg was tutored by a neighbor who claimed that dizzy spells prevented him from leaving his apartment. In exchange, Lina offered to substitute for him on the *trudfront* (labor front), joining the brigades of citizens ordered to assist in the resistance.

She recalled being sent to be part of a workforce digging trenches as panzer tank barriers and traps during that chaotic first winter in Moscow under siege. Though mud had slowed the progress of the pincer formations that Hitler hoped would sever the northern, southern, and western supply routes to Moscow, by mid-November the soil had frozen and the assault intensified. Tens of thousands of people (women and the men exempted from the reserve armies on the front lines) hacked away at the frozen earth with pickaxes and shovels to slow Hitler's advance to the city. Additional tens of thousands were mobilized to jam the roadways with metal spikes and re-outfit civilian factories for the production of armaments. Some businesses were relocated and repurposed during the war. The Second Moscow Watch Factory transplanted its operations to the southeast, where it "served the needs of the front" by producing detonators. The Red October chocolate plant remained on the river island across from the Kremlin, but now it produced rations for the front as well as high-caffeine Kola bars to keep Soviet pilots and submariners awake. Soviet forces suffered appalling losses, but the Wehrmacht was overstretched and undersupplied, turning the German ground offensive into a four-month war of attrition.

Lina remembered Svyatoslav petitioning for her to be exempted from the *trudfront* for health reasons. That left her the option of tending livestock on a collective farm (*kolkhoz*) near Moscow, but she refused. Serge had proposed that she evacuate with the children to a *kolkhoz* in the interior, but that would have meant forfeiting the apartment on Chkalov Street to anonymous authorities. He also offered —out of feelings of guilt and genuine, frightened concern—to arrange for her evacuation by special train to the Caucasus, where he and Mira were waiting out the war. She considered accepting the humiliating proposition for a moment in July 1941, when the attack was at its most ferocious. One night, startled awake by bombs, terrified, and sleep-deprived, she began to frantically pack those things in the apartment that she most wanted to preserve. But she had nowhere to store them and lacked the strength to drag the box out of sight.

Lina tried to track the progress of the war through the radio broadcasts, since newspapers had suspended publication. She hung a map on the wall and marked the changing positions of Soviet and German forces on the Eastern Front with pins and flags. But the radio broadcasts were intermittent, subject to random disruption: either the signal went dead or it was interrupted by a metronomic ticking sound followed by an air-raid bulletin. Neither Lina nor her neighbors could gauge the direction of the conflict nor tell how close the

Germans came to Moscow before having to suspend their assault. Even after the ground campaign was slowed and then repulsed in December 1941, the air campaign continued.

Citizens of Moscow knew little about the state of their city and less about the progress of the war elsewhere. Lina learned about the notorious 872-day blockade of Leningrad and the battles at Kursk and Stalingrad in unreliably piecemeal fashion. The reports were "horrible, horrible—to make your hair stand on end," she recalled: massive starvation, cannibalism, people being sent to the front lines bearing only pitchforks, soldiers turning into frozen statues in the cold. Fear got the better of some of her neighbors, who turned against her. Tongues wagged about her knowledge of the German language, and someone went so far as to suggest that she should set the table to greet the Germans at their arrival.

For help she turned at first to longtime friends, most of whom she had met through Serge. The American Communist Jenny Marling sought, true to form, to convince Lina that she was somehow fortunate. Whereas most people lived in small makeshift spaces, hoarding everything, Lina's apartment was big enough to host several Soviet families, and she had goods to barter in the wartime black markets. Jenny's husband, Alexander Afinogenov, recommended Lina for part-time translation work at Sovinformbyuro and even pledged to try to get her out of the Soviet Union—ironic, given his and his wife's efforts a decade before to bring her there in the first place.

Afinogenov told Lina that he had received instructions from the Central Committee to travel to England and the United States to facilitate the dissemination of pro-Soviet propaganda there. Jenny could not accompany him, since she was pregnant with their second daughter. So Afinogenov proposed that Lina travel with him as translator—her ticket home to the West. The officials with whom Afinogenov needed to consult and from whom he would pick up his passport and travel papers remained stationed at their desks in the capital, though much of the Soviet government had been evacuated to Kuybïshev, southeast of Moscow. The Central Committee was located at 4 Old Square, not far from the walls of the Kremlin, and made an obvious target for German bombers. Afinogenov turned up on October 29, 1941, for his appointment. One of the officials with whom he was supposed to meet had just stepped out to use the toilet.

A single Luftwaffe plane was heard overheard. It dropped a thousand-pound bomb in the inner courtyard of the building, producing a massive explosion. Shrapnel pierced Afinogenov's chest, fatally wounding him. He was just thirty-seven. (The official in the toilet survived.)

Thus Lina lost her chance to leave the Soviet Union. The news of the bombing left her in hysterics.

Sovinformbyuro, Lina's wartime employer, was an organization of about eighty people established by the Central Committee and Sovnarkom (Council of People's Commissars). It churned out propaganda about the Soviet war effort, publishing especially colorful stories of survival for domestic and international readers in newspapers and magazines. The organization also provided broadcast material to eighteen radio stations in twenty-three nations. English-language readers consumed tales about wartime escapades—learning, for example, about a young Soviet nurse who had sung her way out of a Nazi death camp. Sovinformbyuro also released a secondhand account of a soldier who was quite literally saved by his boots. A panzer tank plowed through his dugout, leaving him for dead under a mound of earth. Fellow soldiers found one of his boots sticking up from the mud, then the other, and finally the soldier himself, barely alive, in an air pocket. His boots were returned to him in the hospital with a note attached, describing the rescue. He did not wear them again until Victory Day.

At Sovinformbyuro Lina worked as an English- and French-language translator. Svyatoslav remembers her doing some secretarial work in the first years of the war; she herself claimed that she did translations in 1944–1945. Yet a letter from the spring of 1942 indicates that she began the work early that year, if not before. She picked up her translation assignments, and the scrap paper on which to do them, in the reception area of the building at 10 Stanislavsky Street. (Before the war, the building had housed the German embassy.) At home Lina had two typewriters with English-language keyboards, a Smith Corona and an Underwood, but she wrote up her assignments in longhand. Owning those typewriters was illegal.

Although Afinogenov had vouchsafed her trustworthiness, Lina's work for Sovinformbyuro became part of her 1948 arrest file. She was accused of stealing a secret document from the offices and shown a photograph of it as proof. Lina denied the charge, but she did remember that one of the pieces of scrap paper used for her translations had, on the back side, a few lines of type on it. That recollection proved fateful.

She spent most of her time in the apartment, paranoid about losing her possessions to thieves. Looting was rampant, and she and her neighbors took turns guarding the entrance to the building. The provisional authorities in Moscow had authorized the Red Army to confiscate personal belongings, but it came as a surprise that Serge's car, the blue Ford imported from St. Louis in 1937, was needed at the front. The lieutenant in charge of the division that had been positioned in the courtyard of Lina's building demanded the car's papers (it had been registered with the Kuybïshev auto inspection) as well as her driver's license in November 1941. Sensing that this might happen, she had already asked her longtime chauffeur, Fyodor Mikhaylov, to render it unusable by removing its wheels, carburetor, and ignition. But on November 9, a soldier appeared at her door while she was out, and tried to convince Svyatoslav and Oleg to surrender the missing parts. They refused. When Lina returned home, the same soldier reappeared with the same demand. She told him that she would allow the car to be taken only upon presentation of an official order from the Kuybïshev regional command.

At 9 P.M., just before the air-raid sirens began, a truck pulled into the courtyard. Eight soldiers climbed out and hoisted the car onto the flatbed. Lina, enraged, demanded an explanation from their lieutenant and received in response "a tirade of profanity" along with a handwritten, dubious-looking "instruction" for the removal of the car. The order came from the Krasnogvardeysk rather than the Kuybïshev regional command. She still held on to the crucial parts without which the car would not run. But the next day, the same lieutenant came back again with a brigadier, and Lina had no choice but to surrender them.

Indignant and incensed, Lina stubbornly appealed to the Krasnogvardeysk regional command for an explanation, only to be told that they knew nothing of the confiscation. "Let those 'who took it' answer for it," they said, which was not reassuring. She turned to the

Union of Soviet Composers for assistance, and the matter went as high as General Major Senilov, the commander for the City of Moscow. To no avail—the Ford was gone.

Svyatoslav's bicycle was also requisitioned under mysterious circumstances, as was the Förster piano—claimed for one of the cultural centers operated by the Red Army. Lina telephoned the club in a rage, shouting into the receiver, "Why don't you take everything and leave me naked in the flat?" The person on the other end of the line tried to calm her. She had a stamped, initialed receipt for the piano; she would see it again. Though Lina had her doubts—the car, after all, was gone for good—the piano eventually reappeared. It was damaged and out of tune, but still in one piece. Near the end of her life, Lina claimed that the piano had not been recovered, but she was actually referring to the events of 1948, when agents of the MGB (Ministry of State Security) hauled it away for good after her arrest.

Moscow, the capital of the police state, became lawless at the start of the war. The dacha that Prokofiev had rented for his family in the summer of 1940 was looted. When Oleg went to check in on it, he found it empty. Beds, tables, mattresses, appliances, even books—everything had disappeared. The crime was not unexpected, such was the level of chaos and panic. Emblematic of this breakdown in order, in Lina's recollections, was the image of streams of people fleeing the city, with the smell of burning documents heavy in the air.

In October 1941, with the Germans again bearing down on Moscow, so-called commercial stores, which sold higher-priced, better-quality goods, closed down. The state and cooperative stores that lined Gorky Street were stripped bare, with the exception of preserves (jars of rose petal jam, for example), dried mushrooms, and cereals. Lina scoured the markets for food, draping loop after loop of *sushki* (small dried bread rings) around her sons' necks to free up her hands for whatever else she could find. There was next to nothing available in the farmers' markets; crowds formed well before opening, prepared to buy anything that turned up. Milk was sold for spiked prices, ten times the usual cost, then resold by speculators and double-dealers on the side. The price of butter increased a hundredfold. Meat disappeared altogether; even if one searched the streets *dnyom s ognyom* ("in daylight with a torch," meaning "for a month of Sundays"), it could not be found.

Dacha dwellers guarded fenced-in vegetable gardens, bartering carrots, onions, and potatoes for clothes and household goods. Some of the gardeners, Lina recalled, became frankly greedy, holding out for the highest bidder: "They would say 'Oh, but these are used,' or 'This is not a very good brand'" to those hoping to swap an extra pair of shoes for a sack of carrots or onions. Among the most coveted items was fatback, or *salo*, a Ukrainian peasant staple much celebrated in Soviet soldiers' tales. Sometimes it was eaten raw, having been cured for months in salt in dark, cold cellars. It thickened soups, fried vegetables, and even winter-proofed leather shoes. Lina's housekeeper used a hardened slab to do the washing up.

The ration card system that had been instituted in the Soviet Union during the famines of the 1930s was reestablished. Food and goods were now distributed through official channels: certain things were made available at certain times for certain coupons. Lina and her sons were each issued ration cards, which came in different numbered formats for various categories of people. Lina received them for her work for Sovinformbyuro, and Svyatoslav through the colleges and institutes that he attended after completing his primary education. For the sake of a ration card, he enrolled in a music school; later, he joined a tree-felling operation outside of Moscow, which was followed by a stint at the intimidating Moscow Energy Institute—all to gain the right to foodstuffs. (Toward the end of the war, at the encouragement of a neighbor, the respected architect Ilya Weinstein, Svyatoslav entered the Moscow Architecture Institute and indeed became an architect.) The timber work ended in November 1943, when he contracted dysentery. He recovered—only to contract pulmonary tuberculosis, collapsing and coughing up blood.

In the absence of antibiotics and quick access to a hospital, Lina resorted to ineffectual "folk" treatments thought to kill tuberculosis germs, including lemon juice mixed with honey and salt, along with crushed eggshells to combat hypocalcemia. Eventually Serge arranged, at Lina's insistence, for Svyatoslav to be admitted to a specialized tuberculosis sanatorium in Gagra, on the Black Sea. He returned well fed; his appetite, he explained to his mother, had been stimulated by vodka.

By the spring of 1942, the German assault on Moscow had clearly failed, but the circumstances of its citizens remained dire. Lina had bartered away all but the most essential of her belongings for food and had to turn to her husband for help, even at the risk of "causing him anxiety or disturbing his peace"—a comment she made to him out of respect, without the slightest hint of sarcasm.

The first and most detailed of her petitions to her husband is dated May 9, but it did not fall into Serge's hands until June 16. At the time she was subsisting on bowls of thin soup and tablespoons of oats, grieving at the sight of her "chronically malnourished" sons. She spent most of her time hunting the city for food and now found herself having to ration rations, allotting Svyatoslav and Oleg ever-smaller portions of the high-calorie rock sugar that had become an essential part of their diet. She herself had lost ten kilos—a substantial amount of weight on her small frame. The constant search for means to survive had sapped her strength and even dulled her will, such that she was banging her head against the wall in desperation. "I sell and swap, twist and turn, but I still can't seem to escape this vicious circle," she wrote to Serge. "I can't just give away everything I have that's sellable, that people want, for a song. And since nobody wants furniture, I don't in fact have anything valuable left." Actually she did. Men's clothing was needed, but Lina reassured her husband that his things had not been touched. Yet the time was coming when she might be forced to sell some of them.

The eight-page entreaty was hand-delivered to Serge in Alma-Ata, where he and Mira had been relocated by the Soviet government. Had it been mailed, it would not have made it past the military censors, the details being too grim, too honest. Lina noted the hyperinflation that rendered salaries large and small worthless. Her ration card allotted four hundred grams of bread each day, but miniscule amounts of other staples (only two hundred grams each of butter and rock sugar, six hundred grams of meat—just over a pound, and five hundred grams of fish each month). Her only option was to seek access to the meal halls operated by the House of Scientists or Central House of Arts Workers. She knew that the Union of Soviet Composers operated a cafeteria, but it was inaccessible to the family members of composers. On one occasion she forfeited an entire month of ration card coupons to bring Svyatoslav and Oleg to a "so-called lunch" at the Union, but the food was "miserly both in quality and quantity." The entire operation seemed corrupt.

She begged Serge to write letters on her behalf so that she and the children could access the meal hall. The boys were, she pleaded, at a crucial point in their teen years; the consequences of malnutrition would be severe, causing them lifelong health problems and difficulties with learning. Lina anticipated that Serge would deride her, as he had before, for not relocating to a collective farm, but she preempted him, countering that if the treatment she had received from the Union of Soviet Composers was any indication, living on a *kolkhoz* would be traumatic. There she would have no friends or means of support while living in primitive conditions. And once she left Moscow, there would be no chance of getting a permit to return.

Though she took the position of supplicant, halfway through the letter she found it impossible to conceal her anger. She dropped the polite references to Svyatoslav and Oleg as "their" children. He had abandoned them; they were now hers to defend as well as her only hope, her one consolation. She reminded Serge of their exceptional qualities but also of the threat that his neglect, whatever remorse he might feel, now posed. "You have to agree that it would have been better in every respect for the children if they were 'trapped in the darkness of America,'" she said, mocking anti-American Soviet slander. "If it weren't for the hopelessness of trying to travel right now, I'd of course do anything I could to go back there, where there is a home for me and my children, and where they would neither suffer hunger nor cold nor poverty, and where I have close friends." By "close friends" she seems to have meant Carita Daniell and Gussie Garvin, the two ladies who had doted on her in her youth. She had last seen them in Santa Barbara, California, in 1938, and they had encouraged her interest in relocating there while Serge pursued opportunities with Paramount. Gussie had also proposed adopting the children, should anything happen to Lina. Lina's mother remained in France under the German occupation and was therefore incommunicado.

Lina continued to imagine a future for herself and her family outside the Soviet Union—to plan a life back in the West. After the end of the war, she pursued it actively.

Lina muted her anger on the final page of the letter, when reporting that one of his cousins, Katya, "has for several months been in an insane asylum, partly owing to exhaustion, and all but abandoned there." And her own grief overwhelmed her complaints in mention-

ing the death of the philologist Boris Demchinsky, a longtime friend
of theirs. Demchinsky had known Serge since his youth, serving as
his literary muse for several scores, including *The Fiery Angel* and
Cantata for the Twentieth Anniversary of October. For Lina, he had been
a source of emotional and spiritual support—"a true friend," she eu-
logized, "an oasis of the kind that no longer exists among us."

During the winter, she had tried to send a package of medicine to
his apartment in Leningrad, but it did not arrive. The city was cut
off. Soviet forces gained very limited access through a road etched
onto the hard surface of frozen Lake Ladoga. Sledges and tractors
brought food and fuel into the city when the ice permitted and the
road was not under attack; sick women and half-frozen children were
brought out. Through Demchinsky's son, Lina learned that his father
had starved to death after being brought, too late, for treatment to the
Astoria Hotel. (The Astoria served as a makeshift hospital during the
famine, but access was limited to those with *blat*, the proper connections.) His death went unrecorded by the Leningrad authorities, allowing either his widow or his son to use his ration cards.

"Such is the sad and very difficult outcome of these past months,"
Lina said to conclude her letter to her estranged husband. "May God
protect you."

Even though he must have known something about the plight of
his family, Serge was shocked to learn the details and took immediate steps to help. He wrote letters on Lina's behalf to the chairman of
the Committee on Arts Affairs and the Union of Soviet Composers,
expecting that he had sufficient leverage to arrange special meals for
her. The letters came from Alma-Ata, where Serge was contributing
to the war effort by composing soundtracks for patriotic films. (Both
the Leningrad and Moscow film studios had been relocated there.)
Despite his earnest effort, however, Lina continued to be rebuffed
whenever she tried to access the meal hall of the Union, the argument
being that she had not been registered and did not have the proper ration cards. Neither charm nor tenacity nor effrontery worked for her.
But shouting did. In September she received permission for Svyatoslav and Oleg to take two meals a day; these were exclusive privileges
denied to the families of other composers, but Lina shamed Levon
Atovmyan, who occupied the second-highest position in the financial division of the Union of Soviet Composers, into providing access.

With her sons taking meals at the dining hall, she could conserve her ration coupons for basics, some of which also came through the Union. On one occasion, through special dispensation, she collected twenty-five kilos—over fifty pounds—of potatoes; on another she received butter and eggs. Knowing the desperation of other families, she spread the word about her hard-won access, causing Atovmyan (whom she rightfully did not trust) additional grief.

When he could, Serge sent packages with colleagues traveling on wartime business to Moscow. The financial support he provided his family came from commissions (he took on a lot of hackwork for this purpose), royalties, official prizes, and off-the-books, forgivable loans through the Union. (Here, what Lina called the "slippery" side of Atovmyan's personality proved useful.) Serge was able to increase his support in November 1942, though both he and Lina knew that there was little she could acquire with the rubles he sent through couriers or arranged for her to collect in Moscow. She asked him instead to send rice and dried fruit; he would do what he could, but apologized that he (meaning Mira, who did most of their shopping) found little in the markets. "Don't think for a minute that it's El Dorado—the Lost City of Gold—here," he said, to clarify the situation. "There's nothing like eating cold, semi-cooked macaroni every day to send the stomach into somersaults." Eventually he managed to send her some local honey.

Though he did not mention it to his wife, Serge was now suffering serious health problems, including debilitating headaches and blackouts from high blood pressure, a chronic illness that would bring his life to a premature end. He suffered the first of the blackouts in 1943 in Alma-Ata, while shopping for food.

Lina continued to wield every tool at her disposal, work all her contacts, make any connection to scrape by in Moscow. She benefited from the Red Cross, specifically the attentions of an elderly delegate with the American mission to Moscow. (In September 1941, the American Red Cross reached an agreement with the Soviet Red Cross for the shipment of civilian medical and clothing supplies to Russia from New York. The amount of the relief increased from an initial $500,000 in supplies to over $4.1 million by June 1942.)

The delegate in question worked out of a historic building on Vesnin Street that housed foreign missions. Despite his rather pitiful appearance, he had it in his head that he was irresistible to women. Lina indulged his amorous interest at first, writing him decorous thank-you notes and inscribing a photograph "with love." He provided packages of medicine, leather shoes, and thick woolen military shirts. "Give them away to the neighbors if you don't need them," he advised her.

Lina felt guilty about her own opportunistic streak when she allowed Svyatoslav and Oleg to visit his residence to eat and bathe, since she did not have hot water. That only increased his attentions. When he became a pest, she had to slight him, placing a crucial source of material support in jeopardy. Similar flattery from a Frenchman—in the form of a bouquet of flowers—did not help her situation; the American Red Cross delegate saw the bouquet and became jealous.

She recognized her profound indebtedness to this American only after he left. The young man who assumed his position at the mission maintained protocol, so he offered no succor. At some point—Lina could not remember the year—she had to court his favor when she developed an excruciating tooth infection that required urgent treatment. The dentist on staff, an American naval man, took her under his care, extracting the cotton swab that her previous Soviet dentist had forgotten to remove when inserting a filling. Replacing the infected tooth with a crown required several visits. Each of them was noted by the NKVD agents who monitored her, and they catalogued her movements as fraternizing with foreigners—a criminal act.

Lina also benefited, at no price to her dignity, from her friendship with Varvara Massalitinova, a famous actress in her midsixties. Lina had come to know her during the shooting of *Alexander Nevsky*, in which Varvara played the plump, good-humored mother of the heroic warrior peasant Buslay. She had special access to food, and even wine, through the chamber theater that had employed her for most of her career. At Easter she set a marvelous table for Svyatoslav and Oleg and urged them to fill themselves to the gills, thrilled to be able to "gossip, gossip, gossip" with Lina the entire day.

Such was his disposition that Serge wanted to believe that even in the harshest, most trying circumstances, his wife and especially their children maintained the semblance of a normal existence. Even after being evacuated to Alma-Ata, he conducted his life with exacting precision. He sent two hundred rubles for Svyatoslav's nineteenth birthday in March 1943 and wondered how Oleg was doing at school, hoping to see some of his drawings and play long-distance chess with him.

Still, he focused on his own needs. He wrote to Lina, requesting that she send some of his clothing and bedding from the apartment. It was not a condition of his financial support, but merely a reflection of the material shortages in Alma-Ata. He asked for a warm hat, one of his suits, a pair of dress shoes, and a few of his ties. She obliged, although she also asked him to donate things to his children. His old lacquer shoes went to Svyatoslav, but he refused to let go of his blue suit, suggesting that Lina have another made from her stock of fabric. He would pay for the tailoring so long as the cost was reasonable.

Even in the midst of a world war, with Serge evacuated from Moscow, Lina living in extreme privation, and their marriage all but ended, they had to come together as parents. In May 1943 Oleg became gravely ill, with a fever, chest pain, and swollen neck that made it painful to breathe and swallow. He had contracted diphtheria from contaminated milk and required hospitalization. Through connections at the Union of Soviet Composers, Lina arranged for him to be admitted to the Kremlin Hospital, located at the time across from the Lenin Library in the center of Moscow. Serge transferred three thousand rubles from Alma-Ata to pay the bills. His younger son's condition improved, though he remained under observation through June for abnormal heart rhythms because the tissue in the upper and lower chambers had become inflamed. He recovered, but in a weakened condition that contributed to his premature death in 1998 from congestive heart failure.

The illness spread by cough or sneeze to Lina in July, at the end of Oleg's convalescence. The extreme fatigue that had become her normal condition intensified. A low-grade fever developed, and she had a crippling headache. She assumed that she had contracted louse-borne typhoid, an epidemic in the city. The nature of the treatment she received is unclear. Lina remembered being admitted to the Kremlin Hospital before or after Oleg's discharge. Instead of treatment, however, she was offered food: gruel in the morning, followed by hard- and soft-boiled eggs—a true luxury typically reserved for new nurs- ing mothers—in the afternoon.

In her delirium, Lina remembered the nurses spiriting the food away to their families; she also retained images of a room full of sick children who seemed to have been abandoned. Her fever spiked dan- gerously high. A female doctor from Georgia came to her side, exam- ined her, and concluded that instead of typhoid, she had a pneumonic infection in the right lung that required antibiotics. She had not been eating, so she also needed proper nutrition.

Lina was sent home and convalesced with the help of her thirty- nine-year-old French neighbor, Anne-Marie Lotte, the young mother of two girls and a recent acquaintance. Lina looked on her as an angel sent from heaven, but Anne-Marie had actually ended up on Chkalov Street through an awful series of events. She provided the intimate details as she tended Lina. Their stories had a lot in common.

Like Lina, Anne-Marie had relocated to Moscow for personal rather than political reasons. In Paris as a *lycée* student she fell in love with a Ukrainian sculptor named Saul Rabinowitz and married him. He had expected to remain in Paris but was lured back to Moscow by a commission for a bust of People's Commissar Sergo Ordzhonikidze (an ally of Stalin's who died in mysterious circumstances during the spring of 1937) and taught at the Stroganov Art and Design Insti- tute. Rabinowitz wanted to leave Anne-Marie behind, but she refused to let him go, dispatching telegram after telegram to him announc- ing her decision to relocate to the Soviet Union. In the summer of 1937, Anne-Marie obtained a Soviet permanent residence permit, bade farewell to her widowed mother, and boarded a train. Her first impressions of Moscow after the two-day journey were of heat, dirt, barefoot children, and men sitting on the floor of the train station, cursing as they spat out sunflower-seed husks. Rabinowitz met her at the station but wanted nothing to do with her, declining to kiss her and annulling their marriage almost as soon as she crossed his door- step. Anne-Marie was left with twenty rubles in a bedbug-infested communal apartment.

Her fortunes reversed when, at a gathering hosted by the journal- ist Ilya Ehrenburg and his wife, she met the architect Ilya Weinstein, a recent widower. He had designed the massive apartment complex in which he lived at 23–25 Chkalov Street, almost directly across the street from Lina's building. Weinstein took in the frightened, emaciated Anne-Marie. Their relationship quickly turned romantic, and she twice became pregnant during the war, delivering the first of her two daughters in a shelter.

The comparable experiences brought Lina and Anne-Marie together. Both of them imagined that they might leave the Soviet Union. In the months following the march of captured, mercilessly taunted German soldiers through the streets of Moscow in July 1944, Anne-Marie began petitioning the French embassy for help, using the diplomatic mail to establish contact with her family. Lina also went and, like Anne-Marie, bravely arranged to send and receive foreign correspondence. One evening, both of them attended a reception for Maurice Thorez, the longtime leader of the French Communist Party, who had spent the war in exile in the USSR (he was evacuated by arrangement of the Komintern to Ufa, a city southwest of the Urals). There survives a passport-size photograph of the two ladies standing together on the second-floor balcony of the building—a study in light and dark. The taller, blonde Anne-Marie leans against an intricately decorated corner column, squinting slightly in the springtime sun. Lina stands in the shade, facing her, posture perfect, wearing dramatic makeup, a once fashionable French hat with a birdcage veil, and a flower in her hair.

From Lina's account, Anne-Marie was the much more flirtatious of the two at the embassy gatherings. She found a crucial support in Roland de la Poype, a heroic fighter pilot with the Normandy Squadron, which fought against the Nazis on Soviet soil (under the command of Charles de Gaulle). Thanks to his lobbying on her behalf, she was permitted to contact her family and, in June 1946, was issued a French passport and a ticket for a special flight leaving for Paris. Her husband, Weinstein, advised her to leave, even though it meant that he would never see her or their daughters again. Lina visited Anne-Marie just before her departure and said, optimistically, "Well, my gentle Annette, in a month I'll have a visa and we'll see each other in Paris!"

For Lina, the role of Roland de la Poype was to be played by Stanislas Julien, a French diplomat or perhaps a military officer who was posted in Moscow until July 1945. (He may have been the same Frenchman who, to the dismay of the American Red Cross delegate, had sent her roses.) Julien had promised to help Lina leave the Soviet Union, but ultimately did not—a brutal disappointment. He cut off all contact with her once he had returned to France and performed the small favor of visiting her mother to pass along the photographs he had taken of Lina. Svyatoslav took a couple of additional photos of Lina and Julien together in her apartment in 1944; these show an unsmiling middle-aged man with receding white hair, wire-framed glasses, a wrinkled white shirt, and a bracingly direct expression. Perhaps against Julien's wishes, Lina's friendship with him had remained platonic. He nonetheless became fearful after his return to France, first asking her to write him at a post-office box rather than his home address and then falling strangely silent. Toward the end of her life, Lina vaguely recalled knowing a Frenchman who had a scandalous affair with a translator in Moscow during the war, but she did not provide his name. It might have been the enigmatic Stanislas Julien.

With the end of the German attacks on Moscow in 1942—the first turning point in the Soviet phase of the war, but by no means the end, those upper-level officials who had been evacuated to Kuybïshev began to trickle back into the city. Checkpoints remained in place along the perimeter, and services continued to be sporadic, but residents no longer had to black out their windows with curtains and stock rooftop cannons. Musical life gradually resumed, and it was expected that the strictures placed on the arts before the war would now be relaxed.

Oleg asked his mother to take him to concerts, in hopes of seeing his father. They heard piano and organ recitals at the Moscow Conservatoire at the invitation of one of the professors there, Alexander Gedike, and Lina even sang at the Union of Soviet Writers club. Gedike commented on Oleg's likeness to Prokofiev, especially when he was smartly dressed. Each time Oleg asked, "Where's Papa?" And each time his hopes of seeing his father were dashed. Prokofiev remained in Kazakhstan until October 1943, but in truth, "Papa" never came back.

After his return to Moscow, Prokofiev continued to support his family but declined to see Lina, Svyatoslav, and Oleg in person. He relied, as he had while living in the Caucasus and Kazakhstan, on intermediaries. Lina remembered him once bringing or sending chocolates to her and the children—when what they needed was proper food. There was also a terrible argument over a carpet that he wanted to take with him to the apartment he occupied with Mira. But that incident was toward the end of the war, long after the period from the autumn of 1943 to the fall of 1944 when he was staying in hotels: the National, the Metropole, the Moskva, and the Savoy.

The hotel assignments, secured for him either by the Committee on Arts Affairs or the Union of Soviet Composers, reflected Prokofiev's privileged status as a leading composer, but they were erratic. He often had to change hotels and, at the Moskva, ended up being unceremoniously bumped from room to room, an irritation that increased his feeling of homelessness. His itinerant evacuation in the Soviet Union now paralleled his itinerant years in the West. Since he had few belongings, he needed to arrange with Lina for the clothes he had left in the apartment to be brought to him. Telegrams were also exchanged about retrieving some of his books and a writing table from the apartment. He wanted the table for composing, but Svyatoslav needed it for his studies; Lina negotiated for a secretary desk in exchange. Atovmyan took some of the items to the Moskva, as did Lina's housekeeper, Frosya.

She had now been with Lina for several years, dividing her time between the apartment, where she cooked and cleaned and mended clothes, and outdoor construction brigades. Irrespective of her provincialism (evidenced by her troubles pronouncing the word *composer*), Lina found much to admire about her. Frosya was steel-willed but also kindhearted and morally grounded. She became a member of the family, staying with Svyatoslav and Oleg even after their mother's arrest and imprisonment. Out of loyalty to her employer, Frosya declared that she despised Mira.

Now and then she ran errands for Lina to Serge's rooms at the Hotel Moskva (he moved from the eighth floor up to the thirteenth and then, after his short stint at the Savoy, down to the fourth and the first), finding the scene there unwholesome: "It's not the same. I went into that hotel room and I saw his music on his table, butter, one of her combs and brushes with her hair in it, and I couldn't look at her." Serge came once to the apartment to gather some suits, pleased that Lina "had not exchanged them for sugar, lard, or anything else."

He stayed for an awkward meal. Leaving the apartment, he was confronted by the plumber who lived downstairs in the building. The plumber was a rather straight-laced paterfamilias who, like Frosya, empathized with Lina. "So you've come to see your family?" he inquired, glowering at Serge from the bench he habitually occupied in the courtyard. "You're a fine father." Serge kept his head down, stone-faced.

The tensions increased in September 1944, when Serge and Mira received a small apartment for themselves on Mozhayskoye shosse. From then on, Serge categorically refused to see Lina and accused her of being passive-aggressive, holding on to items of his that neither she nor their children needed. He demanded everything in his room besides the piano, which he offered to leave to accompany her singing, so long as Atovmyan could find another one for him. (He did, a Steinway.) The latest list of book requests included H. G. Wells's *The Outline of History* from 1920, a modern translation of the Bible, and one of the two biographies of Mary Baker Eddy, the founder of Christian Science, which they had brought with them from Europe.

Serge no longer considered himself part of Lina's or his children's lives. He began to refer to Mira as his spouse, as did his colleagues— though all sides knew that she was not. He steeled himself to ask Lina for a formal divorce, but hesitated, perhaps out of residual feelings of guilt, perhaps out of consideration for her ill health. Instead, he asked Atovmyan to broach the subject with Lina on his behalf, if only to see where she stood.

Atovmyan dragged his feet, and Lina rightly resented his role as go-between. She asked Serge to meet her at the apartment of a neutral friend, the actress Yelena Kuzmina, thus sparing Svyatoslav and Oleg the confrontation. Serge refused and wrote a letter requesting a permanent divorce. It ended up in Svyatoslav's hands, and he did not have the heart to give it to his long-suffering mother. Had she received it, she would not have agreed to a divorce, since it would have left her even more vulnerable. She felt shielded enough by her marriage to fraternize with the staff at the embassies of the Soviet Union's wartime allies, even though such contact with foreigners was disallowed by the state as treasonous. Such socializing had its real purpose, though—to escape.

Serge worried about her precarious position without assisting her in her effort to leave. He had become a different person, with a different mindset. Now a true Soviet composer, he had worked hard on behalf of the regime during his evacuation, churning out one patriotic score after another, and had received numerous awards and honors, such as the Order of the Red Banner of Labor on July 27, 1943. Though Serge remained attracted to Christian Science, a religious "sect" that Marxist-Leninist ideology could not countenance, he found a way to adapt it to a Soviet context. And whereas he once talked about his music in terms of divine inspiration, now he referred to it in terms consistent with the regime, as expressing human potential and the triumph of the spirit.

The clearest manifestation of his commitment to the Communist cause was his illustrious Fifth Symphony, which received its premiere on January 13, 1945, in the Great Hall of the Moscow Conservatoire. Lina and Svyatoslav attended. As Serge prepared to give the downbeat for the first movement, the concert's presenter appeared on stage to update the audience on the progress of Soviet troops on their final march into Berlin. There was a pregnant pause as the moment of triumph was absorbed by everyone in the hall. One of the luminaries in attendance recalled that "the hall was probably lit as usual, but when Prokofiev stood up, it seemed as though the light poured down on him from on high . . . There was something deeply significant, deeply symbolic in this, as if this moment marked a dividing line in the lives or everyone present, including Prokofiev himself." To the end of his life, Svyatoslav never forgot the image of his father "standing on the conductor's platform like a statue, pausing as guns blasted in celebration of the progress of the Red Army." The medals that he had earned for his wartime service graced his tuxedo. His blood pressure was dangerously high.

A month before that performance, the zenith of Serge's career in the Soviet Union, he had been invited to a gathering that he did not want to attend, but decided (or was advised) that he should. The occasion was an afternoon reception on December 4, 1944, at the French embassy for the visiting statesman Charles de Gaulle, leader of the Free French during World War II. He had flown to the Soviet Union at Stalin's behest and landed in the remote but militarily significant city of Baku on the Caspian Sea, some nineteen hundred kilometers southeast of Moscow. The trip to the capital was completed by train. En route the French delegation paused in Stalingrad, where de Gaulle marveled at the massive construction projects without realizing he was witness to the expanding prison-camp system. In Moscow he was taken to the ballet, heard a song-and-dance ensemble at the House of the Red Army, and on December 4, received, as protocol demanded, a "cohort of intellectuals and writers, officially catalogued as 'friends of France' by the Soviet authorities."

Lina was welcomed at the French embassy as Serge's still-glamorous wife. When her turn in the receiving line arrived, she and de Gaulle politely chatted. Serge overheard and was appalled. "I've just spoken with your husband," the tall, thin general said by way of introduction, bending to address her. He wondered whether she would return to France. "I miss Paris so much," Lina confessed. De Gaulle graciously responded, "We eagerly await your arrival."

Serge took Lina aside and berated her for asserting that she was still his wife, even though, from a legal standpoint, she had the right to do so. She protested, but the tongue-lashing continued. "Don't be naive. You know the invitation was sent to me and my companion," meaning Mira, who just by her nature would have shied away from attending. "And from what I hear," Serge added, with reference to an unpleasant conversation he had just had with a high-level Soviet official, "you still visit foreign embassies." He warned her that if she persisted and something happened, she could not count on his help. "You can't stop me," Lina countered. "You don't have any control over me."

He did not, and his warning had no effect. Besides her forays to the French embassy, Lina became a regular visitor to the British and American embassies, alternately defying and denying the risk. Frederick Reinhardt, one of the diplomats stationed at the American embassy from 1940 to 1942 and from 1946 to 1948, recalled that "in the early postwar period," Lina brought herself "unfavorably to the attention of the authorities" by persisting in her efforts to obtain an exit permit. He first met her in 1940, when she came to a lunch or dinner at the embassy with Serge, and then again on her own in 1941, following the evacuation of the Soviet diplomatic corps and government to Kuybïshev.

She became well known to British citizens in Moscow, befriending staff members at the weekly newspaper *British Ally* (*Britanskiy soyuznik*), published in the Soviet Union since August 1942 as an emblem of Anglo-Soviet diplomatic friendship. In 1947, however, the Kremlin deemed it a security concern. Memoranda about its nefarious influence as an anti-Soviet propaganda outlet were exchanged between Central Committee and government officials. Distribution was suppressed; the once-enthusiastic letters to the editor from readers grew hostile. The editor, Archibald Johnstone, disappeared, and his supposed letter of resignation, which included an abdication of British citizenship, appeared in *Pravda*. Publication was suspended in September 1950.

Sometime in 1945, the staff organized a cocktail party at the Metropole Hotel. Lina received an invitation, and there she met Anna Holdcroft, a recently arrived translator for the British Ministry of Information. Holdcroft would serve in Moscow from November 1944 for four years as an attaché in the information department of the British embassy. Holdcroft seems to have been in charge of the films that were screened at the embassy on the weekends in 1945. Lina made a point of attending until she began to find them enervating.

Holdcroft lived at the Metropole, and Lina exercised wiliness in slipping in to see her, something that, in Holdcroft's words, "did her no good." She added that Lina moved "freely amidst the foreign embassies of Moscow and was invited to many parties." She ignored the danger, but Holdcroft did not: "I urged her to be more cautious but she never heeded my requests. She was at that time trying desperately to be allowed to go to France to see her mother, but without success."

More problematic was the friendship Lina developed with Holdcroft's colleague George Vanden, third Baron Derwent. Lina found the nobleman attractive and impeccably mannered, as befitted his upbringing and Oxford education, and stimulating in conversation. Derwent blended his diplomatic work with studies in art and music history (he published on Goya and Rossini) and creative writing, turning his perception of the war into a collection of poems published in 1946, called *Before Zero Hour*.

Lina remembered meeting Derwent at British parties in 1947. He was on the prowl (his wife had died in 1941), but she could not provide what he sought. The relationship never became intimate—she dubbed it *amitié amoureuse*—but it at least assuaged her terrible loneliness. Their few dates were tense. Because she had performed official service for Sovinformbyuro and had upper-level connections on the Central Committee, Lina was even less free than other Soviet citizens to fraternize with foreigners, despite her urgent desire to do so. Derwent pledged not to cause her any problems and devised clever ways for them to meet. One evening he arranged a rendezvous in the crowded Arbat Metro station, noting that he would be easy to recognize in his white officer's uniform. She should not make eye contact but could signal her arrival with a word or two at the appointed column atop the escalator before passing through the doors ahead of him. He would follow at a safe distance.

He and the other British officers she met could obtain passes for foreign films, though exposure to decadent capitalist entertainment remained ideologically perilous even after the war. Still Lina went. One film starred Douglas Fairbanks Jr., whom she had met in Hollywood in what seemed like a previous life. She sat in the theater beside Derwent without acknowledging his presence, maintaining a nervous decorum. The implications of even holding his hand were terrible to imagine. When he dropped her off in his car at the entrance to the Metro, he dared not kiss her. Lina exited, and he politely waited to see that she had made it into the station without incident (muggings were not uncommon). He then drove on.

In the early spring of 1947, Derwent left the USSR. He later became engaged to Carmen Gandarillas, the daughter of a staffer at the Chilean embassy in London, whom Lina dubbed "the appropriate person" for him. She recalled her own time with him less as a lost opportunity than a therapeutic distraction. Derwent died suddenly and peacefully in his sleep three months after his well-publicized engagement, on January 12, 1949, in Paris. He was just fifty.

The friendship with Anne-Marie, the pragmatic semi-flirtations with the American Red Cross delegate and the diplomats, the escapist films—these are the stories of the war years that Lina offered to interviewers, not those about hunger, illness, and ration cards. The fractious encounters with Serge also went unreported, likewise the creeping, corrosive suspicion that she had put herself at risk once too often. Cocktails with Holdcroft and films with Derwent took her back to a life that she no longer had, at least for a moment, and strengthened her resolve to reclaim it, to get out of Moscow.

• • •

Lina began to suspect that her movements were monitored, and they were: her activities were reported and added to her personal file at the MGB, a subdivision of the NKVD established in 1946. Riding the Metro home after seeing Derwent for the last time, she became aware of a man across from her in the wood-paneled, wide-aisled carriage. He looked up at her, then down at his newspaper, and then back up again. He repeated the action without variance. Lina was meant to notice him, noticing her.

Unnerved, she got off at her station, traversed the expanded, forty-meter width of Chkalov Street through an underpass, walked along a street without cars, past stores without signs, to her building. She entered the quiet, empty courtyard, passed through the tenth entrance, and then went up the three flights of cement stairs to her apartment. The resonance of her footfalls in the stairwell was as distinct and familiar to her as the mix of odors on each floor. She arrived home safe, alone.

Lina saw the stranger on the train again in 1948, at her brief, perfunctory trial.

Chapter 11

I N MARCH 1947, after the violent death of her husband, Alexander Afinogenov, Jenny Marling arranged permission to leave Moscow, where she had been working as a liaison to foreign journalists, and travel with her daughters Joy and Alexandra (Sandra) home to Los Angeles. They sailed from Odessa to New York, then flew to California. On the plane, Jenny spoke to her daughters in English for the first time. They settled in Hollywood near her mother and an uncle employed by Disney. Yet Jenny found it impossible to reintegrate into American life and just eighteen months later made plans to return to Moscow. When Joy and Alexandra, ages eleven and six, asked why they were heading back, Jenny replied, "Because that's where your father and my husband is buried." She shipped their belongings (including a newly purchased Buick) back to the Soviet Union in August 1948. Once she and her family arrived by ship, she planned on driving the eleven hundred kilometers to Moscow.

As the Black Sea port of Odessa came into view, fire broke out on the vessel—a steamer named *Pobeda* (*Victory*). Manufactured in Germany, it had been transferred to the Soviets as war reparations, and rechristened. Investigators later discovered that the fire had started in a pantry crammed with phonograph records and film canisters. One of the films ignited while being rewound; first the projectionist's clothing, then the entire room caught fire. Flames engulfed the carpeting down the hall and spread along the plywood bulkheads, funneling through shafts into living quarters, the steering room, and the radio room. The radioman saved himself by jumping through a window, without signaling distress. He, like the projectionist, would be convicted of negligence and sentenced to hard labor. Jenny's two daughters survived the inferno: Joy was reading elsewhere, while Alexandra was playing in a corridor with another girl. She remembers seeing her mother for the last time behind a wall of flame.

Guardianship of the girls was assigned to their paternal grandmother, who lived in a building on Lavrushenskiy pereulok managed by the Union of Soviet Writers. From California, Jenny's daughters received a sentimental photograph from Jenny's mother. It was taken just before they left for Moscow and shows the two girls standing in front of the Buick with their mother, wearing white dresses, faces tanned, squinting in the sun. The inscription reads, "Darlings, do you remember this? Your car and my garage. You can see my porch upstairs and me crying. Keep this forever."

Had she survived the fire aboard the *Pobeda*, Jenny would still have been in peril. Alexander Fadeyev, a hard-drinking bureaucrat at the Union, revealed that her name had crossed his desk on a list of those to be arrested. Alexandra believes that her mother anticipated this. From the *Pobeda*, she telegrammed her mother-in-law to the effect that her daughters would soon need her to look after them. Alexandra also later learned that their ship was delayed in New York for four hours while Jenny's baggage was searched by customs officials.

Jenny died on September 1, 1948, at age forty-three. She saw Lina just before leaving for the United States. Lina also saw Anne-Marie Lotte soon after she received the long-hoped-for news that she could travel to France to rebuild her former life. The fates of these two women could not have been more different—from each other's or from Lina's. Though she too had tried desperately to return to the West, on November 1, 1948, Lina was consigned to the purgatory of the gulag.

For American, British, and French nationals who had relocated to the Soviet Union and found themselves effectively imprisoned there, the postwar period—specifically 1946 and 1947—saw the opening of a diplomatic window and the chance to depart. But by 1947, as she approached her fiftieth birthday, Lina knew that she was in a race against time. If she did not get out before that window closed, she had good reason to believe she would be arrested. It was a gamble: either her foreign contacts would come to her rescue, or they would land her in prison. As Frederick Reinhardt, first secretary and consul general of the American embassy, noted in 1948, "Practically all the Russians in Moscow who had been in contact with foreign embassy circles were arrested and disappeared from view. This was true of the Russian language teachers and others who presumably in the past had had official permission to be in contact with foreigners."

Lina must have been afraid, but both Jenny and Anne-Marie saw that she grew less rather than more fearful over time. She worried about her sons, having become more of a mother to them in Moscow during their adolescence than she had been in Paris during their childhood, and despaired that she might never see her own mother again. For this reason Lina used Svyatoslav's recurring respiratory illnesses (tuberculosis had left a hole in one of his lungs) as a pretext for requesting permission from the Soviet government to leave on compassionate grounds. Her husband pledged to help, but it seems that Serge did not, and the petitions came to naught.

Olga Codina remained in France, desperate for the occasional word from her daughter. She lived in modest quarters—a pair of rooms with a balcony overlooking a park in Ozoir-la-Ferrière, a suburban town southeast of Paris—and survived on an allowance that Serge received through his French publisher, Éditions Russe de Musique. The Paris office was managed by one of his confidants, Gabriel Paitchadze, with whom both he and Lina had originally discussed the move to the Soviet Union. On Serge's request, Paitchadze extracted a modest pension for Olga from his royalties.

She wrote frequently to her daughter, but most of the letters went undelivered. Lina saw them only in later years, after her mother's death. Olga also wrote to Paitchadze and his wife, Vera—short notes expressing immense gratitude for their financial support and their concern for her health, along with growing fears about Lina's well-being. Anxiety became anguish during the war, when neither mother nor daughter could reach each other. Their postwar correspondence through the French embassy and via intermediaries crossing borders was intermittent at best. Using his contacts in Moscow, perhaps including Serge himself, Paitchadze sought to answer Olga's pleas for information about her daughter. But at a certain point he had nothing to offer.

Olga could not countenance life in Stalinist Russia, and her frantic letters reveal a confusion that had nothing to do with her advanced age. On September 5, 1946, for example, she cautiously and naively wrote, "Concerning L. I.—Lina Ivanovna—I have little hope of her coming, however three weeks ago I received the following telegram from her: 'Espérons te rejoindre courant automne. Soignes-toi.' [We hope to meet up in the fall. Take care.] Especially at this time it's not so unusual to receive permission to leave. Perhaps she could be helped through S. S.'s—Prokofiev's—influential new relative. It's amazing that she's not taken advantage of this opportunity, and how remarkable that she and the children haven't been pushed out of their apartment. I heard that the children are incensed at their father. Many years ago, when Svyatoslav was 2 years old, the artist Alexandre Benois said that 'this baby' was his—Serge's—best composition."

The "new relative" Olga mentions was Mira's father, Abram Mendelson, and his supposed political influence stemmed from his work as a Soviet economist, for which he had achieved prominence. Like his wife, Abram was a true believer with hard-won political credentials, built on the back of his disavowing involvement during his youth with the Communist Bund, an anti-Bolshevik Jewish labor group. But that political savoir-faire was exactly the reason why he avoided contact with Lina. It would not have entered his mind to involve himself in her efforts to obtain an exit visa—even if, for obvious personal reasons, Mira wanted him to.

On January 3, 1947, Lina sent her mother a New Year's telegram with a kiss and the hope that they would be together in France in the spring: "Embrassons, souhaitons bonne année, espérons ce printemps nous verra ensemble chez toi." That didn't happen, and Lina fell silent. By the time they resumed contact in the summer, Olga's health had drastically declined, and Lina started to believe that she would never see her mother again.

Olga repeatedly expressed her panic at the lack of news from or about her daughter—even after Lina was arrested, something she knew of only from rumors. In the last letter she sent to the Paitchadzes, dated March 8, 1949, she frantically accused them of hiding things from her. The strange matter of Lina's relationship with Stanislas Julien came up: "You don't have news from S. J., who on one occasion requested that I only write to him at No. 622, the post-office box of the city in which he's living? I still don't believe that nobody knew about them." Then Olga indulged the far-fetched rumor that someone had actually managed to visit Lina at Lefortovo prison: "And your acquaintance, the one who saw her last August, she can't see her anymore? Tell me, I beg you!"

No one had seen Lina in August, and no one would. Olga never learned what had happened to her daughter, who would never learn what had happened to her.

Lina's failed efforts to obtain an exit visa, and the despair those efforts occasioned, prompted Svyatoslav to write an aggrieved, strongly worded letter to his father in the middle of August. It begins benignly, with Svyatoslav chatting about a summer stay on the Gulf of Finland at the resort of Terioki, which Soviet forces annexed in 1944. Svyatoslav also conveys his impressions of the museums in Leningrad (his fourth time in that city, the second that he could remember), his still-fragile health, his interest in obtaining a driver's license, and his upcoming exam at the architectural institute.

He also hints about marriage and a desire for a family of his own —pointedly adding, while knowing that his father might take offense, that "if I have children of my own, I hope they'll receive greater warmth" than he and his brother had received from their absent, preoccupied father. His mother, Svyatoslav writes, spent the summer in Moscow in a terrible mental and physical state, "tormented in the knowledge that Grandma's health has seriously declined, and at her age, with all she's been through, I fear it's the end." Appealing to his father's conscience, Svyatoslav reminded him of the consequences of his decision to walk out on his family. "Mama has also endured no shortage of hardship these past few years and the one dream that both she and Grandma share after their difficult, terrible years apart is to see each other again, one last time." The grief in Olga's last letter to her daughter and grandsons was so staggering, Svyatoslav appends, that he could barely hold back his tears while reading it. "How good it would be if you could somehow help Mama," he pleads. "It seems it would be so easy for you, at least much easier than for poor Mama, who has been fighting without success for this for a long time, expending blood and nerve. I would take such pleasure in helping, if only I were able."

Serge did not—and probably could not—help obtain an exit visa for Lina. His intervention, despite Svyatoslav's belief otherwise, would have made their lives worse, and his own situation was at the time precarious. For elite artists living under Stalin, official approbation tended to alternate with condemnation. Rational explanations for such changes in fortune are hard to come by. Vacillations in cultural policies affected careers, but so too did disputes within cultural agencies, miscommunications between those agencies and other tiers of government, and personal rivalries. The power of the regime was absolute in the sense that it followed no consistent rules. When Serge's standing declined radically in 1948, ideological considerations were less to blame than bureaucratic infighting and financial crises.

Serge had benefited from obeisance to the Soviet diplomat Potyomkin, the armed forces commander Voroshilov, and other high-ranking members of the regime in 1938, but not in 1948. On February 10 of that year, the Central Committee issued a resolution condemning the ideological failures of an overpriced opera, called *Velikaya druzhba* (*The Great Friendship*), by the second-tier composer Vano Muradeli. Toward the end of that fateful decree, its actual target comes into view: the Soviet musical elite and the agencies that supported them. Prokofiev, Shostakovich, Myaskovsky, and three others were criticized for absorbing modernist creative techniques, thereby alienating audiences, and for shunning the accessible Russian folk traditions in favor of inaccessible abstraction. Whatever the accolades heaped on them during the war, their works were suddenly reinterpreted by the Central Committee as emblems of decadence.

Soviet music had been through the ritual of denunciation and atonement before, but Serge had always avoided public disgrace. Yet here he was, caught in the crosshairs, found to have benefited from cronyism and kickbacks through the Union of Soviet Composers. His principal connection at the Union, his longtime patron and musical assistant Levon Atovmyan, had granted him a huge interest-free loan in 1946 toward the purchase of a dacha in the suburban enclave of Nikolina gora. A series of audits at the Union brought this and other improper loans and payments to light, and Atovmyan lost his job (but miraculously avoided prison). The off-the-books 150,000-ru-

ble loan became due in full, but Serge did not have the means to re-
pay it, since—as a consequence of the February 10 resolution—he
had lost almost his entire income. Several of his works were banned,
excised from the repertoire for their newfound ideological deficien-
cies, even though, before 1948, they had been officially celebrated.
The menace behind his political rebuke was such that even the works
that avoided censure went unperformed. Olga complained in her last
letter to Paitchadze that Serge had become "terribly miserly" with his
family. But at the time, he was destitute.

Serge submitted dutiful letters of apology to the bureaucrats behind the February 10 resolution, to little avail. The chairman of the
Union of Soviet Composers, Tikhon Khrennikov, was either not inclined or in no position to be forgiving. In addition to the political
blow, Serge suffered a personal one. The Soviet filmmaker Sergey
Eisenstein died the day after the public release of the resolution. He
was just fifty and had yet to finish editing the film he had been working on with Serge during the war, *Ivan the Terrible*. (Revisions were
demanded by Stalin himself.) There survives silent film footage of
Serge at the memorial service, his face drawn and pale.

It took Serge years to recover materially from the crisis, and his
health never did. He spent the remaining five years of his life in and
out of hospitals and sanatoria. Arguably the greatest musical genius
of the twentieth century was reduced to piecemeal labor on unin-
spired and uninspiring scores, the most notorious being an opera titled *Povest' o nastoyashchem cheloveke* (*Story of a Real Man*), about a Soviet fighter pilot who loses both legs in a crash, only to return to
heroic battle. Lina suspected that Mira had suggested the plot, a ridiculous caricature of an actual wartime event. (In truth, an official
within the Committee on Arts Affairs had backed the project, though
Mira eagerly helped to devise the libretto, adding a scene in which the
convalescent hero dances a rumba on double prostheses.) At his sickli-
est, Serge relied on self-interested, semi-employed minders—the disgraced Atovmyan included. Recycling and reworking older compositions became his enfeebled norm in the early 1950s.

Mira remained devotedly at his side, having become his wife on
January 13, 1948, through a nefarious bureaucratic fiat. Serge had
filed a petition in a local court (in Moscow's Sverdlov district) to di-

vorce Lina on November 22, 1947. He had long ago ruled out their reuniting, though Lina continued to hope. She still loved him. Her relationships with other men remained platonic, nurtured for the help
that they might provide to her in her efforts to leave, either temporarily or permanently.

The divorce petition was rejected, for reasons no one could have
anticipated. On November 27, the court ruled that Serge's 1923 marriage to Lina at the Ettal Rathaus had no legal basis, since it had taken
place outside the Soviet Union and had not been registered with Soviet officials. The marriage was null and void the moment they took
up residence in the Soviet Union. Even by Soviet legal standards, the
ruling was a farce, a circumvention of jurisprudence that became infamous in post-Stalinist Soviet classrooms. For one thing, the decision asserted that the marriage had taken place not in 1923, but in
1918, before Serge had left Russia for the United States and before he
had even met Lina; for another, it asserted that the couple had been
Soviet citizens at the time of their union, which, to be sure, they were
not. The status of their two sons went unmentioned.

Serge came to terms with the nonsensical ruling—which obviously left him free, as a single man, to marry—after he had it verified
with a second court. Less than two months after the confirmation
ruling, and unbeknownst to Lina, Serge married Mira. It was then
just a matter of weeks before Lina would be summoned to pick up a
package outside her apartment, dragged into a car, and taken to the
Lubyanka prison for interrogation.

Olga knew nothing about her daughter's arrest on the night of
February 20, 1948, but concluded the worst. "Has something horrible happened to 'her'?" she asked Gabriel and Vera Paitchadze four
months after her daughter's disappearance. "I presume 'she' ended up
na indekse—on a list—as a foreigner?" The pronouns *she* and *her* substituted for *Lina*: Olga avoided writing her daughter's name for fear of
the consequences. Paranoia had infected her communications to even
her most trusted friends in Paris. In August 1948, she wrote a similar letter to Anne-Marie Lotte in search of information, pinning her
hopes on the presence of the deputy foreign minister of the Soviet
Union, Andrey Vïshinsky, in Paris. "He presumably knows her; is it
not possible to approach him and ask where she is, what's happened

to her?" It was a pitiful appeal, especially given Vïshinsky's odious involvement in the Stalinist purges.

At home alone after Lina's arrest, Svyatoslav and Oleg opened the apartment door to confront three MGB officers: Major G. A. Trifonov, Captain N. F. Koytsov, and Lieutenant A. P. Bobrov. Their mother was out, they said, only to be reassured that the officers were well aware of that fact, since they had just stuffed Lina into a car bound for the Lubyanka. There followed a search of the apartment and the itemization and confiscation of supposedly incriminating evidence. It was carried out in the presence of Lina's terrified sons, along with the assistant to the *upravdom* (warden) of the apartment building, V. I. Egorova, whose duties as informant exceeded those of custodian and bill collector. Serge's August Förster piano was tagged for removal, likewise the Smith Corona and Underwood typewriters, the Singer sewing machine, the silver tea service, the 94-volume Brookhouse-Efron encyclopedia, 286 foreign-language books, 68 magazines, numerous never-to-be-recovered photographs and documents.

Svyatoslav flinched when the looters discovered his postcards of Soviet leaders: "The postcards had been with me a long time and in my thoughtlessness I did not recognize that it was necessary from time to time to remove the pictures of those leaders who had been repressed. During the search, one of the MGB officers came across a photograph of the latest enemy of the people. He laid it aside for the file. I attempted a protest: 'I bought them all together, like they were sold at the store.'"

The search had nothing to do with incriminating evidence. The apartment was looted, its contents taken on "special order" for "supply to the MGB USSR." Lina's brooches, rings, bracelets, and watch were stolen. Each item was made of gold, but the four-page list (in four copies) of confiscated belongings described them disingenuously as "yellow-colored." The same ruse applied to the knives, forks, and spoons—the silver inventoried as plain metal cutlery.

The piano was the greatest loss, along with a precious oil painting of opalescent white flowers by the Silver Age artist Natalia Goncharova, whom Lina and Serge had befriended in Paris through her affiliation with the Ballets Russes. The other paintings in the apartment, including a large portrait of Lina, remained on the walls; the ill-tempered female officer who turned up that night to finish the search decided that they were not to her liking. But the Goncharova appealed to her. Sizing up the apartment, her dull eyes landed on the small mother-of-pearl image: "Give it to me but don't enter it on the list." She walked out with it under her arm, covered in a cloth. The shopping spree ended with the bagging of the family record collection: 17 Soviet albums and 147 foreign ones—including precious original recordings of Serge's piano works as well as performances by Duke Ellington, Benny Goodman, and Ray Noble. (The violinist Juri Jegalin recalled Serge playing the coveted jazz records for him at a late-night gathering in the apartment in January 1939.) The albums were left behind in a sealed room in the apartment, to be collected at the end of the summer. Svyatoslav used the time to rescue some of the foreign discs, replacing them in their sleeves with 78s of trivial Soviet ditties found at a local market. The criminal act went unnoticed when it came time to haul away the albums for the enjoyment of a jazz-loving interrogator or investigator. Some of the thick, brittle 78s were smashed as men in uniform dragged the sack down the stairs.

Just one of the items taken could have been interpreted as anti-Soviet, contravening Stalinist social or political policies. This was item number 44: Mary Baker Eddy's *Science and Health with Key to the Scriptures*, the textbook of Christian Science, in an edition published in Boston in 1937. (The title is written in Russian on the confiscation list, but the book was printed in English. The first Russian-language edition did not appear until 1961.) Lina possessed other Christian Science–related publications; not all of them were confiscated by the MGB. One of them is a postcard-sized book on thick paper, printed with a Communist Red frame but bearing Mary Baker Eddy's—as opposed to Stalin's—thoughts on good versus evil. It dates from 1909, in a bilingual French-English edition, and contains the statement "There is no door through which evil can enter, and no space for evil to fill in a mind filled with goodness." Eddy's publication seems to have been left untouched, even though its title alone could have been interpreted as an anti-Stalinist provocation: *Ce que dit notre leader—What Our Leader Says*.

There were other materials of this sort in the apartment. The most poignant is a tiny card printed in 1936 in the United States by the trustees of the Mary Baker Eddy Estate—a children's prayer, brought by Lina to the Soviet Union in the year of her permanent relocation. It reads: "Father-Mother-God, Loving me—, Guard me when I sleep; Guide my little feet up to Thee."

Svyatoslav and Oleg were permitted to remain in the apartment after the search but were locked out of the two rooms used for storing items to be collected later. They stayed there, in fact, for almost two years. In October 1949 they received an eviction notice; that December, they relocated from the third to the sixth floor in the same entrance of the same building, from apartment 14 to 19. The new apartment comprised two rooms plus kitchen, bath, and toilet—forty-eight square meters in total.

The furniture that had not been bartered during the war or pilfered by the MGB took three days to move up the stairs. The elevator operator refused to help with the move, so Svyatoslav recruited a broad-shouldered friend from the institute for the task. The previous tenant in apartment 19, the popular graphic artist Mikhaíl Kupriyanov, had left it in pristine condition, except for the fairy-tale-like mural that his daughter had painted on the glass-paned, thick wooden door to the kitchen. As Svyatoslav and a friend lugged chairs and mattresses up the stairs, another artist favored by the regime, the Stalin Prize recipient Nikolay Sokolov, moved into their former home. First, though, Sokolov remodeled it, erasing all trace of its prior occupants. "Such a renovation Sokolov has made to No. 14," Svyatoslav wrote to his imprisoned mother in 1950, "and how very sad that our No. 14 has so completely disappeared."

In 1949 Svyatoslav successfully defended his diploma project at the Architectural Institute, but it took him a long time to find work, owing to his mother's arrest. Eventually, he found a rather dull position as a draftsman for electric station designs; later, he translated articles on construction and architecture from English and French into Russian for a research institute. It took several months for Svyatoslav, his wife, Nadezhda, and Oleg to adjust to their cramped abode. Marking birthdays and the New Year were painful in their mother's absence, since Lina had always insisted on making them family events.

• • •

In accordance with MGB arrest order No. 3939, Lina was detained first at the Lubyanka, briefly, and then Lefortovo prison for a total of nine and a half months. Three and a half months of her imprisonment involved protracted interrogations, otherwise known as the "investigation." After passing through the gates of the Lubyanka, she was photographed from the front and side, her gaze defiant, the blackness in her eyes making the irises and pupils almost indistinguishable. A haggard crone barked at Lina to undress, then sheared the buttons, hooks, and zippers from her sweater and dress. After her purse was emptied, Lina was given a doubly signed receipt from the Internal Prison of the MGB USSR for the "29 rubles and 95 kopecks" it contained, another one for her Soviet passport, and yet another for her wristwatch and bracelet.

The serial numbers and brand names of the jewelry were itemized, just like the belongings removed from her apartment. An intrusive search the next day revealed that Lina had concealed an additional five thousand rubles on her person; for that amount too she received a doubly signed receipt. Despite running a low-grade fever, she was made to take a cold shower. She remembered the water barely dribbling down on her head as she tried to wash her hair with anti-lice soap. Once her fingerprints were taken, she was shoved into a tiny cell with a low ceiling. There was no chair or bed, and not enough room to stand. She heard bells ringing and the sound of other people being photographed and strip-searched. Lina spent most of her time alone. When overcrowding forced a second or third person into her cell, mattresses were thrown onto the floor. Her first meal consisted of sour black bread and water; the next a plate of unpalatable, rust-colored herring soup.

She summoned a guard and said that she needed to contact her children, let them know what had happened. Rambling, shaken, she mentioned that Svyatoslav's twenty-fourth birthday was coming up and she wanted to make it special for him. Callous reassurance came in reply: "They will be notified in good time."

Seeking information about their mother's whereabouts, Svyatoslav and Oleg went to a police information outlet on the old cobblestone lane running between Gorky Street and Lubyanka Square. They were told that Lina had been transferred to Lefortovo prison in southeast

Moscow. The next day they took the suburban train to the village of Perkhushkovo and, in the absence of buses, walked the remaining fourteen kilometers to Nikolina gora, to report the news to their father. Mira opened the door of the dacha in her housecoat, wide-eyed with alarm. She recoiled and retreated to summon Serge. When he appeared fifteen minutes later, Svyatoslav and Oleg recounted what had happened to their mother. The three men walked together in the cold; Serge asked one or two questions, shocked and shaken, but his political standing was so reduced that there was no thought of his trying to help. The boys also appealed to Dmitri Shostakovich for assistance. Despite also being censured by the Central Committee in 1948, he occupied a position of influence as a deputy to the Supreme Soviet of the RSFSR. But he was powerless when it came to the MGB.

The routine roundups left the MGB overextended, so Lina was taken outside Moscow for interrogation in a makeshift building. On the way, through a crack in the back door of the unmarked truck, she recognized the streets near her apartment; before being pulled from the vehicle she heard barking dogs and glimpsed chickens. At the Lubyanka, her interrogations occurred at irregular intervals on the fourth and sixth floors of the main administrative building adjacent to the prison itself, in long, narrow, cramped rooms with pale red cement floors and faded green-and-white walls. Each room had a shelf, a small barred window, a single stool, and a pair of vents to dispel the stench of disinfectant and human fear. Some of the rooms had parquet floors—a vestige of the building's benign past, when it served as the headquarters of an insurance firm.

The four men who interrogated her were semi-educated thugs who knew nothing of the world beyond the Soviet Union and who lived in squalid quarters on small salaries supplemented by bribes and extortion. Unlike the staff of the labor camps where Lina would later find herself exiled, where men and women were required to fulfill production quotas, those at the prisons specialized in torturing people for the purpose of extracting confessions. They could take their time. The methods ranged from beatings to lashings to the injection of truth serums. The sadistic rituals numbed their minds and inured them to the horrors they were committing and the fact that they too were at risk, isolated in their ranks, susceptible to denunciation from subordinates and superiors as one wave of postwar repression spawned another.

Pyotr Malikov was one of her tormentors. Born in 1901 to peasant parents in the village of Krasovka, he served four years in the army, from 1919 to 1923, before joining a trade union in the southern Russian city of Saratov. He petitioned for membership in the All Union Communist Party of Bolsheviks and was accepted into the second district Party organization in Saratov in 1927. His social service included teaching peasant women in his village how to read; in later years, he taught and led discussions on the history of the Party. In Moscow, he took up residence in a communal apartment and found work supervising builders and mechanics while also serving in the agitation and propaganda department of a scientific institute. Malikov assisted the director of Moscow Aviation Factory No. 261 in dismissing suspect employees; he did the same at an iron and steel works in the Ural Mountain city of Nizhniy Tagil. Regarded as "disciplined and politically literate," Malikov earned several honors and medals. The photograph in his personal file shows a glassy-eyed, thin-lipped man of forty, wearing a buttoned suit, knotted striped tie, and starched white shirt. His left brow is arched, emphasizing his skeptical, penetrating gaze.

Among Malikov's comrades was Nikolay Kuleshov, who joined the ranks of the political police in 1933, after several years of work in a Moscow metal plant called Hammer and Sickle. He served during the war at the Stalingrad and Ukrainian fronts as part of the SMERSH (the Russian acronym for "death to spies") counterintelligence operation, absorbing a smattering of German. He performed his duties adequately but suffered mental problems stemming from a loveless childhood. His father had died in 1917 or 1918, when he was eight or nine; his impoverished mother abandoned him in an orphanage. He claimed no brothers or sisters on his résumé, no exposure to cosmopolitan influences, and no hesitation of any sort in his work. Kuleshov's MGB uniform and brush cut make him look older than thirty in his photo, which dates from 1939. He is thick-necked and pudgy-faced, his features more brutish than Malikov's.

Joined by two other agents, Malikov and Kuleshov beat Lina; deprived her of light, sleep, and warmth; and bound her limbs in excruciating positions. Once she was thrown into a cell filled with ice. Under such extraordinary duress, Lina signed a confession for a random assortment of charges. Her file already contained political denunciations and fabricated accusations, but their authors remain unknown. Mira is not presumed to be one of them.

Lina faced four charges: The first was the theft of the document from Sovinformbyuro. This she categorically denied, pointlessly explaining that her translation services did not include work with confidential materials. The second charge concerned one of the numerous letters and notes that she had sent abroad with confidants or through the embassies. The letter in question was written by a certain Engineer Shestopal, the husband of Lina's Parisian friend Susanna Rotzenberg, who worked in Moscow for Soyuzintorgkino, a bureau that imported and exported films.

For ensuring the letter's delivery, Lina was accused of facilitating the illegal transfer of information about a factory in the city of Gorky to a foreign source. In her most detailed petition for help with her case, written to Shostakovich, Lina described the accusation while also revealing something more about the methods of her interrogators. First she had been "interviewed" about her relationship with Shestopal and his wife — as had Shestopal himself, who had denounced her. Then her interrogators arranged a confrontational meeting with Shestopal in order to "expose" her. "Shestopal was in a terrible, unrecognizable state," she commented, "and he couldn't even look me in the eyes, evidently confessing under duress to the effect that he had not given me just an ordinary letter addressed to his wife, but something about a factory in Gorky.

"I read this letter and there was nothing suspicious in it; otherwise I wouldn't have passed it along. I considered Shestopal a decent person and couldn't understand how he could have come up with such a lie about his wife and I having 'conspiratorial liaisons.' His wife was not anti-Soviet and, my friendship with her, given her age, was of a maternal sort, nothing more. The investigator cursed at me after the confrontation and said that I was a coward, that this would be the ruin of me."

Lina repeatedly "confessed" to the investigator that in 1940 she had indeed passed the letter along as a favor to Shestopal, but that the letter was innocuous. She had given it to Fannie (Theophania) Chipman, the French-born, thirty-five-year-old wife of Norris Chipman, diplomat at the American embassy in Moscow in the late 1930s. At Lina's request Fannie had taken Shestopal's letter with her to Paris in 1940 and made sure that Susanna Rotzenberg received it. Whatever its contents, Lina knew passing the letter through foreign diplomatic channels was in and of itself sufficient grounds to be charged with treason. But she admitted to doing so nonetheless, clarifying that she had opened it to make sure that its contents were benign, nothing anti-Soviet. Lina also admitted to sending a package to Fannie Chipman in Paris through Frederick Reinhardt.

The interrogations circled around and around these matters, to the point that Lina felt, as intended, that she was losing her mind. The most serious accusation hurled at her concerned her persistent efforts to leave the Soviet Union with the aid of foreign embassy workers. Besides the Chipmans and the Reinhardts, focus fell on Anna Hold-croft of the British embassy and a random assortment of staffers at the French embassy. Lina had also visited the Japanese embassy, incriminating herself there as well. She had been tracked for so long that the MGB knew the dates and times of most of her personal meetings with foreign diplomats.

She defended herself as simply trying to visit her ailing mother in Paris. Her desire to see Olga was interpreted as a collusional conspiracy to defect, though that was surely not her intent. Her requests to travel always made it clear that she intended to return to her two sons, who were to remain in Moscow. And all the while, she pointed out that she was as much a stranger in the Soviet Union as the foreigners she had befriended.

From the Lubyanka, Lina was transferred to a cell, four square meters in size, at Lefortovo. Journalists writing about the prison note that the K-shaped building has yellow brick walls, three floors, and narrow staircases, and it houses up to two hundred prisoners. These trivial details are repeated as evidence of just how little is known about the prison's operation, past and present.

Historians have been thwarted in their efforts to write about Lefortovo, since even the museum devoted to the history of the surrounding neighborhood avoids mentioning it. The prison is largely hidden behind an apartment building at the corner of Lefortovsky Val and Ulitsa Energeticheskaya (Electric Power Street). A corner of its dilapidated, thick outer wall can be glimpsed between the apartments and the campus of an eighty-year-old aviation engine research institute. Both the campus and the prison wall are ringed with barbed wire. Spotlights and an inward-slanted, shoddy sheet-metal shield block sound and sight into and out of the prison.

What scant information exists about Lefortovo in the 1930s and 1940s comes from the reminiscences of those inmates fortunate enough to have survived. The sound of executions and interrogations was concealed by (depending on the source one consults) the roar of a turbine from the neighboring aviation institute or the snarl of tractors running on the prison grounds. Prisoners were kept isolated, save for occasional ersatz cellmates—informants working for the MGB. There were accounts of prisoners being locked in wooden closets in the corridors to conceal them from each other while being taken to the toilet, the bath, and the interrogation cell. These elaborate measures prevented prisoners from learning the layout of the building. They also ensured that they were deprived of even the basic human comfort of hearing someone speak.

Having been accused of a crime against the state, Lina was not allowed any contact with the outside world while at Lefortovo. The prolonged isolation exacerbated her psychological deterioration, as did her awareness of the torture, murders, and suicides occurring all around her. She knew about these things not because she saw them, but because her interrogators told her. She did hear the screams emanating from the interrogation cell. It may be that her sons were allowed to leave packages at the service entrance at 5 Lefortovsky Val; even so, she would not have received them. Svyatoslav and Oleg did not see their mother again until after she had been transferred to the north. Oleg was the first to visit, once restrictions for traveling to the gulag were lifted, following Stalin's death.

On November 1, Lina was court-martialed by a three-member Military Collegium (Voyennaya kollegiya) of the Supreme Court of the USSR and sentenced to two decades of hard labor in accordance with the treason statute (58-1a) of the Soviet Penal Code. The trial lasted less than fifteen minutes. Lina laughed when she heard the verdict.

• • •

SIMON MORRISON · 255

Beyond revealing that single detail—her laughter—Lina refused to
speak about the months preceding her conviction and sentencing.
Svyatoslav and Oleg learned nothing beyond the scattered details
that their mother provided in her numerous, pointless petitions for
a review of her case. Lina sent these from the labor camp of Abez, in
the Komi Autonomous Soviet Socialist Republic of the gulag system.
Besides the February 28, 1954, petition to Shostakovich, she submitted one on May 27 of that same year to the prosecutor general of the
USSR. On the first pages of both, she lists her address as 388/16b—
the number of her mail slot in the gulag, where she had been living
for six years.

For the prosecutor general, Lina first listed the charges made
against her and then tried, in confusing fashion, to demonstrate that
they were baseless. Besides theft, treason, and illegal foreign contacts,
she had been forced to sign a statement admitting to being an American agent in consort with her anti-Bolshevik immigrant husband.

"The evidence was distorted to the point of non-recognition," she
shouted into the dark,

> and this is what they called recasting "my balderdash" into legal lan-
> guage. They said to me: "Don't be foolish—sign the confession. We
> know you're not a spy, but it has to be this way." They intimidated me
> by saying that the lives of my children would be destroyed. Investi-
> gator Zubov spit on me and kicked me. For three and a half months
> (the length of the investigation) I wasn't permitted to sleep, neither
> during the night nor the day. I was driven to the point of madness.
> Two days out of five I was made to sit, in truth, "stand," my legs
> as swollen as logs. In freezing temperatures they took me from my
> cell for interrogation outside, without proper clothing. At night dur-
> ing the interrogations I heard shrieks of pain from the offices of the
> investigators at Lefortovo prison. Having been made sick, disorien-
> tated, the investigator "consoled" me: "Don't worry, you'll be scream-
> ing even louder when you feel this truncheon on your ass!" I was sub-
> ject to profanity of this sort all the time. Lieutenant Kuleshov called
> my husband a "white émigré" who'd hoarded money abroad, and that
> I'd covered this fact up and would be severely punished for it.
> At the end of the investigation I tried to mount a protest, wanted to
> commit my side of the story to paper, but I was not allowed. Fragile,
> debilitated by everything that had happened and in a precarious psy-

chological state after the investigation—how could I defend myself?
—is it no wonder that after all I've described above I was prepared
to sign any protocol, willingly, knowing that there wasn't a word of
truth in it?

And so she became a "dangerous criminal," living in frail health,
now fifty-six years old, in the harshest of conditions. She asserted
her rights to rehabilitation and justified her return to the civilized
world by including an autobiographical sketch that highlighted her
appearances as a singer with her husband, "the Soviet composer S. P.,"
in Europe and America and the Soviet embassies. She had also sung
with the Moscow Philharmonic, in Kharkov, and in Arkhangelsk. Although "a nervous condition" had forced her to retire early from the
stage, she had found fulfillment as a Soviet citizen through her children and her husband's creative work.

Lina's petition was reviewed and rejected on June 26, 1954, exactly
a month after its receipt. She remained in her barracks just beneath
the Arctic Circle.

Chapter 12

LITTLE REMAINS OF the camps where Lina fought for eight years to survive—or of the entire gulag system. *Gulag* is an acronym, a contraction of *Glavnoye upravleniye ispravitel'no-trudovikh lagerey i koloniy*, which translates as the cumbersome "main administration of the correctional labor camps and colonies." Prison camps spread across the Soviet Union to form what the Soviet writer Alexander Solzhenitsyn, himself a prisoner, famously called the "Gulag Archipelago." They were an integral part of Stalin's Five-Year Plans for the industrial expansion of the Soviet Union, because the gulag provided slave labor in places with harsh climates, where no one could be enticed to go.

The Soviet camps differed from the Nazi camps for mass extermination. Even so, millions upon millions of innocent people were worked to death in the glorious service of the regime. Conditions were appalling, production inefficient and wasteful. According to eyewitness accounts, and the intrepid research that substitutes for a reckoning by the government of the Russian Federation, murders, rapes, suicides, and acts of sadism were common in the gulag. Recreation, such as it was, took the form of ideological reeducation programs. In the 1930s and 1940s, those who managed to outlive their sentences tended to be resentenced—or routinely, banally, executed. Lina survived for various reasons: the material support she received from her sons, her gender (death rates among men were higher than among women), the less taxing work assigned to older prisoners, good fortune, her own wit, and her relationship to an eminent Soviet composer. Ultimately, she earned release as a result of the political upheaval that followed Stalin's death on March 5, 1953 — the same day as Serge's.

Lina spent the first four years of her incarceration at Inta, the center of a massive cluster of camps in the desolate northern reaches of Russia. She was then transferred ninety-one kilometers south to Abez, the name given to a sub-cluster of six camps established in 1942 just beneath the Arctic Circle. (In the ancient dialect of the region, Komi, the word *abez* denotes "lack of cleanliness, slovenliness.") In January 1956, almost two years after Stalin's death, Lina was relocated again — this time to a sub-cluster of camps near Potma, southeast of Moscow, with a large foreign population. Six months later, she was released.

At Inta, a sculpture of a burning cross marks the entrance to a makeshift graveyard and bears the inscription TO THOSE WHO DID NOT RETURN in three languages, including Komi. It is the one monument to what happened there. Dark green diesel trains, three or four carriages long, crawl along the rail line to the dreary town, located atop one of the world's largest mineral deposits. It is an odious place, built on corpses — along the river and in the Siberian forest, human bones still surface from the earth during the spring thaw.

Prisoners died of malnutrition and exposure to subzero temperatures while building the older wooden residences of the town, the mineshafts, the power grid, and the railroad. The landscape, such as it is, is dominated by a water tower bearing the regional coat of arms. In the summer, the area becomes a sea of mud, leaving the power poles canting at bizarre angles in the muck. The train station is seventeen kilometers away, connected to the town by bus 101, but there is no central bus station, which hinders getting from point A to point B. Wooden walkways made from the sides of shipping cartons run helter-skelter between the newer, five-story brick apartment buildings. Homeless dogs run around idle children. The travel agency Intatur organizes excursions throughout the area and the Polar Urals, catering to visitors who might like to see the huge national park of virgin forest. Tourists can choose between two hotels, one of which offers a single shower for sixty-five guests, though it never has that many.

In the mottled, weed-covered wasteland of Abez, almost nothing remains. There was once a settlement that served six camps, two of which were built for women, some fifteen hundred prisoners in each. But the wooden barracks, barbed-wire fences, and watch towers were razed in 1959 by the prisoners themselves, under orders from Moscow, in a crude effort to conceal the crimes of Stalinism. Climate conditions ensured that any remaining structures would dissolve into the tundra. For the prisoners held there in the 1940s and 1950s, the treacherous terrain was a greater deterrence to escape than the guards. But even the crowded, infested barracks offered little protection from the elements, since they were never meant to be permanent. Now the once-sprawling compound is reduced to graves marked by wooden signs with no names, just letters and numbers. A taller sign above a portion of a water or sewage pipe reads THIS WAS THE LOCATION OF THE EARTHEN DUGOUT FOR THE GRAVEDIGGERS. Another sign shows where the morgue once stood. The dead would have been kept there; so too the dying.

It now takes nearly forty hours by train—not including transfer and waiting times—to reach Inta from Moscow, a distance of sixteen hundred kilometers northeast. In the 1940s and 1950s, the trip lasted four days. It would have taken Lina at least this long to reach Inta and her camp at Abez after departing from the *étap* at Kirov, a way station for prisoners eight hundred kilometers inland from the Soviet capital.

Kirov was the hub of a group of prisoner logging operations known as the Vyatlag (after the Vyatka River). The trip there from Moscow marked the first stage in Lina's conversion into a nameless labor camp inhabitant, or zek (from *zaklyuchyonnïy*, "locked in"). The most horrible moment would have been the first, when the train full of the condemned—men, women, and perhaps even children—lurched into motion. They traveled from Moscow along a freight line. Some were held in a barred, locked passenger carriage, others in a livestock car with planks for beds, a small heater in the middle, and a hole carved into the floor to be used as a toilet. Some prisoners were even caged. If the train stopped at a regular civilian train station, it was possible to acquire food from the local villagers; if not, rations consisted of frozen bread, strips of dried, salted fish, and precious cupfuls of water. Upon arrival in Kirov everyone was hauled off the train, stuffed into a truck, and unpacked into a prison cell that would have reminded Lina of her incarceration at Lefortovo.

On November 22, 1948, from the Kirov *étap*, Lina sent her nine-teen- and twenty-four-year-old sons a telegram with the number of her prison mailbox (22/23) and eight additional words in Russian. They attest to her disorientation and denial, or maybe to her resolve: "Awaiting your arrival. By appointment. Inquire with the police. Kiss. Mama." Of course her children could not visit her. In fact, when Oleg bravely traveled to Inta to try to see her—a harrowing trip that left him in fear for his life—he was rebuffed. The system did not permit meetings between prisoners and their relatives; seeing his mother, even for a few minutes, was out of the question. Oleg returned to Moscow traumatized.

In December, Lina left the transit prison in Kirov for the Komi Autonomous Soviet Socialist Republic. The camps at Inta bore the general name Dubravnïy lager, after the Russian word for *oak*, and the mining region to which she was first sentenced was known as Mineralnïy lager—the kind of name given to the therapeutic spas in the Crimea. Her home became a mattress on a plank bed in a claustrophobic wooden barracks for women. The air would have been easier to breathe on the upper bunks than the lower ones. There may or may not have been an aisle between the mattresses. Either an outhouse or a slop bucket served as a toilet; maintaining a semblance of cleanliness and preventing diseases such as botulism were critical. The zone, or prison grounds, that Lina inhabited was part of a huge central camp dedicated to mining and building the town of Inta. Beyond the barbed-wire fences in the adjacent zones, men worked the mines; most of them were doomed. The women cleared roads and plastered walls—easier work, which allowed them to live longer.

Given the horrors of the trains and transit prisons, Lina's arrival in Inta was cause for relief. Nothing could be worse than what she had already endured. Her fellow inmates were, by and large, low-risk political prisoners mixed in with informants, thieves, and (perhaps) workers from outside the zone. There were Muscovites and Leningraders who had interacted with foreigners and who, like Lina, had been forced into confessing to espionage; peasants from Belarus and Ukraine accused of resisting collectivization or collaborating with the Nazis; ethnic Estonians, Latvians, and Lithuanians suspected of anti-Soviet liaisons with the Germans. Some of the prisoners were uneducated, others people of great culture—like the Sorbonne-educated daughter of the onetime Latvian minister of enlightenment. The guards mocked her by making her keep guard over a cesspit.

Before moving to the barracks, an event that might have taken several days, Lina was forced to strip naked, examined, and sent to the bathhouse for disinfecting. Many prisoners were ordered to shave their heads and bodies, or it was done for them. After being cleared by a doctor to enter the zone for additional processing, Lina received a standard camp uniform: *valenki* (felt boots) and galoshes that were too big for her, a well-worn outer coat of pleated wool, and a head covering. She also received a few pairs of used underwear. A number on the back of her clothes identified her, and she took her place in a building with other women serving twenty-year sentences for treason. The clothes she later received from home could be worn within the zone, but when allowed outside the zone into civilian areas, Lina had to wear her camp uniform.

She emerged from the bathhouse to see standing before her Inna Chernitskaya, a former Russian staffer at the British embassy in Moscow, with whom she had become acquainted in 1944 at the Metropole Hotel. Chernitskaya was just twenty-three when she was arrested. She was picked up in the same month and year as Lina. A knock at the door at one in the morning awoke her, with the command, "Passport check, open the door!" The men who entered her apartment had dirty boots. She would have to wash the floor when she returned home, Inna thought to herself—but she did not return for eight years. Like Lina, she endured a protracted interrogation that forced her to narrate fictional accounts of treason in copious detail. Repeating the made-up stories condemned her further, because she would forget her own lies, inadvertently omitting or adding details that her investigators then used against her as evidence of a cover-up. (Since the accounts weren't true, they couldn't be remembered, and so the variants on the fictions became proof of more treason.) One of the men quoted Dante as she passed through the gates of the Lubyanka: "Abandon hope all ye who enter here." Her possessions were stolen and offered for sale at discount rates to the wives and mistresses of bureaucrats in a special store.

For her, as for Lina, the journey to Inta was traumatic and the arrival humiliating. Now the two of them were hugging and kissing each other in the frost—a moment of tender human contact. Inna knew the routines of the zone extremely well, since she had arrived several months before Lina. For a time, she worked in the *kaptyorka*, or supply depot, dispensing rations of rice and raisins to the prisoners and helping with the piecemeal distribution of packages (prisoners received only what was left over after the guards had helped themselves). Because her eyesight was poor and she had either lost or broken her glasses, Inna was not permitted to leave the prison grounds and did not participate in the construction detail supporting the mining projects that to this day define the place. Had she ventured out, even by innocent mistake, she would have been shot. She remembered the command of the guards as she was being marched to and from the barracks with the other prisoners: "A step to the right or a step to the left will be considered an escape attempt." At least she had endeared herself to the guards to the extent that none of them wanted the burden of killing her.

On December 19, 1948, Lina wrote a cramped four-page letter to Svyatoslav and Oleg, the first of the two she was allowed to send each month. She claimed to be "feeling a little better" after a month at Inta. The experience of the hideous six-week trip to the north had begun to recede from her body, if not her mind: she would have nightmares about it for the rest of her life. It was frigid outside, she acknowledged —minus forty-seven degrees Celsius. (It was not uncommon for the temperature to drop even lower.) The brilliance of the sun appearing over the desolate subarctic horizon brought to mind the sunrise music in Serge's *Scythian Suite*. It set before two in the afternoon, leaving her unable to gauge the time of day. The air was "very good" but blinding, howling blizzards were frequent, she wrote, an observation that confirms she was working outside. She would take ill for three weeks at the end of the year. Thereafter, she would work in a camp hospital—most of the staff would have been prisoners—and did secretarial work for camp administrators. There is also oblique reference in her letters to working in a sewing factory, six days a week.

Lina did not describe her daily routine, but likely she worked eight to ten hours a day and ate two meals in the communal meal hall. She would line up for porridge or herring with black bread in the morning, and a weak soup, or *balanda*, in the afternoon. The prescribed beverage was yeast-based and somehow meant to prevent scurvy. The clearing and building work was backbreaking; barrels, buckets, and shovels became instruments of slow torture.

Because of her age and physical limitations, Lina had a lighter workload than other women in the zone, but still it was grueling. She cleaned the bedbug- and lice-infested barracks when their residents were working, in the meal hall, or standing in line at the bathhouse. Lina ached to the core. Soon her back would begin to hunch, and her stride would shorten. Yet even while cleaning latrines, Lina sought to preserve her dignity. She wanted to hear and speak French again, to lose herself in memories of Paris. And she was just as social as ever, lingering between the barracks in the cold, in hopes of finding someone to talk to. Pulling buckets of human waste through the snow and ice, she struck up "intellectual conversations" with others in her brigade. One of the women knew the constellations and would point out stars and planets in the subarctic sky; another had studied Tolstoy, and yet another discussed the French writers Honoré de Balzac and Marie-Henri Beyle. Lina, of course, shared her knowledge of music.

Surprisingly enough, she actually pursued musical activities in the gulag. Inta permitted *kul'turno-vospitatel'naya rabota* (cultural education activities), which assumed both professional and amateur forms. Imprisoned actors, singers, and dancers could obtain at least partial exemption from hard labor by organizing agitprop shows for the guards and prisoners. It was not unusual for theatrical and even operatic entertainments to be mounted in the communal spaces, along with agitprop poster and placard exhibits and lectures on political themes. Some eligible prisoners refused to participate on moral grounds, but most did so as a practical means of survival—Lina among them. Prisoners were also allowed on occasion to form their own choruses or instrumental ensembles. Such activities were perceived by the authorities as motivational, a spur to produce more during the workday so as to enjoy the cultural activities at night. Prisoners used their agitprop activities as bargaining chips for reduced time on the labor front, and reportedly some prisoners were assigned easier tasks, thanks to their artistic endeavors.

Cultural education took other forms in the gulag. Films about Lenin, the heroes of the Komintern, and the defeat of the Nazis were shown on limited occasions as rewards to prisoners who exceeded their production quotas in the mines and timber operations. The projectors tended to break down, however, and replacement parts were hard to find. In the 1940s and 1950s, larger camp centers operated low-grade radio stations; smaller ones distributed agitprop newsletters lauding the achievements and denouncing the failings of the imprisoned builders of socialism. Prisoners took refuge from the bombast by playing board games. Facilities for sports did not exist at Inta, but they were nonetheless decreed an essential part of the ideological rehabilitation of the prisoners, exhaustion and starvation notwithstanding.

Lina petitioned to join a makeshift orchestra in Inta: a bizarre ensemble of singers, orchestral instruments, and folk instruments; some were shipped or brought to the camp, others handmade on the spot. Had she not taken ill at the end of 1948, she would have sung in a New Year's concert. Her description of the short-lived ensemble is redundant, indicative of her exhaustion, but also of the fact that she was competently performing a role—less for her sons than for the censor reading the letter. Lina tries not to complain, seeks to describe something positive. Besides "mixed instruments," she reports, "there's also a chorus, violins, flutes, accordions, squeezeboxes, a guitar, a very good conductor who's a serious musician, and a male chorus, and in all likelihood I'll be singing with them here."

Later she mentions an oboe, a French horn, and drums. Because her camp was only for women, the "male chorus" comprised either bored guards or prisoners from a neighboring camp for men. One of the violinists was in special demand because he actually built instruments. "He made a violin that's being used in the orchestra and sounds not bad at all. Now he's making a bass, but of course there are no strings for it, so you have to send a set of bass strings. It's a big request, I know, but absolutely essential."

She wanted her sons to send vocal music for her to perform, including arias from Soviet operettas, songs from recent Soviet films, arrangements of Strauss waltzes for soprano, and arias from Dvořák's *Rusalka*, Puccini's *La bohème* and *Madama Butterfly*, and Musorgsky's *Sorochinsky Fair*. She added a poignant selection: Chopin's tiny love song "The Wish," about a maiden imagining herself as the sun, and then as a bird, for the pleasure of her beloved. The last line speaks to her own longing: "Why can't I turn myself into a bird?"

Though she had almost lost her voice entirely, during the years she spent farther north at Abez, she sang in an ensemble that toured a portion of the gulag. When she could no longer muster any voice, she moved on to choral conducting, "with broad gestures and widespread arms." By that time there was no longer an orchestra, not even an accordionist, in her camp.

In November 1955, she led a pair of concerts in an army club. Female prisoners sang revolutionary songs; soldiers accompanied on brass instruments. The imprisoned musicologist David Rabinowitz slipped Lina a note of advice. She was "conducting as though in front of an orchestra, while one should lead choruses with small confined gestures in front of the body."

She persisted in her requests for music from her sons, adding a lament composed by Serge to the list—"I Shall Go out Across the Snow-Covered Field" from *Alexander Nevsky*.

The last item suggests that she did not at this point believe Serge had been arrested. Eventually, his silence would imply that he had. But he was never actually detained by the authorities, nor even investigated. The composer spent his final years relatively secluded in his dacha at Nikolina gora, a series of strokes having rendered him incapable of composing for more than an hour or two a day, bringing his life to a bathetically premature end. He confessed to Mira Mendelson in the last week of his life that his "soul hurt."

Other items that Lina asked to have sent to her were more practical. Food was of course the most pressing concern, then clothing. She had been told that she could receive as many food parcels as she liked, the assumption being that the guards would swindle some of the items and that others could be bartered for personal favors. Area villagers sold food to the prisoners, but Lina did not want cash mailed for this purpose—at least not at first, since she knew it would be confiscated. At a bare minimum, she needed butter, sugar, and vitamins ("A, C, B_1, B_2, or, even better, multivitamins"). She asked for additional supplements: fish oil, glucose tablets, and boxes of sinestrol in ampules as well as syringes and hypodermic needles. Sinestrol was used to treat, among other things, rapid hair loss.

Fatty foods were crucial to combating the cold. Lina needed butter, *salo*, brisket, and *kolbasa*. Onion and garlic appear on the list for their medicinal attributes; Svyatoslav and Oleg needed to be sure to wrap these and the other vegetables and dried fruits well so as to prevent them from freezing solid en route. Since the camp *balanda* (hot water mixed with some oats, roots, or fish bones) had deprived her of the sense of taste, she requested salt and pepper. She wanted her own bowl and utensils, since these were in short supply and sometimes had to be shared.

Likewise fresh bed linens could be sent along with whatever dresses and blouses remained in the apartment. For emotional and practical reasons, Lina also hoped to receive some of her sons' shirts and thick sweaters, including the pullover that Jenny Marling had given to Svyatoslav before she left for California. Though the guards did not permit food in the barracks, they turned a blind eye to tea and coffee and certain sweets, and so Lina asked for those items, along with a miniature coffeepot. For exchange with the guards and the other women, she wanted unfiltered cigarettes, tobacco, and cigarette papers. Like cosmetics, which she also desired, these were worth their weight in gold. Maintaining one's appearance meant maintaining self-respect, although her efforts were hampered by the absence of mirrors, which were prohibited because they could be shattered and made into weapons. Perhaps Svyatoslav and Oleg could send her something that might protect her skin against the elements? Lina was rumored to have been resourceful enough to make a face cream for herself out of potatoes. She smuggled food into the barracks and mastered the art of cooking on the coal heater in the middle of the building. Fish bones were converted into needles after the example of the Ukrainian peasant women who killed time with cloth and thread. Lina learned to embroider in the camps and made a tote sack with a Ukrainian rhombus design. Her sons sent her the fabric.

She apologized for filling the letter with endless requests, for writing one long shopping list. "But what's to be done if it's like this now?" she asks—meaning that she had no choice but to beseech them for help. The final fold of the fourth sheet is crowded with what she wanted most: information about her sons' lives. She asked to hear everything, hoping to have something to think about beyond the relentless nothingness of Inta and the out-of-tune din of the camp band. She used her memories to create an alternative image of her present

SIMON MORRISON · 267

circumstances and to generate hope for her future. While recalling family birthday celebrations of years past, she imagined having spent Oleg's most recent birthday together with him. He had graduated in 1947 from Middle School 110 and went on to graduate studies at the Moscow State Pedagogical Institute while also taking lessons with the famous Russian modernist artist Robert Falk. In 1952 he matriculated at the Pedagogical Institute, subsequently becoming a successful painter and sculptor honored by the USSR Academy of Arts. Perhaps, Lina asked the rising artist, he would include one of his "still lifes" in the package — or maybe a photograph of him and his brother. She had met a painter in the camp but he had nothing to work with, she noted. Maybe Oleg could find a few tubes of oil paint for him?

Lina remained her children's proud, no-nonsense mother, reminding them to practice the piano, read, and attend concerts, not to waste time making new friends, and to learn from their mistakes. Later, she would admonish Oleg for not eating enough — he lost a great deal of weight in his early twenties. Lina embraced from afar her erstwhile, newlywed housekeeper Frosya, who remained in her thoughts, and wondered if one of her foreign friends, Victoria, had managed to leave the Soviet Union — a question that could have added years to her sentence, had the censor flagged it. "You haven't heard anything about Grandma?" she pleaded, meaning her mother, Olga. They had not, and the terrible silence would persist, even though she encouraged her sons to try to contact Olga in Paris.

According to one of her companions in the camps, the writer Yevgeniya Taratuta, Lina possessed tremendous powers of denial, inner faith, and firm will — all the product of her immersion in Christian Science. She refused to "believe that what had happened to her was real, did not believe that the situation would persist, and did not believe at all in her 20-year sentence." She also did not appear to believe that her marriage to Serge had ended, though by this point they had been apart for almost ten years. She longed for him still. Even if he could not help her to obtain release, she wanted his support, and so asked her sons to approach him for advice about how to arrange his music for performance by the ragtag gulag ensemble. At the close she asked, as she would in all of her letters from Inta and Abez, about "Papa's" (Serge's) health, and sent him a hug.

The abjectness of her petition cannot be overstated.

Her sons responded. Lina received parcels from home and shared what she could with Chernitskaya, Taratuta, and the other women she befriended after the guards had stolen (among other things) the tobacco. But little arrived during the first year of her sentence in the north—or the second for that matter. Another list she mailed on October 31, 1949, asks for the same music and some of the same foodstuffs. She had evidently received the aria from *Alexander Nevsky*, which would have been much more manageable for her now-faded, hoarse voice than the Puccini or Musorgky arias. New appeals are made for candles, gauze, and sackcloth, together with "*glucose in ampules for injection*," a request underscored as urgent.

Permission to write was sometimes reduced, sometimes increased, which made Lina all the more anxious to hear from her children. Mail days were more precious than rest days. Lina complained that Svyatoslav and Oleg seldom wrote and that their letters tended to be cautiously brief, terse. But "this wasn't always their fault," explained Taratuta. The guards simply threw away many letters and packages rather than bothering themselves with delivering them. "Lina Ivanovna missed her children, but she left the impression that in her former life she had not been very involved with them. But, of course, she was tormented more than the others. A southerner born in Spain, she suffered unbearably from the terrible cold; and the comfortable life that had been taken from her was altogether unfamiliar to most of the prisoners."

The packages she did receive required a signature at pickup, so Lina completed the back side of the shipping labels or filled out receipts. Upon collecting a package on June 16, 1950, Lina declared: "This will confirm receipt of parcel No. 121 whose contents have the following value: priceless." There follows her signature, along with that of the guard who handed the box to her. Another such shipping label, on a package valued at one hundred rubles, confirms her relocation from Inta to Abez. It is dated April 1, 1953.

In Abez, Lina continued to participate in camp musical activities. As "the wife of our great composer Prokofiev" she was awarded special "invalid" status that eased her workload and allowed her to immerse herself in cultural-educational activities inside and outside the House of Culture (Dom kulturï). It was located in the village adjacent to the camp, where the guards and their families resided. Taratuta recalled that "the prisoners formed a chorus, and some of the young women also sang solo. The repertoire comprised, on balance, folksongs from popular films . . . They sang by rote—no music, no instruments, just a balalaika as accompaniment. Lina Ivanovna sang in the chorus. She barely had any voice left at the time, and greatly pitied the loss." The ensemble had been organized by a Ukrainian ballerina named Tamara Veraksa, who had been imprisoned under the same treason statute (58-1a) as Lina. Veraksa had performed after the war for German prisoners in Soviet prisons, and so was condemned for giving aid to the cause of fascism.

The chorus was sometimes also accompanied by an accordion, which was played by a gifted pianist who had once been a student of a student of Serge's. The women rehearsed in a bookroom after work, "almost dropping from fatigue" but participating nonetheless. They performed opera arias, even singing through Charles Gounod's *Faust* —without props, in identical camp clothing, with women taking the male parts. Near the House of Culture, Abez had a theater where artists charged with political crimes performed as many as four times a week. Besides mounting approved classics, they also directed the amateur artistic activities of the village residents—the gulag support staff. Lina would have been one of the artist-prisoners granted this privileged task.

A single photograph survives from her time in the north, one that documents her theatrical activities. It was taken in Abez on June 29, 1955. None of the surviving members of Prokofiev's family can explain its origins. The image is weird, showing Lina sitting on a narrow wooden bench on a platform in front of two small birch trees. She wears a faded, scuffed gray-striped dress, her hands tucked into the slats behind her back, and looks upward and outward with a blank expression that attempts but fails to convey some emotion. The image was printed with a white embroidered pattern as frame and was likely to have been intended for official purposes—as documentation of artistic affairs in the camps. It is not a photo taken from real life, but from a grotesque theatrical spectacle at the Abez House of Culture. Lina appears on the gulag stage.

The accounts of the women who knew Lina in the camps are ineluctably confused, with dates and events overlapping. Chernitskaya recalls Oleg bravely visiting Lina at Abez before Stalin's death, for example, but he only managed to do so afterward. She remembers as well that perfume was forbidden, and that political prisoners "were not allowed to pronounce the words 'Motherland' or 'Stalin.'" When Chernitskaya earned release, the identification number was removed from her uniform, and she was told to forget it under threat of death.

Taratuta's account suffers from similar vagaries. She had been sentenced to the camps for espionage in 1937 but was amnestied three years before the end of her term in 1954. Lina was lonely, she recalls, kind, and justifiably obsessed with personal hygiene.

According to another eyewitness, the writer Vladimir Pentyukhov, women in the camps at Abez worked under the command of an aged diva known as "Major Baba" or "Babushka," the grandmother of the gulag. She was tall, stout, and big-chested, the convivial caricature of a female Soviet officer. The Major was herself a former prisoner who had atoned for the anti-Soviet hooliganism of her youth by joining the Voyska vnutrenney okhraní respubliki (Forces of the Internal Guard of the Republic). Over time, she lifted the restrictions on letter writing for her prisoners, and Lina was allowed to communicate more often with her sons. If she wrote to anyone else, the letters might not have been welcome, since receiving mail from convicted "enemies of the people" attracted unwanted attention and suggested collusion. Lina did not write to Serge, and he did not write to her, though he sent money to her through Svyatoslav and Oleg. She had dreams about him, and even once thought she saw him in a brigade of male prisoners. He must have been arrested, she concluded, because of her. That was in 1953, just before Serge died of a sudden, massive stroke. Afterward, she continued to see him in her dreams, "smiling and always talking to me, and wanting to tell me more, but what—I don't know."

Lina heard the news of his death from one of the prisoners who had been listening to the radio in the bookroom. She hung her head and walked away, tears flowing down her face.

The details came from Svyatoslav in a letter dated October 13. It includes a sad birthday wish—at the camp at Abez, Lina was about to turn fifty-six—along with the day-to-day details of his and his brother's life. He and his wife had just toured the North Caucasus and painted their room in the apartment; Oleg married Sofya Korovina, a children's writer, and they were planning to have a baby. (Lina would become the grandmother of a boy, Sergey Olegovich Prokofiev, in January 1954.) Svyatoslav added that Oleg was excelling in his studies at the Pedagogical Institute.

Then Svyatoslav hesitantly turns to the death of his father, admitting, at the start, that he was still in shock and trembled sharing the details. "On March 5 Papa was cheerful and felt well. He was working on the final corrections to *The Stone Flower*—a ballet score—in connection with the beginning of a production at the Bolshoy Theater. He even went out strolling for a bit with the doctor's wife. But in the evening he came down with a terrible headache, and it became increasingly difficult for him to breathe. He suffered a brain hemorrhage, long-threatened, and then respiratory paralysis. He wasn't in pain for a long time—it was over in an hour." The next line in the letter cannot be read: it was thickly crossed out by the censor. Fortunately, Svyatoslav kept the rough draft of the letter in his files, allowing the missing words to be reproduced. "And what a cruel—tragic—coincidence: Papa died at the very same time as Stalin: on March 5 at 9 P.M." The censor left only the word *tragic* visible.

Svyatoslav described the preparations for Prokofiev's burial, lamenting that he and his brother were not summoned in time to see their father before he died and that they had seen him all too rarely in the last few years of his life (Svyatoslav blamed Mira for the first offense, but not the second). He was interred in the graveyard on the grounds of the Novodevich convent, while Stalin was interred in the necropolis in the Kremlin walls. The coincidence of their deaths meant that there were no flowers available for Prokofiev's memorial service on March 7 at the House of Composers. One of his neighbors graced his casket with potted plants, the blooms living rather than dead. Musicians from around the world sent telegrams and letters of condolence, according to Svyatoslav, "but unfortunately they were sent to another address" in Moscow—meaning Mira's. He described the memorial concerts he and his wife, Nadezhda, had attended, noting that one of the performances brought back memories of November 1937, when Lina sang *The Ugly Duckling*, with Serge conducting. Svyatoslav closed by reassuring his mother that a parcel containing the music of Rimsky-Korsakov's opera *The Snow Maiden* was on its way, as she had requested, along with a parcel of food. He and Oleg were now alternating the task of keeping their mother fed and clothed at the camp at Abez.

They also worked to secure her release, writing a series of petitions to the prosecutor general and the Ministry of Internal Affairs (the renamed NKVD). In August 1953, Oleg sent the first of these on his and his brother's behalf to Lavrentiy Beria, the mastermind of the atrocities committed in the gulag, just days before Beria's own arrest for treason—presumably on the order of Nikita Khrushchev. For the glory of the Communist Party, Beria oversaw mass murders, invented torture methods, and himself raped women with sadistic delight. The appeal to this monster for a humanitarian reconsideration of Lina's case was rejected on May 8, 1953, just days after its receipt. Beria did not review the case to see if a legal error had been made, as the letter asked.

As part of the appeal, Oleg was obliged to declare that he had not noticed anything suspicious in his mother's activities prior to her arrest, and that his father, a "Stalin Prize laureate and RSFSR People's Artist," had died on March 5, 1953, "unfortunately unable to realize his desire to petition on Mama's behalf." In the spring of 1954, Lina's own request for a review of her case was again denied, this time because it had been sent to the wrong person—to Shostakovich, who was no longer a deputy to the Supreme Soviet of the RSFSR.

That summer, while traveling to the Crimean resort of Koktebel for a stay of two to three weeks, Oleg met a woman named Liya Solomonovna, who had been in Abez with Lina for two and a half years. From this meeting he learned that Lina had been relocated to a somewhat more civilized camp within the Abez sub-cluster. He also heard that her sentence had been reduced. Oleg and Svyatoslav knew so little about her case, however, that the length of her sentence was in dispute: "Her sentence is not 25 but 20 years," Oleg wrote to Svyatoslav. "By general decree it's been reduced by a third—do the math—though that's still a lot."

The good news among the bad was that her new camp did not involve hard labor. "It's by no means a sanatorium," Liya told Oleg. The camp was overcrowded and the conditions unpleasant, "but at least it's not *katorga*" (penal servitude). Now six years into her sentence, Lina's burden had eased. She did clerical work and, for her ideological betterment, sang folksongs. She also taught opera arias to three other women and was allowed to read newspapers and books—even some in foreign languages. The disgusting *balanda* served in the meal hall could be supplemented with food bought from a small stall run by peasants on the other side of the barbed-wire fence. Even so, Liya urged Oleg to hasten his efforts on his mother's behalf, to "claw her out of there."

Stalin's death (reportedly from a stroke) occasioned a first reckoning with his crimes by the new Soviet leader, Nikita Khrushchev. His critique of the excesses of the Stalinist regime began with a commission that considered freeing gravely ill prisoners and would culminate in his "secret speech" denouncing the Stalinist cult of personality in 1956. Lina's case, Liya noted, had not been taken up by the commission, even though she was arthritic and suffering choroiditis, an eye inflammation caused by tuberculosis. Oleg, Liya proposed, should take comfort in the fact that his mother was still strong, that she was not yet debilitated enough to be freed.

By September 20, 1954, Oleg had resolved to try to visit his mother again. Ultimately, he saw her four times in Abez, each meeting lasting three hours. Her looks had not changed significantly; she had not even gone gray. For the first time, he heard the story of her arrest and the nature of her conviction, about "the unjust charges (not at all what we had imagined) and the monstrousness of their devising." He was relieved to hear that her life had become easier over the past year —though "everything's relative!"—and there remained hope that for health reasons she would be relocated to a camp for invalids closer to Moscow.

Sixteen months later, on January 5, 1956, Lina sent a telegram to her sons with word that she anticipated being transferred to the Russian Republic of Mordovia. The harsh labor camps at Abez had been liquidated. Instead of four days from Moscow, she would now be only eight to ten hours away. That same month, she was relocated to one of three camps for older women and the infirm at Yavas, some fifty kilometers from Potma, a village with a present-day population of forty-one hundred. The Ministry of Internal Affairs did not assign Yavas a physical address until May 1948—three months after Stalin ordered the construction of special camps and prisons for supposedly danger-

274 · LINA AND SERGE

ous political criminals. Lina's address there was Potma, Yavas post office, mail slot 385/14.

Until Stalin's death and the beginning of the liquidation of the gulag in 1954, most of the three thousand or so women in Yavas—out of an approximate total population of twenty-three thousand—spent long days in factories and mills, followed by farm work with cows and pigs or tending crops. Idlers were subject to beatings, forced marching drills, and sleep deprivation. Over the years the unpaid workers of Yavas produced everything from shoes to dominoes to railway ties. In the camps for women, work exemptions were granted to those who were pregnant and nursing; there were special barracks for mothers with babies. (Though men and women did not live in the same barracks, contact between the sexes was not prohibited; in the annals of the gulag, there are numerous accounts of heterosexual and homosexual romances, successful and unsuccessful pregnancies—even accounts of married couples living together in separate spaces.) Lina again worked in a sewing factory, though for seven days a week rather than the six required while in the north.

When she was transferred to Mordovia in 1956, prisoners were organized and processed at Potma and then dispatched along the camp rail line by *teplushka* (stove-heated boxcar) to their destinations, which were identified by number. Elsewhere in the Soviet Union, the boxcars were used to transport livestock; here they moved people. In warmer months, when the side panels of the cars were kept open for ventilation, a crossbeam and metal caging prevented prisoners from falling out or escaping. The first camp sub-cluster was at Molochnitsa, a settlement for men fifteen kilometers from Potma. (The name means "dairymaid," but it also has a gynecological connotation, referring to vaginal candida, or "thrush.") Molochnitsa was followed three kilometers farther by Sosnovka, a sub-cluster for men serving life sentences, and then Lepley, for foreigners and stateless citizens and the endless number of Soviet prosecutors and judges charged with conspiring with them. Further down the line the male and female camps at Yavas appeared, and then the farthest settlement at Barashevo, which included a hospital for the terminally ill and a morgue.

Both of Lina's sons went to see her in Yavas on February 24, 1956. Svyatoslav remembered traveling south to the station at Saransk, then changing to a local train that stopped for two or three minutes at the short-platform station at Potma (Zubova-Polyana). There he and his brother waited an entire day before boarding the *teplushka* running on the side-branch line perpendicular to the main line. For an hour the sickly-looking steam locomotive crept through forestland, and then perimeter lights and an endless expanse of camps came into view— "like some sort of nightmare," Svyatoslav recalled. These camps cover much of Mordovia and remain in operation, though they have been refurbished and fall under different government regulation. Successive generations of the civilian population of Potma have worked as guards.

Svyatoslav and Oleg arrived at Yavas late in the evening. They were permitted to spend the night in an administrative annex, sleeping on tables. In the morning, they arrived at the Dom svidanii (Meeting House), a modestly furnished building at one end of the zone. One door led to the outside world, another to the barracks. There, for the first time in eight years, Svyatoslav saw his mother. The visit was unsupervised (a practice unheard of in the gulag before Stalin's death) and lasted four or five days. Svyatoslav commented on the thoughtfulness of the guards, which made them "unrecognizable" from their former selves, according to Lina. He recounted the reunion in his diary as follows: "After the noisy, stuffy barracks, the narrow and uncomfortable plank beds, to have a separate room, to sleep in a real bed, to have endless conversations with us on the most sensitive of subjects (freedom in the past, freedom in the future) was for poor Mama a true celebration." Svyatoslav added that, despite swollen eyes caused by sleep deprivation, his mother looked much the same as he remembered her in 1948, though mentally she had dulled, slowed. He also records his mother emphasizing that "despite her harsh and unjust conviction, she suffered the breakup with Papa more than the imprisonment that was its main consequence." Her two "heartaches" were "'Papa and this monstrous injustice.'"

Oleg returned to Moscow from Potma on March 1, promising his mother another visit in May, with his wife. Svyatoslav stayed in the guesthouse until March 4, living with Lina as though they were at a dacha, lighting the stove with firewood and even baking on it. The zone in which she lived had both a "commercial" and a "common" canteen. From the former, she ordered a napoleon torte and obtained "raw" homemade lemon vodka. The two of them belatedly celebrated Svyatoslav's thirty-second birthday. Lina told him that despite the improved conditions, Potma was harder for her than Abez had been, since in the north everyone had known her and she had received permission, for good conduct, to leave the zone on occasion for the neighboring village and Inta—though never in civilian clothes and under the threat of severe punishment, had she not returned on time. Fear, like the cold, had been the greatest deterrent to escape. In Potma, she hadn't found a place for herself, hadn't become part of a network with the other prisoners or the administration. She would be there just four more months.

Svyatoslav left Potma on March 4. He said goodbye to his mother outside in the snow, at the third post on the open road from the camp to the railroad. Lina was not allowed to venture past that post. They kissed and hugged each other. Svyatoslav walked through the field that led to the train, looking back at his mother as she receded from view. She lingered, waving goodbye with both hands. He thought of running back to her but continued on, the visit over.

Upon his return to Moscow the next day, Svyatoslav placed yellow irises on his father's grave in the Novodevich cemetery. Prokofiev had been dead exactly three years. Svyatoslav described his visit to the grave, after seeing his mother in prison, in terms that suggest a macabre family reunion: "Now we are all together," he confided to his diary. "No one has come between us." That evening he decided against visiting Mira Mendelson, as he had on previous anniversaries.

On June 13, 1956, Lina was granted release from the gulag by order of the Military Collegium of the Supreme Soviet. She had written numerous times on her own behalf for a review of her case, as did her sons, and as did the preeminent composer in the Soviet Union, Dmitri Shostakovich. In 1936, Serge had sought to capitalize on Shostakovich's political problems, seeing in his rival's misfortune a chance to burnish his standing with the Stalinist regime. Had Lina not supported her husband's self-delusion, everything might have been different in their lives. They might not have moved to the Soviet Union in the first place. Now, twenty years later, Shostakovich had used his political clout to come to her rescue. Svyatoslav and Oleg's 1955 appeal to Shostakovich for intervention was referred to the office of the chief military prosecutor for processing and "supplemental verification." (Although, back in 1948, Shostakovich could do nothing for Lina, by the mid-1950s he had risen to a position of influence in Soviet political circles, and each week received numerous requests for interventions in cases like hers.) This referral proved decisive.

The dismissal of Lina's original case was based on a ruling forwarded from the chief military prosecutor to the Military Collegium. After reviewing her file, the prosecutor decreed that the allegations leading to her arrest and imprisonment in 1948 had no justification. There were no contacts with spies, no treacherous political conversations at lunch with foreign friends, and no efforts to smuggle sensitive documents to fascist imperial governments—as the protocols she had been tortured into signing at Lefortovo indicated. The ruling came down on May 15, 1956, but Lina had to wait six weeks for her release. Meanwhile 90 percent of the prisoners in the camp neighboring hers at Potma had been freed. Having not yet heard the prosecutor's decision, Lina worried that her release would be conditional, subject to the caprice of lower-level bureaucrats working for a lower-level commission.

The commission summoned her for an interview on May 18, 1956, and she recounted the proceedings in a letter to her sons, noting that on this occasion, as in the past, the bureaucrats reviewing her case were interested in the negative, not the positive. At the start of the interview she was asked to explain the reasons for her twenty-year sentence, to which she replied, "While I don't precisely know how my indictment was formulated, I'm aware of the accusations made against me. To these, I can only honestly and sincerely declare that I was never recruited by anyone and never used my foreign contacts to undermine the Soviet State. The investigation was so difficult that I ended up slandering myself. Not only was I unable to defend myself but, under pressure, I was forced to sign outrageously distorted confessions."

Lina told the commission that, owing to her foreign upbringing and "political illiteracy," she "did not always take into account what was considered proper and improper Soviet conduct." She burst into tears after adding, "Now I understand that I should have curtailed my meetings with foreign acquaintances so as not to attract undeserved suspicion."

The commission then asked her about her current relationship with her famous husband. Lina answered, "Unfortunately he hasn't been among the living for three years now. If he were still alive I'm sure that he would be advocating for me. My case was reviewed a long time ago now. I was questioned (reinvestigated) by the *starshiy oper-ativniy upolnomocheniy* [a senior camp official with the power to recommend cases for reinvestigation] at Abez, and he gave me cause for hope."

There were no further questions. The commissioners referred the matter to Moscow for supporting documents, since they had nothing in hand but a record of her sentencing, and told her that she would be called to appear before them later on.

As her account to her sons makes clear, Lina refused to increase her chances of release by becoming one of "the repentant," since, from the start of the eight-year ordeal, she had insisted on her innocence. She dreaded a conditional release: bail might be set; she might remain exiled, unable to travel within 101 kilometers of Moscow. Transfer to another camp was also possible since political prisoners were generally the last to be amnestied. Oleg took the train to Potma on May 22 to provide moral support. He arrived at 3 A.M. in order to take the 5 A.M. *teplushka* to her camp. He reassured his mother, over and over again, that she would be freed.

Svyatoslav marked the official date of his mother's release—June 13, 1956—on his desk calendar with a single word: *rehabilitation*. A woman had called him from the Military Collegium to confirm its decision. Relieved, ecstatically overcome, he bellowed "Thank God!" into the receiver. The "female voice" on the line deadpanned: "What, you mean to say you believe me?"

Lina left her barracks at Yavas on Friday, June 29, after sending two packages of her belongings home to Moscow. From the village of Potma, where she stayed for a night at a hospice for the aged and infirm while awaiting a passport, she telegrammed her sons: "Leaving tonight at 8:30. Kiss. Mama." She arrived in Moscow at 10:25 in the morning on July 1, her prison camp release form allowing her to obtain a passport from the Zubova-Polyana regional police division. The photograph shows a tight-faced, thin-lipped woman with cropped hair—a ghost of her former self, but soon to return to it. Svyatoslav and Oleg met her at the Kazan train station, after a week of taking turns waiting by the telephone for word from her. They did not know when her train would arrive, and so went to the terminal three times on the morning of July 1 to meet it. Finally, the steam locomotive from Saransk pulled in. Lina alighted into the arms of her sons, who escorted her through the ornate central arcade into Komsomol Square and its thick crowds of arriving and departing passengers.

Two days later, after a homecoming that brought Lina into contact, for the first time, with Svyatoslav's wife, Nadezhda, and Oleg's wife, Sofya, Svyatoslav took his nervous, frail mother into the center of Moscow to collect her rehabilitation certificate. Their destination was the fourth floor of 13 Vorovsky Street, the mid-eighteenth-century building that housed the Military Collegium. Before obtaining the certificate, Lina was required to sign an oath of silence about her experience in the gulag. The bureaucrat whom Svyatoslav summoned on the internal telephone said to one of his colleagues, "Look for the file belonging to Lina Ivanovna Prokofiev—it's, you know, one of the fabricated ones." The trauma of Inta, Abez, and Potma was waved away with cynical disregard.

Her first public outing after her return was on September 24, 1956. Lina received an invitation to a performance of Shostakovich's First Violin Concerto, among other works, at a lavish concert celebrating his fiftieth birthday. The next day, she sent the composer a tender note of thanks that referenced the help he had given her: "I'm so happy that I was able yesterday to attend the triumph of your jubilee concert . . . For a long time I was deprived of the opportunity to hear good music and thus especially valued this evening." To the embarrassing and sometimes hypocritical accolades that Shostakovich received from officials and colleagues at the performance, Lina added that she considered him a "wonderful person—honest, kind, sympathetic, and good." Then she thanked him, again, for his attention to her.

Epilogue

F OR THE REST of her life Lina feared being picked up on the street, flinched whenever a car passed close to her on the sidewalk, and relived the interrogations in her sleep. She was released from the camps in 1956 and finally left the Soviet Union in 1974, but she never escaped her experience there. The memories flooded back in the final days of her life, which she spent at a foreign hospital in a foreign city—the Johanniter Hospital in Bonn, Germany. As she slipped in and out of consciousness, her room became a cell at Lefortovo and the barracks at the camps. "The nurses and nurses-aides were guards and wardens in disguise," Svyatoslav recalled from her bedside. She believed "that the needles administered to her were meant to force her into a confession; and that someone was being beaten on the other side of the wall. And she repeatedly cried out that she wasn't guilty of anything."

When she returned from Potma, Lina had nowhere to live in Moscow, no local identification papers, and no belongings other than the clothes on her back and two parcels of personal items from the camps, which included some of the music she sang and the photographs and letters her sons had sent. Nothing confiscated from her apartment after her arrest in 1948 was ever returned, and the financial compensation for the loss of her valuables would be trifling. From July 1956 to 1959 she lived intermittently in apartment 19 on Chkalov Street, occupying one of the two rooms in the overcrowded home, with Svyatoslav's family in the other. (During the first and second summers after her release, she also stayed at the dacha Svyatoslav rented north-west of Moscow in Povarovka.) Oleg moved with his wife and son into a building operated by the Union of Soviet Composers on Third Miusskaya Street. Although he still used his former room as a studio, Lina was registered as its official occupant. Svyatoslav's son remembers Oleg's painting supplies and his amusingly diverse jazz and classical record collection; he also remembers the aroma of the tiny pots of coffee and toast that Lina would prepare in the morning, the marine color she painted the walls in her room, the cheerful blinds she hung, and the chaotic clutter—the cosmetics, jewelry, and clothes—that concealed the secrets of her gradual return to elegance.

Neither she nor her sons would return to the original family apartment on the third floor of the same building. It was gone for good. In 1959, Lina received her own apartment in a new but drab-looking brown brick building near the Kiev train station, in what was considered at the time a prestigious neighborhood, where Soviet leaders and foreign diplomats resided in the grander Stalinist edifices on the avenue. She was assigned a small unit with a balcony facing the inner courtyard, number 177 at 9 Kutuzovsky prospekt. The layout was ludicrous: a single large room doubling as bedroom and living room on one side; a kitchen, toilet, and entrance on the other. It soon became overstuffed with personal belongings and items purchased from the Russian souvenir shop on the first floor: nesting dolls, headscarves, and collectible china plates embossed with scenes from Russian fairy tales. Lina dined at the restaurant of the Hotel Ukraine (that hotel, in a Stalinist skyscraper, is now part of the Radisson chain).

She received the apartment from the Moscow mayor's office thanks to the general secretary of the Union of Soviet Composers, Tikhon Khrennikov. Music historians tend, with good reason, to scorn Khrennikov for his role in the ideological denunciation of the leading Soviet composers—Prokofiev included—in 1948. But he supported Lina before and after her release from the gulag, even writing a letter urging a review of her arrest and conviction. His empathy with her plight counterbalances his antipathy toward Serge's second wife, Mira Mendelson, with whom he repeatedly clashed.

Besides helping Lina obtain an apartment, Khrennikov was also instrumental in securing her a pension of seven hundred rubles a month—the same amount allotted to Mira. Payment was approved on November 3, 1956. The political historian Leonid Maksimenkov points out that Khrennikov's support for Lina was part and parcel of a grand effort by the Soviet government to commemorate Serge's life and work. It may be that her release from the gulag also owed to what Maksimenkov calls the government's "immortalization" of the composer as a classic Soviet artist. Given his posthumous stature, his first wife could not be allowed to fend for herself on the streets.

Yet she had to fight to be recognized as Serge's legal heir. As Lina learned from her sons, her marriage was dissolved by bureaucratic fiat just before she was sent to the gulag, and Serge married Mira. Exactly when she found out is unclear, but from the camps she began the process of having the dissolution of her marriage overturned. On April 27, 1957, the oversight committee for the Moscow courts reversed the decision of November 27, 1947, that had invalidated her marriage, on October 8, 1923, to Serge.

The reversal, which restored Lina's rights as Serge's legal heir, reflected a July 8, 1944, decree by the Supreme Soviet to the effect that marriages abroad remained valid in the USSR. This reversal, however, was itself reversed after a protracted judicial wrangle that pitted Lina and Mira and their allies against each other. On March 12, 1958, the Russian Supreme Court affirmed Mira as Serge's widow based on the evidence she provided, including their 1947 marriage certificate, the 1941 evacuation order in which Serge incorrectly listed Mira as his wife in order to secure her passage out of Moscow, and a personal letter that he sent to a friend in 1944 about his separation from Lina.

The argument supporting the annulment did not deny that Serge and Lina had been married but, once again, found that the marriage had not been registered with the Soviet government. Eventually, but unhappily to all concerned, both marriages were recognized. Prokofiev was deemed to have two widows, and his estate was distributed among his two wives and his two sons. The arrangement necessitated annulling the composer's will of November 28, 1949, in which he bequeathed his dacha, belongings, and manuscripts exclusively to Mira, and instructed that his royalties be shared between her and his two sons. Lina successfully lobbied for the estate to be distributed four ways—among her, Mira, Svyatoslav, and Oleg.

In her diaries, Mira referred to Lina's release from the camps and rehabilitation in the most cryptic terms, as "the return of L. I." She accused Lina of heaping "a mountain's worth of dirt" on her reputation and portrayed herself as a victim. Recounting her side of the legal struggle, she bemoaned the stress and upset that it caused her through the winter of 1957–1958. Besides narrating the actions of her supporters and opponents in the courts—she did not represent herself—she detailed her efforts to preserve the manuscript of *War and Peace*, among other scores.

Mira led a fearful, joyless existence, both before and after Serge's passing. She died on June 8, 1968, at just fifty-three years of age, from a presumed heart attack while talking on the telephone. She collapsed on the floor, with the receiver still in her hand. The Glinka Museum in Moscow inherited the documents and manuscripts in her possession, along with her share of the Prokofiev Estate.

Throughout the 1960s, interest in Serge's music increased—more so in the West than in the Soviet Union, and Western visitors sought to make contact with Lina. But great effort was made to keep her out of sight of foreign politicians, cultural officials, and academics interested in her and her husband.

When, in 1962, the American musicologist Malcolm Hamrick Brown traveled to Moscow on a Fulbright fellowship to conduct research for a book on Serge's life and works, he was stymied in his efforts to obtain Lina's telephone number by the Soviet musicologist Izraíl Nestyev, among others. Yet he persevered, and eventually succeeded. On the phone, Lina responded to his request for an interview with a long silence, then told him to call her back the next day, since she did not know her schedule. Later he learned that she had made up an excuse in order to check with Nestyev and her sons to see if it was safe for her to host a foreigner. They met on June 14, two days after Brown visited with Mira Mendelson—a brief, terse encounter that never strayed from template remarks about Serge's commitment to socialist realist aesthetics and the search for the ideal Soviet sound. Brown took less than a page of notes.

Lina insisted on speaking English to Brown when they finally met, and questioned him at length about his background and credentials. He left the apartment with a "profound sense of regret that she would never have the privilege that I had of getting on a train and leaving Moscow and the Soviet Union."

After saying goodbye to her, he discovered that he had left his ad dress book in her apartment. He telephoned Lina, but she did not answer (she had gone to a friend's to watch a television broadcast of a performance of Tchaikovsky's First Piano Concerto by the visiting American pianist Van Cliburn). He called again the next morning. This time she picked up, exclaiming, "It's a miracle that you forgot that notebook. I so wanted to see you again before you left." During his return visit, she openly acknowledged her arrest, trial, and subsequent time in the camps, noting that MGB agents had not only accused her of working on behalf of the American embassy, but even proposed that she had married Serge for the purpose of anti-Soviet espionage. (She was likewise accused of colluding with Frederick Reinhardt, first secretary of the embassy, in a money-laundering scheme.) To his dismay, Brown could not continue the conversation, since he was leaving Moscow for Warsaw late that afternoon. Lina "grasped my hands in both of hers and with tears in her eyes said: 'I'm trusting you with my life. If you reveal the information I've given you, they will see that I pay for it. But I've told you these things because someday the world must hear the truth about me and my husband.'"

Such interactions with foreigners in the Soviet Union were severely limited, as was the ability to travel abroad. Lina received invitations to Prokofiev performances and festivals in Western and Eastern Europe, and the Soviet Ministry of Culture assisted in granting her permission to attend those events in the Soviet-controlled eastern bloc. In 1966, she traveled to Bulgaria for a performance of the ballet *The Prodigal Son*, as well as to Berlin and Leipzig in East Germany for a staging of *The Fiery Angel* and a colloquium titled "The Contemporary Interpretation of Opera." In May 1968, she went to Prague, Czechoslovakia, for a music festival. Three months later, Soviet and Warsaw Pact forces invaded Prague, putting an end to the political and economic reforms initiated by the Czechoslovakian leader Alexander Dubček.

Despite similar invitations from around the world, she was repeatedly denied the opportunity to venture beyond the Iron Curtain. In 1968, Lina applied for a tourist visa to London but was summarily turned down. The disappointment was tempered by news that she would soon receive an invitation to Paris from the French minister of culture for the unveiling of a Prokofiev memorial. A small plaque would be placed on the side of the eggshell-colored apartment build-ing at 5, Valentin Haüy, where he, Lina, and their sons had lived from 1929 to 1935. According to Maksimenkov, Lina was denied permis-sion to go to Paris because she had not been sanctioned by the Foreign Travel Commission of the Central Committee "to travel to capitalist countries." Lina attributed the rejection to a bad character reference from Khrennikov and the Union of Soviet Composers. Khrennikov denied the accusation, blaming the Soviet Ministry of Culture.

Other blocked invitations included trips to Italy, Switzerland, and West Germany for performances of Prokofiev operas and ballets. Lina was also asked to travel to Australia for the first public perfor-mance at the Sydney Opera House on September 28, 1973—a pro-duction of *War and Peace* under the direction of Edward Downes. Intentional bureaucratic dithering ensured that her request was not considered until after the performance, and then denied—in a typi-cal twist of Soviet logic—because the event had already taken place. The administration of the Sydney Opera House marked Lina's ab-sence by placing a rose on the front-row seat that, had it not been for political malfeasance, she would have occupied.

Though she never resigned herself to life in the Soviet Union, con-tinuing to petition to travel, Lina made a home for herself in Moscow at her small apartment and spent time with her sons at Nikolina gora. Following Mira's death, the three of them together purchased the dacha. Mira had also bequeathed it to the Glinka Museum, expect-ing that it would be converted into a museum. That was prevented by the regulations of the Nikolina gora housing cooperative, which do not permit state enterprises (such as a museum) to possess private homes. After another tedious and emotionally fraught legal process —one that rivaled the fight to have her rights as Serge's wife restored —Lina and her sons took possession of the dacha. A renovation to the balconies made them safe and comfortable, so Lina could inhabit the top floor. Svyatoslav and Oleg and their families used the bottom floor.

Svyatoslav's son Sergey (Serge Prokofiev Jr.) remembers attending camps for Soviet pioneers near Nikolina gora in the summers. Twice a day, he and the other scouts would amble past the dacha to the lo-cal river for a swim, not noticing that the lane on which it stood was named after his grandfather and namesake. He knew little about his grandmother's life and had never heard of Mira Mendelson. Sergey would marry and have two daughters, who themselves spent summers at the dacha playing with other children, unaware of the historical significance of the place.

Though Lina's children and grandchildren were raised in the Soviet Union as Soviet citizens, eventually all made it to the West—a striking reversal of the path that she herself had taken. Oleg was the first to leave. Divorced from his first wife, he received long-awaited permission in 1969 to wed the British-born Russian art historian Camilla Gray. They had met in Moscow in 1962 while Gray was researching what would become an outstanding book on the Soviet avant-garde; the next year they decided to get married, but Soviet officials had to sanction it. They celebrated the birth of their daughter, Anastasia, in October 1970 and bought a picturesque house in the northwest outskirts of Moscow. It was on the shore of the Khimki reservoir, in the former village of Novo-Butakovo. The canal that leads to the reservoir, which provides Moscow with an economic connection to the Volga River and the seas beyond it, was dug by hand by gulag prisoners in the 1930s.

In December 1971, Gray died suddenly of liver failure caused by viral hepatitis. She was pregnant with their second child at the time and on vacation with Oleg on the Black Sea. Neither she nor the baby could be saved. Oleg thereafter petitioned on compassionate grounds for permission to leave the Soviet Union to attend his wife's funeral in England. He received a five-year external passport and left for good, with a toddler in his arms and a suitcase containing several of his canvases. (The art was damaged, since the suitcase was declared to have no value.) Camilla's parents assumed Anastasia's care, and Oleg received a Gregory Fellowship in painting at the fine arts department of the University of Leeds, which enabled him to support himself. His home in Khimki, a rare acquisition of private property in the Soviet Union, was sold by Lina to another artist.

Svyatoslav's son, Sergey, his daughter-in-law, Irina, and his granddaughters, Lina and Nika, left the Soviet Union for France during their summer vacation in June 1990. They decided to settle in Paris, acquiring French citizenship in 2000. Though Sergey had enjoyed a contented childhood in Moscow, the place he had known no longer existed—a loss emblematized by the disappearance of the fountain and flowers in the courtyard of the apartment on Chkalov Street and by the ever-increasing traffic and pollution in the once-tranquil enclave of Nikolina gora. Svyatoslav and his wife, Nadezhda, did not have as strong a desire to relocate as their son did, and imagined living out their cautious, careful lives in the apartment and the dacha. Partly to be near his son and grandchildren, Svyatoslav nonetheless applied for and received French citizenship as his 1924 birthright. Despite their advanced age, he and Nadezhda traveled back and forth between Moscow and Paris. Svyatoslav died in Paris on December 7, 2010, eight years after his wife. His apartment in Moscow remains vacant at the time of this writing; the dacha is up for sale, with no thought of turning it into a memorial museum.

On August 16, 1974, Lina again requested permission to leave the Soviet Union to see her son and granddaughter, Oleg and Anastasia. Her letter was addressed to Yuriy Andropov, then the chairman of the Committee for State Security, or KGB—and later the leader of the Soviet Union as head of the Communist Party. The invitation abroad had come from Camilla Gray's parents in 1973, and Lina had since then been trying without success to obtain permission through the Office of Visas and Regulation (OVIR), a point that she made to Andropov. The initial refusal had come after eight months of waiting —a long time for a pensioner approaching the age of seventy-seven. Her letter offers a strikingly blunt catalogue of grievances along with heartfelt pleas for compassion. She asserted, bravely, that she could not "come to terms with the harsh injustice inflicted on me by the OVIR . . . the thought of dying without seeing my granddaughter and son is unbearable." Then she used an even more daring tactic, advising the head of the KGB that "as Prokofiev's widow I am well known in the world of culture abroad. Denying me permission to leave would attract detrimental interest in the press. I would like to avoid a scandal, but with every passing month it becomes more difficult to claim that the documents for my departure are in process." And more: Lina emboldened herself to write to Leonid Brezhnev, Khrushchev's successor as leader of the nation, arguing that she had been repeatedly mistreated by Soviet officialdom, despite having adopted the Soviet Union as her "second homeland" in 1936 and rejoicing in the nation's "successes and achievements" to the present day. She had, for example, obligatorily donated fifty-nine thousand francs of her own income to the Soviet Fund for Peace. Suggesting that the state owed her some consideration, she described her eight years in the camps as a "terrible mistake made at her expense." That harrowing injustice was being compounded by the inexplicable rejection of her requests to travel to the West for premieres of her husband's music. Worst of all, she was being kept apart from her son and granddaughter, whom she missed terribly.

Given all the years of denials, she had no real hope of the request being approved. Lina was shocked when, just a few days later, she received an external passport with a three-month visa to England.

Permission was granted through Andropov's rather than Brezhnev's office. On November 17, 1974, Lina flew to London on a three-month visa, with twenty rubles in her purse and an excess-baggage-claim ticket. She was not a defector; in fact, she took care to extend her visa through the appropriate consular channels in London and Paris. But she never intended to return. In 1979, she arranged for her thirty-square-meter apartment on Kutuzovsky prospekt to be reassigned to Oleg's son, Sergey, following the completion of his required service in the Red Army.

Lina lived her remaining years in London and in Paris and spent extensive periods in the United States and Germany, serving as a cultural representative for the Prokofiev Estate and Foundation, the latter established on her initiative in 1983. She traveled widely, retracing the steps of her life before the move to Moscow. To recuperate from her nagging health problems, she visited Tunisia and Spain, where she located the house in which she was born.

Invitations from Italian musical societies allowed her to look up her former haunts in Milan. Following a trip to the Steirischer Herbst Festival in Graz, Austria, for a performance of Serge's first opera, *Maddalena*, she returned to Ettal for a day of reminiscing in the company of the prior of the Kloster there. In the United States in 1976, she exhausted herself attending concerts and receptions in her honor and sparring with journalists across the country: Boston, Chicago, New York, Washington, and especially New York all brought back memories. In 1977, she accepted invitations to concerts in Texas. She was given the key to the city of Austin, saw a bronco busted, and enjoyed a "stupendous lunch" in what she called a "Gone-with-the-Wind-style" mansion. From there she traveled to Los Angeles and San Francisco, where her friends from long ago lived. But Carita Daniell and Gussie Garvin, she learned, had died in 1969 and 1955 respectively. Of the diplomats she had known in the Soviet Union in the 1930s and 1940s, she managed to reconnect with Anna Holdcroft of the British embassy. She also restored ties with her beloved former neighbor in Moscow, Anne-Marie Lotte, who lives in Brittany.

Even though she had long since lost her singing voice, she even found her way back to the concert stage. On November 11, 1985, Lina narrated *Peter and the Wolf* at Alice Tully Hall in New York. The performance, celebrating the fiftieth anniversary of the composition of the score, was part of an all-Prokofiev concert organized by Michael Spencer, the executive director of Hospital Audiences, a nonprofit organization that brings cultural events to the underprivileged. Spencer had visited Lina in Paris the previous year and proposed that she take part. Several phone calls and letters later, she agreed, deciding that even if her eyesight was now very poor, she still had superb diction. Spencer had the text of *Peter and the Wolf* copied out for her in enormous letters in an oversized book. Lina prepared for the performance by listening to the various recordings, including one narrated by David Bowie, which she liked. Oleg accompanied his mother to New York and exhibited a pair of sculptures and several drawings in the hall. Lina read with "élan and dry amusement," according to one reviewer, and delighted the audience. A year later, she recorded *Peter and the Wolf* with the Scottish National Orchestra under Neeme Järvi.

After she left the Soviet Union, her correspondence with the American musicologist who had managed to meet with her in Moscow, Malcolm Hamrick Brown, intensified. They had kept in touch intermittently throughout the 1960s and 1970s, the hope being that she would collaborate with him on a book about Serge. Lina often expressed her disgust at the amateurishness and tendentiousness of the books and articles on her husband that she saw—she read everything she could on his life and works—vowing to set the record straight about his career in her own terms. She was exceedingly protective of his legacy. Lina promoted Serge's music in the West; ensured, through her lawyer, that his scores were placed under secure copyright; blocked the sale of stolen manuscripts at auctions; and supplemented the collections of Prokofiev-related documents in New

York, London, and Paris. Yet her relationship with Brown soured, and she instructed her lawyer, André Schmidt, to send the equivalent of a cease-and-desist letter in June 1982. Cordial relations were restored in the fall, however, and Brown even interviewed Lina again. But their long-planned book went unrealized.

Lina seriously considered writing her own book—an autobiography—or at least collaborating on a biography. In June 1977, in her Paris apartment, Lina met with the composer Phillip Ramey for a series of interviews that were meant to provide the backbone for a chronicle of her relationship with Serge. Ramey had met Lina in New York the previous February at the apartment of his composition teacher, Alexander Tcherepnin. Impressed by the thirty-page essay on Serge's music that he had written for Time-Life Records, she invited Ramey to her room in the Salisbury Hotel and proposed that he collaborate with her. The Scribner publishing house reneged on a promised contract, but Ramey nonetheless flew to Paris with a tape recorder and portable typewriter to begin work on what promised to be a sensational publication. The interviews, which took place at Lina's apartment at 8, rue Récamier, were unsuccessful. Lina refused to address the subjects that most interested him about her marriage to Serge and their hardships in the Soviet Union. Ramey learned a great deal about her distant relatives, but little about the north. The fiasco was encored two years later when Lina provided a series of interviews to the writer Harvey Sachs. Though some of the material in those interviews has been included in this book, a lot of it is confused and inaccurate. As much as she wanted to tell her story, she did not—for fear of the consequences. In that sense, she never escaped the Soviet Union.

Nor could she, in the end, make sense of her husband's life, their life together, or her own life after their separation and his passing. Those who knew her at the end found her baffling, compelling, disdainful, exasperating, flirtatious, humorous, stubborn, and high-spirited. The interview transcripts leave the impression of someone seeking to prevent anyone from reaching the obvious conclusion: that she was a tragic victim of Serge's genius and the self-delusion that he shared with his nation. Having learned to despise Soviet propaganda stories of self-sacrifice, she would not abide their being applied to her own life by commercial biographers in the West. Rejecting the clichés of the places and events she seemed to define became her paradoxical purpose.

In October 1988 Lina went to Bonn, the capital of West Germany, to visit the Mexican diplomat and exhibition curator Norma Sanchez, a friend of comparatively recent acquaintance. Shortly after arriving for her planned two-week stay she suffered a gallbladder attack and was admitted into the Johanniter Hospital. Svyatoslav received a telegram on October 8: "Your mother seriously ill wishes to see you before dying. Sorry to inform she does not have many days left."

Her son came to her side from Moscow on an expedited visa, as did Oleg from London. She marked her ninety-first birthday in the hospital (her sons posed with her for a toast), signed documents relating to the Prokofiev Estate and Foundation and the preparation of her will, and received visitors. She asked to be buried beside Serge's mother, Mariya, outside of Paris in Meudon. Neither she nor her sons ever discovered what had happened to her own mother, Olga.

To ensure Lina's continued care during her final weeks, Oleg arranged for her to be transported from the Johanniter Hospital in Bonn to the Churchill Clinic in London. She spent Christmas and New Year's Eve in hospice, the hallucinations of her eight years in the north strengthening as she weakened. Before the end, she scribbled a note with a shaking hand that can only be hypothetically deciphered. Svyatoslav's son, Sergey, the dedicatee of this book, thinks that it reads: "En vous souhaitant beaucoup de chance dans la vie" (Wishing you great success in life).

The soprano Lina Prokofiev (née Codina) died on January 3, 1989, age ninety-one. No recordings of her singing are known to survive.

Acknowledgments

The guiding force for this book, from the first page to the last, is its dedicatee, Serge Prokofiev Jr., with whom I have worked for several years as editor of *Three Oranges Journal* and, since 2010, as president of the Serge Prokofiev Foundation. Without his enthusiasm and inspiration, *Lina and Serge* would not exist. He provided all of the letters, documents, and photographs credited to the Estate, as well as access to closed archival sources in Moscow and London. Serge Jr. answered numerous questions by e-mail in 2010–2011, and he brought several people in Lina's life to my attention, including Anne-Marie Lotte and Stanislas Julien.

I inherited my positions with the journal and foundation from Noëlle Mann, who died on April 23, 2010. I miss her, as does everyone involved in Prokofiev studies. In 2008 Noëlle challenged me to write an essay on Lina's childhood, which became the first chapter of this book. I began to research the rest, knowing that there existed a Russian-language memoir of Lina Prokofiev by Valentina Chemberdzhi, *XX vek Linï Prokof'yevoy* (Moscow: Klassika-XXI, 2008). That book highlights Lina's later Soviet years, especially 1960–1974, when Lina and Mme Chemberdzhi befriended each other; it includes interviews with Lina's children and grandchildren, first and foremost Svyatoslav Prokofiev. I was delighted when the author, a music critic and translator based in Barcelona and Moscow, agreed to publish excerpts from *XX vek Linï Prokof'yevoy* in the November 2010 issue of *Three Oranges*. Earlier, Mme Chemberdzhi and I had discussed collaborating on an

English-language book about Lina—one that would include the hundreds of unpublished letters and documents about her life that had been made available to me—but the idea did not pan out, through no fault of either of us. I hope that *Lina and Serge* complements Mme Chemberdzhi's personal account. I also hope that it properly realizes Malcolm Brown's, Phillip Ramey's, and Harvey Sachs's separate efforts to piece together Lina's life through interviews and correspondence with her.

For generous research assistance, I am grateful to Galina Zlobina, the deputy director of the Russian State Archive of Literature and Art and my longtime friend; Natalya Strizhkova, the archive's head of communications; and Dmitriy Neustroyev, the manager of the reading room. I am also grateful to Fiona McKnight of the Prokofiev Archive in London for her expertise and help throughout. Special thanks to my cherished friend and closest colleague Caryl Emerson for believing in these pages, making them better, and turning me to the Real Science. Thanks also to Alexandra Afinogenova, Michele Cabrini, Megan Conlon, Warren F. Daniell Jr., Maria Ibrahimova, Peter Kenez, Pilar Castro Kiltz, Nelly Kravetz, Chris Mann, Leonid Maksimenkov, Roger Parker, Anthony Phillips, and Boris Wolfson.

My heart to Elizabeth Bergman, who read and reread the text with her expert editorial eye and gifted verbal touch, and who unearthed the Americana of the opening chapters. To her also goes credit for authoring the greatest text of all: our daughter, Nika.

Finally, thanks to my brilliant editor at Houghton Mifflin Harcourt, George Hodgman, and to Bruce Nichols, who took over the project from George in the final stages. Susanna Brougham and Dan Janeck did wonderful copyediting and proofreading. My agent Will Lippincott made it all happen with an élan Lina would have envied.

Notes

ARCHIVAL SOURCES

LPF — Lina Prokofiev Fonds of the Serge Prokofiev Archive at Goldsmiths, University of London
MHB — Malcolm Hamrick Brown
RGALI — Russian State Archive of Literature and Art
SPA — Serge Prokofiev Archive at Goldsmiths, University of London
SPE — Serge Prokofiev Estate (Paris)

INTRODUCTION

Sources include a photograph of the sack Lina fashioned in the gulag and a letter from Lina Prokofiev (LP) to her sons dated December 19, 1948, both provided by the Serge Prokofiev Estate. The photograph of Oleg in the apartment; the MGB inventory of its contents of February 21, 1948; and LP's petition of May 29, 1954, to the USSR attorney general, which details her 1948 interrogations, also come from the Estate. The confiscation of the Goncharova painting and 78s from the apartment is described in Svyatoslav Prokof'yev, "O moikh roditelyakh: Beseda sïna kompozitora s muzïkovedom Nataliyey Savkinoy," in *Sergey Prokof'yev, 1891– 1991: Dnevnik, pis'ma, besedï, vospominaniya*, edited by M. E. Tarakanov (Moscow: Sovetskiy kompozitor, 1991), 226–28. The narrative of the events leading up to and including the arrest is derived from this source and, primarily, an interview transcript in the Lina Prokofiev Fonds (LPF) of the Serge Prokofiev Archive (SPA) at Goldsmiths, University of London. Harvey Sachs conducted the interview with LP on May 21, 1984. Additional details are from an unpublished letter from Anna Holdcroft to Malcolm Hamrick Brown (MHB) dated October 10, 1964. I remain grateful to Professor Brown for donating his archive of Prokofiev materials to me. The account of the trip to the Soviet Union in 1927 is from Sergei Prokofiev, *Soviet Diary 1927 and Other Writings*, edited and translated by Oleg Prokofiev (London: Faber & Faber, 1991), 3–10, 15, 29–30, 68–69, 43–44.

3 *"the privileges awaiting him"*: LP interview with MHB, July 18, 1968.
6 *"What's happened?"*: LPF 1/9.
7 *"What have I done?"*: LP interview with MHB, April 1–2, 1985.

CHAPTER 1

Sources include, on LP's grandparents, parents, and early childhood, Sviatoslav Prokofiev, "Little-Known Facts About People Close to Prokofiev," *Three Oranges Journal*, vol. 1 (January 2001): 20–21; notes taken by MHB in a November 1967 interview with LP; autobiographical notes and interview transcripts (LP and Harvey Sachs) in the Lina Prokofiev Fonds (LPF) of the Serge Prokofiev Archive at Goldsmiths. *Le Journal de Genève* lists the 1904 recitals of Juan and Olga Codina in Geneva. The dates of LP's travels to and from the United States and her addresses between 1907 and 1910 come from the Bureau of the Census and the passenger lists of the Immigration and Naturalization Service, National Archives, Washington, DC, accessed through Ancestry.com. McClellan's term as New York mayor is celebrated at Thebowerboys.blogspot.com/2009/01. Information on Charles Wherley, the construction in Brooklyn during LP's childhood, the public schools she attended, and her father's performance at the Chiropean Meeting in 1909 is from the indispensable *Brooklyn Daily Eagle* (editions of March 3, 1893; September 27, 1895; January 22 and November 10, 1909; May 31 and August 27, 1911; October 4, 1912; June 25, 1913); that on the subway construction accident is from the *New York Times*, August 7, 1910. Details about Carlo E. Carlton are from the *New York Clipper*, January 30, 1909; and the *New York Times*, March 9, 1909. On Juan Codina's singing career and the recording of "Para jardines Granada" he made with Columbia Records, see Serge Prokofiev Jr., "Juan Codina —A Singer," *Three Oranges Journal*, vol. 15 (May 2008): 36. On Vera Danchakoff: Ida Clyde Clark, editor, *Women of 1923 International* (Philadelphia: John C. Winston, 1923), 174; on Charles Johnston, H.B.M., "Charles Johnston," *Theosophical Quarterly Magazine*, 1931–1932 (New York: The Theosophical Society, 1932), 206–11. The details on LP's evening aboard the *Kursk* are from the *Brooklyn Daily Eagle*, February 23, 1915; those on Yekaterina Breshko-Breshkovskaya's stay in the United States are from the *New York Times* (January 20, 25, 26, 30; February 11, 15, 26; April 7; May 21, 1919). LP's encounters with Aleksey Stahl and Vera Janacopoulos are recalled in LPF. The address of the cooperative bank where LP worked is from Prokofiev's 1918 address book; RGALI f. 1929, op. 4, yed. khr. 41.

9 *"eight years in prison"*: Donal Henahan, "Is She the Only Wife of Serge Prokofiev?" *New York Times*, December 20, 1976, p. 59.
10 *"Can't we turn on the light"*: LPF 1/9.
12 *"Kiss her on the forehead"*: LPF 1/9.
13 *"To live happily"*: Henahan, "Is She the Only Wife of Serge Prokofiev?"
14 *"Avez-vous une aussi belle"*: Letter from LP to Sergey Prokofiev (SP), December 29, 1920, RGALI f. 1929, op. 4, yed. khr. 300.
15 *"made-up language"*: LPF 1/1.

17 *"The Southerner tried to speak"*: The Speaker's Garland and Literary Bouquet (Philadelphia: P. Garrett, 1876), 140.
19 *"the cheapest high-class apartments"*: Brooklyn Daily Eagle, August 27, 1911, p. 15.
21 *"People had strange ideas then"*: LPF 1/1.
23 *"You're such a polite little Russian"*: LPF 1/1.
24 *"cock of the walk"*: LPF 1/4.
27 *"far from totalitarian"*: LPF 1/9.
   "It is difficult to speak of Russia": "Exposes Bolshevik Misrule in Russia," *New York Times*, January 30, 1919, p. 3.
   "enticed, tempted, and mislaid": Letter of August 23, 1919, Folder 10 (Reel 2) of the Lillian Wald Papers, Columbia University.
   "fundamental good foundations": LPF 1/9.
28 *"The Cooperatives will endeavor"*: The Russian Cooperative News: Bulletin of the American Committee of Russian Cooperative Unions, vol. 1, no. 1 (June 1919): 15.
   "The peace treaty has been signed": The Russian Cooperative News, vol. 1, no. 3 (August 1919): 1.
30 *"Oh, I'd like to go too!"*: LPF 1/1.

CHAPTER 2

Sources for the details of the life of Serge Prokofiev (SP) in Russia and his first years in the United States include Sergey Prokofiev, *Diaries 1907–1914: Prodigious Youth*, translated by Anthony Phillips (London: Faber & Faber, 2006), 167–68, 425–32, 658–64, 704–8; and Prokofiev, *Diaries 1915–1923: Behind the Mask*, translated by Anthony Phillips (London: Faber & Faber, 2008), 175–83, 272, 316–21, 328, 343–46, 354–56, 363–65, 369, 373–74, 380, 388–90, 392–93, 406–7, 427–28, 434–35, 445–50, 480–81, 486–87, 500–501, 509–10, 529–34, 537–40. I am grateful to Phillips for permission to use his translations in this chapter. Information also from Prokofiev, *Prokofiev by Prokofiev: A Composer's Memoir*, translated by Guy Daniels (Garden City, NY: Doubleday & Co., 1979), 129–30, 151–53, 161–62, 219–21. On *Love for Three Oranges*: Stephen D. Press, "'I Came Too Soon': Prokofiev's Early Career in America," in *Sergey Prokofiev and His World*, edited by Simon Morrison (Princeton: Princeton University Press, 2008), 334–75. The obituary of Harriet Lanier in the October 28, 1931, edition of the *New York Times* provided her and her husband's addresses; that of Stella Adler in the December 22, 1992, edition supplied the details about the actress's career and teaching. Details on the Bohemian Club from Archive.org/details/bohemiansnewyork ookrehuoft. For background on Stahl, I thank Natalya Strizhkova of RGALI; information also from RGALI f. 1929, op. 4, yed. khr. 360, the letters Stahl wrote to SP from 1918 to 1924. Biographical information on Janacopoulos is from an unpublished lecture by Noëlle Mann on "The Rose and the Nightingale." On Carita Spencer and Gussie Hillyer Garvin I am grateful to research by Pilar Castro Kiltz. LP recalled the flower delivery mix-up in a December 22, 1982, interview with MHB; other information on her relationship with SP from LPF and

RGALI f. 1929, op. 4, yed. khr. 300. The photograph of the Wagner reenactment on Staten Island is from the Serge Prokofiev Estate; the general location of Stahl's house on Prince's Bay was deduced by visiting the area in the summer of 2009.

32 *"tease the geese"*: Prokofiev, *Prokofiev by Prokofiev: A Composer's Memoir*, 345.
   "astonishingly beautiful": Prokofiev, *Diaries 1907–1914: Prodigious Youth*, 431.
33 *"plague of abscesses"*: Prokofiev, *Diaries 1915–1923: Behind the Mask*, 406.
34 *"Did I love him?"*: Prokofiev, *Diaries 1907–1914: Prodigious Youth*, 168.
   "gloomy-looking Negro": Prokofiev, *Diaries 1915–1923: Behind the Mask*, 328.
   "beautiful, flat-chested": Ibid., 380.
   "limping badly": Ibid., 346.
35 *"conquered"*: Ibid., 343.
   "Prokofiev may well be": Unsigned, "Concert and Reception at the Brooklyn Museum," *Brooklyn Daily Eagle*, October 30, 1918, p. 7.
36 *"the thoughts of the young"*: Prokofiev, *Diaries 1915–1923: Behind the Mask*, 373.
   "sold his soul to the devil": Ibid., 369.
   "psychologist of the uglier": Richard Aldrich, "Serge Prokofieff a Virile Pianist," *New York Times*, November 21, 1918, p. 13.
   "hell-broth": Nicolas Slonimsky, *Lexicon of Musical Invective: Critical Assaults on Composers Since Beethoven's Time* (New York: W. W. Norton & Co., 2000), 130.
37 *"coughing like a lunatic"*: Prokofiev, *Diaries 1915–1923: Behind the Mask*, 344.
38 *"a sort of nightclub"*: Ibid., 510.
39 *"Etude in Rhythms"*: James Gibbons Huneker, "Music: The Russian Symphony Orchestra," *New York Times*, December 11, 1918, p. 13.
   "Don't you understand?": LPF 1/1.
40 *"hell of a girl"*: Prokofiev, *Diaries 1915–1923: Behind the Mask*, 393.
41 *"I lived only for my pleasure"*: Dagmar Godowsky, *First Person Plural: The Lives of Dagmar Godowsky* (New York: Viking Press, 1958), 249.
   "Your talent is in": Peter B. Flint, "Stella Adler, 91, an Actress and Teacher of the Method," *New York Times*, December 22, 1992, Section B, p. 10.
42 *"Lately I have thoughts"*: RGALI f. 1929, op. 4, yed. khr. 215, l. 1 [January 14, 1921].
   "I arrived to New York": RGALI f. 1929, op. 4, yed. khr. 44, l. 1 [January 31, 1921].
43 *"Look, I saved your life!"*: LPF 1/1.
   "new admirer": Prokofiev, *Diaries 1915–1923: Behind the Mask*, 428.
44 *"Vidish'-li tï inogda"*: RGALI f. 1929, op. 4, yed. khr. 300, l. 8 [December 29, 1920].
   "My child": LPF 1/4.
45 *"Just what do you think"*: RGALI f. 1929, op. 4, yed. khr. 27 [December 4, 1919].
   "Do you know what time": LPF 1/1.
46 *"it is a long time since"*: Prokofiev, *Diaries 1915–1923: Behind the Mask*, 445.
47 *"Oh, he did that for effect"*: LPF 1/1.
   "So, are you getting married?": Ibid.
48 *"I revolve between"*: Prokofiev, *Diaries 1915–1923: Behind the Mask*, 486.
49 *"Olga Vladislavovna"*: LPF 1/9.

"You don't really think": Ibid.
"Where did you hook": LPF 1/1.
"I'm probably one of the only": Ibid.
52 *"un petit bijou"*: Prokofiev, *Diaries 1915–1923: Behind the Mask*, 539.
"many miles of briny deep": RGALI f. 1929, op. 4, yed. khr. 300, l. 4 [December 14, 1920].

CHAPTER 3

The bulk of the narrative draws from LP's letters to SP from 1920 to 1922, preserved in RGALI f. 1929, op. 4, yed. khr. 300. His letters to her during this period (f. 1929, op. 4, yed. khr. 127) are generally unrevealing; it seems not all of them have survived, though. RGALI is also the source for the details about SP and Nina Koshetz and, in the archive's press clipping files, the American critical reception of *Love for Three Oranges*. I rely throughout on Prokofiev, *Diaries 1915–1923: Behind the Mask*, 542–44, 564–67, 571–74, 589–90, 593–94, 598–610, 612–16, 619–20, 622–28, 634–57. The March 28, 1921, edition of the *New York Times* includes a review, by an unimpressed Richard Aldrich, of Koshetz's recital with the Schola Cantorum. Information on Balieff's cabaret is from Lawrence Sullivan, "Nikita Baliev's Le Théâtre de la Chauve-Souris: An Avant-Garde Theater," *Dance Research Journal*, vol. 18, no. 2 (Winter 1986–87): 17–29. On the Dadaists and their haunts: Arlen J. Hansen, *Expatriate Paris: A Cultural and Literary Guide to Paris of the 1920s* (New York: Little, Brown, 1990), 21–22. On "Kiki de Montparnasse" and Prokofiev's aversion to Paris's seamier, steamier side: *William Wiser: The Crazy Years: Paris in the Twenties* (New York: Atheneum, 1983), 86, 148–50. Photographs of LP's ski trip and her convalescence from appendicitis are from the Serge Prokofiev Estate.

55 *"to the grave!!!!!!!"*: RGALI f. 1929, op. 4, yed. khr. 284, l. 10 [April 27, 1921].
"like a lover for a rendezvous": Ibid., l. 1 [December 4, 1920].
56 *"The spirits told me"*: Ibid., l. 4 [December 15, 1920].
57 *"One of them (the longest)"*: Ibid.
"It's strange, but lately": RGALI f. 1929, op. 4, yed. khr. 300, l. 7 [December 29, 1920].
58 *"Bus'ka, I must warn you"*: Ibid.
60 *"contrôler le trac"*: Ibid., l. 5 [December 19, 1921].
"'Takaya gadost'": Ibid., l. 9 [January 5, 1921].
61 *"old dear"*: Ibid., l. 3 [December 14, 1920].
"How lucky some people are!": Ibid., l. 4.
"You never make any reference": Ibid.
62 *"I understand that your successes"*: Ibid., l. 19 [January 17, 1921].
"posting a letter": Ibid., l. 12 [January 5, 1921].
63 *"stupid situation"*: Ibid., l. 23 [March 1, 1921].
"a freak nor an idiot": Ibid.
64 *"Lina (not Nina)"*: Ibid., l. 30 [March 23, 1921].
65 *"In the morning I drank coffee"*: Ibid., l. 27 [March 24, 1921].
"an entire battalion of fleas": Ibid., l. 31 [March 26, 1921].

66 *"to acquire all the sense"*: Ibid., l. 35 [April 23, 1921].

67 *"alarmingly* décolletées *cocottes"*: Prokofiev, *Diaries 1915–1923: Behind the Mask,* 603.

69 *"conniving little Yid"*: RGALI f. 1929, yed. khr. 300, l. 41 [June 15, 1921].
"pure coloratura": Ibid., l. 42.
"she's a marvelous person": Ibid., l. 43.
"How encouraging": Ibid.

70 *"I owe it all to Mme Calvé"*: Ibid., l. 48 [June 20, 1921].
"Your letter from the 17th": Ibid., l. 49 [June 21, 1921].

71 *"If only you knew how wonderful"*: Ibid., l. 50.
"It seems to be the only thing": Ibid.
"j'ai peur qu'elle n'a pas": Ibid., l. 76 [January 7, 1922].

72 *"confounded colds"*: Ibid., l. 64 [November 20, 1921].
"The old witch": Ibid., l. 73 [December 8, 1921].

73 *"dangerously attractive"*: Ibid., l. 66 [November 28, 1921].

75 *"bodyguard" to protect himself*: Ibid.
"string of $1,000 dates": RGALI f. 1929, op. 1, yed. khr. 921, no. 371 [September 29, 1921, letter from Fitzhugh W. Haensel to Mr. Liebling of *Musical Courier*].
"anything else the company has": Ibid., no. 387 [Karleton Hackett, "'Love for Three Oranges' Said to be Russian Jazz," *Chicago Evening Post*, December 31, 1921].

76 *"prophet of the music of the future"*: Ibid.
"two tunes": Edward Moore, "'Love for Three Oranges' Color Marvel, but Enigmatic Noise," *Chicago Daily Tribune*, December 31, 1921, p. 11.
"hurdy-gurdy rhythms": RGALI f. 1929, op. 1, yed. khr. 921, no. 389 [Ben Hecht, "Around the Town," *Chicago Daily News*, December 30, 1921].
"best-dressed man in Chicago": Prokofiev, *Diaries 1915–1923: Behind the Mask,* 635.

77 *"It's impossible to struggle"*: RGALI f. 1929, op. 4, yed. khr. 300, l. 72 [December 8, 1921].

CHAPTER 4

This chapter relies on the RGALI correspondence between SP and LP, along with Prokofiev, *Diaries 1915–1923: Behind the Mask,* 663–65, 670–72, 676–84, 696, 699, 702–6, 710–13. The account of SP's time in Ettal includes details from LPF and a 2002 article by Svyatoslav Prokofiev in *Three Oranges Journal* available at Sprkfv.net/journal/three03/ettal1.html. On *The Fiery Angel,* Simon Morrison, *Russian Opera and the Symbolist Movement* (Berkeley and Los Angeles: University of California Press, 2002), 242–307. I am grateful to Phillip Ramey for a copy of his interviews with LP in 1979 and to Malcolm Hamrick Brown for the letters from SP to his longtime friend Fatma Khanum. The Ramey interview of July 9, 1979, contains the tale about the incubator. Thanks to Peter Kenez for vetting the details on the Russian civil war; the statistics on casualties are from Necrometrics.com. Details on SP and LP's recital in Milan are from a bulletin in the May 17, 1923, edition of *Corriere della Sera;* the performance was not reviewed. On the carnival: My-milano.com/carnevale_milano.html; Files.meetup.com/85466/ carnevale_in_italy.pdf. On the Oberammergau Passion play: Nicholas Kulish, "Church Crisis Shakes Faith of German Town," *New York Times*, May 15, 2010, p. A4; James Shapiro, *Oberammergau: The Troubling Story of the World's Most Famous Passion Play* (New York: Vintage, 2001), 3–43, esp. 26–27; 101–36, esp. 126–27; and *Time* magazine at Time.com/time/magazine/article/0,9171,717218,00.html; Time.com/time/magazine/article/0,9171,933678,00.html.

81 *"temperamental as her"*: Unsigned, "Eva Didur Wins Throng," *New York Times*, March 11, 1918, p. 9.
82 *"very chic"*: RGALI f. 1929, op. 4, yed. khr. 127, l. 9 [April 6, 1922].
"for me it is the spiritual union": RGALI f. 1929, op. 4, yed. khr. 300, l. 91 [June 1, 1922].
"So if I do decide to take a vacation": Ibid.
83 *"I'm reading* Le Grand Secret*"*: Ibid., l. 92.
"elements of growth": Ibid., l. 56 [July 2, 1922—letter out of order in the file].
"Such is possible only for a person": RGALI f. 1929, op. 4, yed. khr. 127, l. 16 [July 9, 1922].
"pose before the world": Ibid.
84 *"I must feel that you accept"*: RGALI f. 1929, op. 4, yed. khr. 300, l. 55 [July 2, 1922—letter out of order in the file].
"frying pan": RGALI f. 1929, op. 4, yed. khr. 127, l. 14 [June 8, 1922].
"I'd be sad in Ettal": Ibid., l. 16 [July 9, 1922].
"I sincerely love and value": RGALI f. 1929, op. 4, yed. khr. 300, l. 93 [July 13, 1922].
"green" or "sour apples": RGALI f. 1929, op. 4, yed. khr. 127, ll. 15, 18 [July 9 and 29, 1922].
"If I were the vain and empty": RGALI f. 1929, op. 4, yed. khr. 300, ll. 94–95 [July 13, 1922].
"ein paar Wochen": RGALI f. 1929, op. 4, yed. khr. 127, l. 17 [July 18, 1922].
"kind and gentle ptashka": Ibid., l. 18 [July 29, 1922].
87 *"Once when I was at"*: Interview transcript, LP and Phillip Ramey, July 8, 1979, p. 6.
89 *"Do you know I am becoming"*: RGALI f. 1929, op. 4, yed. khr. 300, l. 103 [October 16, 1922].
"my wife": RGALI f. 1929, op. 4, yed. khr. 127, l. 19 [December 17, 1922].
91 *"very well poised in mind"*: RGALI f. 1929, op. 4, yed. khr. 301, l. 14 [February 27, 1923].
"Il Re—the King—came": Ibid., l. 39 [April 12, 1923].
92 *"There are times when I hate"*: Ibid., l. 12 [February 18, 1923].
93 *"tendency towards excess"*: Unsigned, "Il 'Rigoletto' al Carcano," *Corriere della Sera*, March 4, 1923, p. 5.
"just one note": RGALI f. 1929, op. 4, yed. khr. 301, l. 20 [March 9, 1923].
94 *"gracious"*: "Il 'Rigoletto' al Carcano."
"Under the circumstances": RGALI f. 1929, op. 4, yed. khr. 301, l. 33 [March 30, 1923].
95 *"stupid visas"*: Ibid., l. 25 [March 17, 1923].
"helpless Italian businessman": Ibid., l. 40 [April 15, 1923].

96 *"She needn't be jealous"*: Ibid., l. 44 [April 17, 1923].
"*evidently your Prokofiev*": Ibid., l. 51 [May 9, 1923].
"*had little hope of Verdi's*": Sprkfv.net/journal/threeo3/ettal1.html.
"*Could it be you have nothing*": RGALI f. 1929, op. 4, yed. khr. 360, l. 20 [received July 21, 1923].
97 *"dulcet rhythm of the life"*: Letter of May 30, 1923, from SP to Fatma Khanum; MHB.

CHAPTER 5

Information in this chapter is from Sergey Prokof'yev, *Dnevnik 1907–1933*, edited by Svyatoslav Prokof'yev, 2 vols. (Paris: sprkfv, 2002), 2:236–51, 263–86, 291–94, 338–49, 365–80, 386–92, 402–26, 439, 445–53; on *Le pas d'acier*, the 1925 invitation for SP to visit the Soviet Union, and his conversion to Christian Science, I also draw from my book *The People's Artist: Prokofiev's Soviet Years* (Oxford and New York: Oxford University Press, 2008), 3–11. SP wrote to Boris Krasin concerning the commission for a "film-symphony about 1905" on June 24 and July 28, 1925; RGALI f. 1929, op. 4, yed. khr. 117. On Paris, I consulted Ernest Hemingway, *A Moveable Feast: The Restored Edition* (New York: Scribner, 2009), 34–39, 81–86. Serge Prokofiev Jr. confirmed the names of the restaurants the Prokofievs frequented. Serge Moreux conducted his interview with SP in 1933, but it was not published until 1949.

100 *"what Mozart did after Bach"*: RGALI f. 1929, op. 1, yed. khr. 927, no. 562 [Bruno David Ussher, "Prokofieff Believes in the Advent of a 'New' Simplicity," *Los Angeles Evening Express*, February 19, 1930].
101 *"sail about 20"*: RGALI f. 1929, op. 4, yed. khr. 301, l. 82 [February 7, 1924].
102 *"stomach-less"*: Prokof'yev, *Dnevnik 1907–1933*, 2:242 [February 27, 1924].
"*hoyden*": Ibid., 2:245 [March 14, 1924].
104 *"the principal cafés"*: Hemingway, *A Moveable Feast*, 82.
105 *"wondrous garden"*: Ibid.; Prokof'yev, *Dnevnik 1907–1933*, 2:284 [October 7, 1924].
106 *"At 12:15 in the morning"*: Ibid., 2:294 [December 12, 1924].
"*God's motherhood*": SPA VIa/105 [July 28, 1924].
"*Turn thought away*": Ibid.
107 *"if you only knew the role"*: RGALI f. 1929, op. 4, yed. khr. 110, l. 2 [December 25, 1927].
109 *"Owing to Christian Science"*: Prokof'yev, *Dnevnik 1907–1933*, 2:425 [July 30, 1926].
111 *"eye of Moscow"*: Ibid., 2:344 [July 24, 1925].
"*To agree would mean*": Ibid.
"*It'll cost you dearly*": Ibid.
112 *"So might we conclude"*: Ibid., 2:346 [July 27, 1925].
"*Bolshevizia*": Prokofiev, *Soviet Diary 1927 and Other Writings*, 8.
"*The government consents*": As quoted in Morrison, *The People's Artist: Prokofiev's Soviet Years*, 7.

113 *"To take a neutral stance"*: Prokof'yev, *Dnevnik 1907–1933*, 2:338–39 [July 12, 1925].

114 *"Your career is finished"*: Interview transcript, LP and Phillip Ramey, July 8, 1979, p. 4.

115 *"famous for its ugliness"*: Prokof'yev, *Dnevnik 1907–1933*, 2:368 [January 8, 1926].

"sincerity, charm and no little": SPA cutting 047 [Blanche Lederman, "Serge Prokofieff Heard," *Musical America*, February 6, 1926].

"graceful, attractive type": SPA cutting 041 [Unsigned, "Russian Pianist, Here for Concert, Says Native Land Is Music Hungry," *Saint Paul Pioneer Press*, January 9, 1926].

"I think there should be": RGALI f. 1929, op. 1, yed. khr. 923, no. 479 [Unsigned, "Russian Composer Seeks New Art," *Portland Telegram*, January 15, 1926].

115 *"under the terms"*: Ibid., no. 483 [Unsigned, "Prokofieff Plays Piano Concerto to Audience of Two," February 27, 1926].

116 *"the ritual was almost always"*: Interview transcript, LP and Phillip Ramey, July 9, 1979, pp. 2–3.

"horrifying" list: RGALI f. 1929, op. 4, yed. khr. 301, l. 98 [January 15, 1926].

"I realize that I'm still": Ibid.

"stupid review": Ibid.

lack of *"assurance"*: SPA cutting 042 [Lindsay B. Longacre, "Russian Composer Presents Own Works to Pro Musica," *Denver Times*, January 13, 1926].

"May God grant you success": RGALI f. 1929, op. 4, yed. khr. 301, l. 98.

121 *"Foreign air does not suit"*: Sprkfv.net/journal/three11/intimate2.html.

CHAPTER 6

The chief source for the first half of this chapter is Prokofiev, *Soviet Diary 1927 and Other Writings*, 3–157. I expand at the start on Oleg Prokofiev's observation, on p. xiv of the introduction, that "Stalin's rule was only beginning" in 1927, "the Great Famine was yet to come and so were all the hardships of industrialization, not to mention the purges of the 1930s. It is doubtful if anybody could even start to imagine what it would all turn into." LP's interviews with Harvey Sachs on November 12–13, 1982, and Phillip Ramey on July 13, 1979, provide additional details about the 1927 trip. SP protests the absconding with his piano in a November 12, 1923, letter to Lunacharsky; RGALI f. 1929, op. 4, yed. khr. 126. On Soviet music after the Revolution: Francis Maes, *A History of Russian Music: From Kamarinskaya to Babi Yar*, translated by Arnold J. Pomerans and Erica Pomerans (Berkeley and Los Angeles: University of California Press, 2002), 246–50; and Richard Taruskin, *Defining Russia Musically* (Princeton: Princeton University Press, 1997), 91–92. The Moscow descriptions come from my own observations of the surviving architecture of the 1920s and photographs of the Prokofievs in the Soviet Union from the Serge Prokofiev Estate. On Gorchakov, I relied on Noëlle Mann, "Georgii Gorchakov and the Story of an Unknown Prokofiev Biography," *Three Oranges Journal*, vol. 11 (May 2006): 9–13; details on the period from 1927 to 1929 (apartment relocations, automobile mishaps, *The Fiery Angel*, Arens, Gorchakov, the trip to London, and the birth of Oleg Prokofiev) from Prokof'yev, *Dnevnik 1907–1933*, 2:556–59, 569–78, 593–601, 608–11, 635–37, 656–61, 714–16, and 724–25; I consulted, passim, David Nice, *Prokofiev: From Russia to the West, 1891–1935* (New Haven and London: Yale University Press, 2003), 243–67.

123 *"provincial appearance"*: Prokofiev, *Soviet Diary 1927 and Other Writings*, 10.
125 *"behind a curtain"*: Ibid., 17.
126 *"You can imagine the hellish"*: Ibid., 38.
127 *"Serge was exhausted"*: LPF 2/1.
   charges of "hooliganism": As quoted in Taruskin, *Defining Russia Musically*, 92 n. 19.
128 *"But I said 'How can I?'"*: LPF 2/1.
129 *"a glass of champagne"*: Prokofiev, *Soviet Diary 1927 and Other Writings*, 104; LPF 2/1.
132 *"The telephone has only"*: Prokofiev, *Soviet Diary 1927 and Other Writings*, 136.
   "a somewhat leprous appearance": Ibid.
   a "beautiful" sight: Ibid., 140.
133 *"always had something up"*: Interview transcript, LP and Phillip Ramey, July 13, 1979, p. 4.
   "Where do you see that?": Ibid., p. 3.
   saying, "no, no": Ibid., p. 4.
   "Who is that man?": Ibid.
   "Why did you have to ask": Ibid.
134 *"My visit here"*: Prokofiev, *Soviet Diary 1927 and Other Writings*, 150.
   "a kind of huge jar": Ibid., 14; LPF 1/9.
135 *"Those seeing us off"*: Prokofiev, *Soviet Diary 1927 and Other Writings*, 156.
136 *"935 francs pour reparations"*: RGALI f. 1929, op. 4, yed. khr. 301, l. 103 [April 23, 1929].
137 *"so absorbed in the progression"*: Mann, "Georgii Gorchakov and the Story of an Unknown Prokofiev Biography," 11.
   "made too much noise": Ibid.
138 *"twitching and tapping"*: Ibid., 12.
   "shattered by the amount": Ibid.
   "stopped working before": Ibid.
143 *"Respirez tranquillement!"*: Prokof'yev, *Dnevnik 1907–1933*, 2:656.
   "freakish" sight: Ibid.
144 *"Walking home, I thought"*: Ibid., 2:658.

CHAPTER 7

Information in this chapter from LP's correspondence with SP in 1935–36: RGALI f. 1929, op. 4, yed. khr. 302 and f. 1929, op. 1, yed. khr. 655. I also quote the letters of February 22 and 24, 1936, from LP to SP in *The People's Artist: Prokofiev's Soviet Years*, 42–43. For the descriptions of Polenovo, I relied on the "closed" 1935 letters from SP to LP preserved in the Serge Prokofiev Archive at Goldsmiths, University of London. On LP and La Serenade: Prokof'yev, *Dnevnik*

1907–1933, 2:798–99. I am grateful to Malcolm Hamrick Brown for the letters and postcards from SP to Olga Codina. Information on LP's Moscow house-keepers is from Elena Krivtsova, "'Placeless, Dateless' Documents in the Sergei Prokofiev Collection (Based on Materials in the Glinka State Central Museum of Musical Culture)," *Three Oranges Journal*, vol. 22 (November 2011): 3–4. On Alberti de Gorostiaga and Lily Pons: James A. Drake and Kristin Beall Ludecke, editors, *Lily Pons: A Centennial Portrait* (Portland, OR: Amadeus Press, 1999), 24, 44–45, and 48; and "Lily Pons Sings Before Record-Breaking Crowd of 175,000 in Chicago," *Life*, September 6, 1937, 28–29. For the points about Moscow on July 1, 1936, I consulted *Pravda* and *Vechernyaya Moskva* (*Moscow at Dusk*). On the attacks in *Pravda* on Shostakovich, the best English-language source remains Laurel E. Fay, *Shostakovich: A Life* (Oxford and New York: Oxford University Press, 2000), 82–85.

146 *"the music that's needed"*: RGALI f. 1929, op. 4, yed. khr. 320, ll. 33–34 [September 20, 1931].
"*I think that matters*": RGALI f. 1929, op. 4, yed. khr. 147, l. 17 [October 6, 1931].
148 *"of the merits of moving"*: As quoted in Morrison, *The People's Artist: Prokofiev's Soviet Years*, 17.
"*Your letter is so interesting*": RGALI f. 1929, op. 4, yed. khr. 302, l. 80 [May 25, 1934].
149 *"V. F. asks why you"*: Ibid., l. 99 [November 19, 1934].
"*our Prokofiev*": Prokof'yev, *Dnevnik 1907–1933*, 2:680 [March 5, 1929].
"*very lively and interesting*": RGALI f. 1929, op. 4, yed. khr. 302, l. 48 [August 16, 1933].
"*How sorrowful it's all become*": Ibid., l. 105 [January 4, 1935].
151 *"The thing about last night's concert"*: As quoted in Elena Mironenko, "Sergei Prokofiev and Moldova: Creative and Biographical Ties," *Three Oranges Journal*, vol. 22 (November 2011): 11.
"*the concert was such a success*": Interview transcript, LP and Phillip Ramey, July 9, 1979, p. 3.
"*Those are from your military admirer*": Ibid., p. 4.
153 *name as "Protopief"*: RGALI f. 1929, op. 4, yed. khr. 302, l. 74 [April 18, 1934].
"*a little too much*": SPA XXXIX – 289 [March 31, 1935].
"*large buildings trying to scrape*": Ibid.
155 *"acquaintances of acquaintances"*: RGALI f. 1929, op. 4, yed. khr. 302, l. 118 [July 25, 1935].
"*I can't tell you how lonesome*": Ibid., l. 117.
156 *"Bath house a prison cell"*: Ibid., l. 119 [August 11, 1935].
"*had big success with the ladies*": Ibid., l. 121 [October 31, 1935].
157 *"who needs folklore"*: Ibid., l. 123 [November 27, 1935].
"*Well that's it then*": Ibid., l. 124 [November 30 and December 1, 1935].
"*It'd been so long since*": SPA Closed 10.
158 *"superior vocal technique"*: Ibid.
"*But concerning Radio*": Ibid.
"*They're not remarkable*": RGALI f. 1929, op. 4, yed. khr. 302, l. 126 [December 19, 1935].

"cocktail" hosted by Americans: Ibid., l. 124 [November 30 and December 1, 1935].

159 *"enticing voice, feline":* LPF 2/1.

160 *"I saw part of the parade":* RGALI f. 1929, op. 4, yed. khr. 302, l. 122 [November 8, 1935].

161 *"The musical idiots and cretins":* RGALI f. 1929, op. 1, yed. khr. 655, l. 1 [February 22, 1936].
     "to be the one who is showing": Ibid., l. 2 [February 24, 1936].
     "Be a little more careful": Ibid., l. 1 [February 22, 1936].

162 *"Don't rush with the furniture":* Ibid.
     "It seems to me that in all": Ibid., l. 2 [February 24, 1936].
     "When's it over?": Ibid., l. 5 [March 1, 1936].

163 *"flirting corner":* Ibid.
     "How many evening dresses": Ibid.
     "I wish I had thought of all": Ibid.

164 *"Every day something new":* Ibid.
     "much more interesting": Letter of September 11, 1935, from SP to Olga Codina; MHB.

165 *"Each morning I sit":* MHB.

166 *"some big hero":* LPF 2/1.

167 *nasally as "cam-pan-zer":* Oleg Prokofiev, "Papers from the Attic: My Father, His Music, and I," *Yale Literary Magazine*, vol. 148, no. 2 (September 1979): 21.

CHAPTER 8

Information in this chapter is from the correspondence between LP and SP at RGALI and SPA, and from the interviews conducted with LP by Harvey Sachs and Malcolm Hamrick Brown. Details on William C. Bullitt's outrageous 1935 ball is from Will Brownell and Richard N. Billings, *So Close to Greatness: A Biography of William C. Bullitt* (New York: Macmillan, 1987), 174–75, and, passim, Charles W. Thayer, *Bears in the Caviar* (Philadelphia and New York: J. B. Lippincott, 1951), 158–63. The ball was reimagined in Moscow in 2010: Moscow. usembassy.gov/news-enchantedspas0102910.html. On Jay Leyda and Stella Adler: RGALI f. 1929, op. 4, yed. khr. 44, l. 3. On Alexander Afinogenov: Jochen Hellbeck, *Revolution on My Mind: Writing a Diary Under Stalin* (Cambridge, MA: Harvard University Press, 2009), 285–345. Details on Jenny Marling from her daughter, Alexandra Afinogenova, whom I met in Moscow on August 30, 2011; thanks also to Professor Boris Wolfson of Amherst College. On John Bovingdon: Hoover Institution Archives, Joseph Freeman Collection, box 16, folder 29. Source documents on SP's Ford and chauffeur provided by the Serge Prokofiev Estate. On *Romeo and Juliet, Cantata for the Twentieth Anniversary of October,* and the tours of 1937 and 1938, I draw from *The People's Artist: Prokofiev's Soviet Years,* 29–40, 50–66, 70–77, 79–82; I quote a longer excerpt from the letter from Lawrence Creath Ammons to LP on p. 81. Information on LP and SP's 1937 stay in New York is from Alice Berezowsky, *Duet with Nicky* (Philadelphia and New York: J. B. Lippincott, 1943), 207–14. Details on SP in Kislovodsk in 1937 is from

Krivtsova, "'Placeless, Dateless' Documents in the Sergei Prokofiev Collection (Based on Materials in the Glinka State Central Museum of Musical Culture)," 5–6; these pages include images from SP's Kislovodsk dance-hall manual. Besides LP's letters to her mother, details on the closing of the English-language school in Moscow is from Prokof'yev, "O moikh roditelyakh: Beseda sïna kompozitora s muzïkovedom Nataliyey Savkinoy," 222–23, and Valentina Chemberdzhi, *XX vek Lini Prokof'yevoy* (Moscow: Klassika-XXI, 2008), 171–72. Thanks to Serge Prokofiev Jr. for the details about School N336 and Ephraim F. Gottlieb's gift calendars.

169 *"a red-headed timid boy"*: LPF 2/1.
   "because Stalin is there": Ibid.
   "locked eyes with Stalin": Prokof'yev, *Dnevnik 1907–1933*, 2:834.
   "You don't know what": LPF 2/1.
   "Your children will not get": Ibid.
170 *"they didn't like me speaking"*: Ibid.
172 *"people would sell a diamond"*: LPF 1/9.
174 *"a very convinced Communist"*: Ibid.
176 without its *"particularities"*: RGALI f. 1929, op. 4, yed. khr. 224, l. 2 [August 7, 1932].
   "The concerned Latvians": Ibid.
   "nothing serious": Ibid.
177 *"At last I can speak"*: LPF 1/9.
   "I like it here": Ibid.
   "the musical advancement": As quoted in Morrison, *The People's Artist: Prokofiev's Soviet Years*, 73.
   "unpleasant seriousness": Prokofiev, "Papers from the Attic: My Father, His Music, and I," 21.
179 *"Just what do you think"*: As quoted in Morrison, *The People's Artist: Prokofiev's Soviet Years*, 65.
   "no form or physical": As quoted in ibid., 39.
180 *"For never was a story"*: As quoted in ibid., 36.
181 *"Why don't you sleep?"*: LP interview with MHB, April 1–2, 1985.
   "I want to go back": LPF 2/1.
   "What I promised then": LP interview with MHB, December 20, 1982.
   "nervous atmosphere": RGALI f. 1929, op. 1, yed. khr. 655, l. 12 [December 6, 1936; unsent].
182 *"If it were up to me"*: Ibid.
   "I completely understand": Ibid.
   "today there was a demonstration": Ibid., l. 13.
183 *"stunning"* attire: Berezowsky, *Duet with Nicky*, 209.
   "Thank you, I rather like it": Ibid., 211.
   "When Madame Prokofieff took": Ibid., 212.
184 *"poker-face expression"*: Ibid., 210.
   "The government hasn't": Ibid., 213.
   "You know, it's too bad": Ibid., 211.
185 *"Sergey Sergeyevich"*: As quoted in Morrison, *The People's Artist: Prokofiev's Soviet Years*, 52.
   "What about your boys?": Ibid.

"*later learned*": Ibid., 52–53.

186 "*whimpers now and then*": Ibid., 53.

"*exceptionally uninteresting*": RGALI f. 1929, op. 2, yed. khr. 464, l. 6 [received August 11, 1937].

187 "*I can well imagine*": SPA Closed 18 [September 11, 1937].

188 "*The composer got it*": Paul Harrison, "How Hollywood Receives One with High Rank in World of Music," *San Jose Evening News*, April 11, 1938, p. 7.

"*Well, our slang may not be*": Ibid.

"*The three days in London*": Postcard of January 29 [?], 1938, from LP to Olga Codina; MHB.

"*We received a letter*": Ibid.

189 "*in connection with some*": Prokofiev, "Papers from the Attic: My Father, His Music, and I," 24.

"*I'm not getting a swelled head*": RGALI f. 1929, op. 2, yed. khr. 249, l. 2.

"*I send your wife and you*": Ibid.

190 which was "*inconvenient*": Letter of March 4, 1938, from SP to Olga Codina; MHB.

"*There was a flicker*": As quoted in Morrison, *The People's Artist: Prokofiev's Soviet Years*, 76.

"'*You know, Dima'*": Ibid.

191 "*I want to tell you*": As quoted in Peter J. Hodgson, "Lina Prokofiev and Christian Science" [unpublished]; SPA.

"*It was a relief to know*": Ibid.

"*spiritual and human*": Ibid.

"*Hollywood sounds promising*": Ibid.

192 "*He didn't ask*": LPF 2/1.

CHAPTER 9

This chapter draws on the interviews conducted with LP by Harvey Sachs, the painful 1938–1940 correspondence between LP and SP housed at RGALI, and the "closed" 1938–1939 letters from SP to LP at SPA. Valentina Chemberdzhi quotes discrete sections of the SPA letters in *XX vek Lini Prokof'yevoy*, 189–91 and 197–204; I indicate the passages she consulted before me in the notes below, but relied on the uncut originals. LP's disdainful description of Mira Mendelson (MM) is balanced by the glowing one in another memoir by Chemberdzhi, *V dome muzika zhila: Memuari o muzikantakh* (Moscow: Agraf, 2002), 99–104; MM is recalled by the author as "the embodiment of goodness and meekness" and the "ideal wife for Prokofiev." The gossip about MM in the diplomatic corps is described by the American embassy staffer Frederick Reinhardt in a letter to MHB of March 4, 1963. On the beginning and early years of SP and MM's relationship I referred to M. A. Mendel'son-Prokof'yeva, "Iz vospominaniy," in *Sergey Prokof'yev, 1891–1991: Dnevnik, pis'ma, besedi, vospominaniya*, 236–54; I also draw from *The People's Artist: Prokofiev's Soviet Years*, 85–86 (*Hamlet*), 96–106 (Meyerhold's arrest and *Semyon Kotko*), 113–17 (*Zdravitsa*), 157–62 (MM and SP), 167–73 (*The Duenna*), 175–76 (the war and evacuation), 218–24 (*Alexander Nevsky*), 436–37 (MM and her parents). On Hitler in Paris: ww2today.com/23r-june-1940-hitler-tours-paris; on the Narzan mineral waters: Themoscowtimes.com/guides/travel/2011/eng/ar ticle/436913.html; and on the Castle of Wile and Love and other attractions of Kislovodsk: Russia-travel.ws/regions/Kislovodsk.

195 *"So tomorrow I have to stand"*: RGALI f. 1929, op. 1, yed. khr. 655, ll. 16–17 [May 14, 1938].
"I kiss and hug you": Ibid., l. 16.
197 "grand légume": LPF 1/9.
198 *"You're insane—he has a wife"*: Ibid.
199 *"to a blossoming poet"*: As quoted in Morrison, *The People's Artist: Prokofiev's Soviet Years*, 158.
201 *"the composition of new works"*: SPE.
"Alas, I have nothing special": RGALI f. 1929, op. 1, yed. khr. 655, l. 26 [July 16, 1939].
202 *"It seems that two days"*: Ibid.
"I still can't get my head": Ibid.
owing to the *"spasmodicism"*: Ibid.
203 *"rehabilitate" herself*: Ibid.
"What a horror": Chemberdzhi, *XX vek Lini Prokof'yevoy*, 199; SPA Closed 23 [July 19, 1939].
"a tragic romantic fate": Ibid.
a single word: *"perverse"*: SPA Closed 25 [August 1, 1939].
wisecracking *"metallurgist"*: RGALI f. 1929, op. 1, yed. khr. 655, l. 29 [August 20, 1939].
204 *"a branch stuck up"*: SPA Closed 26 [August 10, 1939].
"You'll be manning": Chemberdzhi, *XX vek Lini Prokof'yevoy*, 203; SPA Closed 27 [August 20, 1939].
the petite *"poetess"*: RGALI f. 1929, op. 1, yed. khr. 655, l. 29.
"subordinate home and hearth": Letter of July 18, 1939, as quoted in Mendel'son-Prokof'yeva, "Iz vospominaniy," 243.
"horrible bazaar": Ibid.
205 *"the scratching of the pencil"*: Ibid.
"I haven't danced": Ibid.
"Each passing day brings": RGALI f. 1929, op. 2, yed. khr. 465 [July 16, 1939].
206 *"British lion"*: SPA Closed 28 [September 7, 1939].
"inject itself": Ibid.
207 *"just some girl"*: As quoted in Morrison, *The People's Artist: Prokofiev's Soviet Years*, 157.
"get rid of her": LPF 2/1.
"Well, go ahead and see her": As quoted in Morrison, *The People's Artist: Prokofiev's Soviet Years*, 157–58.
"I'm telling you this": LPF 1/9.
"incredibly lonely it seemed": As quoted in Morrison, *The People's Artist: Prokofiev's Soviet Years*, 116–17.
208 *"the little girl with her daddy"*: LPF 1/9.
"She lives very near": Ibid.

"Probably some had already": Ibid.

209 *"He's never used the car"*: LPF 2/1.

210 *"The life of somebody"*: Ibid.

"Please read through this": RGALI f. 1929, op. 1, yed. khr. 464, l. 12 [June 1, 1940].

"the past eight months": Ibid., l. 13.

"spiritual suicide": Ibid., l. 16.

211 *"Even though it's difficult"*: Ibid., l. 13.

"machinations" in her attempts: Ibid.

"Could you possibly believe": Ibid.

"Remember what you wrote": Ibid., l. 15.

212 *"Never travel to the south"*: Ibid.

"despotism" of Mira's: Ibid., l. 17.

"It's only now": RGALI f. 1929, op. 1, yed. khr. 290, l. 1.

213 *"for it cannot be"*: Ibid.

"disgraceful" accommodation: LPF 1/9.

CHAPTER 10

LP's interviews with Harvey Sachs (SPA) and the letters she exchanged with SP in 1942–1943 (RGALI) provide the details about her wartime experience at the heart of this chapter. Svyatoslav Prokofiev mentions LP's work for Sovinformbyuro and friendship with Anne-Marie Lotte in interviews with Valentina Chemberdzhi: *XX vek Linï Prokof'yevoy*, 213 and 219–20; details vetted by Serge Prokofiev Jr. Information on SP's evacuation, return to Moscow with MM, his support of LP and their children, and the Fifth Symphony premiere are from *The People's Artist: Prokofiev's Soviet Years*, 179–80, 215–16, 252. Footage of the German invasion of the USSR, including the rooftop firebomb defenders and the shelter provided by the Metro, is available at YouTube.com. On the Red October chocolate plant: Weburbanist.com/2011/04/24/soviet-yum-yum-russias-red-october-chocolate-factory/. On the Red Cross: *Annual Report for the Year Ending June 30, 1942* (Washington, DC: The American National Red Cross, 1942), 106–7; thanks to Lindsay Flanagan Huban for providing a scan of this document. I am grateful to Professor Nelly Kravetz of Tel Aviv University for permission to quote from the typescript of the memoirs of Levon Atovmyan, to be included in her forthcoming book *Ryadom s velikimi: Atovm'yan i yego vremya* (Moscow: Rossiyskiy universitet teatral'nogo iskusstva—GITIS, 2012). Details about Afinogenov's death were confirmed by his daughter Alexandra Afinogenova; interview of August 30, 2011. Information on the staffing and structure of Sovinformbyuro is from Natalya Strizhkova of RGALI. The Sovinformbyuro tales about the nurse and the soldier's boots from the RIA Novosti online archive: Eng.9may.ru/eng_album/. Biographical information about Anne-Marie Lotte, who is ninety-eight at the time of this writing, is from Anna Shaparova (scenarist), Rodrigo Saludes (director), and Lyosha Rebrov (producer), *Russkaya Annet* (Moscow: TV Tsentr, 2008); thanks to Serge Prokofiev Jr. for providing a copy of this television broadcast, which includes footage of Mme Lotte in conversation with Svyatoslav Prokofiev. Photographs of Anne-Marie Lotte, LP, and Stanislas Julien from the Serge Prokofiev Estate. I also referred to Yekaterina Sazhneva, "Anyutina 'skazka,'" *Alef*, vol. 952 (August 2006): Alefmagazine.com/pub972.html. Besides Mme Lotte, one of LP's housekeepers, the French national Marquella Paquita, somehow managed to leave the Soviet Union after the war. How she met LP and how long she worked for her is unknown. Upon returning to France, she wrote a letter to Mme Lotte from Marseille. It is dated June 10, 1947, and begins: "My dear Linette: Of course you know already, through Lina, that I have arrived in France just a month ago. As you could imagine, I am enchanted, finally I was able to get out of that 'paradise,' which was a difficult thing, since I waited two years" (letter from the Serge Prokofiev Estate). On *British Ally:* "Moscow Briton Deserts," *Glasgow Herald*, April 25, 1949, p. 38; Time.com/time/magazine/article/0,9171,813277,00.html. On Lord Derwent: Cracroftspeerage .co.uk/online/content/index940.htm; Thepeerage.com/p7189.htm; Charlotte Mosley, *The Mitfords: Letters Between Six Sisters* (New York: HarperCollins, 2008), 253–54.

214 *"unfit" for combat:* E-mail of June 6, 2011, from Serge Prokofiev Jr. to me.
216 *"served the needs of the front":* Slava-moscow.ru/factory.htm.
217 *"horrible, horrible—to make":* LPF 1/9.
219 *"a tirade of profanity":* Letter of June 9, 1942, from LP to the Union of Soviet Composers; Serge Prokofiev Estate.
      "Let those 'who took it'": Ibid.
220 *"Why don't you take everything":* LPF 1/9.
      dnyom s ognyom: RGALI f. 1929, op. 1, yed. khr. 655, l. 37 [May 9, 1942].
221 *"They would say 'Oh, but these'":* Ibid.
222 *"causing him anxiety":* Ibid.
      "chronically malnourished": Ibid.
      "I sell and swap": Ibid.
      "so-called lunch": Ibid., l. 38.
223 *"You have to agree":* Ibid.
      "If it weren't for the hopelessness": Ibid.
      "has for several months": Ibid., l. 39.
224 *"a true friend":* Ibid., l. 40.
      "Such is the sad": Ibid.
225 the *"slippery"* side: Ibid., l. 38.
      "Don't think for a minute": RGALI f. 1929, op. 3, yed. khr. 82, l. 17 [November 3, 1942].
226 photograph *"with love":* LPF 2/1.
      "Give them away to the neighbors": LPF 1/9.
      "gossip, gossip, gossip": Ibid.
229 *"Well, my gentle Annette":* E-mail of July 11, 2011, from Serge Prokofiev Jr. to me [quoting the telephone conversation he had just had with Annette].
230 *Oleg asked, "Where's Papa?":* LPF 1/9.
231 *"It's not the same":* Ibid.
      "had not exchanged them": LP interview with MHB, July 19, 1968.
232 *"So you've come to see":* LPF 1/9.
233 *"the hall was probably lit":* As quoted in Morrison, *The People's Artist: Prokofiev's Soviet Years*, 252 [memoir of the pianist Svyatoslav Richter].

"standing on the conductor's": Letter of May 30, 2009, from Svyatoslav Prokofiev to me.
234 *"cohort of intellectuals"*: Charles de Gaulle, *Mémoires* (Paris: Éditions Galli-
mard, 2000), 650.
"I've just spoken with": Levon Atovm'yan, *Vospominaniya* [typescript], ch. 3, p.
24.
"Don't be naive": Ibid.
"You can't stop me": Ibid.
"in the early postwar": Letter of March 4, 1963, from Frederick Reinhardt to
MHB, p. 3.
235 *"did her no good"*: Letter of October 10, 1964, from Anna Holdcroft to MHB,
p. 2.
"freely amidst the foreign": Ibid.
"I urged her to be more": Ibid.
236 *"the appropriate person"*: LPF 2/1.

CHAPTER 11

Much of the detail in this chapter, verbal and visual, comes from the Serge Prokofiev Estate (SPE); I am grateful to Serge Prokofiev Jr. for contextual information on Olga Codina, Svyatoslav and Oleg Prokofiev's forced relocation, and the
individuals named in LP's trial as co-conspirators. The narrative of the night of
LP's arrest comes from her May 21, 1984, interview with Harvey Sachs; that of
Jenny Marling's final eighteen months from Alexandra Afinogenova, with additional details provided by Boris Wolfson. On the *Pobeda* fire and the rumors
about its cause: Centrasia.ru/newsA.php?st=1223497260; Argumenti.ru/history/
n149/38608. Special thanks to Leonid Maksimenkov for the information on
Pyotr Malikov and Nikolay Kuleshov, which he obtained from the Russian State
Archive of Social-Political History in June 2008; "Investigator Zubov" remains
unidentified. On the 1948 scandal, see Maksimenkov, "Stalin and Shostakovich:
Letters to a 'Friend,'" in Laurel E. Fay, editor, *Shostakovich and His World* (Princeton: Princeton University Press, 2004), 51–53. Also on the scandal and the illegal
dissolution of LP and SP's marriage: *The People's Artist: Prokofiev's Soviet Years*,
295–96, 306–7; Prokof'yev, "O moikh roditelyakh: Beseda sïna kompozitora s
muzïkovedom Nataliyey Savkinoy," 226. In the latter source, pp. 226–28 include
specific details on the looting of the Prokofiev apartment. On Prokofiev's record collection: Juri Jelagin, *Taming of the Arts*, translated by Nicholas Wreden
(New York: Dutton, 1951), 302–3. Thanks to Abbey Harlow of the Mary Baker
Eddy Library for the detail about the Russian-language edition of *Science and
Health with Key to the Scriptures*. Information on Lefortovo from Aleksandr I. Solzhenitsyn, *The Gulag Archipelago, 1918–1956: An Experiment in Literary Investigation, Volumes I–II*, translated by Thomas P. Whitney (New York: Harper & Row,
1973), 180–81; Anne Applebaum: *GULAG: A History* (New York: Anchor, 2004),
131–33, 148; "New Times Loom for Fabled Lefortovo Prison," *St. Petersburg
Times*, June 7, 2005: Sptimes.ru/index.php?action_id=2&story_id=3758; the essay
by Irina Borogan at Agentura.ru/infrastructure/specprisons/lefortovo/; and my
own strolls around the neighborhood.

238 *"Because that's where your father"*: Interview of Alexandra Afinogenova, August 30, 2011.
239 *"Darlings, do you remember"*: Ibid.; private archive of Afinogenova.
240 *"Practically all the Russians"*: Letter of March 4, 1963, from Frederick Reinhardt to MHB, p. 2.
241 *"Concerning L. I.—Lina"*: SPE.
  "Embrassons, souhaitons": SPE.
242 *"You don't have news"*: SPE.
  "if I have children of my own": RGALI f. 1929, op. 1, yed. khr. 653, l. 40 [August 12–19, 1947].
  "tormented in the knowledge": Ibid.
  "Mama has also endured": Ibid.
  "How good it would be": Ibid.
244 *"terribly miserly"*: SPE [letter of March 8, 1949].
245 *"Has something horrible"*: SPE [letter of July 7, 1948].
  "He presumably knows her": SPE [letter of August 1948].
246 *"The postcards had been"*: As quoted in Morrison, *The People's Artist: Prokofiev's Soviet Years*, 308.
  "special order": SPE [p. 1 of February 21, 1948, list of confiscated belongings].
  "yellow-colored": Ibid.
247 *"Give it to me but"*: E-mail of July 22, 2011, from Serge Prokofiev Jr. to me.
  "There is no door through": SPE.
248 *"Father-Mother-God"*: SPE.
  "Such a renovation": SPE [letter of April 20, 1950, p. 4].
249 *"29 rubles and 95 kopecks"*: SPE.
  "They will be notified": LPF 1/9.
251 *"disciplined and politically"*: Russian State Archive of Social-Political History; document provided by Leonid Maksimenkov.
252 *"Shestopal was in a terrible"*: February 28, 1954, letter from LP to Shostakovich, as quoted in an e-mail of August 29, 2011, from Serge Prokofiev Jr. to me.
255 *"The evidence was distorted"*: SPE [pp. 3–4 of handwritten copy]; abbreviated variant reproduced in Chemberdzhi, *XX vek Linï Prokof'yevoy*, 254.
256 *"dangerous criminal"*: SPE [p. 4 of handwritten copy].

CHAPTER 12

Besides the documents from SPE, I relied for the details of LP's experience in the camps on Inna Chernitskaya and Nelli Kravets, "Zhertvï stalinskikh repressiy: O lagernoy zhizni Linï Ivanovnï Prokof'yevoy i sobstvennoy sud'be," *Muzikal'naya akademiya*, vol. 2 (2000): 236–41; and E. A. Taratuta, "Iz vospominaniy," in *Sergey Prokof'yev, 1891–1991: Dnevnik, pis'ma, besedï, vospominaniya*, 232–36. For essential additional information, I drew from Applebaum, *GULAG: A History*, xv–xvi, 160–65 (transport), 175–78 (arrival), 186–215 (barracks, bathing, food), 231–41 (cultural education), 252–54 (meetings with relatives), and 385–86 (musicians). I also consulted the few references to Abez, Inta, and Yavas in V. P. Kozlov et al., editors, *Istoriya stalinskogo Gulaga. Konets 1920-kh—pervaya polovina 1950-kh go-*

dov, 7 vols. (Moscow: ROSSPEN, 2004–2005), 2:41, 135, 244, 329, 340, 621; 4:579, 595; 6:200, 277, 386, 572, 574, 655. Through Dissercat.com, I referred to Viktoriya Geyorgiyevna Mironova, "Kul'turno-vospitatel'naya rabota v lageryakh GULAGa NKVD-MVD SSSR v 1930–1950-e godï," PhD diss., Irkutskiy gosudarstvennïy pedagogicheskiy universitet, 2002. Descriptions of Abez and Inta are from a 1990 Latvian film narrated by the gulag survivor Alfred Geidans: YouTube.com/watch?v=NtnKdKFhjyA; YouTube.com/watch?v=8Coolywn6RM. Additional information on the region is from Inta-rk.narod.ru/turizm.html and Tour-ural.narod.ru; that on the camps near Potma from Delmor.ru/base/sudar/archive/l4.htm. My thanks to Galina Zlobina for these references and for scoping out the evening train service from Moscow to Saransk with me at Kazanskiy vokzal. Something of the current situation at Potma can be gleaned from a website that has been developed by and for the relatives of prisoners: Zubova-polyana.ru/raspisanie-poezdov-do-stancii-potma-zubova-polyana. Although the site is incomplete, it offers instructions for obtaining travel permits and directions by bus and taxi to the ten administrative settlements and fourteen work colonies. The walk from the bus stops to the camps extends up to seven kilometers—the advantage, according to the site, being "fresh air," the disadvantage being the burden of walking an hour and a half with luggage. People taking the train from Moscow to Potma tend to haul enormous bags of food, clothing, and sundries with them. The site also offers advice on where to stay (some of the settlements have guesthouses; at others local residents offer rooms for rent); the names and phone numbers of administrators; and the location of churches, marriage bureaus, hair salons, and toilets. Relatives are informed "that it is not permitted to bring liquor, narcotics, mobile phones, and weapons if you do not want to complicate the lives of those you are traveling to visit."

258 *TO THOSE WHO DID NOT RETURN:* Sakharov-center.ru/asfcd/pam/pam_carde 223.html?id=619.
259 *THIS WAS THE LOCATION:* YouTube.com/watch?v=NtnKdKFhjyA.
260 *"Awaiting your arrival":* SPE.
261 *"Passport check, open":* Chernitskaya and Kravets, "Zhertvï stalinskikh repressiy: O lagernoy zhizni Linï Ivanovnï Prokof'yevoy i sobstvennoy sud'be," 237.
   "Abandon hope all ye": Ibid.
262 *"A step to the right":* Ibid., 239.
   "feeling a little better": SPE [letter of December 19, 1948, p. 1].
   air was "very good": Ibid.
263 *"intellectual conversations":* Chernitskaya and Kravets, "Zhertvï stalinskikh repressiy: O lagernoy zhizni Linï Ivanovnï Prokof'yevoy i sobstvennoy sud'be," 239.
264 *"mixed instruments":* SPE [letter of December 19, 1948, p. 1].
   "He made a violin": Ibid.
   "Why can't I turn myself": Czilaucik.com/tag/Szmytka.
265 *"with broad gestures":* LP interview with MHB, November 12, 1985.
   "conducting as though": Ibid.
   his "soul hurt": As quoted in Morrison, *The People's Artist: Prokofiev's Soviet Years,* 386.

"A, C, B,, B₂": SPE [letter of December 19, 1948, p. 2].

266 *"But what's to be done"*: Ibid.

267 *his "still lifes"*: Ibid. [p. 3].

"You haven't heard anything": Ibid. [p. 4].

"believe that what had happened": Taratuta, "Iz vospominaniy," 235.

"Papa's" (Serge's): SPE [letter of December 19, 1948, p. 4].

268 *"glucose in ampules"*: SPE [1-page list dated October 31, 1949].

"this wasn't always their fault": Taratuta, "Iz vospominaniy," 234.

"Lina Ivanovna missed": Ibid.

"This will confirm receipt": SPE.

"the wife of our great composer": SPE [diary of Svyatoslav Prokofiev, February 24–March 5, 1956].

269 *"the prisoners formed a chorus"*: Taratuta, "Iz vospominaniy," 235.

"almost dropping from fatigue": Chernitskaya and Kravets, "Zhertvï stalinskikh repressiy: O lagernoy zhizni Linï Ivanovnï Prokof'yevoy i sobstvennoy sud'be," 239.

270 *"were not allowed"*: Ibid., 240.

"Major Baba": Memorial.krsk.ru/memuar/Pentyuhov2/1.htm.

"smiling and always talking": SPE.

271 *"On March 5 Papa was"*: SPE [letter of October 13, 1953, pp. 2–3].

"And what a cruel—tragic": SPE [p. 3 of both versions].

"but unfortunately they were": SPE [p. 4].

272 *"Stalin Prize laureate"*: SPE [undated petition to Beria; rejected on May 8, 1953].

"Her sentence is not 25": SPE [letter of August 30, 1954, p. 1].

"It's by no means a sanatorium": Ibid.

273 *"claw her out of there"*: Ibid. [p. 2].

"the unjust charges": SPE [diary of Svyatoslav Prokofiev, October 4, 1954].

"everything's relative!": Ibid.

275 *"like some sort of nightmare"*: Chemberdzhi, *XX vek Linï Prokof'yevoy*, 254.

which made them "unrecognizable": SPE [diary of Svyatoslav Prokofiev, February 24—March 5, 1956].

"After the noisy, stuffy barracks": Ibid.

"despite her harsh and unjust": Ibid.

a "commercial" and a "common": Ibid.

276 *"Now we are all together"*: SPE [diary of Svyatoslav Prokofiev, March 5, 1956].

277 *"supplemental verification"*: SPE [letter of May 28, 1955].

"While I don't precisely know": SPE [letter of May 18, 1956, p. 1].

"political illiteracy": Ibid. [p. 2].

278 *"Unfortunately he hasn't been"*: Ibid.

one of "the repentant": SPE [diary of Svyatoslav Prokofiev, May 22, 1956].

a single word: rehabilitation: SPE.

he bellowed "Thank God!": SPE [diary of Svyatoslav Prokofiev, June 13, 1956].

"Leaving tonight at 8:30": SPE [diary of Svyatoslav Prokofiev, June 30, 1956]; Chemberdzhi, *XX vek Linï Prokof'yevoy*, 257.

279 *"Look for the file"*: Prokof'yev, "O moikh roditelyakh: Beseda sïna kompozitora s muzïkovedom Nataliyey Savkinoy," 231.

"I'm so happy": RGALI f. 2048, op. 1, yed. khr. 151, l. 25.

EPILOGUE

Information on LP's housing in Moscow, the dacha at Nikolina gora, Oleg Prokofiev's marriage to Camilla Gray, and her sudden death are from Serge Prokofiev Jr. I drew from Leonid Maksimenkov, "Prokofiev's Immortalization," in *Sergey Prokofiev and His World*, 285–332, esp. 299–301 (on LP's and MM's pensions) and 314–17 (on the refusal to permit LP to travel to Paris for the unveiling of the memorial plaque). MM summarizes the legal proceedings concerning the status of her and LP's separate marriages to SP in her 1958 diary: RGALI f. 1929, op. 3, yed. khr. 370, l. 28 [January 13], l. 44 [February 15]. Additional documents about the case in RGALI f. 1929, op. 2, yed. khr. 560. Information on LP's trips to Soviet-controlled Eastern Europe to hear performances of SP's music from her June 1966, May 18 and 31, 1968, letters to MHB. LP's non-attendance at the *War and Peace* performance at the Sydney Opera House in 1973 and the final weeks of LP's life are described in Chemberdzhi, *XX vek Lini Prokof'yevoy*, 264, 321–24. LP's petition to Yuriy Andropov, which Chemberdzhi typed for her, is reproduced in ibid., 272–73. Edward Morgan's translation of this same letter is included in Valentina Chemberdji, "Excerpts from *The Twentieth Century of Lina Prokofiev*," *Three Oranges Journal*, vol. 20 (2010): 28. The original is preserved with LP's petition to Leonid Brezhnev in SPA. LP's 1974 air and baggage claim tickets and currency declaration, the 1979 letter concerning the reassignment of her apartment on Kutuzovsky prospekt, and her regular requests for extension of her visas are also preserved in SPA. My thanks to Fiona McKnight for providing copies.

281 *"The nurses and nurses-aides"*: Prokof'yev, "O moikh roditelyakh," 228.
283 *"the return of L. I."*: RGALI f. 1929, op. 3, yed. khr. 370, l. 30 [January 22, 1958].
284 *"a mountain's worth of dirt"*: Ibid., l. 31.
     "profound sense of regret": Letter of November 6, 1962, from MHB to Anna Holdcroft, p. 3.
285 *"It's a miracle that you forgot"*: Ibid.
     "grasped my hands in both": Ibid.
286 *"to travel to capitalist countries"*: Maksimenkov, "Prokofiev's Immortalization," 317.
288 *"come to terms with the harsh"*: As quoted in Chemberdji, "Excerpts from *The Twentieth Century of Lina Prokofiev*," 28.
     "as Prokofiev's widow": As quoted in ibid.; translation adjusted.
     "second homeland": LPF 8/3/5, p. 3.
289 *"terrible mistake made"*: Ibid.
     "stupendous lunch": Letter of April 21, 1977, from LP to MHB.
290 *"élan and dry amusement"*: "HAI Celebrates 'Peter and the Wolf,'" *HAI News*, Spring 1986, p. 3.
292 *"Your mother seriously ill"*: SPE.
     "En vous souhaitant beaucoup": SPE.

Index